ATLANTA

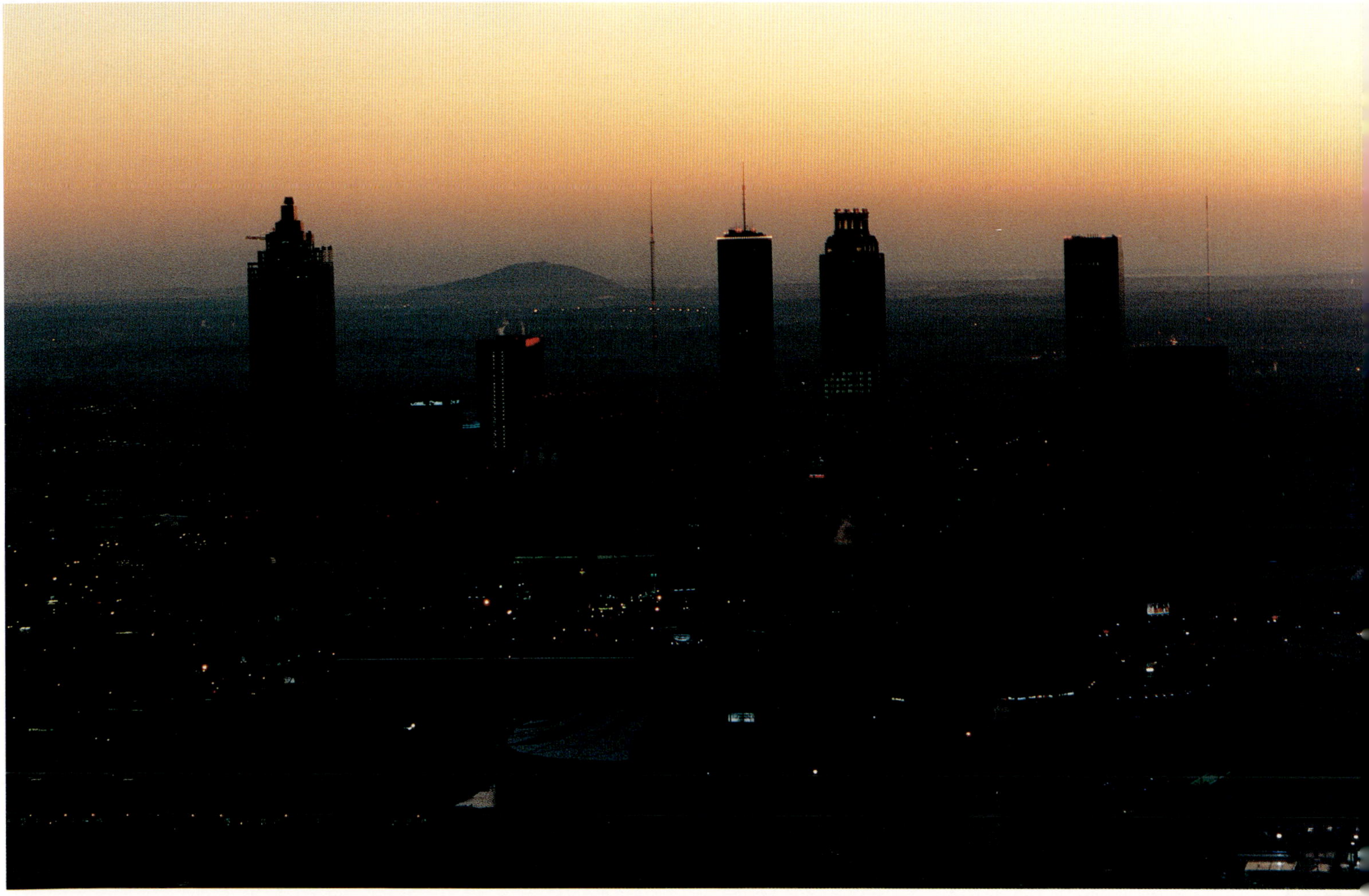

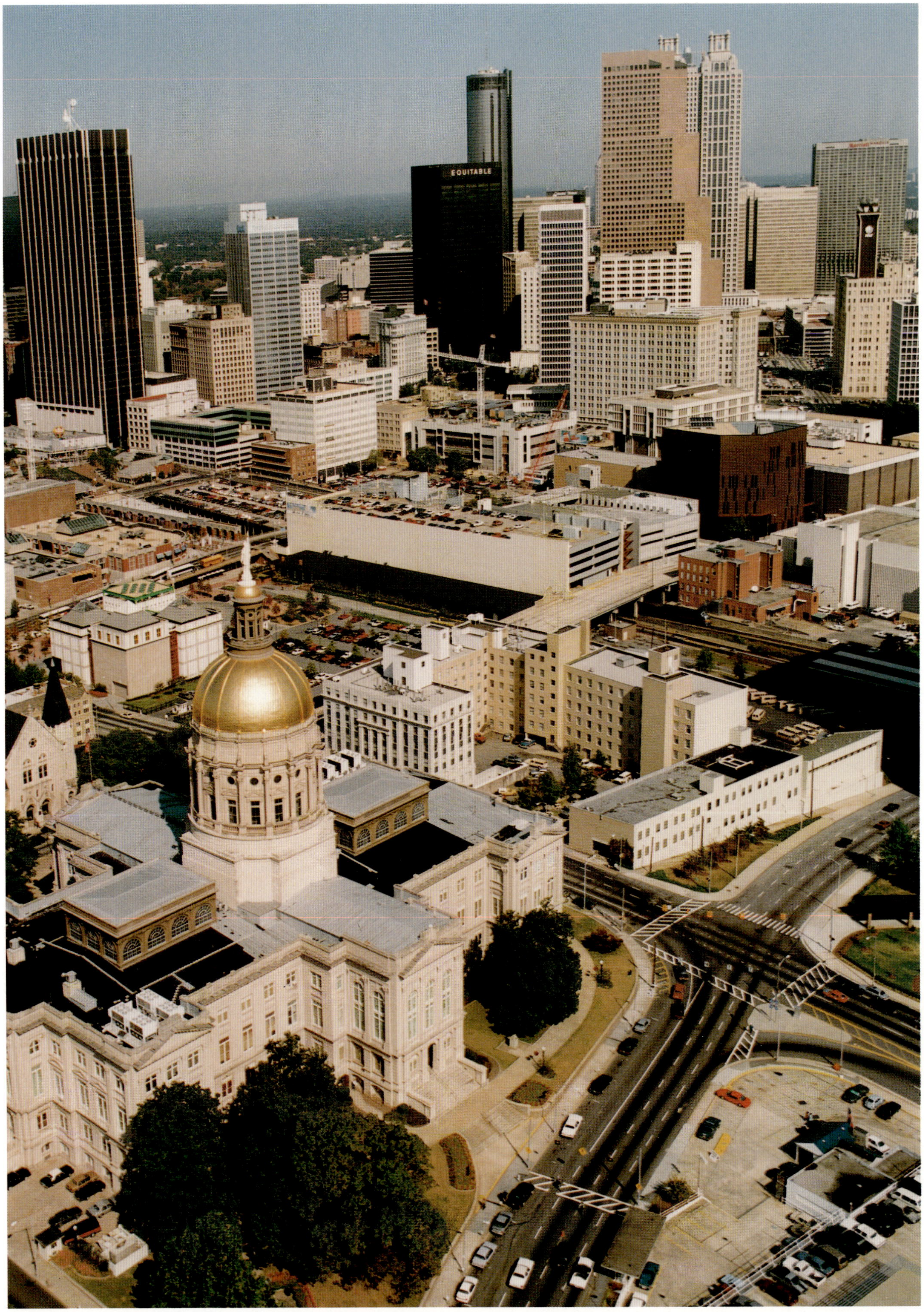
EQUITABLE

ATLANTA

Photographs by
DAVID KING GLEASON

Text by
DON O'BRIANT

Introduction by
JOHN STONE

LOUISIANA STATE UNIVERSITY PRESS Baton Rouge and London

Manufactured in Hong Kong
First printing
03 02 01 00 99 98 97 96 95 94 5 4 3 2 1

Designer: *Amanda McDonald Key*
Typeface: *Adobe Garamond*
Printer and binder: *Palace Press International*

Library of Congress Cataloging-in-Publication Data

Gleason, David K.
Atlanta / photographs David King Gleason; text by Don O'Briant; introduction by John Stone.
p. cm.
Includes index.
ISBN 0-8071-1937-7 (c : alk. paper)
1. Atlanta (Ga.)—Description and travel. 2. Atlanta (Ga.)—Pictorial works. I. Title.
F294.A84G57 1994
975.8'231—dc20 94-14529
CIP

Photo Credits
All of the photographs in this book are by David King Gleason except the following: pp. 14, 15, Phyllis Picardi, Stock South; p. 16, Butler Day; p. 18, Michael Portman; p. 19 (bottom), Aerial Innovations; p. 20, Jonathan Hillyer; p. 21 (top), Michael Portman, (bottom) Timothy Hursley (all photos pp. 18–21 courtesy of John Portman & Associates); p. 24, Phyllis Picardi, Stock South; p. 30, David Murray, Jr., Stock South; pp. 60–61, Carol Christensen, Stock South: p. 64, Mike Moreland; p. 73 (both), Butler Day; p. 75, Andre Jenny, Stock South; p. 82, Arni Katz, Stock South; p. 109, Phyllis Picardi, Stock South; p. 111, courtesy of Fernbank Museum of Natural History; p. 134, Ken Hawkins, Stock South; p. 154, Michael H. Siede, Stock South.

The paper in this book meets the guidelines for permanence and durability of the Committee on Production Guidelines for Book Longevity of the Council on Library Resources. ♾

Contents

Downtown and Midtown

1. Georgia State Capitol
2. Atlanta City Hall
3. Fulton County Courthouse
4. Atlanta–Fulton County Stadium
5. Grant Park (Cyclorama, Zoo Atlanta)
6. Oakland Cemetery
7. Georgia State University
8. Underground Atlanta
9. Grady Statue, *Constitution/Journal* Building
10. Atlanta University Center
11. Herndon Home
12. Georgia Dome
13. Omni
14. CNN Center
15. Candler Building, Woodruff Park
16. Georgia-Pacific Center
17. Martin Luther King, Jr. Birthplace and Center
18. Inman Park
19. Callan Castle
20. Carter Presidential Center
21. Old Sears Building
22. Peachtree Center
23. The Varsity
24. Georgia Tech
25. Coca-Cola Headquarters
26. Fox Theatre, Georgian Terrace, The Ponce, BellSouth
27. The Dump
28. Piedmont Park, Atlanta Botanical Garden
29. Callanwolde
30. Druid Hills
31. One Atlantic Center
32. Promenade II
33. High Museum, Woodruff Arts Center
34. The Temple
35. Ansley Park

Suburbs and Environs

36. Six Flags over Georgia
37. Charlie Brown Airport
38. Wren's Nest
39. Hartsfield International Airport
40. Agnes Scott College
41. DeKalb County Courthouse, Decatur
42. Fernbank Museum of Natural History, Fernbank Science Center
43. Emory University
44. Centers for Disease Control
45. Peachtree Battle
46. Atlanta Historical Society (Swan House, Tullie Smith House)
47. Georgia Governor's Mansion
48. Fort Peachtree
49. Galleria Mall
50. Oglethorpe University
51. Mercer University
52. White Water Park, American Adventures
53. Kennesaw Mountain National Battlefield
54. Big Shanty Museum
55. Roswell (Bulloch Hall, Roswell Mill)
56. To Alpharetta
57. To Lake Sidney Lanier
58. To Road Atlanta
59. Stone Mountain Park

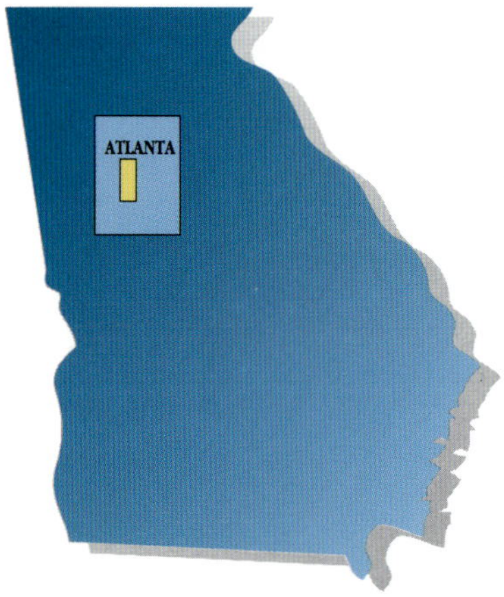

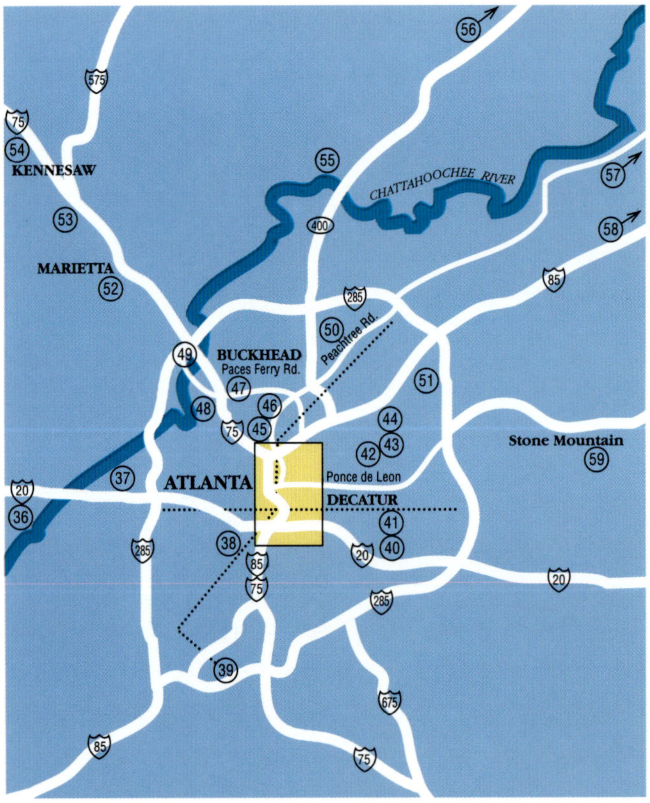

Suburbs and Environs

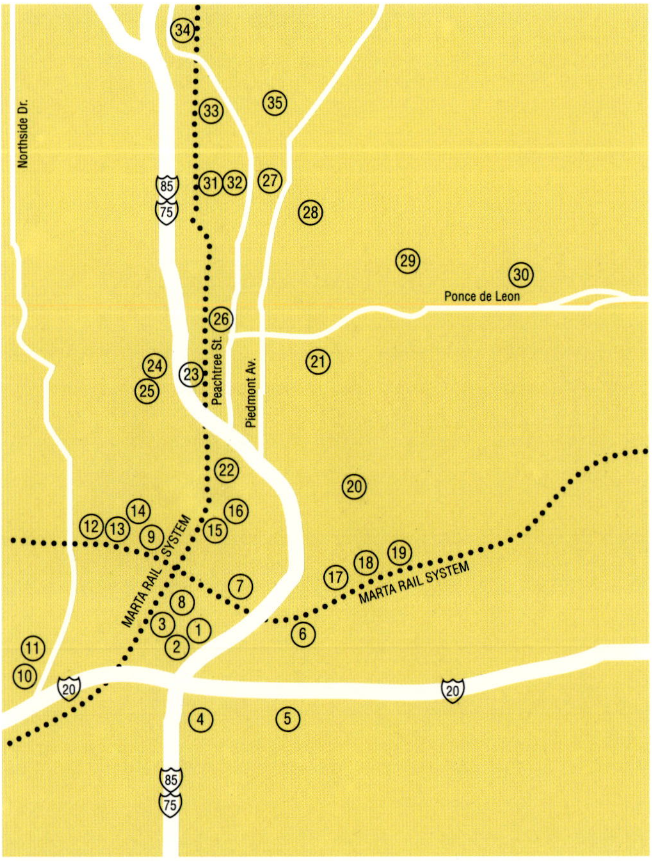

Downtown and Midtown

INTRODUCTION

To choose a time: early March. Bradford pear trees are lighting up all over Atlanta. Daffodils, too, have decided the time is right. The dogwoods are still hesitant, but passing the word. Outside my office, tall maples are tinged with their annual pointillistic green, their countable branches just beginning to catch the slightest wind, as Philip Larkin said they would:

> . . . still the unresting castles thresh
> In fullgrown thickness every May.
> Last year is dead, they seem to say,
> Begin afresh, afresh, afresh.

As it happens, Atlanta has a well-deserved reputation for doing just that.

• • •

The River and the Rock came first, eons ago. The Railroad came much later, and with it came Atlanta. This "brave and beautiful city" had an inauspicious beginning, one that centered on a railroad stake driven in 1837 to locate the terminal point of the Western & Atlantic Railroad. The railroad was to run between middle Georgia and the north, to a place then called Ross' Landing, later Chattanooga.

For about five years, the village around the railroad stake was known simply as "Terminus." In 1842 the thirty or so residents of the settlement christened it "Marthasville," honoring the daughter of Governor Wilson Lumpkin, a proponent of railroad expansion. But in 1845 the locals began calling the place "Atlanta," a word coined to be the "feminine" version of *Atlantic*. Credit for the name that stuck to the early settlement goes to J. Edgar Thomson, chief engineer of the Georgia Railroad. Early Atlanta, then, had its origins in transportation. But its biggest beginning was yet to come.

• • •

On my way home, by the side of LaVista Road in a suburb of Atlanta called Tucker, there is a small white building. A sign reads "Tucker Courthouse 1860." The structure, about twenty by thirty feet, encloses a single simple room, with separate entrances for the judge and the general public.

Peering through the windows, one can make out long wooden benches, a few armchairs, a gavel that brought order to the proceedings, a metal document seal that gave them legitimacy. My brief visit backward in time puts me in mind of the young Atlanta, a much less tranquil place than Tucker was back in 1860. By that year, Atlanta's population had grown to approximately 10,000. The 138 miles of track between Atlanta and Chattanooga had been in place for over ten years. But times were hard—typhoid and pellagra were common, smallpox and malaria still major threats. Most important, with the election of Lincoln as president, the southern states were poised for secession. Four years later, General William Tecumseh Sherman and his Union troops marched into Atlanta. The Atlanta campaign began in May of 1864 and lasted until early September, when the town surrendered. By mid-November, Sherman and his army were prepared to leave on their "march to the sea." But the general was determined that Atlanta would never again assist in the Confederate effort: his soldiers put the torch to the great majority of the city's buildings, military, residential, and commercial, in the great fire that Margaret Mitchell and Metro-Goldwyn-Mayer were to immortalize in *Gone with the Wind.*

• • •

Thus, the symbol of Atlanta became the phoenix, the mythical bird that rose out of the ashes of its own funeral pyre; and its Latin motto became *Atlanta Resurgens.* By 1870, the town was on its way to recovery. The population had climbed past 20,000. What was to become the nucleus of the largest African-American university complex in the nation, Atlanta University, had been founded the year before. A healing of the national psyche was taking place: the death of Robert E. Lee, in October, 1870, was mourned by northerners as well as southerners; and by 1871, one of the Western & Atlantic Railroad's forty-four locomotives was named the U. S. Grant.

In 1872, a bright young newspaperman named Henry W. Grady came to Atlanta. In late 1886, Grady, editor of the Atlanta *Constitution,* journeyed to New York to speak before the New England Society about "the vigorously growing, 'living and breathing' New South." William Tecumseh Sherman was in the audience—and before Grady's talk, the Seventh Regiment Band in the balcony couldn't resist playing "Marching Through Georgia." When Grady finally got to the platform, he spoke of the progress Atlanta had made, of its rebirth and return to commerce after the war. But he couldn't resist temptation either and made this pointed remark: "I want to say to General Sherman, who is considered an able man in our parts, though some people think he is a kind of careless man about fire, that from the ashes he left us in 1864 we have raised a brave and beautiful city; that somehow or other we have caught the sunshine in the bricks and mortar of our homes, and have builded therein not one ignoble prejudice or memory." If the latter part of his statement were not entirely true, it was something to hope for.

• • •

In 1929, at the threshold of the Great Depression, the lives of two of America's important future leaders began to touch temporally in Atlanta. Their concerns would be intertwined until their deaths within a few months of each other nearly forty years later. The two men? First, Ralph Emerson McGill came from Tennessee in the spring of 1929 to be assistant sports editor of the Atlanta *Constitution.* In 1938 he was named executive editor, and in 1959 he won the Pulitzer Prize for his daily columns, which regularly reminded not only Atlanta and the South, but also the world, of the necessity for equality between the races. McGill wrote eloquently, courageously, of the need for goodwill and progress despite the hatemongers, and he challenged and disparaged the venom, noise, and ignorance that came out of the White Citizens' Councils and the Ku Klux Klan. His columns spoke not only for the civil rights of African Americans, but for those of all. After the Atlanta Jewish Temple was bombed in 1958, he wrote, "When the wolves of hate are loosed on one people, then no one is safe." After McGill's death from a heart attack (on February 3, 1969), his pastor, Frank Ross, said of him, "He made you feel better about yourself and about the human race. He called out in you some strengths, some instincts for good you maybe hadn't paid much attention to before. And you found yourself wanting to do what he wanted done." McGill's honesty and compassion earned him the nickname "The Conscience of the South." But others also deserved that accolade.

On January 15, 1929, Martin Luther King, Jr., was born in a house on Auburn Avenue in Atlanta. He would rise, despite epithet and invective, jeering and jail, to international prominence and win the Nobel Peace Prize. His strategy of "nonviolence," of passive resistance, which he adapted from the example and teachings of Gandhi, helped bring sorely needed focus to the civil rights struggle of the late 1950s and 1960s. As co-pastor (with his father) of the Ebenezer Baptist Church in Atlanta, King in his eloquent sermons, his thrilling use of the language, galvanized and gave hope not only to African Americans, but also to millions of others throughout the world. His diagnosis of societal ills was straightforward: "We have learned to fly the air like birds and swim the sea like fish, but we have not learned the simple art of living together like brothers." We are much better off as a society because he had his dreams and the courage to articulate them. He was thirty-nine years old at the time of his tragic assassination on April 4, 1968, only months before Ralph McGill's death. McGill appraised King's importance just after he was awarded the Nobel Prize. The world, McGill noted, has "watched Dr. Martin Luther King and seen in him manifestation of the American promise." Dr. King's memorial tomb, on Auburn Avenue near his birthplace, is lit by an eternal flame.

Let these two, then, be emblematic of all the great leaders it has been our good fortune to have.

• • •

First there was the River—the Chattahoochee. And the Rock—Stone Mountain. And certainly not last, the Railroad. Then, in a series of triumphs, came civil leaders of the highest caliber. Consider only the recent mayors of Atlanta, all people of vision: William Hartsfield, Ivan Allen, Sam Massell, Maynard Jackson, Andrew Young. And the business leaders, symbolized by Robert Woodruff, the Coca-Cola magnate, and his brother, George, also a major philanthropist. Ted Turner, of course. As for sports figures, let us simply note two of the internationally famous Bobby Jones and Hank Aaron. Let Robert Shaw stand for all those who have made music here. And, finally, former president Jimmy Carter, whose Presidential Center and Library continue to remind us of what he cared about most deeply while he was in the White House: human rights. Still hard at work long after his retirement from politics, Carter has emphasized to us all the plight of those who live in the inner cities of our country. And he has urged us, with his imaginative Atlanta Project, to address and correct those intransigent problems. The project seeks to coordinate the ongoing efforts of governments, churches, social organizations, and schools to more effectively help the indigent. The poetic prediction of Robert Frost applies, of course, to all major urban areas: that their citizens must learn "how to crowd but still be kind." In Atlanta, when we have needed leaders, they have come forth.

• • •

The skeleton of the city may be concrete and steel. But it rises out of water, trees, grace, and words. Mellifluous words such as Atlanta, Lullwater, Marietta, LaVista, Chattahoochee, and Sandy Springs; Buckhead, Peachtree, Chamblee, Tucker, Riverdale, and Roswell. These are only some of the words, the places, the roads and rivers from which we have sprung, wherein we live and have our beings.

When I fly back to Atlanta after an out-of-town trip, when the plane cants and wheels toward Hartsfield International Airport, when I can see for a long moment Stone Mountain thrusting up like a prehistoric sphinx, surrounded by trees of every description, the Chattahoochee rushing southward, downtown Atlanta glistening in the late afternoon sun, I know how Ralph McGill felt: "Certainly I love the South. I fancy I can detect the beginnings of its fields and the colors of its soil high up from an airplane when flying home from a distant region. They seem to call out to me, saying, 'You're back home.'"

And so I am.

John Stone

Publisher's Note

Our association with David King Gleason began in 1982, with publication of *Plantation Homes of Louisiana,* and continued until his death in a helicopter crash in April, 1992, while he was taking photographs of Atlanta for this book. In the interim, we had worked together on six other books, ranging from Boston through Virginia and Georgia to Miami and Baton Rouge. With *Atlanta,* we have published eight books of his magnificent photographs in a little over ten years.

To publish books as lavish and complex as these at twelve-to-eighteen-month intervals meant that Dave was immersed in one practically all the time. He would finish his work on one book and immediately plunge into the next, even before the first was published. After the first two or three, we established with Dave a list of subjects, and his work flowed seamlessly from one to the next. If there was an gap of as much as two years, it was because of seasonal demands or the need to cover a large geographic area, as in the case of *Virginia Plantation Homes.*

Because of the nature of these projects and Dave's deep involvement in all aspects of their publication, he soon became more a member of the family than an author. He and his retriever, Goldy, were frequent visitors to the Press offices, especially when a book was in production. They were as familiar and as welcome as dear old friends, which is exactly what they were. And we were frequent visitors to his studio, to review with Dave and Josie, his wife, progress on the new book, looking at 8 x 10 work prints spread out on yards and yards of tables.

Some time after the accident, when we had each been able to make our own separate peace with the fact of his death, we discussed with Josie the possibility of completing and publishing this book. No one knew how far along Dave had been with the shooting, but after printing and reviewing all the rolls of film he had taken, it became apparent that the book was largely complete. We needed to enlist the services of someone knowledgeable about Atlanta to identify the photographs we had and to tell us what further images, if any, were needed. Since Dave had always written his own text—which he did after the book had been laid out—we also needed someone with the knowledge and talent to prepare the captions. Don O'Briant, a veteran Atlanta *Journal-Constitution* feature writer, filled these needs admirably, and he joined the team. John Stone, poet and physician and Atlantan, graced the book with a wonderfully evocative introduction that captures in words what Dave captured on film. Betty Lightfoot, Timothy Crimmins, and Dana White provided valuable insights into Atlanta and its history, and we are grateful for their assistance.

No book of this nature can be entirely comprehensive, but to make *Atlanta* complete in the same manner as Dave's earlier books, we have included a few photographs of key sites from other sources. These are identified on the copyright page. But the vast majority of the images are Dave's; they bear his hallmark and reflect his own special—indeed, unique—artistry. We were all committed to completing this book because of our devotion to Dave, but it is not simply a tribute. It is, rather, his triumph, the magnificent conclusion to David King Gleason's life and work.

Part I

Downtown

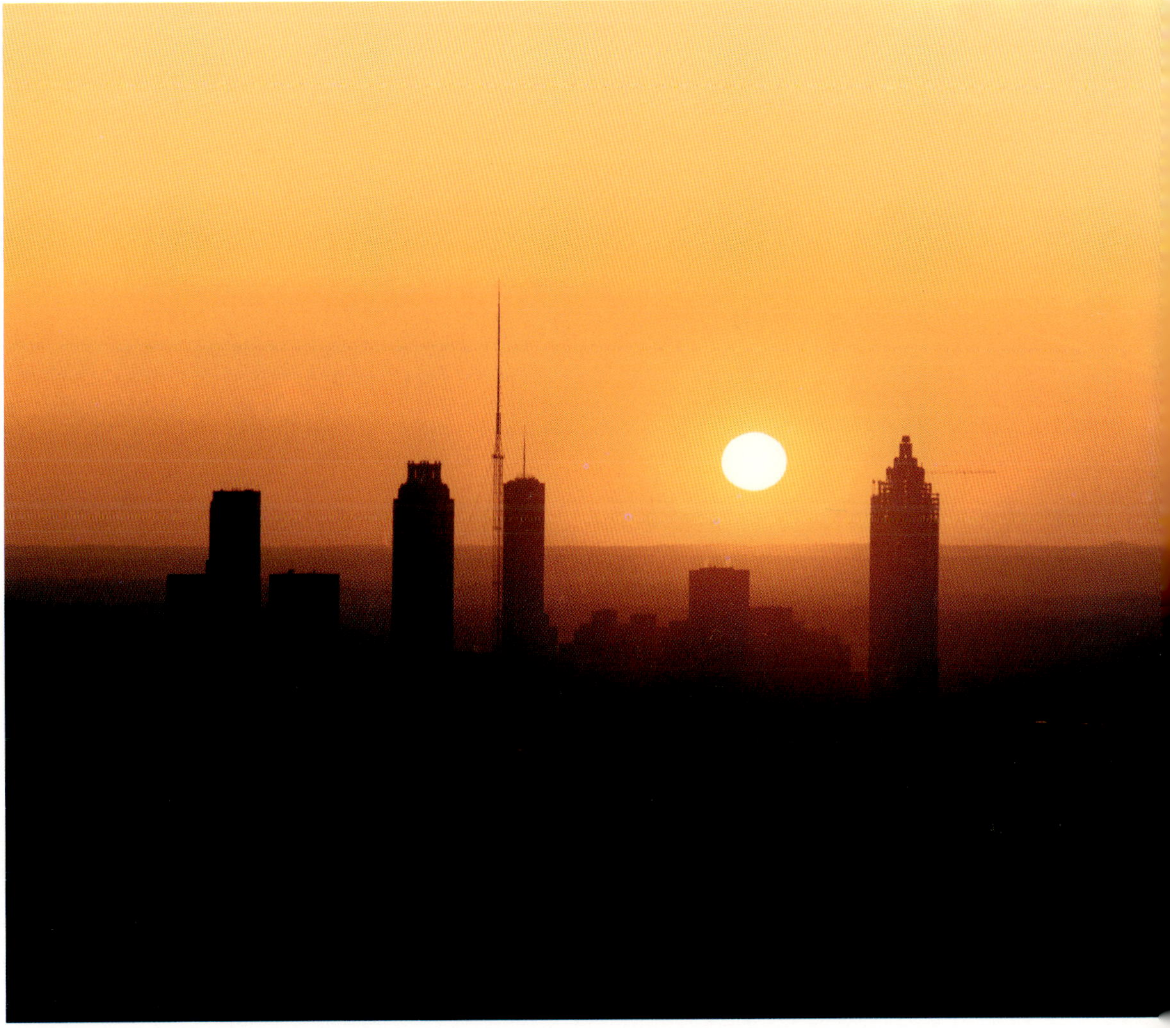

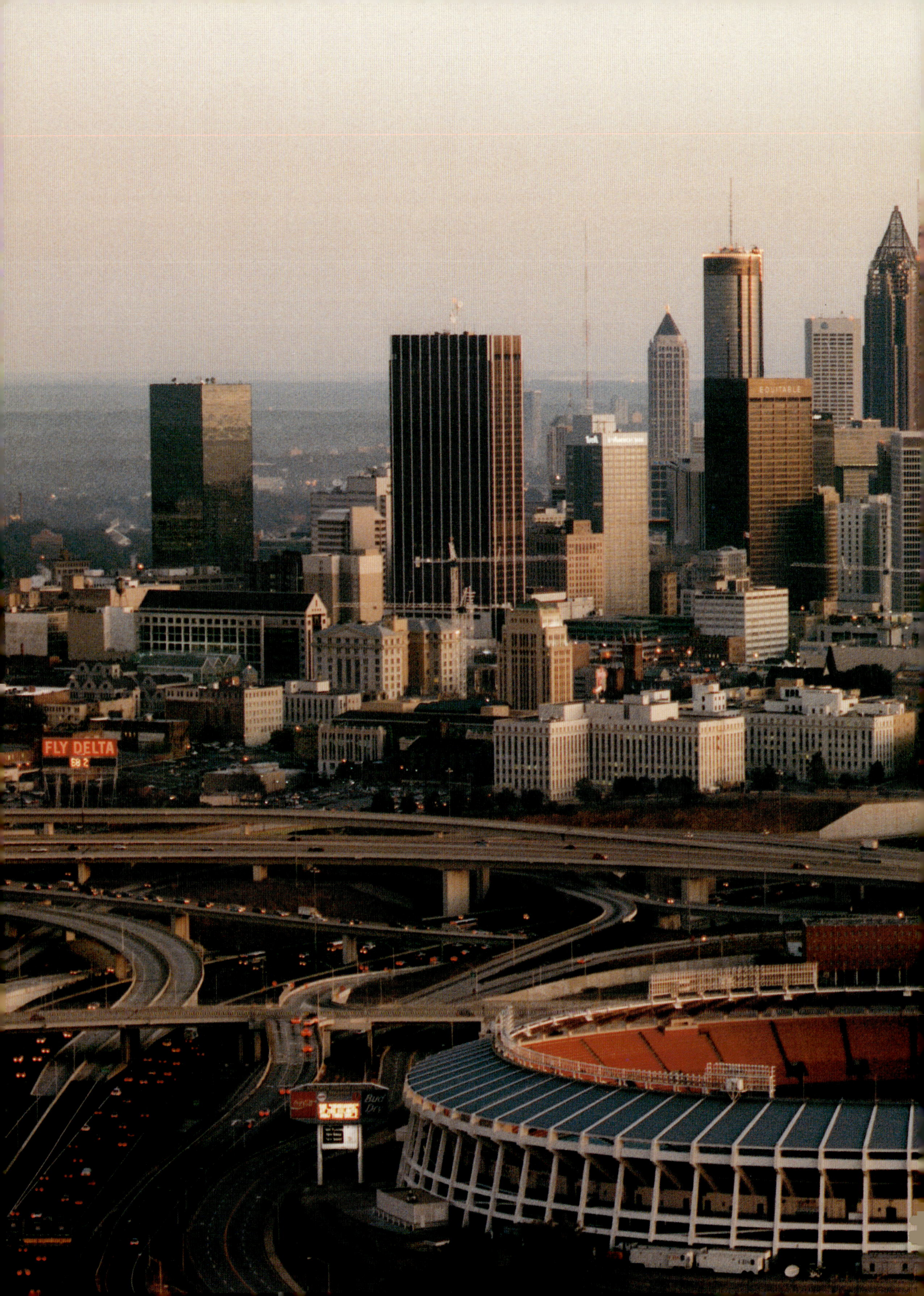
FLY DELTA
EQUITABLE

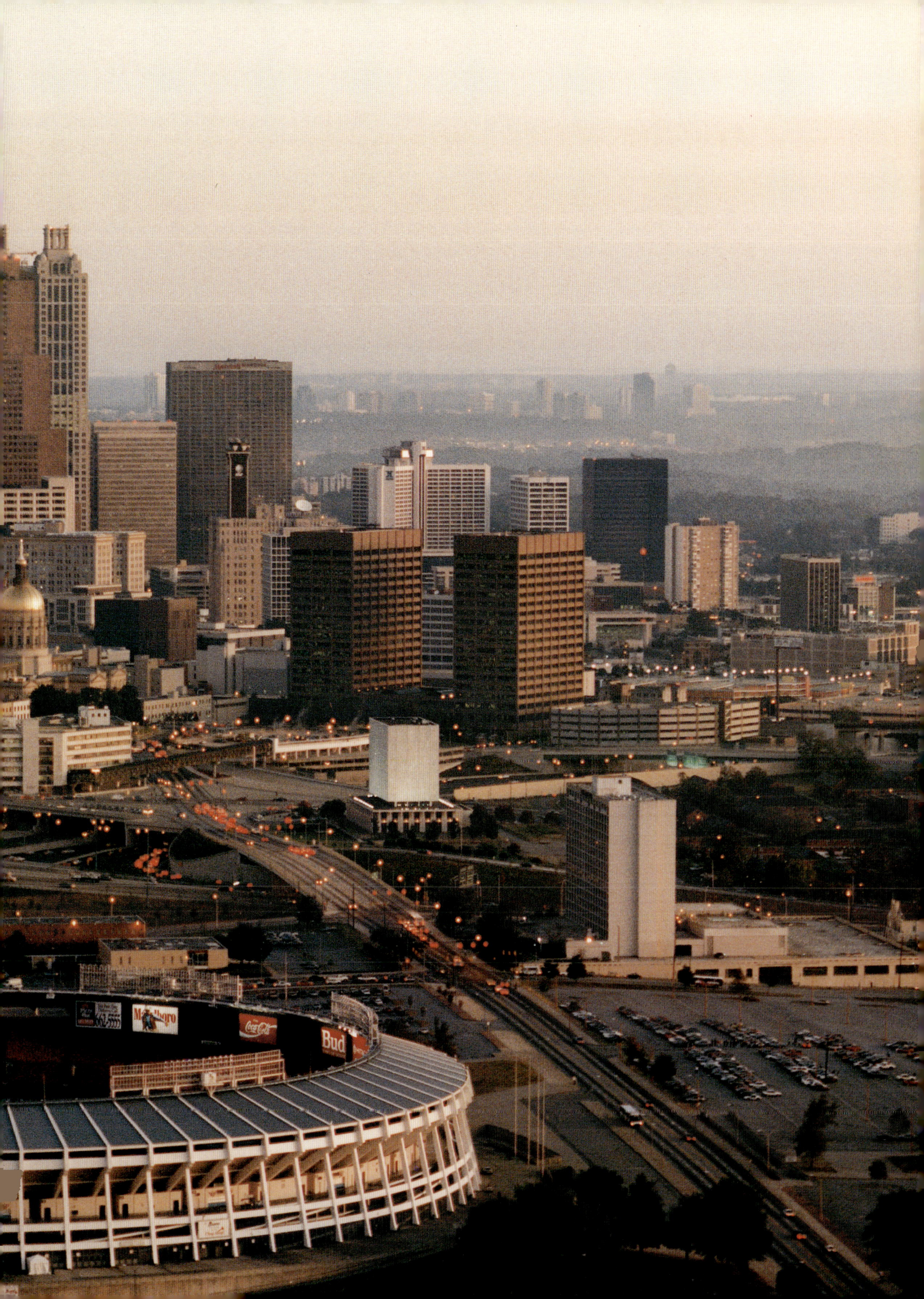
Coca-Cola
Bud

Atlanta Skyline

As business development has spread northward from downtown Atlanta, new skyscrapers have seemed to spring up almost overnight. Among the most distinctive are (from left to right near the horizon) the campanilelike One Atlantic Center; Promenade II with its Mayan-pyramid setbacks; the straightforward BellSouth Center; NationsBank Plaza, photographed just before its final spire was added; the sleek glass cylinder of the Westin Peachtree Plaza Hotel; One Peachtree Center with its multifaceted top; and the twin-capped 191 Peachtree Tower with, directly in front of it, the austere, stepped-back Georgia-Pacific Center.

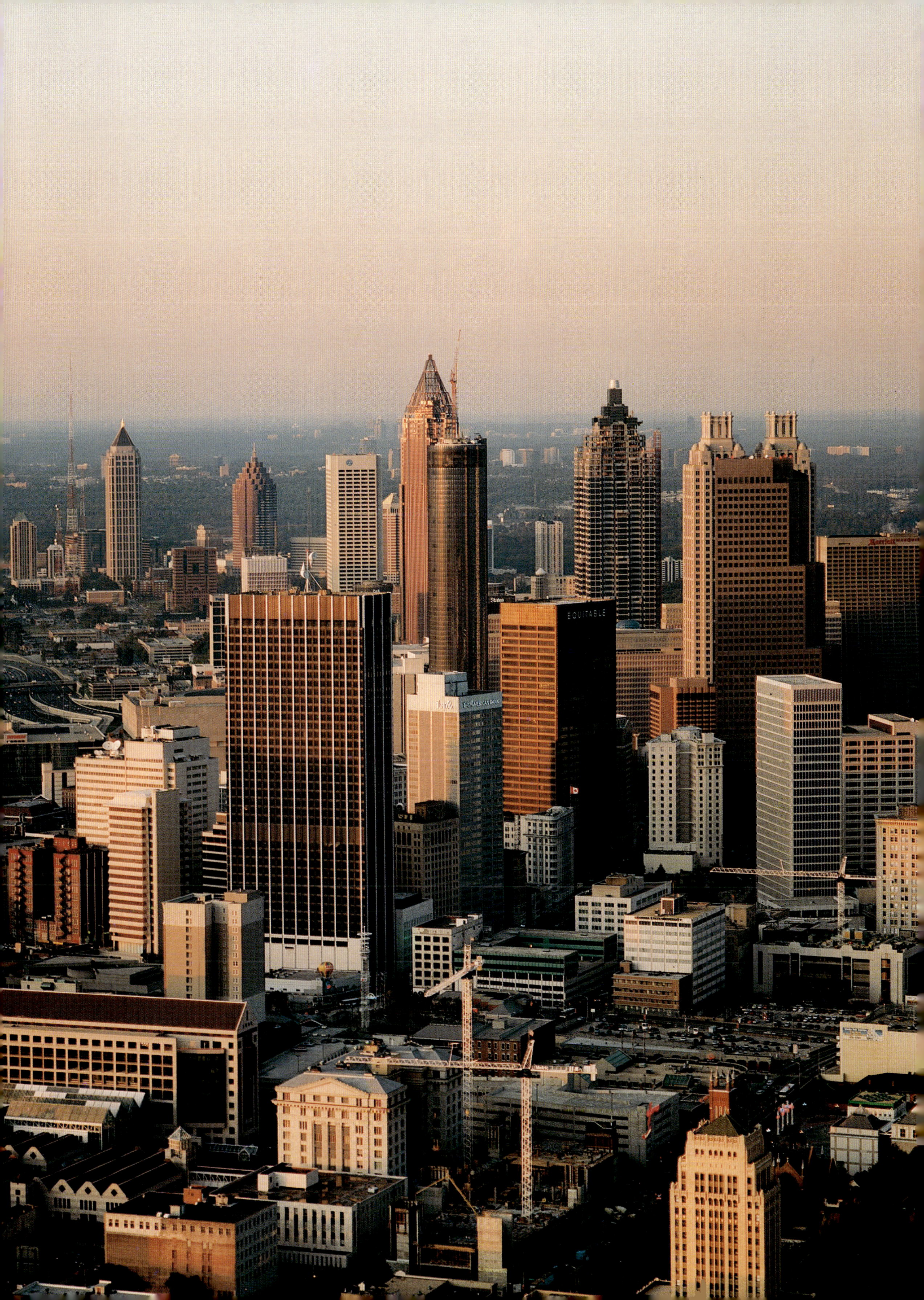
EQUITABLE
Marriott

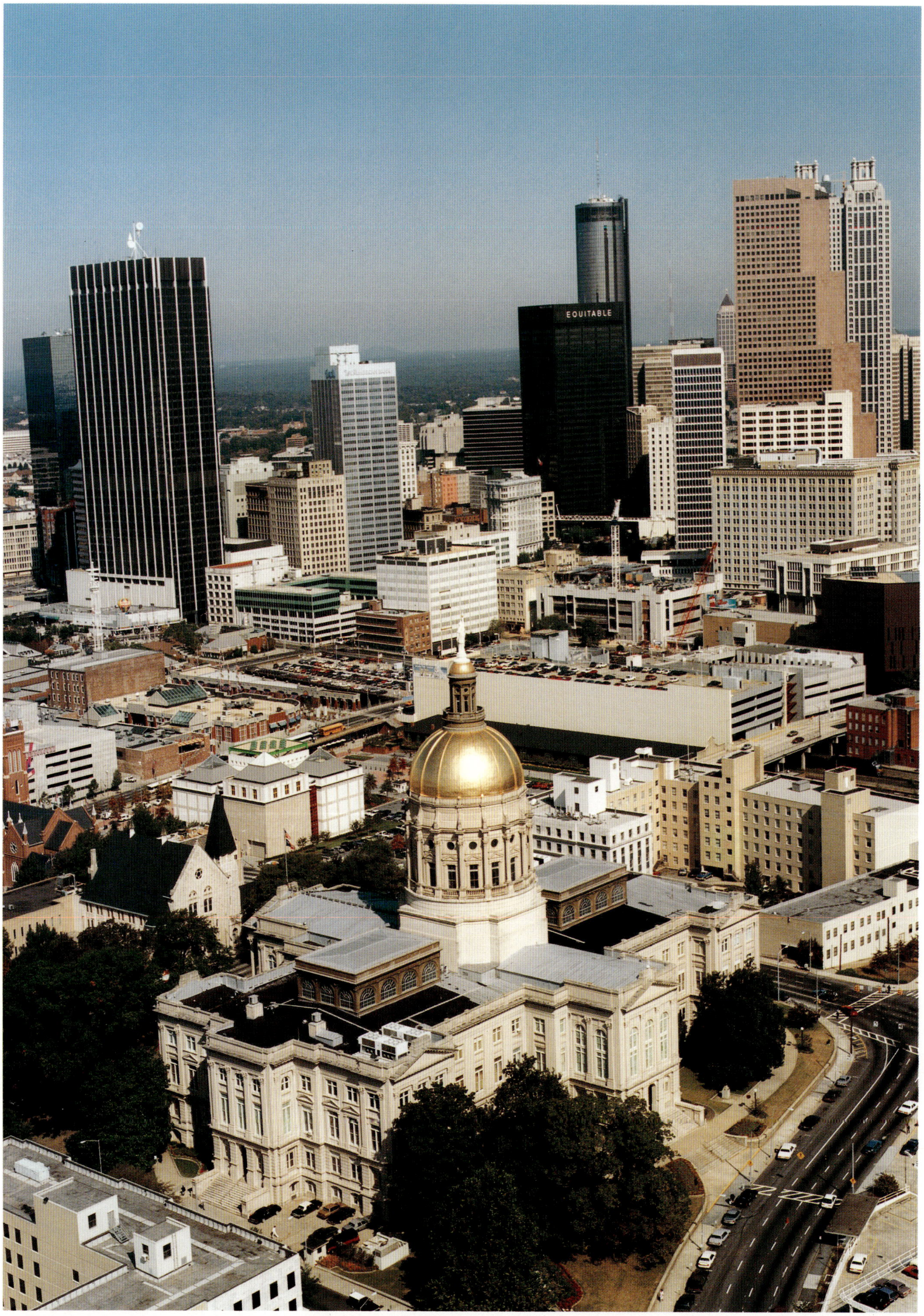
EQUITABLE

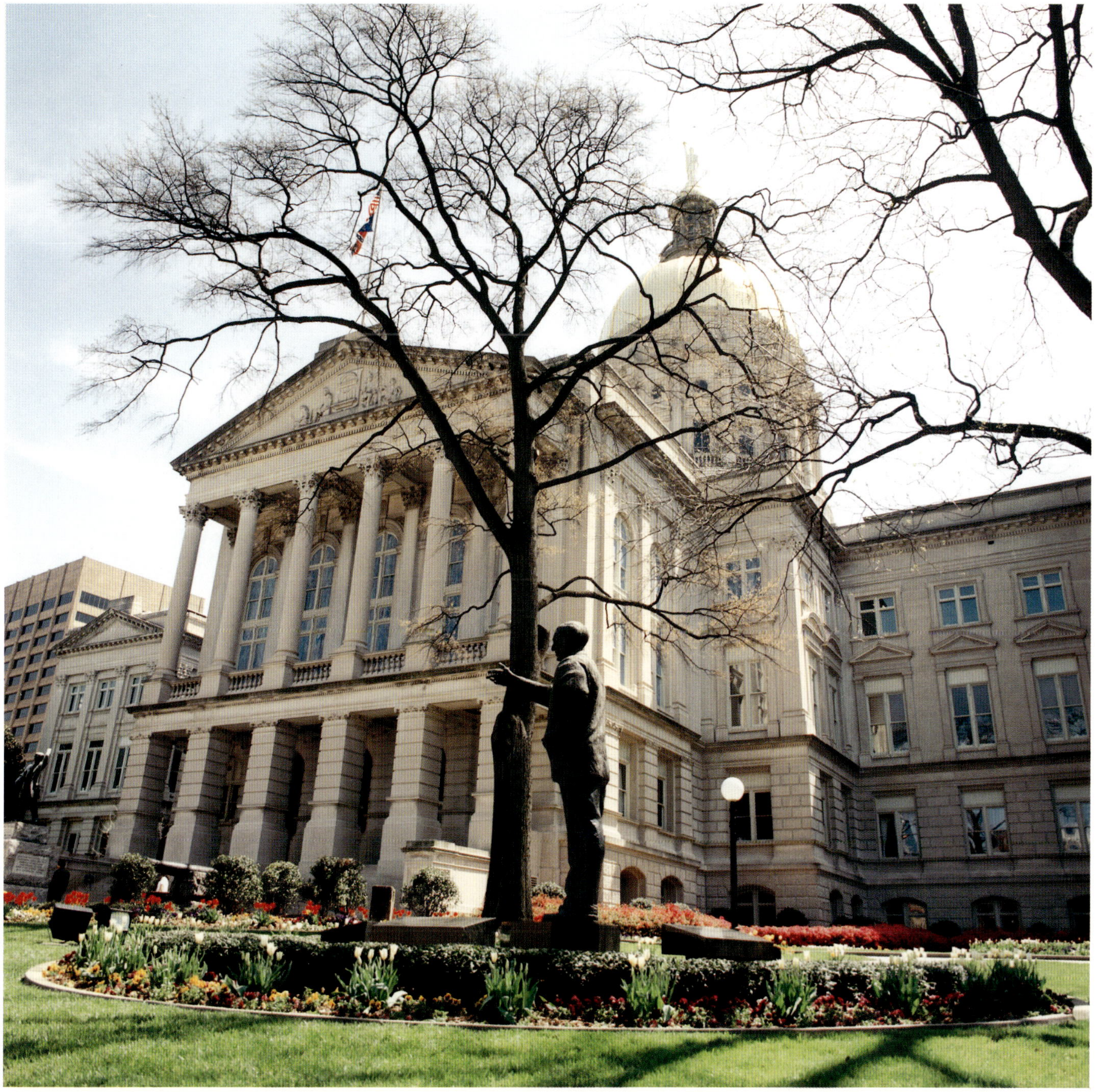

Georgia Capitol

The Georgia Capitol's dome glows like a golden lamp amid the forest of skyscrapers towering over it. In its unmistakeable similarity to the nation's Capitol in Washington, D.C., the building, completed in 1889, eloquently reaffirmed Georgia's allegiance after the Civil War.

The dome was coated in 1958 with a thin sheet of gold from the north Georgia town of Dahlonega, site of the nation's first gold rush after discovery of the metal in 1829 on what was then Cherokee land. Gilding the dome was the suggestion of Dahlonega native Gordon Price. Hearing of Mr. Price's idea, a Lumpkin County widow contributed a bottle of gold dust that had rested in a safe-deposit box for years. Soon citizens were turning out in droves to participate in Gold Panning Days. The gold was hauled to Atlanta by wagon train and presented to then-governor Marvin Griffin. It is a gift that still shines, especially after a touch-up of Dahlonega gold leaf in 1981.

A statue of United States senator Richard B. Russell stands on the capitol grounds. As chairman of the Armed Services Committee from 1955 to 1969, the Georgia Democrat was one of the most influential members of the Senate.

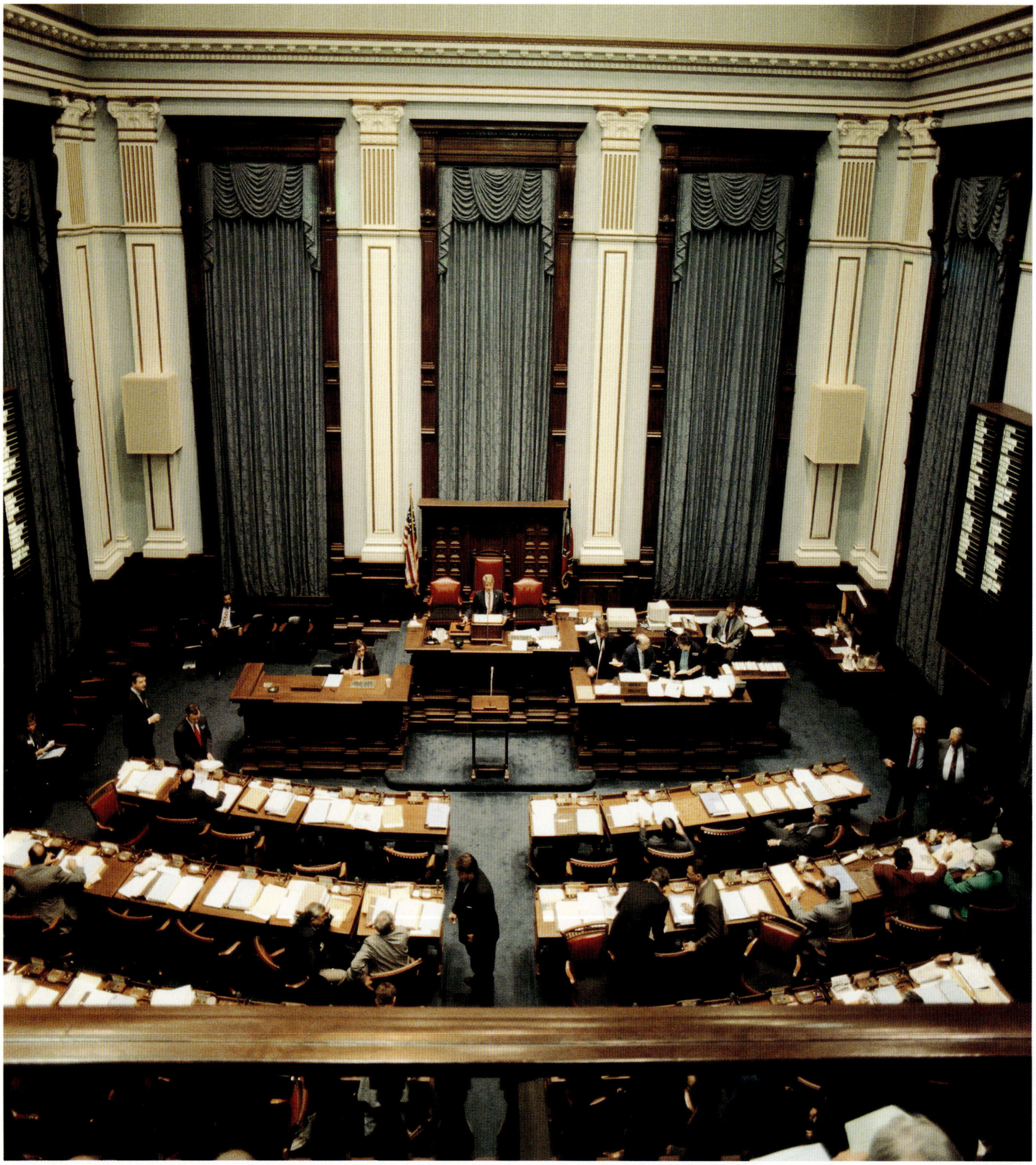

Senate chamber, Georgia State Capitol

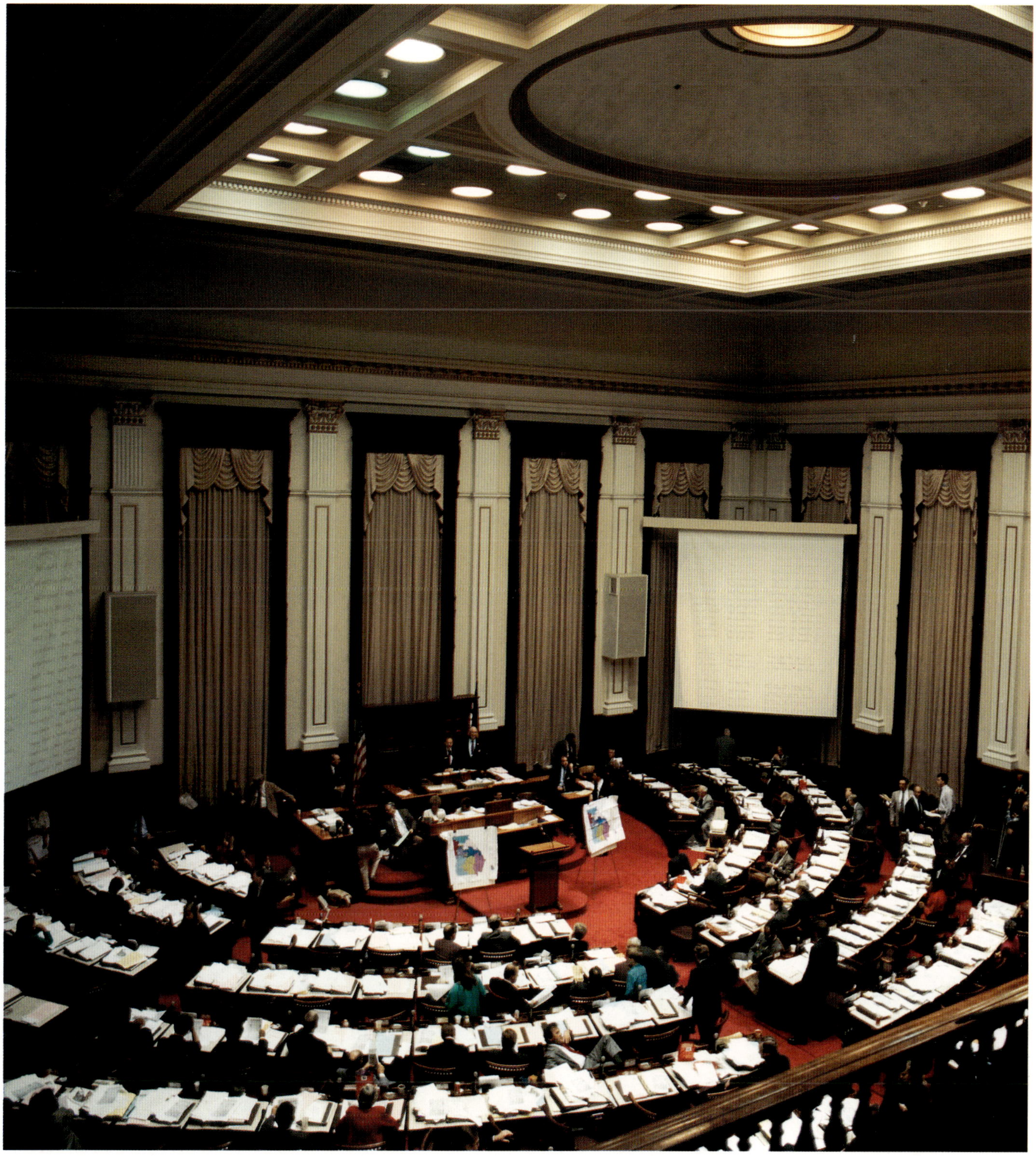

House chamber, Georgia State Capitol

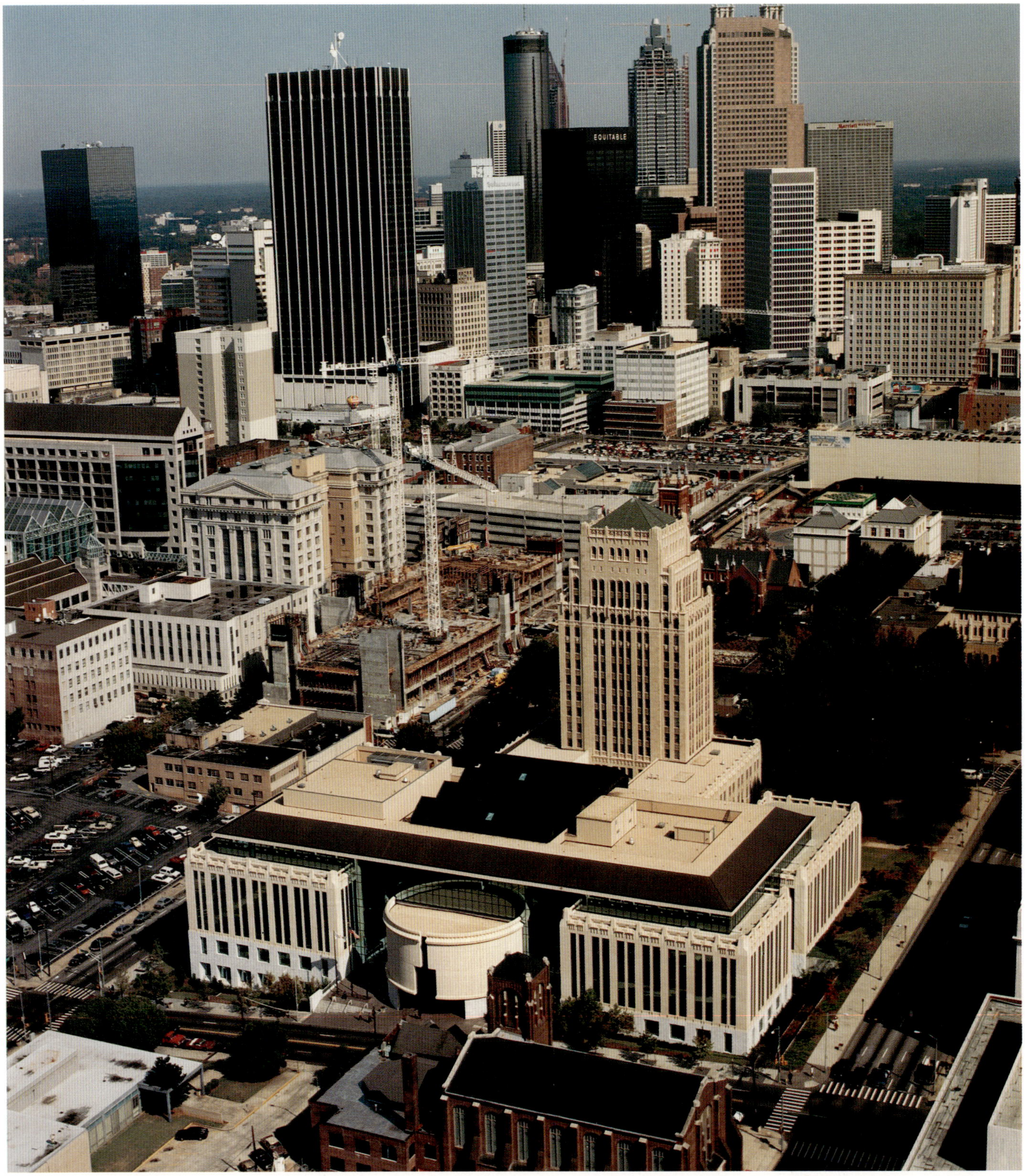

Atlanta City Hall

The original fourteen-story tower was completed in 1930 to a design by G. Lloyd Preacher. All the materials used in the structure were extracted or made in Georgia. The old building's highly ornate interior received a meticulous renovation in the late 1980s, at the same time that the $27-million postmodern addition was constructed. The new building now houses many of the key city offices, including the mayor's, around its dramatic, skylighted atrium.

Across the street from the addition stands Trinity United Methodist Church. Behind the old City Hall tower and partly obscured by it is the Shrine of the Immaculate Conception (constructed 1869–1873), one of the oldest buildings in Atlanta.

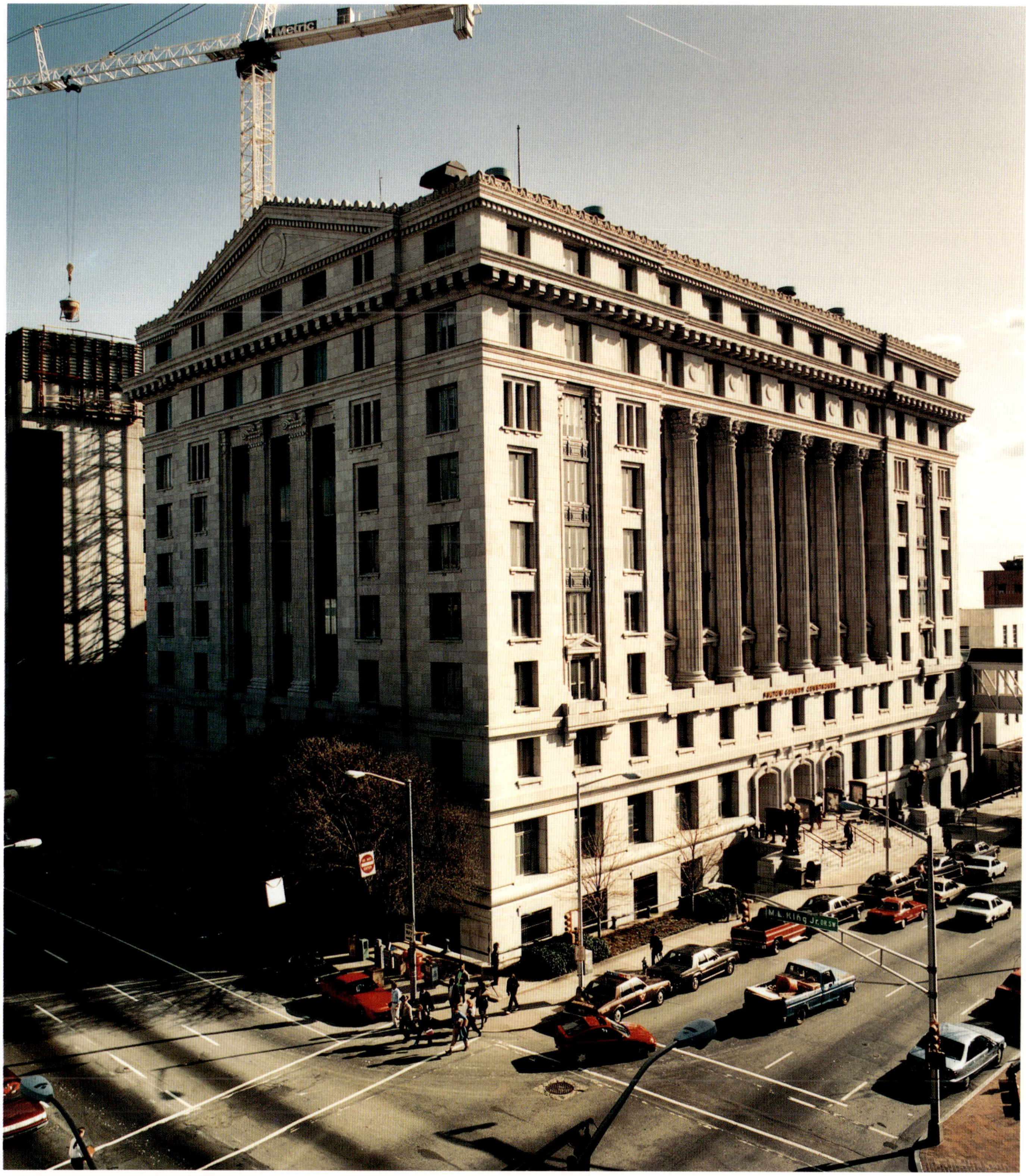

Fulton County Courthouse

With its six Corinthian columns and massive presence, the Fulton County Courthouse sacrifices elegance for an impression of solidity and power. Judges, lawyers, and lawbreakers have crossed paths in this imposing structure ever since its completion in 1914.

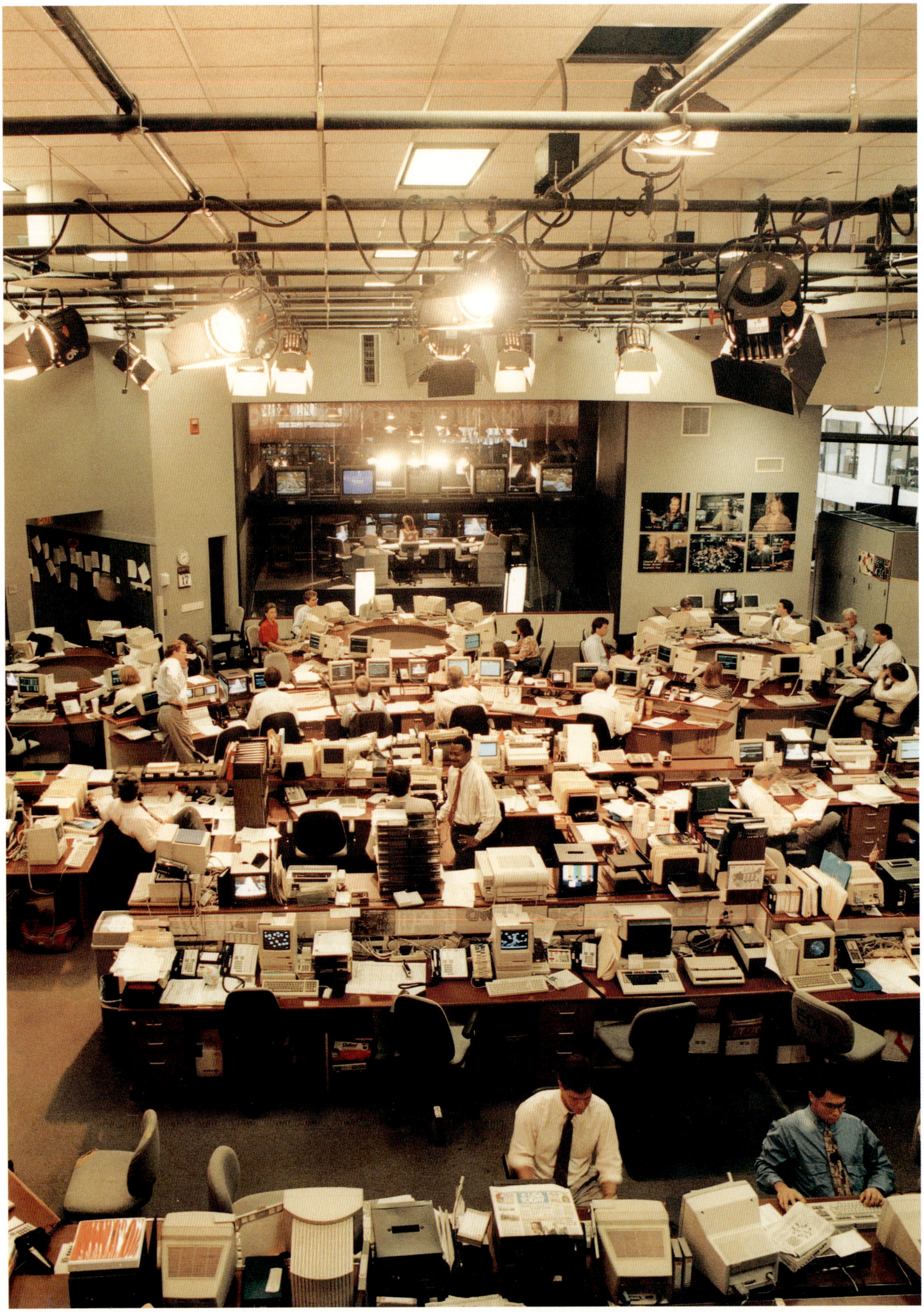

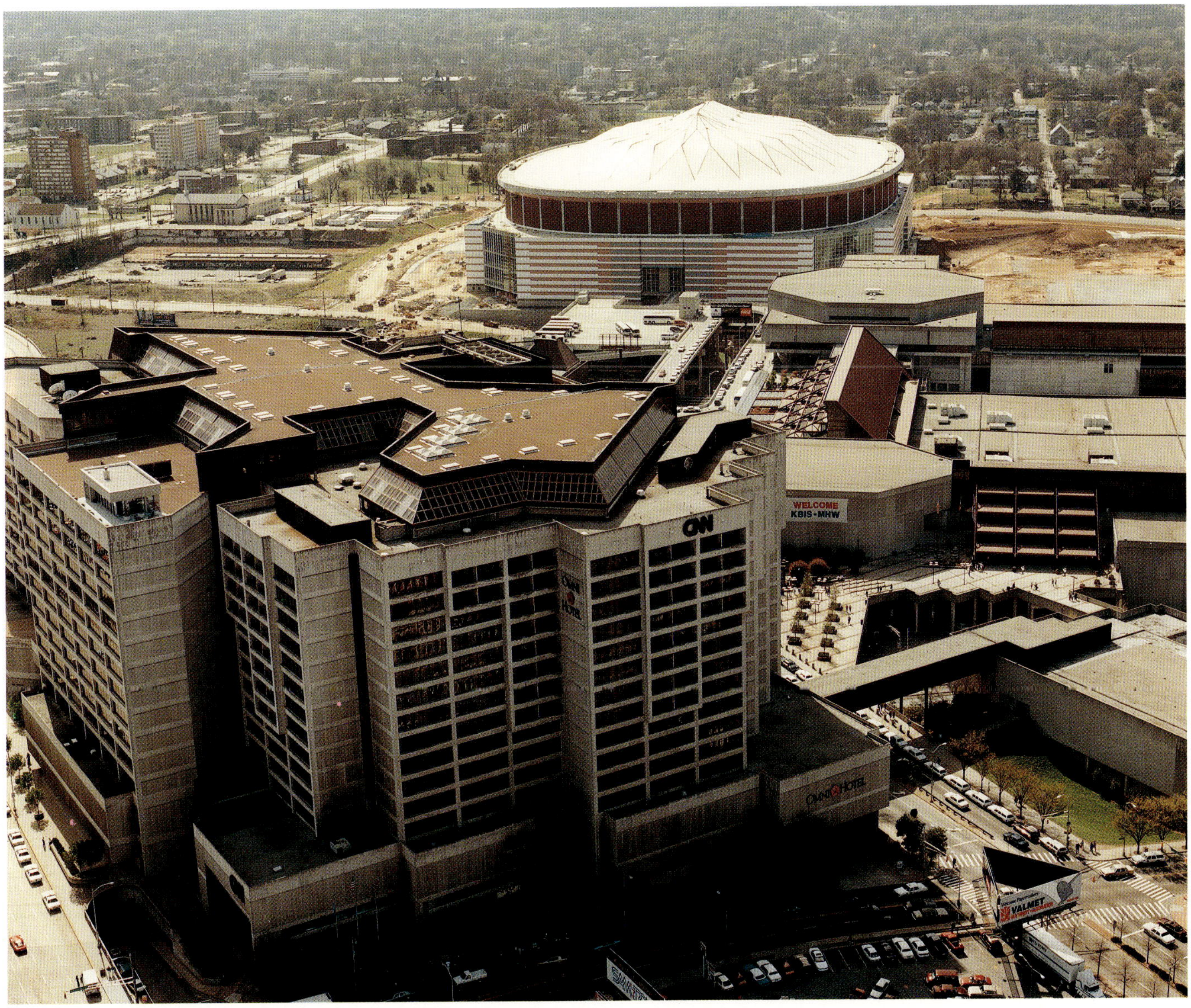

CNN Center

When media mogul Ted Turner suggested a twenty-four-hour television news network in the early 1980s, nearly everyone scoffed. Today Turner's Cable News Network keeps average citizens and heads of state alike abreast of world events. The CNN Center downtown is also headquarters of the Turner Broadcasting System, Headline News, and the Turner Publishing Company. It was once Omni International, an elaborate family-recreation facility and hotel-office complex adjoining the Omni sports arena (here hidden except for a pyramid on its roof, between the CNN Center and the Georgia Dome to the rear). When Omni International failed to draw enough visitors, Turner bought the property for his enterprises.

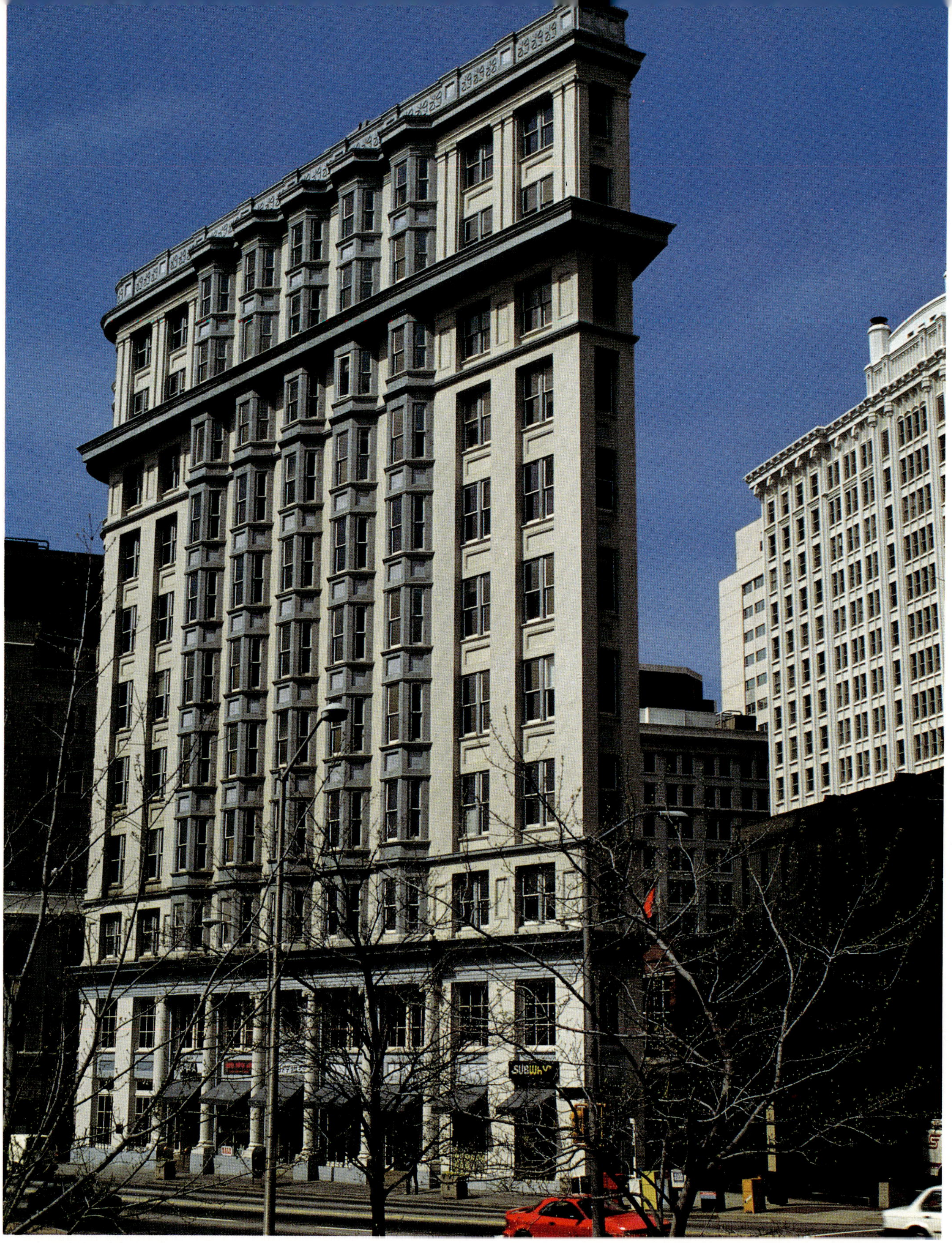

Flatiron Building

A thin, eleven-story wedge sculpted to fit a small triangular site, the Flatiron Building was the tallest in Atlanta when it was completed in 1897, and today it is the city's oldest "skyscraper" still in existence. Originally known as the English-American Building, it predated New York's famous Flatiron Building by four years. However, the New York structure—a similar tall, thin wedge—became so well known and popular that Atlantans eventually adopted the same name for their landmark.

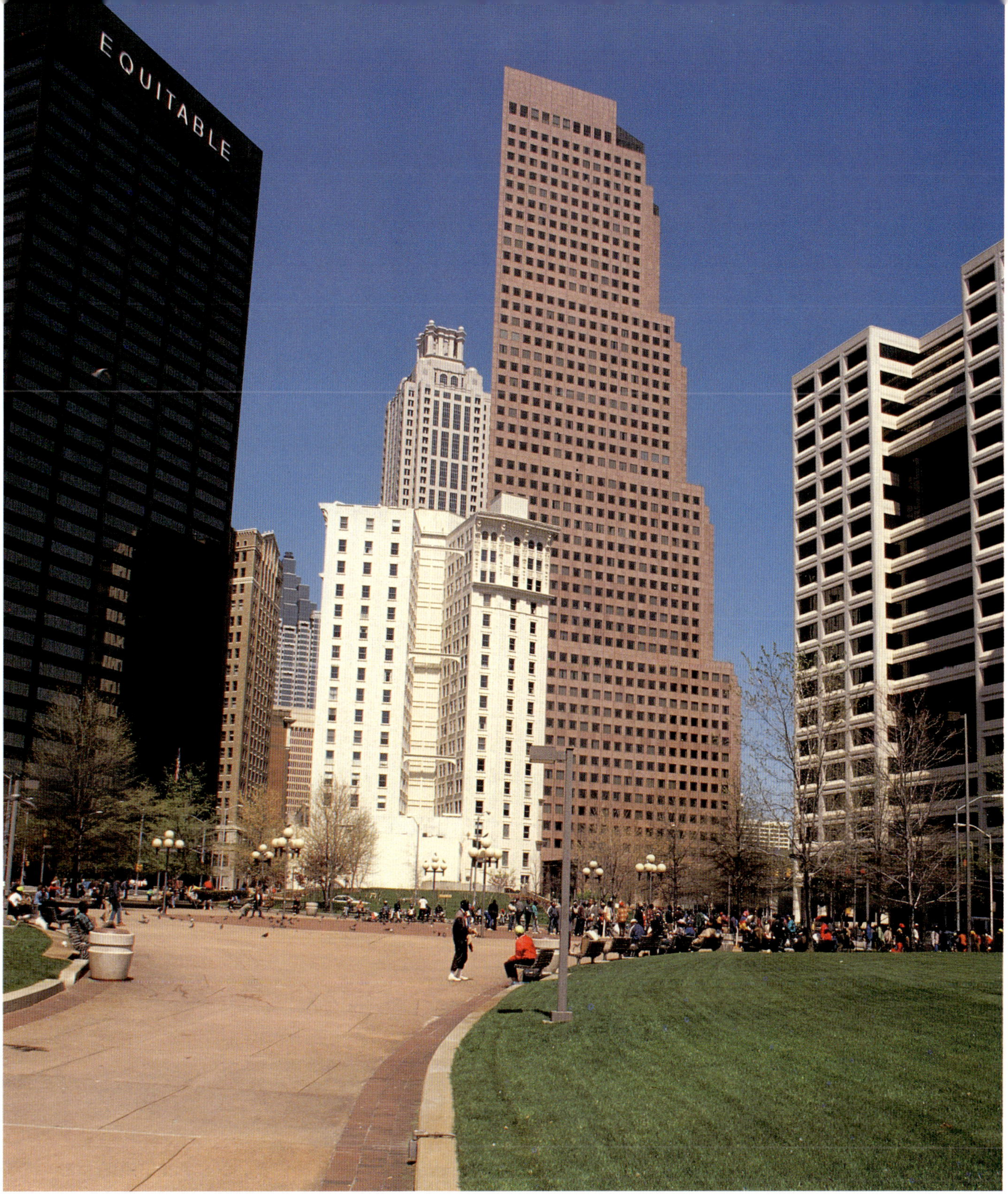

Candler Building and Woodruff Park

A V-shaped, seventeen-story tower clad in Georgia white marble at the head of Woodruff Park, the Candler Building once reigned as Atlanta's predominant skyscraper, and it remains an architectural treasure. Asa Griggs Candler, the founder of Coca-Cola and one of Atlanta's wealthiest citizens, poured his heart and a great deal of his money into the building, which was completed in 1906. The exterior is merely a foretaste of the interior, a masterpiece of marblework prolifically depicting fanciful birds and beasts, famous Atlantans, and Candler's parents. Woodruff Park, five acres of downtown greenery created in the 1970s and named for another Coca-Cola family famed for its philanthropy, is a favorite lunchtime lounging spot for office workers.

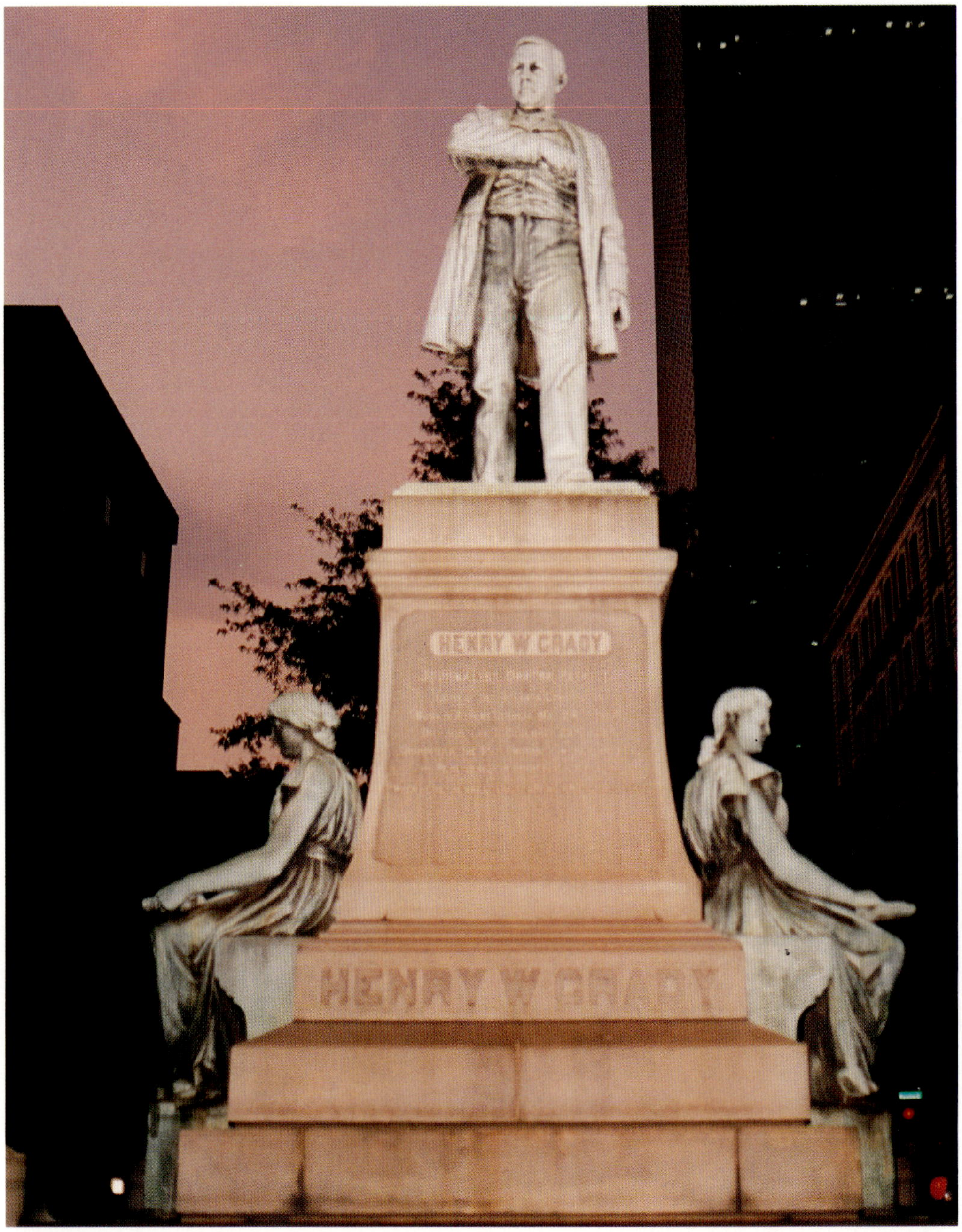

Henry Grady Statue

In 1891 some 25,000 Atlantans gathered on Marietta Street for the unveiling of a statue of journalist Henry Grady. Following his death at thirty-nine in 1889, a hospital, a high school, and the journalism department at his alma mater, the University of Georgia, were named for him. Even in his brief lifetime, Grady was recognized as a personification of the "New South"—a phrase he himself popularized. As managing editor and part owner of the Atlanta *Constitution,* he relentlessly campaigned for the metropolis and the region. Toasting Atlanta's nemesis, former Union general William T. Sherman, during an 1886 visit to New York, Grady claimed proudly that "from the ashes he left us in 1864 we have raised a brave and beautiful city."

At the left to the rear of the statue is the Atlanta *Journal* and Atlanta *Constitution* Building, which houses the newsrooms, offices, and presses for the afternoon and morning newspapers. The papers have produced a number of Pulitzer Prize winners, including *Constitution* editor Ralph McGill, whose crusade for civil rights helped awaken the region during the 1950s and 1960s.

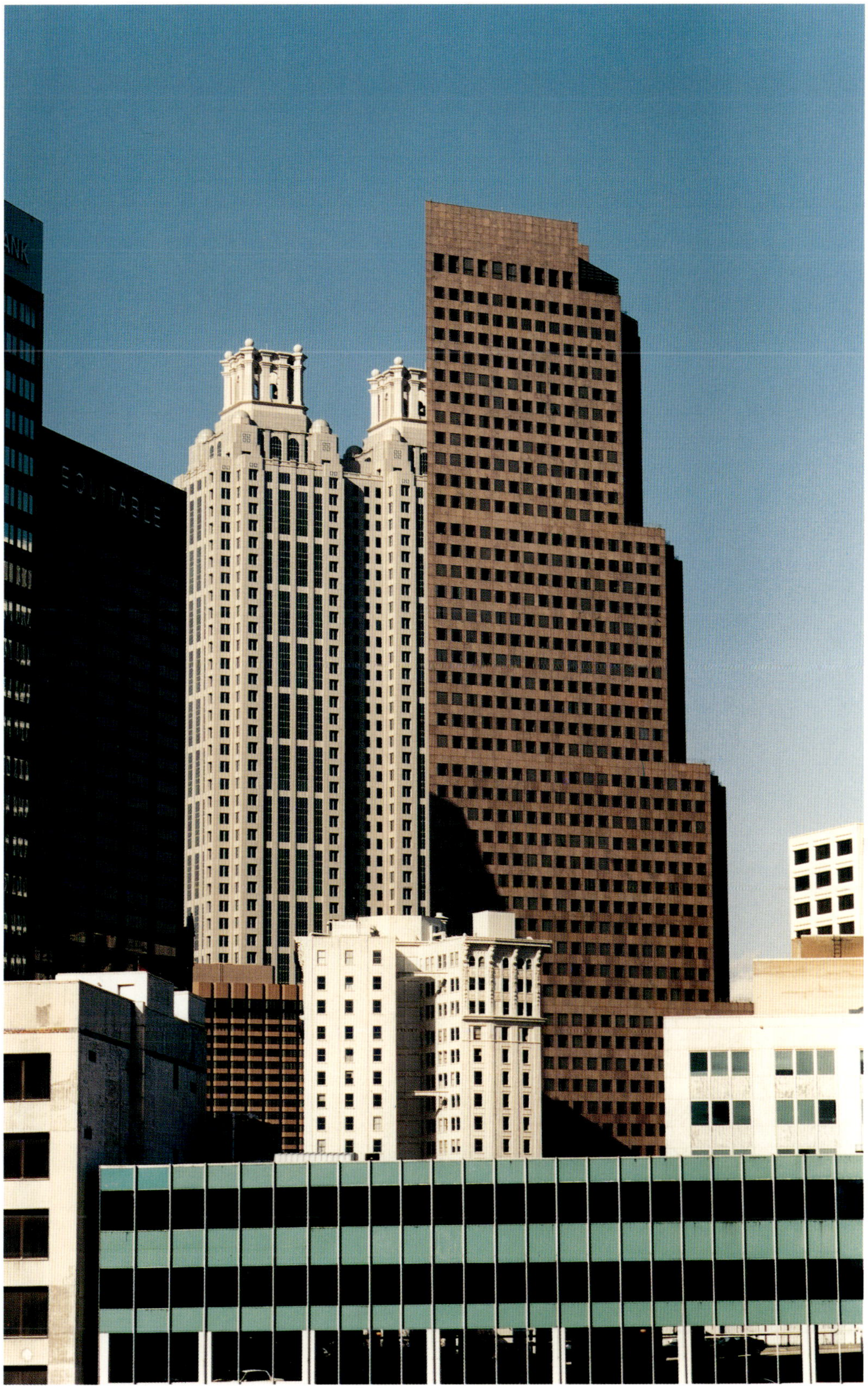

Georgia-Pacific Center

The multistepped Texas-granite profile of the Georgia-Pacific Center, home base of a giant forest-products corporation, has become a familiar landmark for Atlantans since 1982. It occupies an even more familiar site: the building rises on the ashes of Loew's Grand Theatre, where the film *Gone with the Wind* had its world premiere in 1939. Built as DeGive's Opera House (1882), Loew's was one of the great, elegant venues for cinema lovers. It was gutted by fire in 1978.

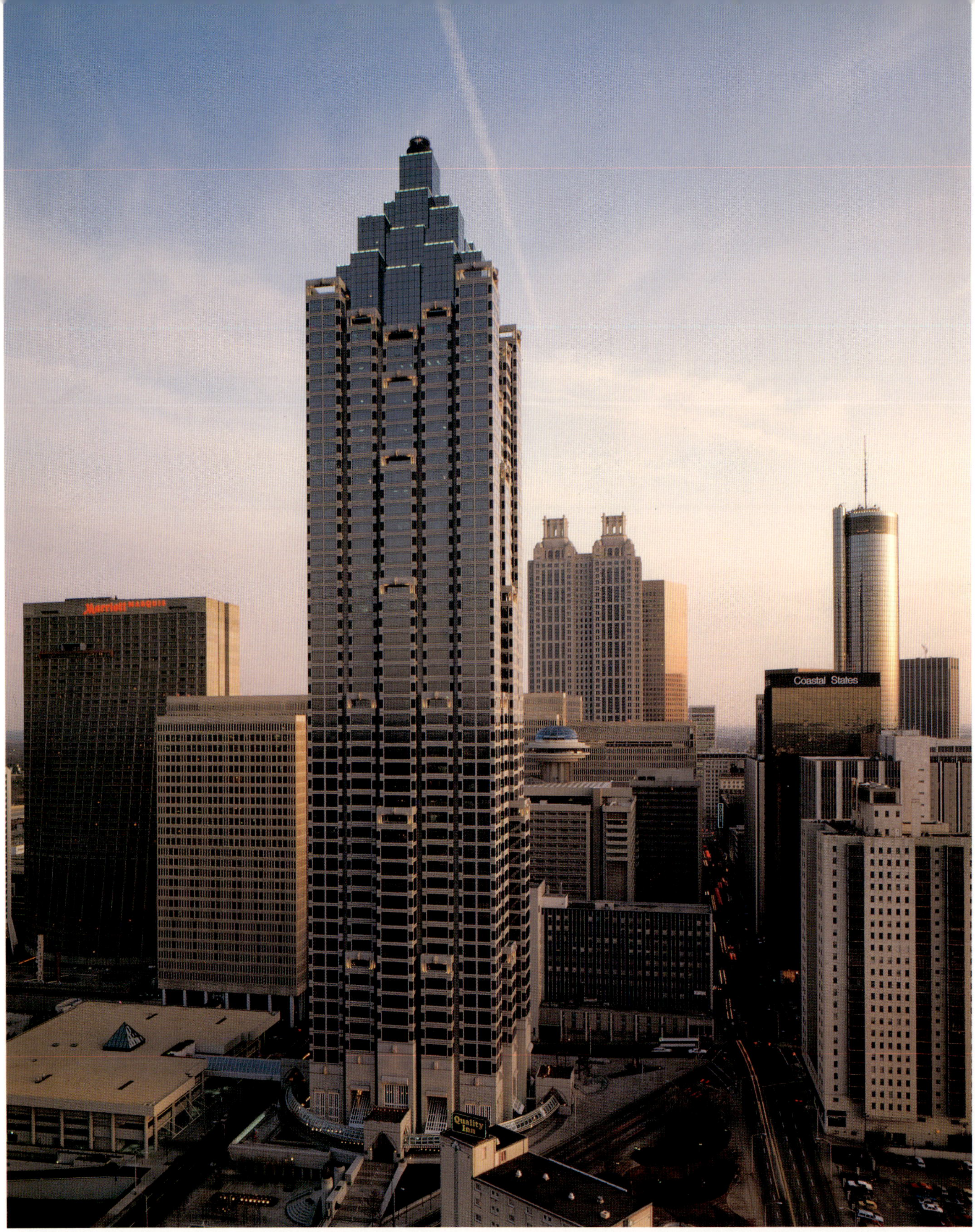

Peachtree Center

The phenomenal growth of Peachtree Center not only reflects the rejuvenation of downtown Atlanta but in large part fueled it. The complex, expressing the ongoing vision of developer and architect John Portman, extends from its newest structure, the sixty-story One Peachtree Center office building (foreground), on the north to the double-crowned 191 Peachtree Tower on the south. In between, among numerous office towers, trade centers, and other facilities, rise three of the city's largest and best-known hotels: the Atlanta Marriott Marquis (left), the Hyatt Regency Atlanta (blue dome, center), and the seventy-three-story mirrored-glass Westin Peachtree Plaza (right).

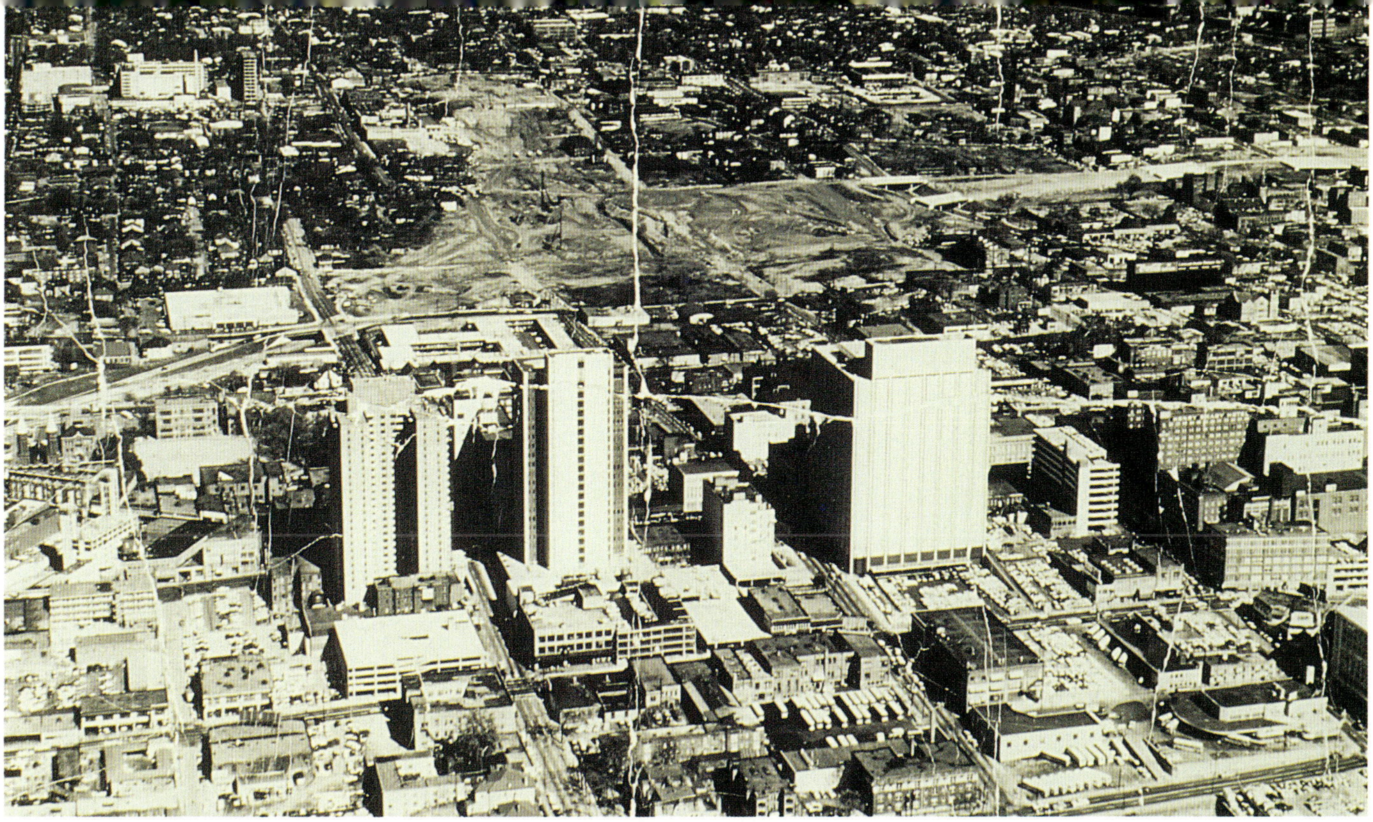

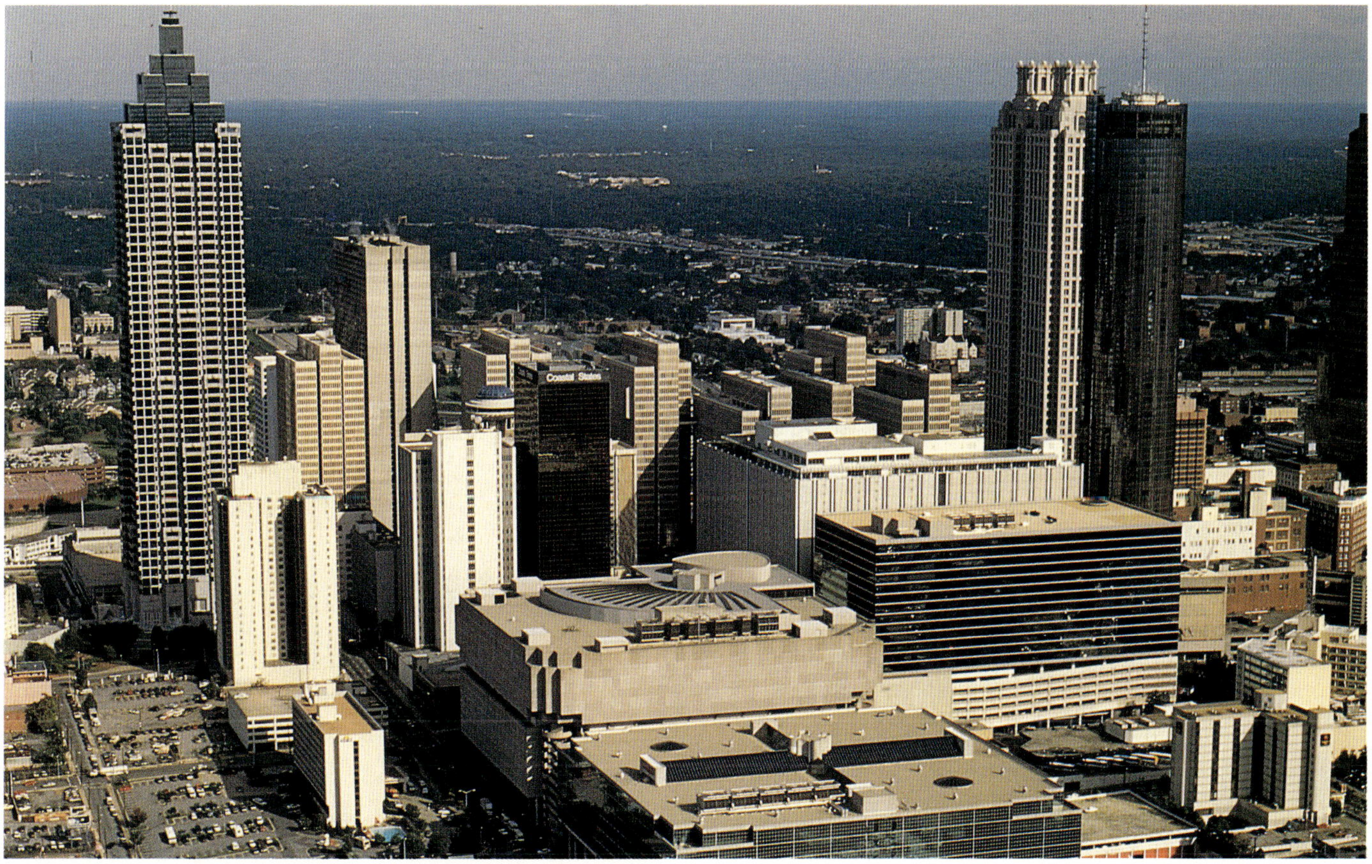

Peachtree Street near its branch with West Peachtree once showcased the mansions of wealthy Atlantans, but after decades of decline the area was a nondescript backwater in 1962 (top). Its most prominent architectural features were two office buildings (left and center) and the huge, newly opened Atlanta Merchandise Mart (right), designed by John Portman as a wholesale trade center.

Portman's plan, essentially, was to use business to attract business. A view of the same area in 1992 (bottom) shows the idea's success. The Merchandise Mart—which had the greatest square footage of any building in the South when it was built—is now nearly three times larger but half hidden by other wholesale-trade giants: the Inforum (foreground), for computer-related products; the Atlanta Apparel Mart (behind the Inforum); and the Atlanta Gift Mart (in front of the Merchandise Mart).

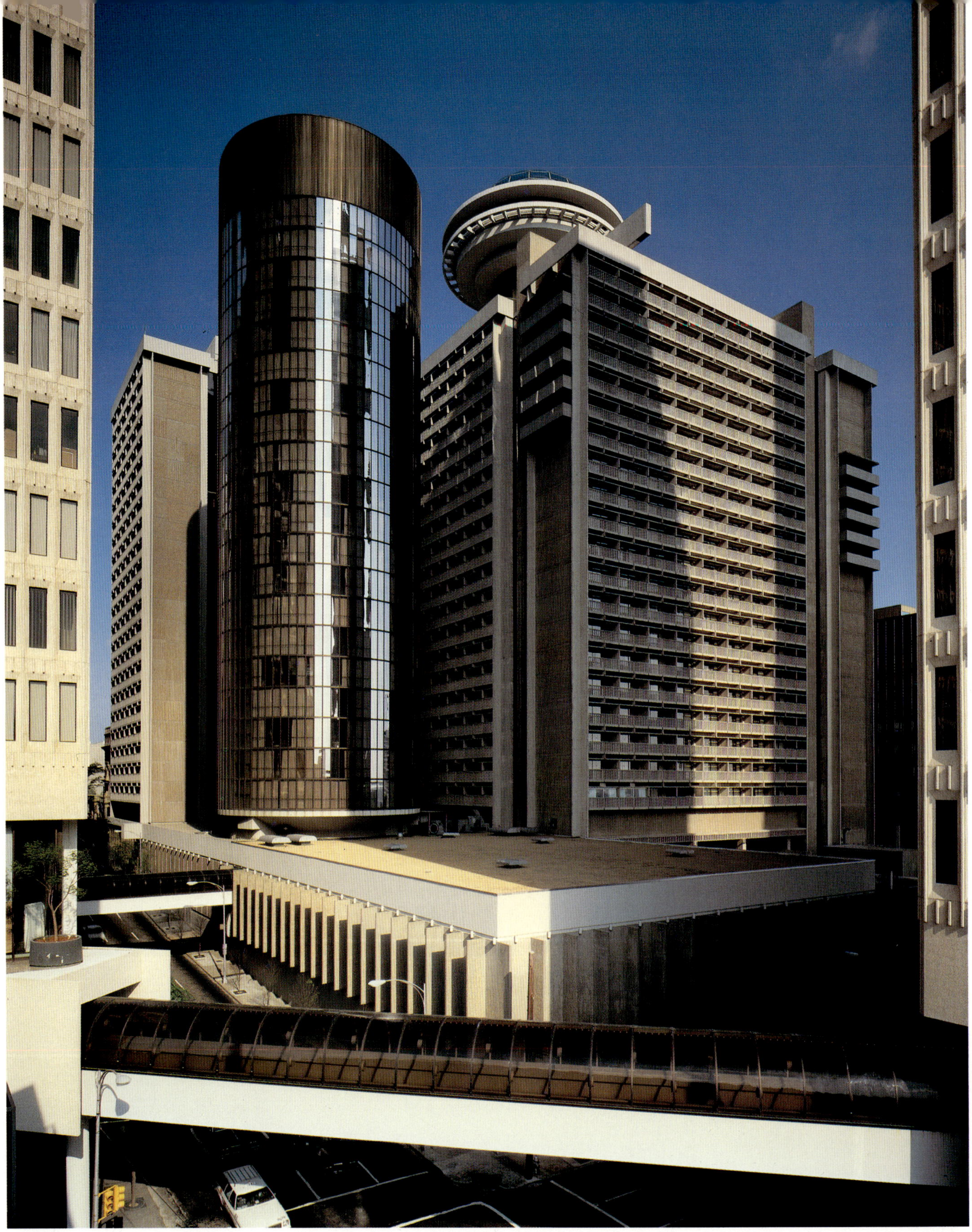

Hyatt Regency Atlanta Hotel

After its opening in 1967, the Hyatt Regency—the first major new hotel built in downtown Atlanta since the 1920s—soon became an internationally recognized icon of the city's resurgence. John Portman's revolutionary design, in particular the hotel's stunning atrium lobby (facing page), was copied worldwide.

The UFO-like dome atop the building houses a revolving lounge that—although increasingly hemmed in by taller structures—still offers spectacular views of Atlanta. The glass tower, added in 1971 as one of two major expansions of the hotel since its opening, was a prototype for Portman's Westin Peachtree Plaza, completed in 1976.

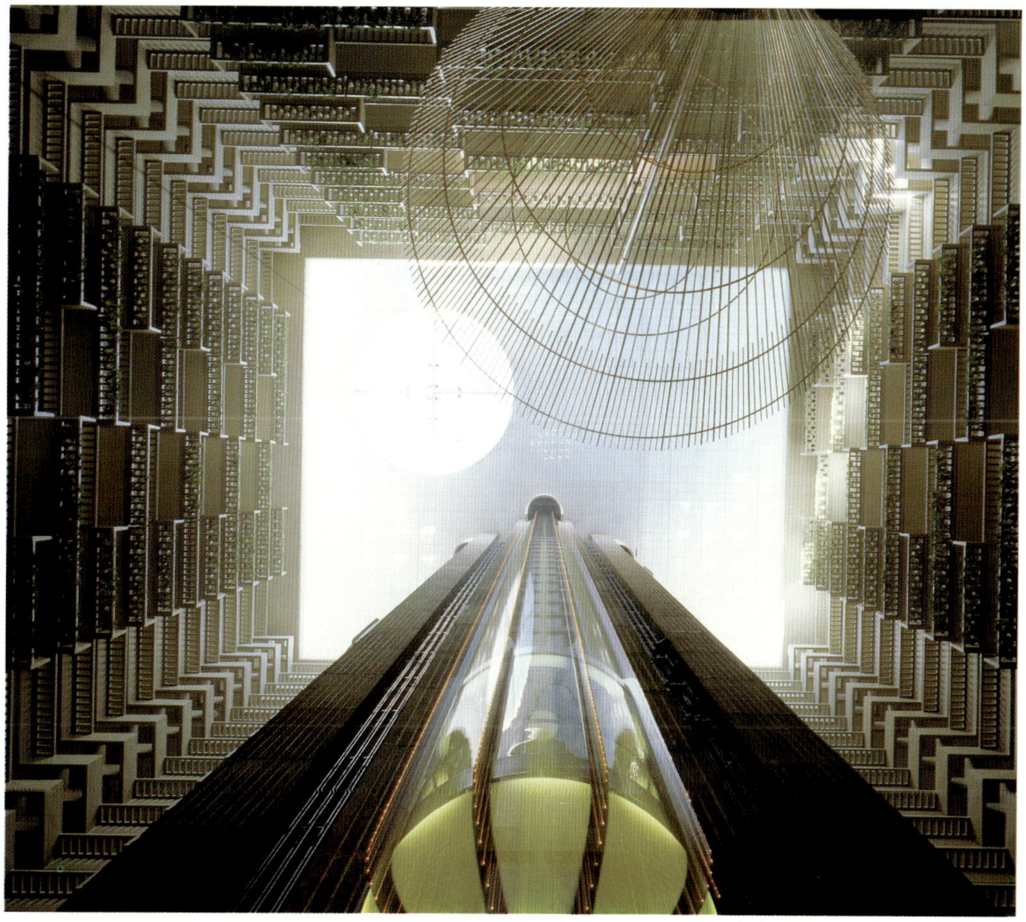

Hyatt Regency Lobby

The Hyatt Regency's twenty-two-story, sky-lighted atrium lobby with its bubble elevators remains the hotel's hallmark. This view is from floor level straight up. The top of Richard Lipphold's 120-foot sculpture *Flora Raris* spreads its wiry bloom opposite the elevator bank.

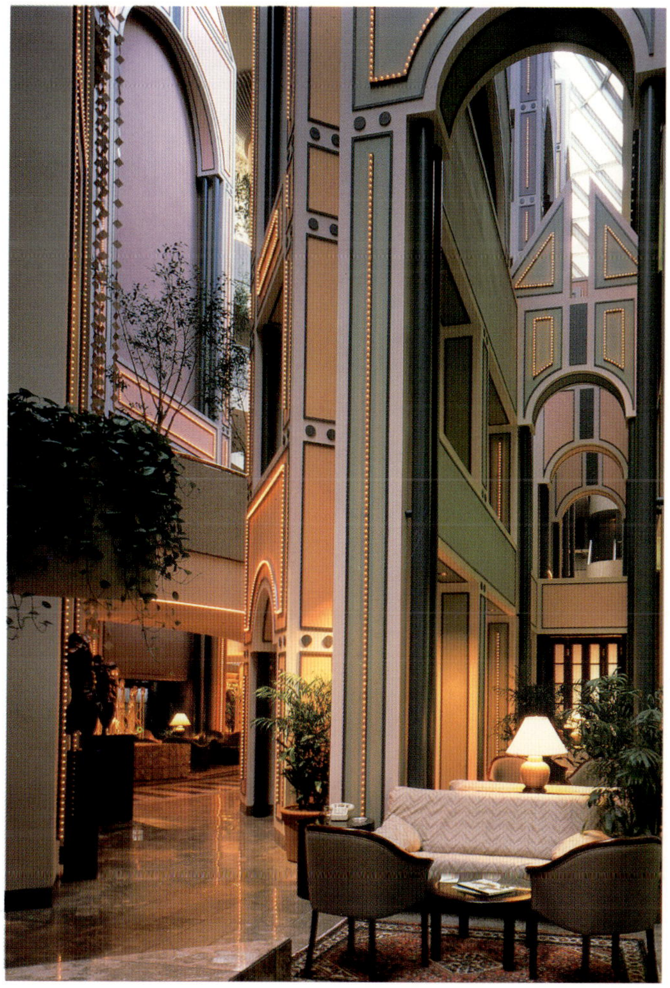

Westin Peachtree Plaza Lobby

Completely renovated in 1986, the Westin Peachtree Plaza Hotel welcomes travelers with a playful, oversized stage-set of a lobby, reminiscent of Copenhagen's Tivoli Gardens.

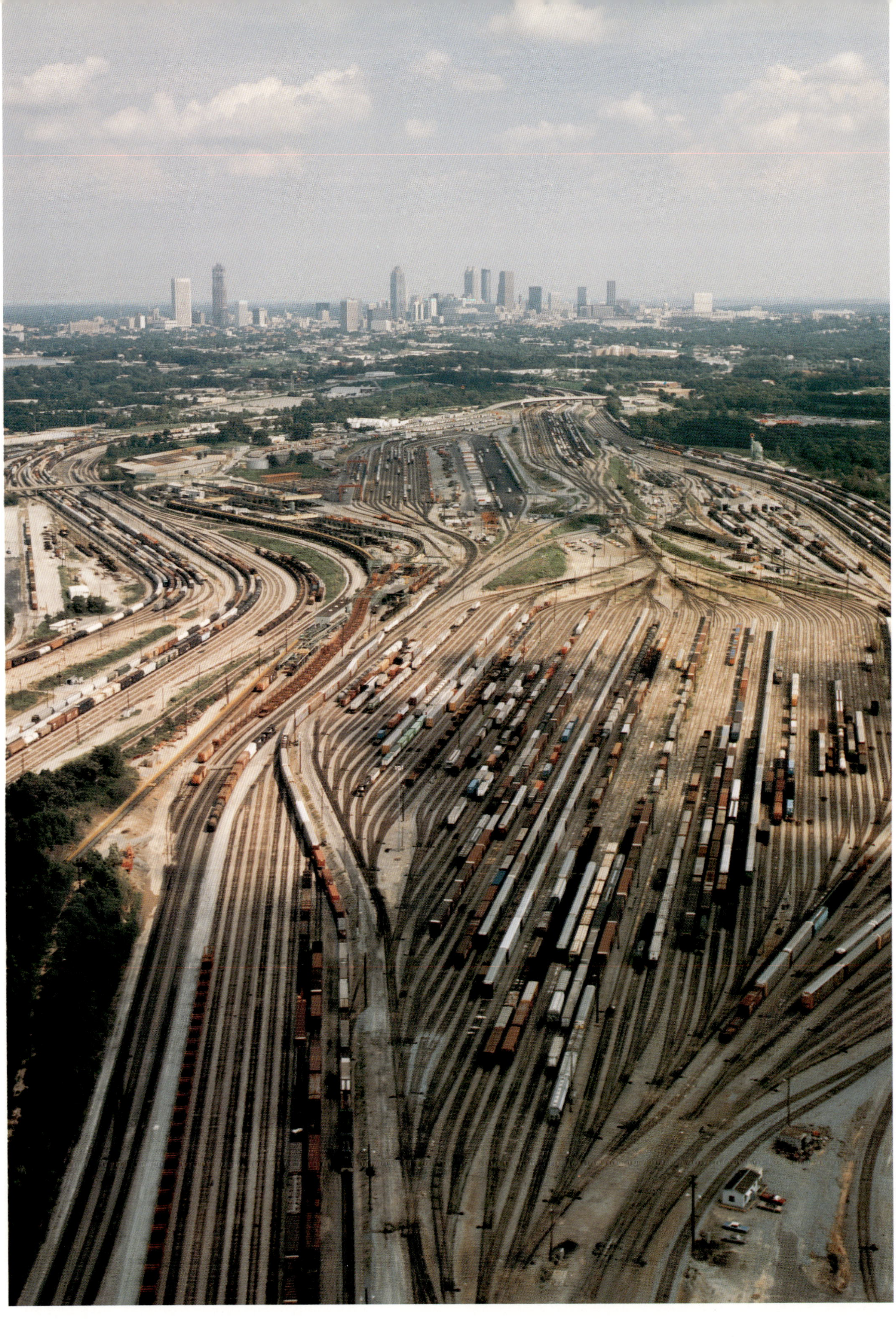

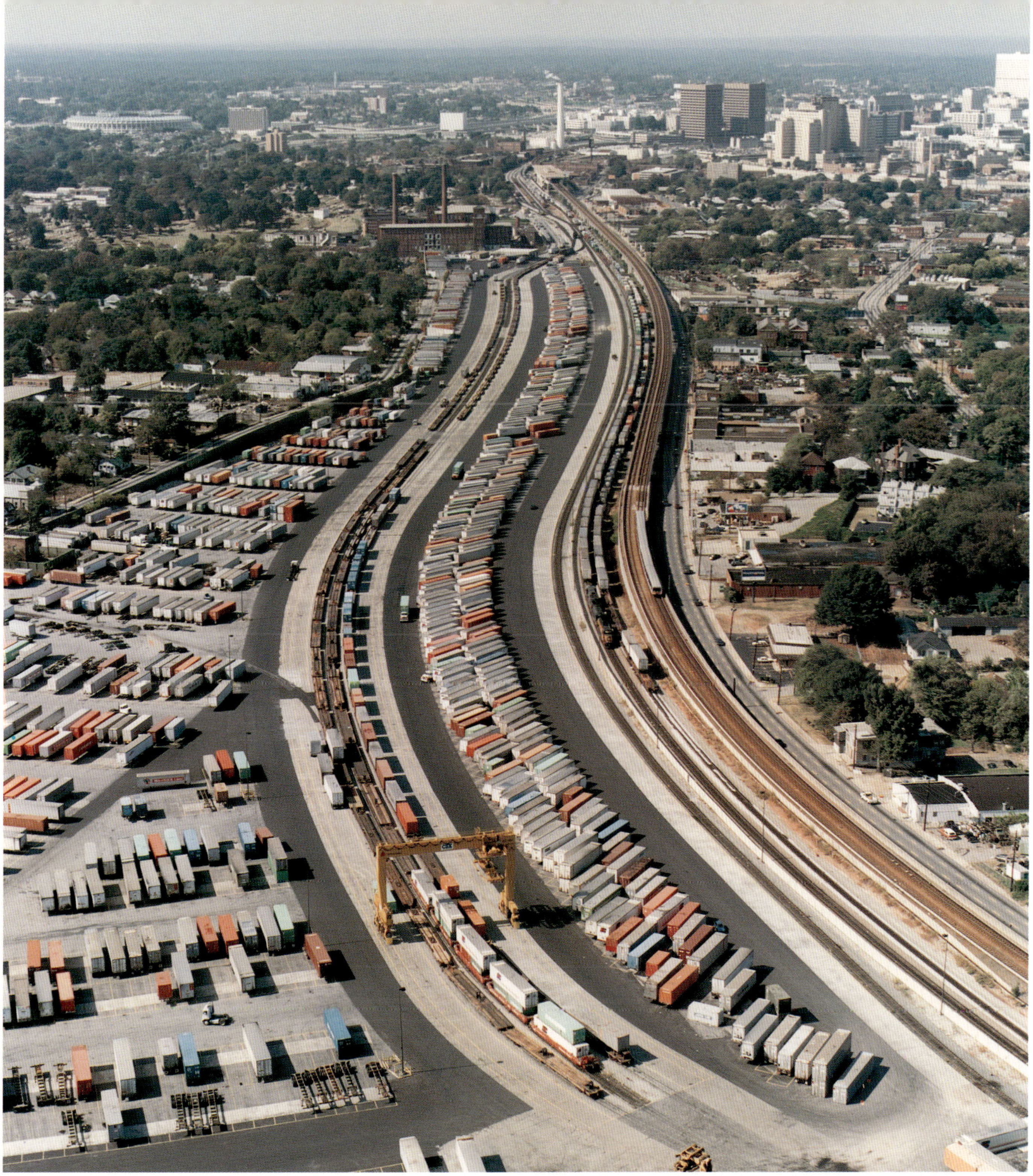

Rail Yards, Piggyback Rail Terminal

Beginning as the tiny railhead of Terminus in 1837, Atlanta evolved into a hub of rail transport for the South. At one time, fifteen different lines met in the city. Passenger-train service has long been eclipsed by air travel, but Atlanta is still the nation's second-largest inland freight-distribution center, after Chicago. Intermodalism—the shipping of goods in readily transferrable containers—has taken a dominant hold in the transportation business. Companies find it makes sense to base regional operations in Atlanta because of its rail lines and trucking headquarters. Cargo containers unloaded from ships at Jacksonville, Charleston, Savannah, or Brunswick are moved by train to piggyback yards in Atlanta and transferred to trucks for regional distribution.

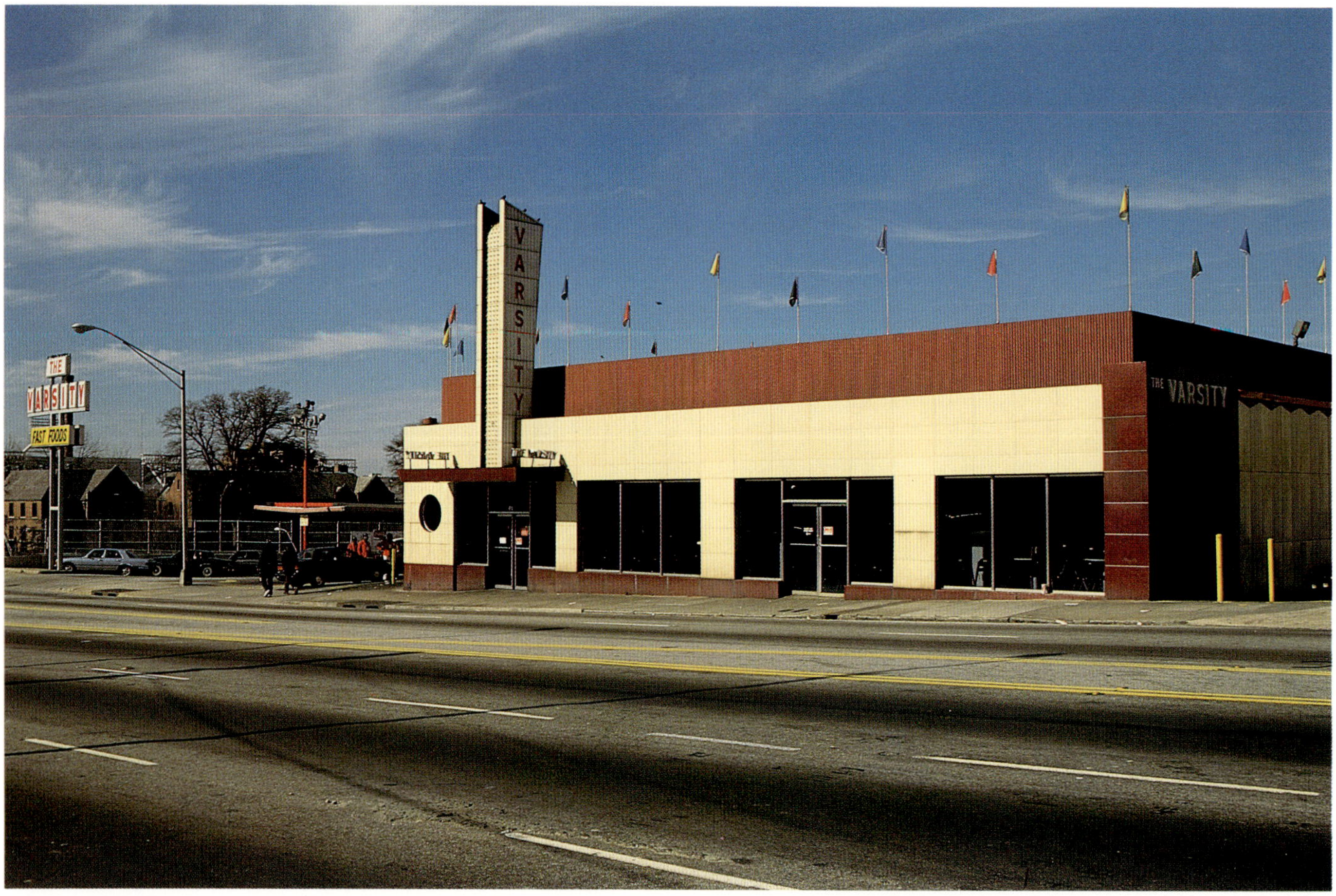

The Varsity

The "world's largest drive-in" has served hot dogs, onion rings, chili steaks, and fried pies to generations of Atlantans. Frank Gordy opened a small restaurant in 1928 as a hang-out for students from nearby Georgia Tech. Business boomed, especially after Gordy hit upon a system for serving customers in their cars and installed awnings under which they could park. The present restaurant building, a period piece in a substyle of art deco known as "streamlined moderne," was begun in 1940, with numerous additions since. Our inclusion of this location in the "downtown" section is arbitrary; it might as easily be called "lower Midtown."

Part II

Colleges and Universities

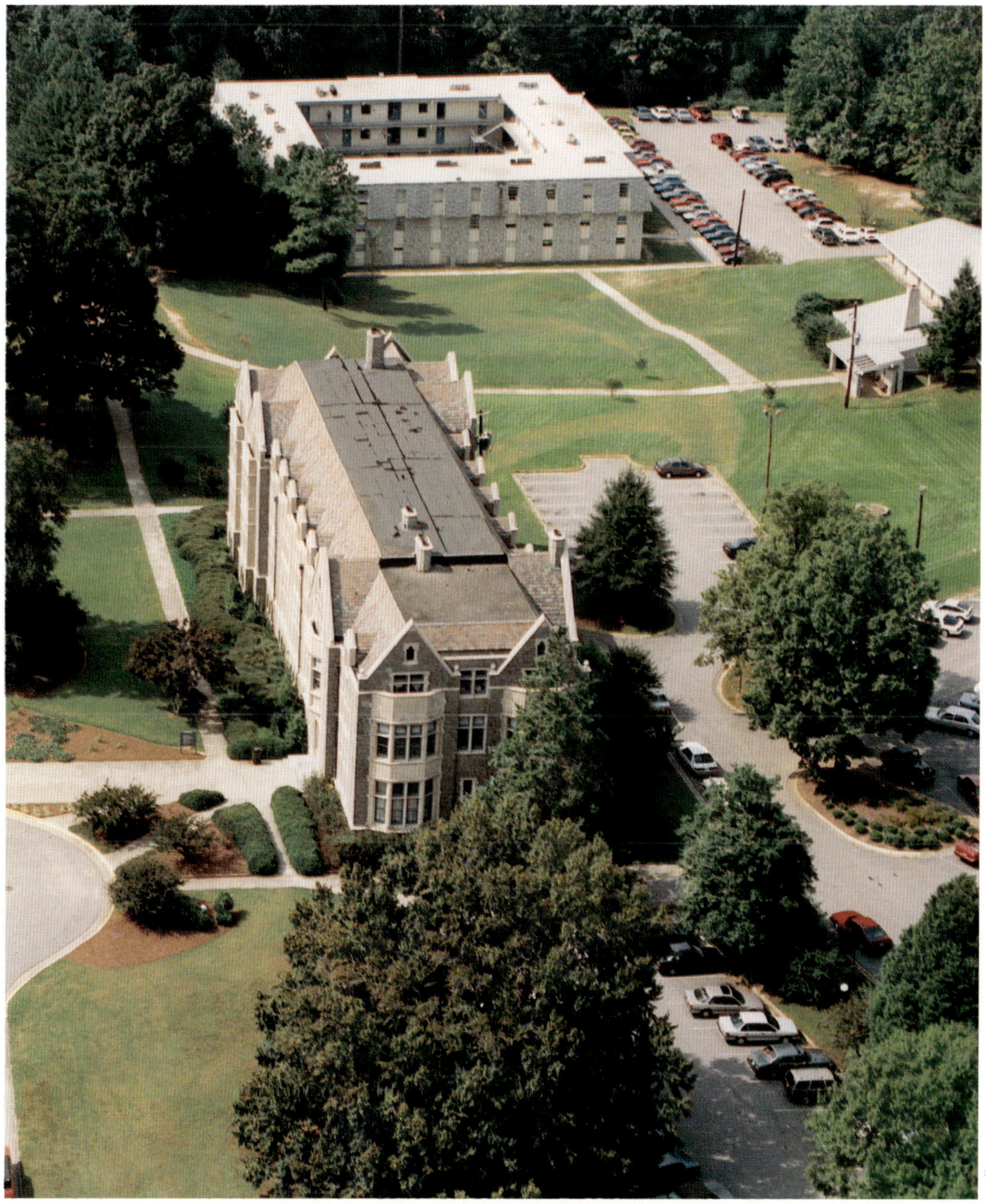

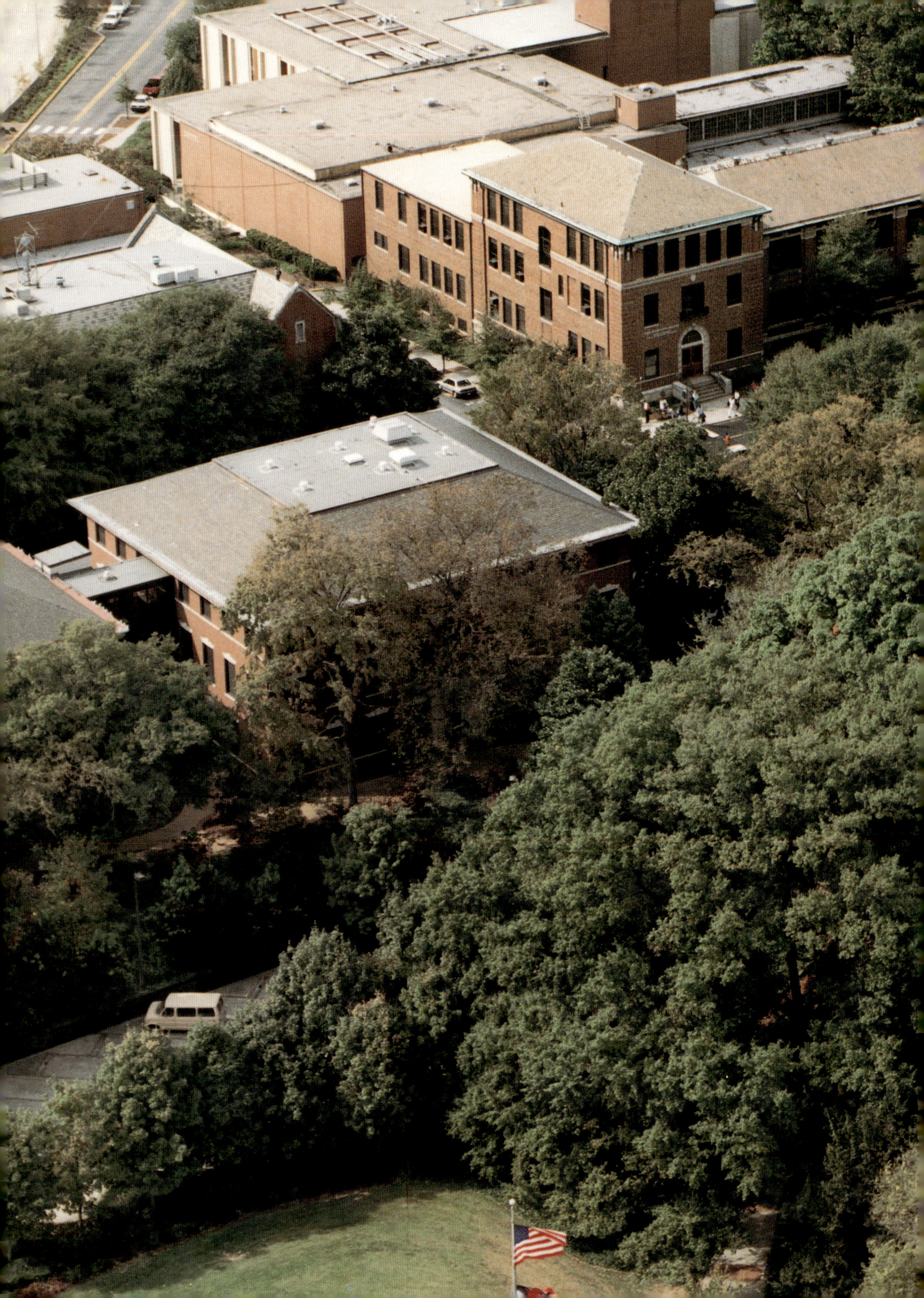

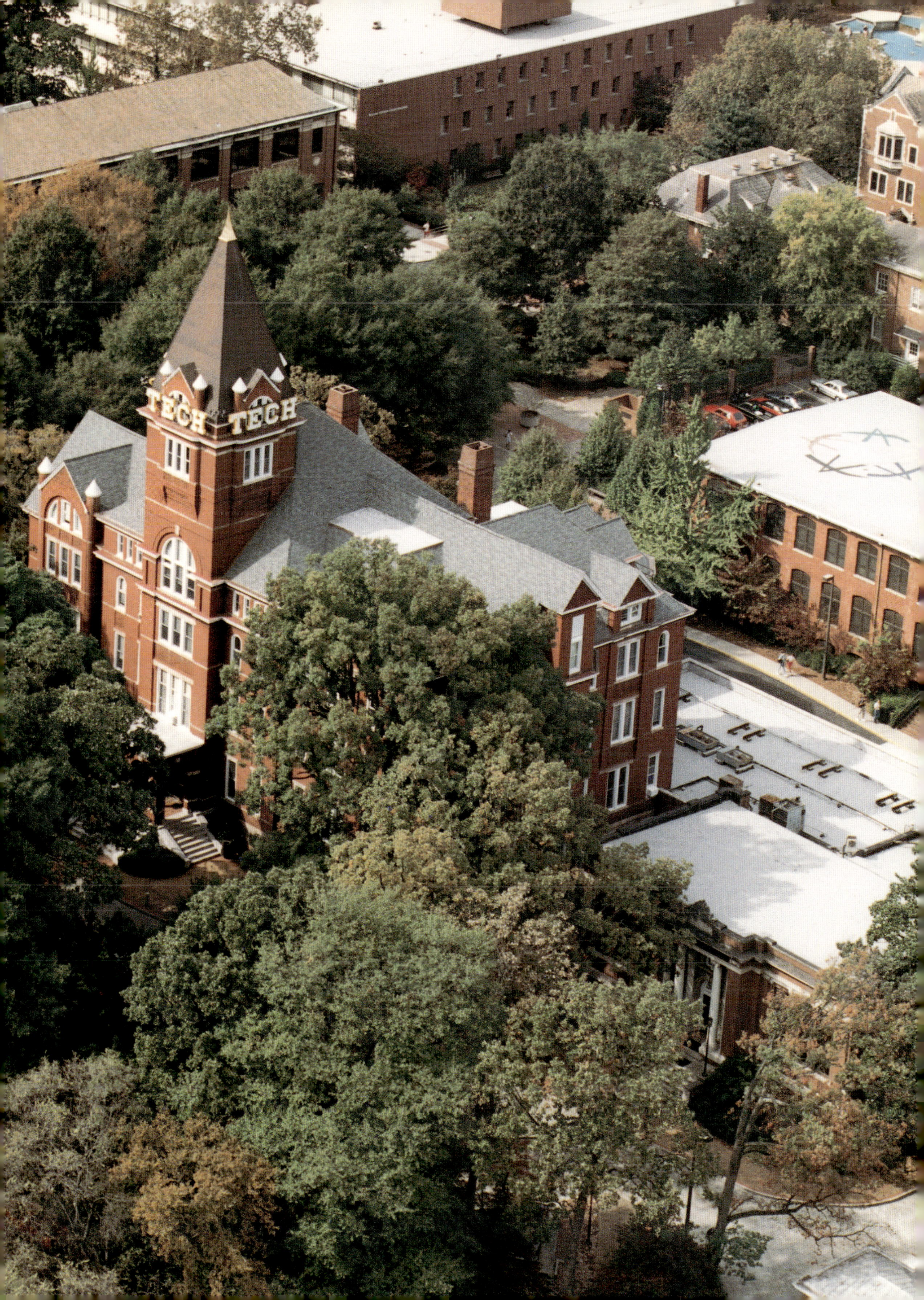
TECH TECH

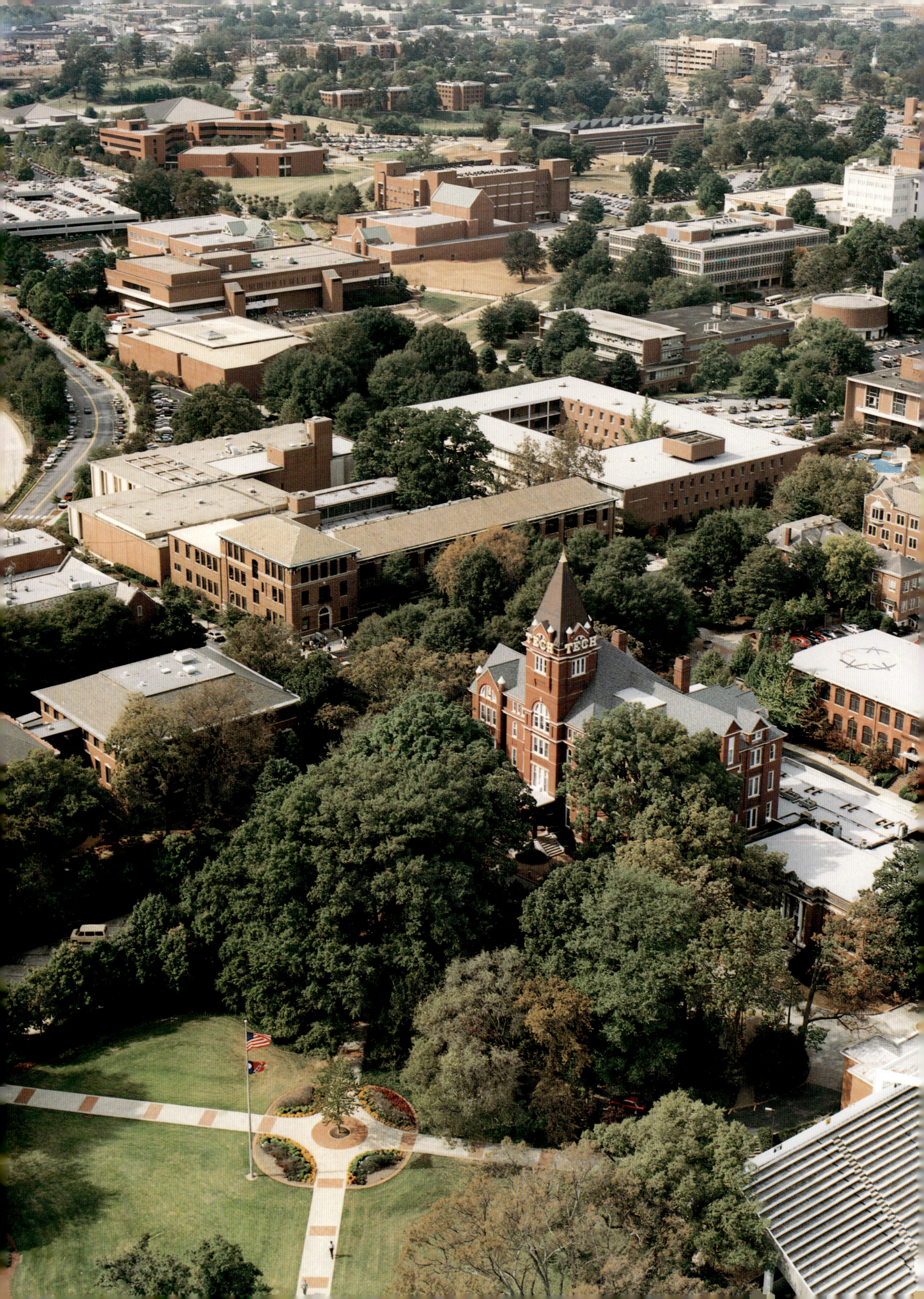
TECH TECH

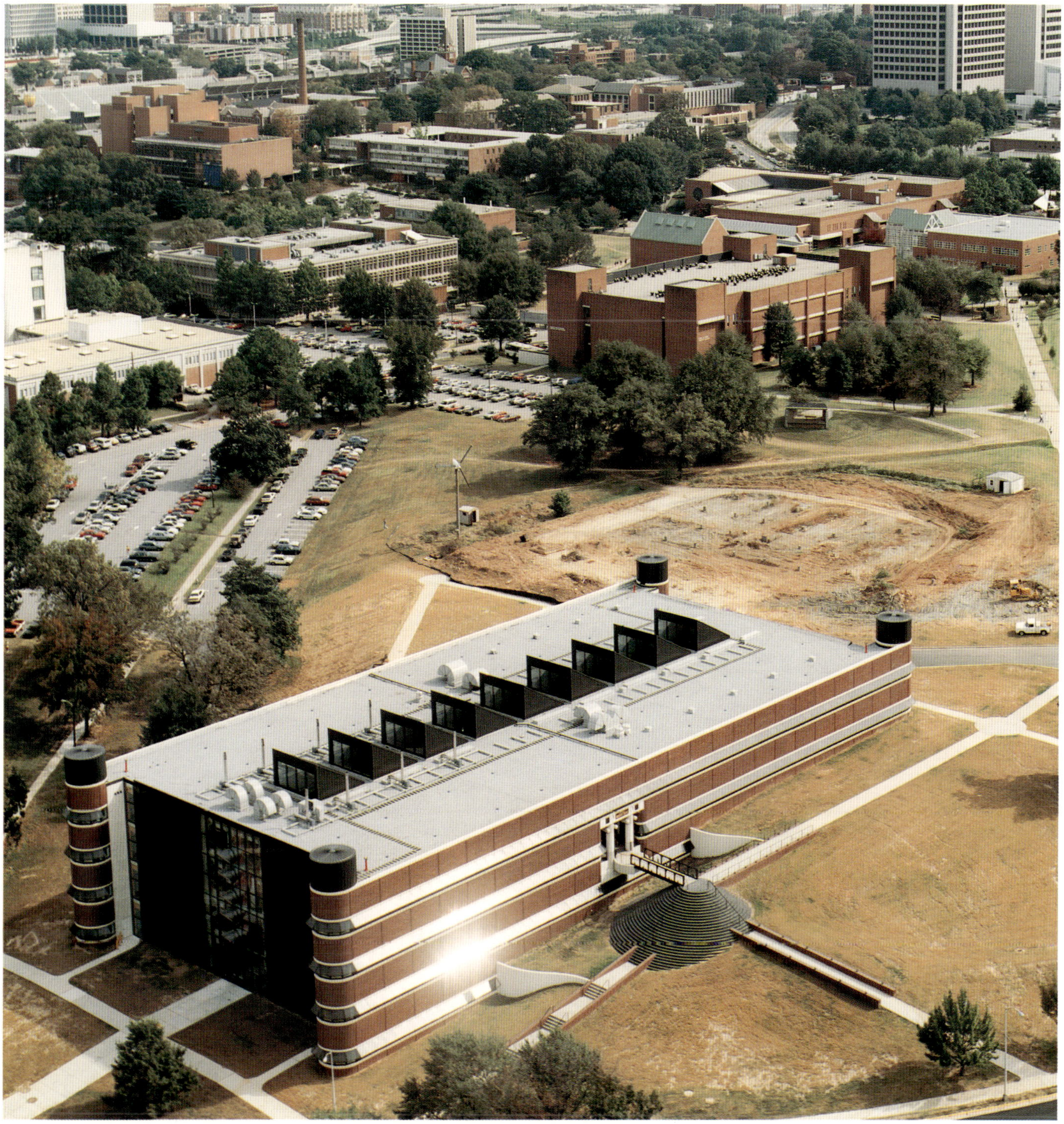

Georgia Institute of Technology

Atlanta won a fierce competition for the state technological school when citizens in 1885 offered to contribute $170,000 plus a building site for the institution, beating out bids from Athens, Macon, Milledgeville, and Penfield. Georgia Tech began holding classes in 1888 with 129 students and a single building. Today its campus has enlarged to more than three hundred acres and its enrollment to more than 12,000. With a worldwide reputation, the school offers highly regarded programs in computers, aerospace engineering, microelectronics, information management, and other cutting-edge technologies. The institution's original 1888 home continues to serve as its Administration Building (left, center foreground). Built 102 years later, the Manufacturing Research Center (above, foreground) playfully expresses the school's technological emphasis.

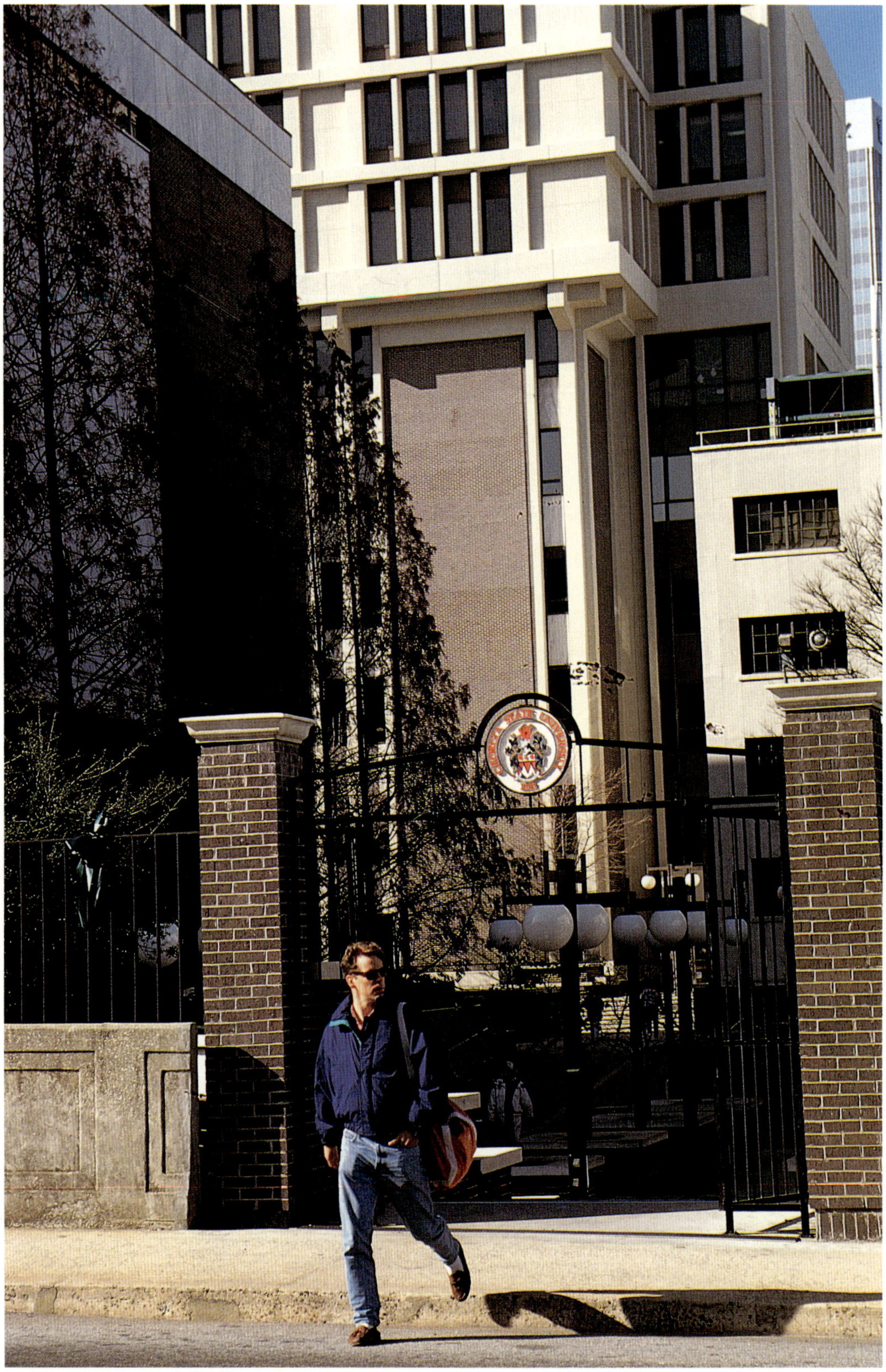

Georgia State University

A few blocks northeast of the capitol is Georgia State University, a rapidly growing institution that began as an offshoot of Georgia Tech in 1913. Originally called the Evening School of Commerce, it was intended for working people who wanted to complete degrees or do graduate work in their fields. Competing for space in Atlanta's crowded business district, the school built upward rather than outward, creating a quintessentially urban campus. Georgia State's Colleges of Arts and Sciences, Business, Education, and Law are considered to be among the best in the region.

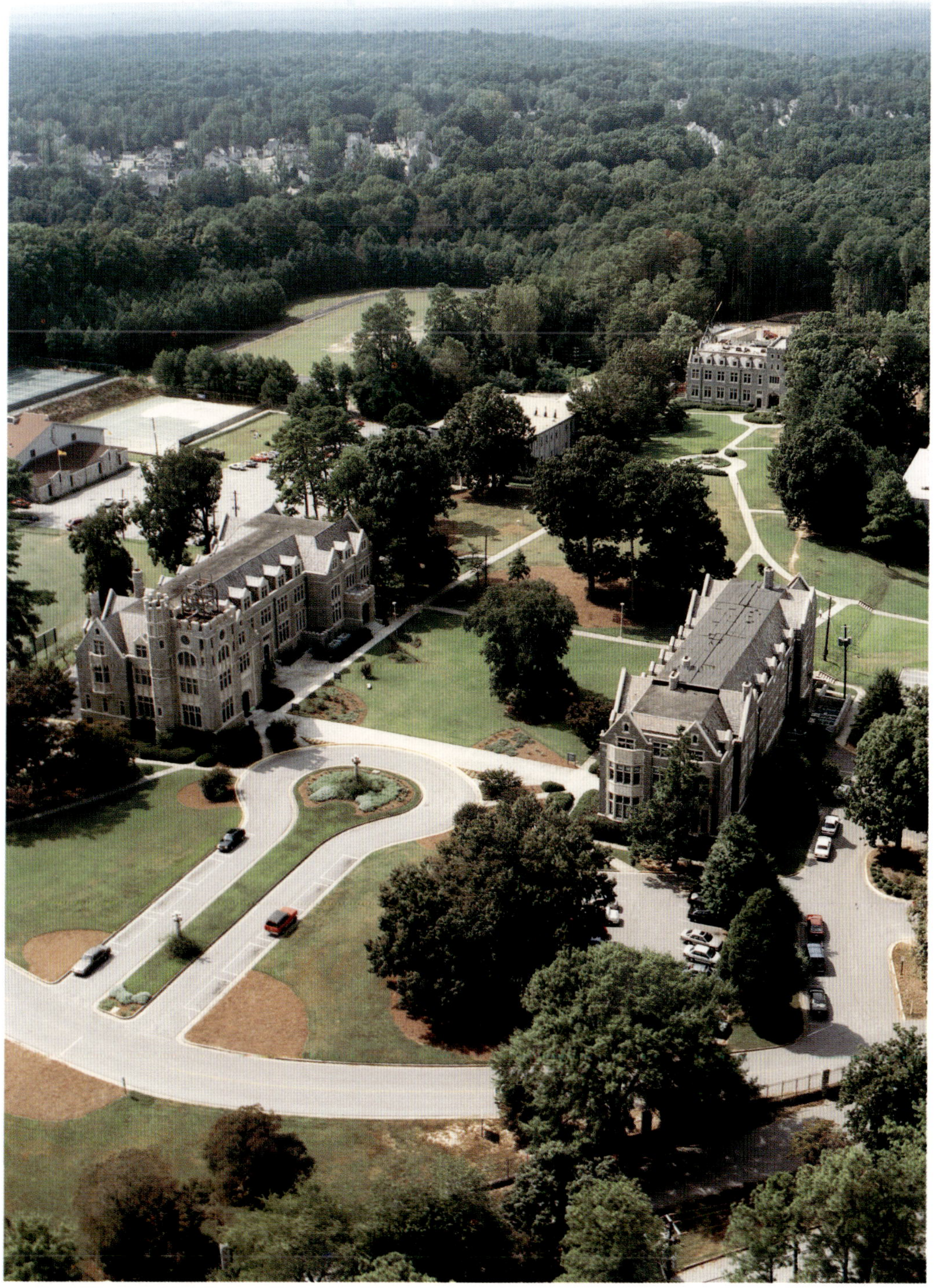

Oglethorpe University

Oglethorpe opened in Atlanta in 1870, the reincarnation of a college founded near Milledgeville in 1835 but closed during the Civil War. The new school failed after only two years but, remarkably, was resurrected again in 1915, when groundbreaking ceremonies took place for a new campus on donated land that was then far out in the country on Peachtree Road. John Thomas Lupton, a Coca-Cola bottler from Chattanooga, was an early patron of the school, giving $100,000 initially, then monthly donations of $10,000 to keep the college growing. The newspaper magnate William Randolph Hearst contributed land in California and $250,000. Stone Mountain granite was used to build a campus designed to resemble that of Corpus Christi College at England's Oxford University. The school is named for James Edward Oglethorpe, founder of the Georgia colony.

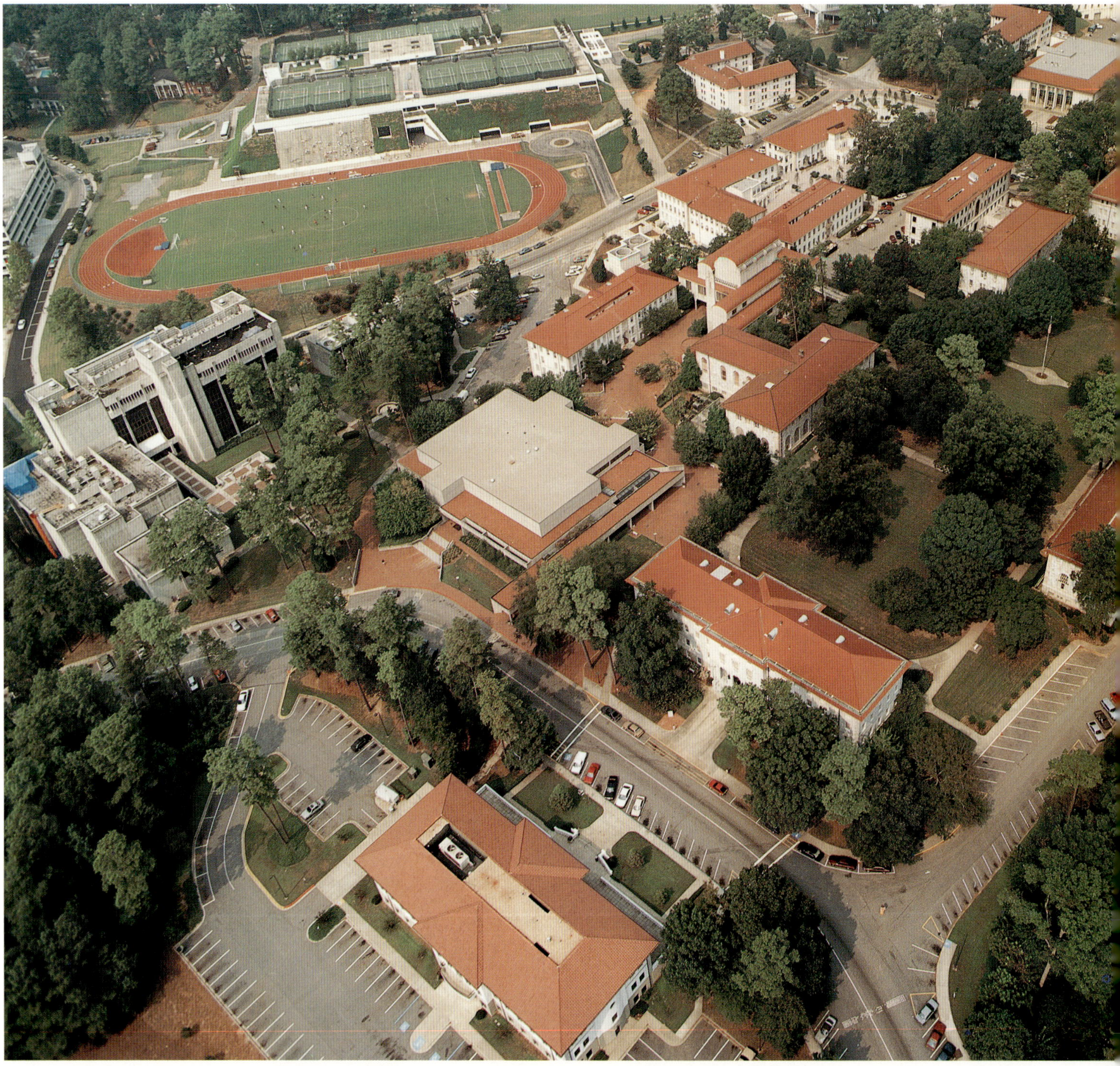

Emory University

Named for a Methodist bishop of Maryland, Emory College was chartered in 1836 and spent most of its early existence in Oxford, Georgia (where a branch of the school still exists). In 1914, Asa G. Candler, who wanted a Methodist university for Atlanta and whose brother Warren had been president of Emory, put up $1 million to attract the school to the city. He later donated seventy-five acres of his Druid Hills land development as a site. In this peaceful, wooded setting, Henry Hornbostel, the architect of Carnegie Tech in Pittsburgh, created a campus of tile-roofed Italian Renaissance buildings. Rechartered as a university in 1915, Emory has continued to thrive with large donations of Coca-Cola money, and today has an enrollment of nearly 10,000.

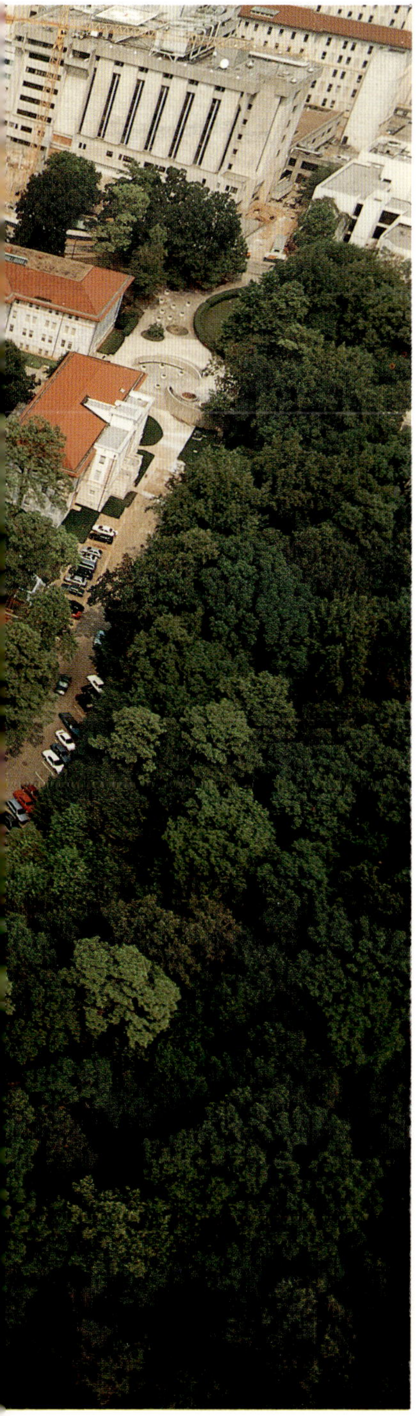

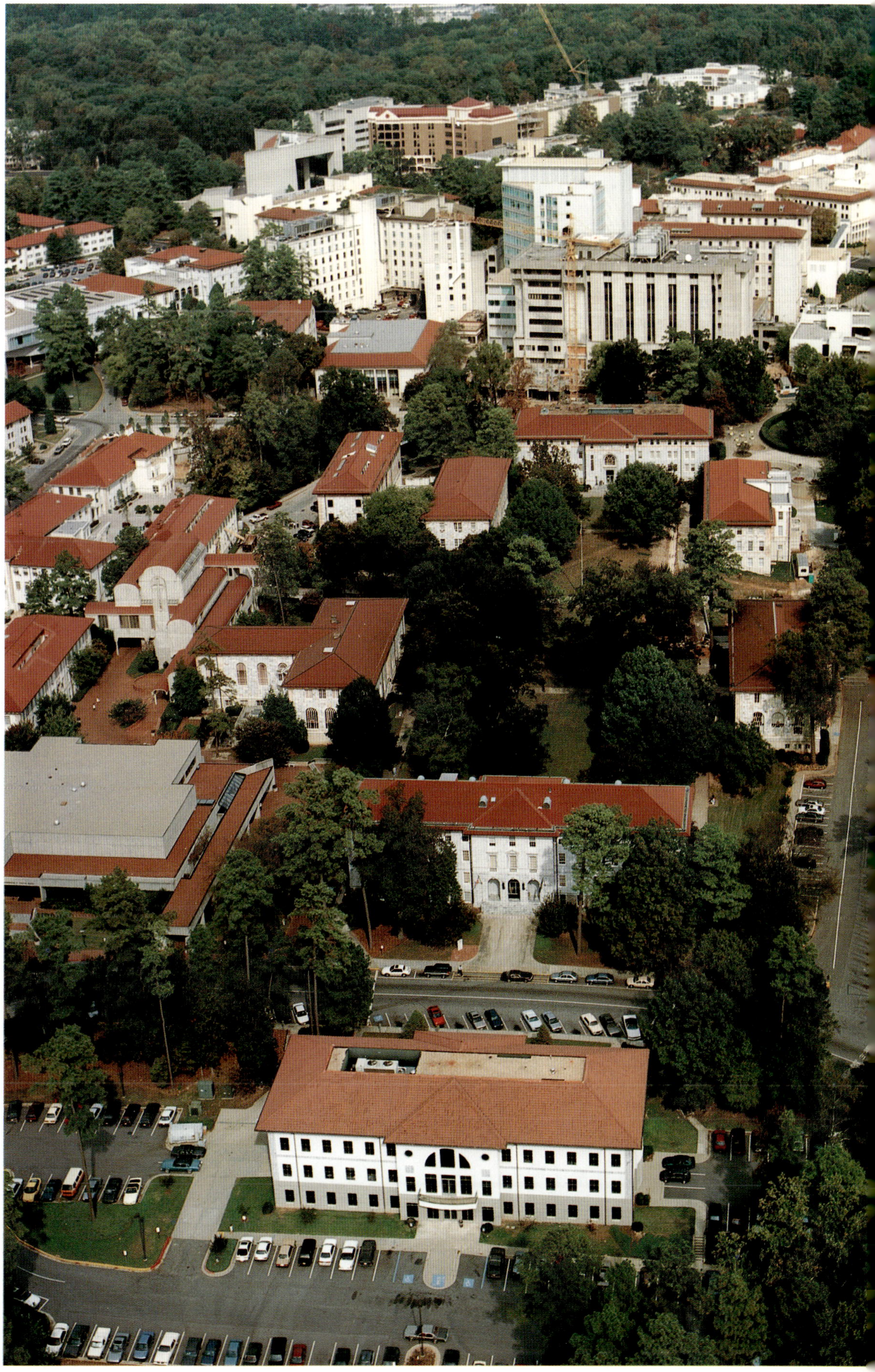

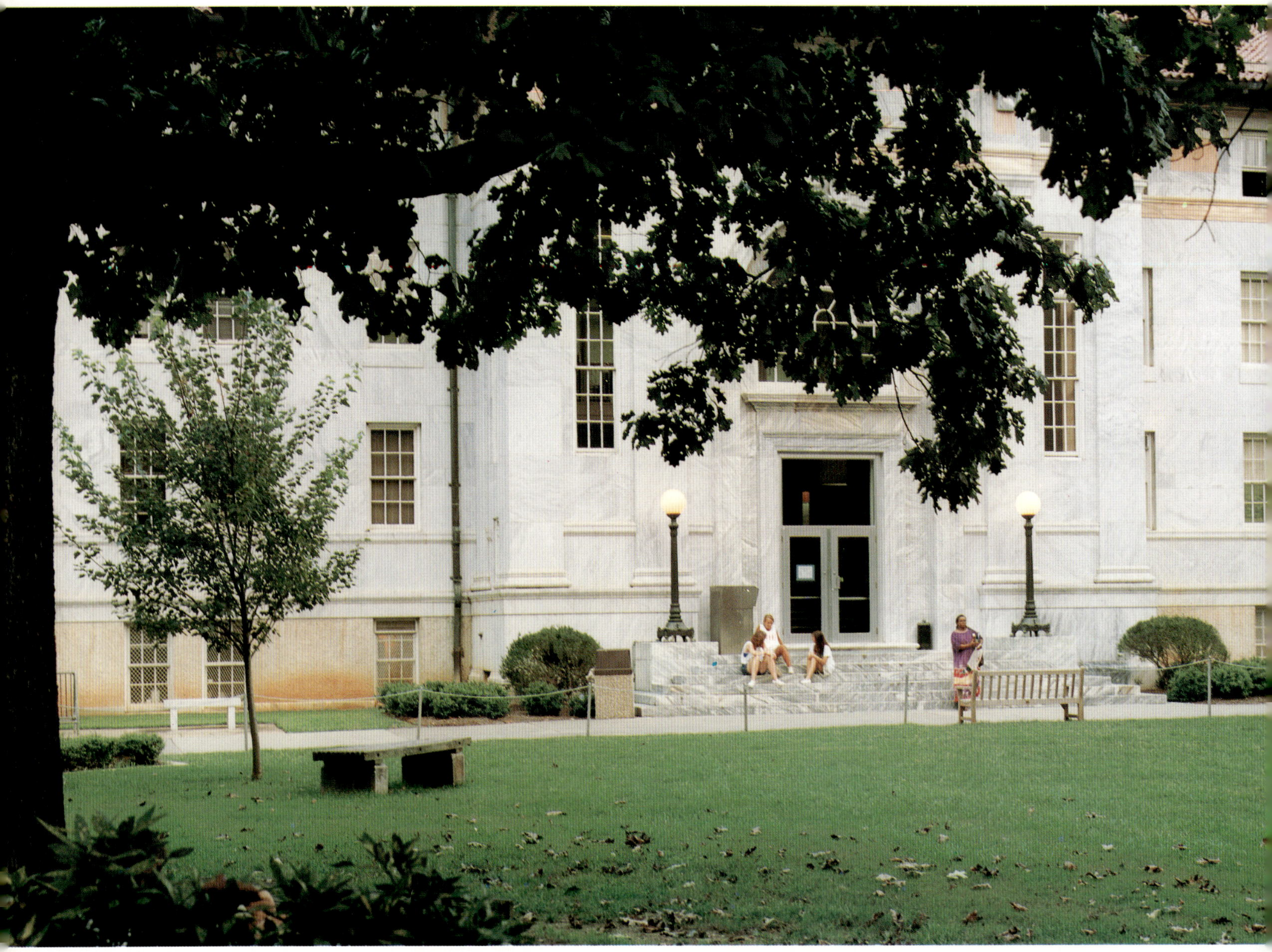

Candler Library

Students relax on the steps of the Asa Griggs Candler Library on the Emory University quadrangle.

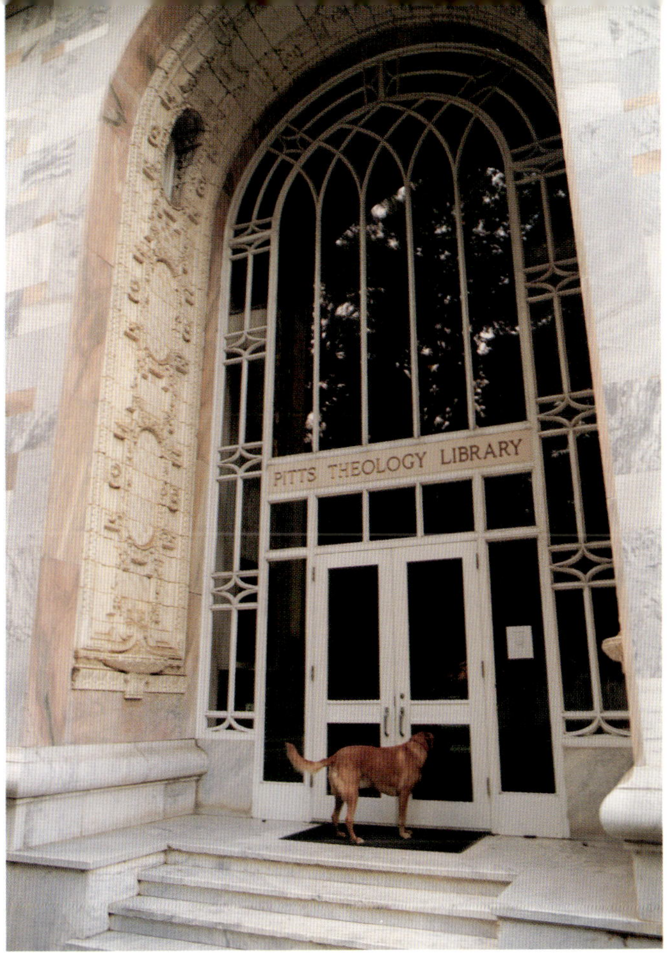

Pitts Theology Library

The Candler School of Theology at Emory has the second-largest theological library in North America, with more than 400,000 volumes. The library was named for Atlanta banker William Pitts and his family, which supported its 1965 renovation and expansion. The exterior features decorative use of thin, varicolored marble "scraps" produced in trimming the original rough blocks to size.

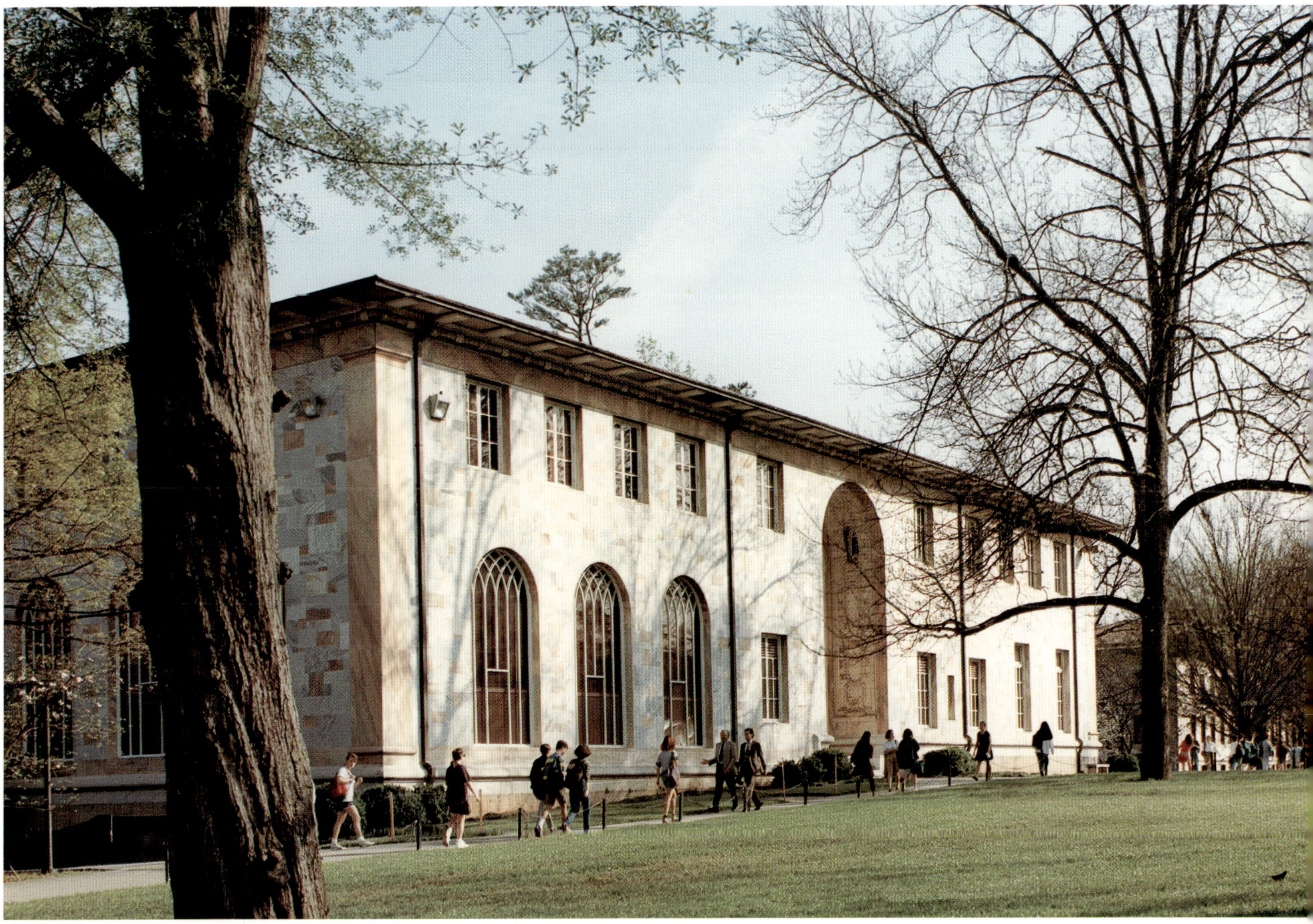

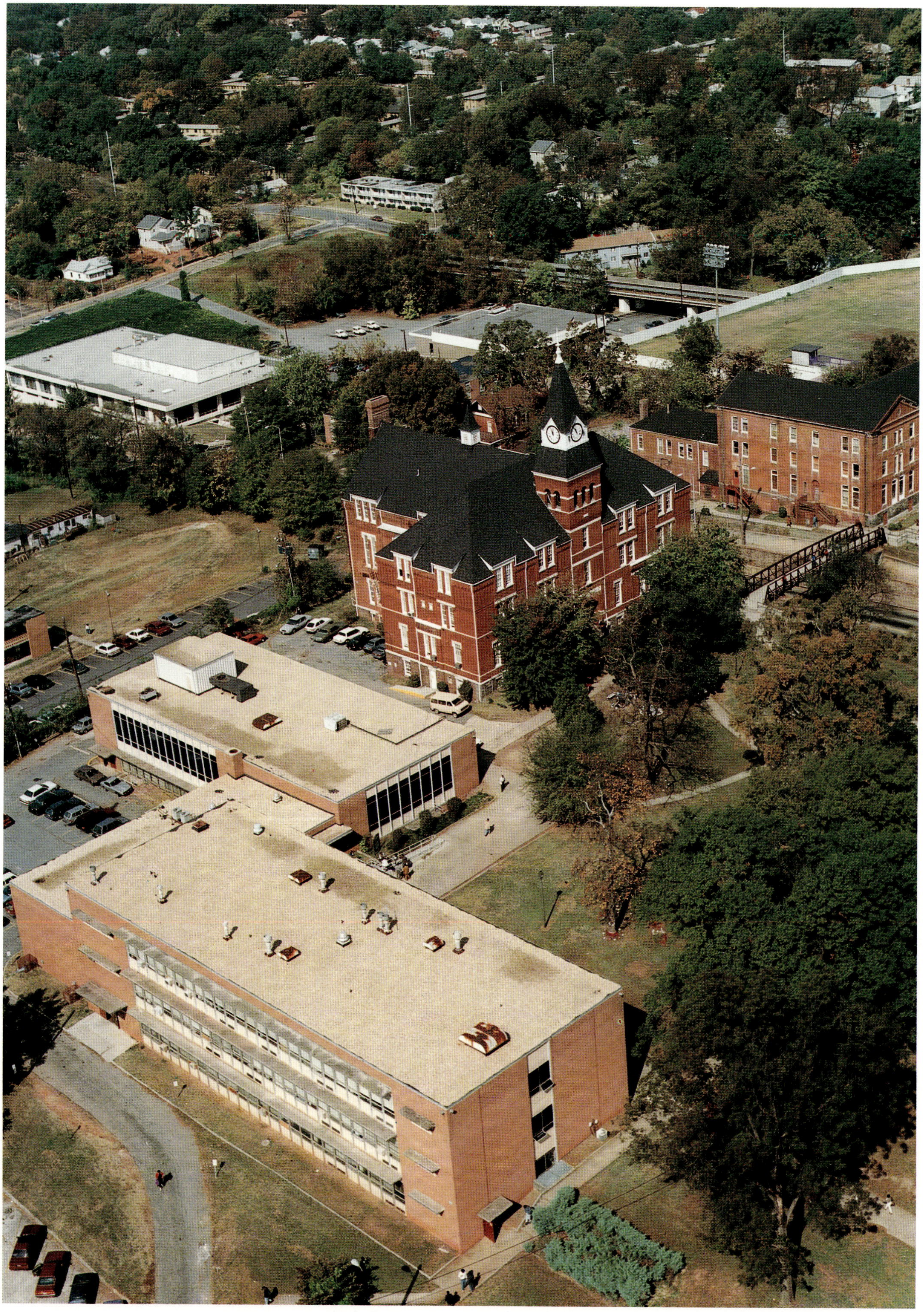

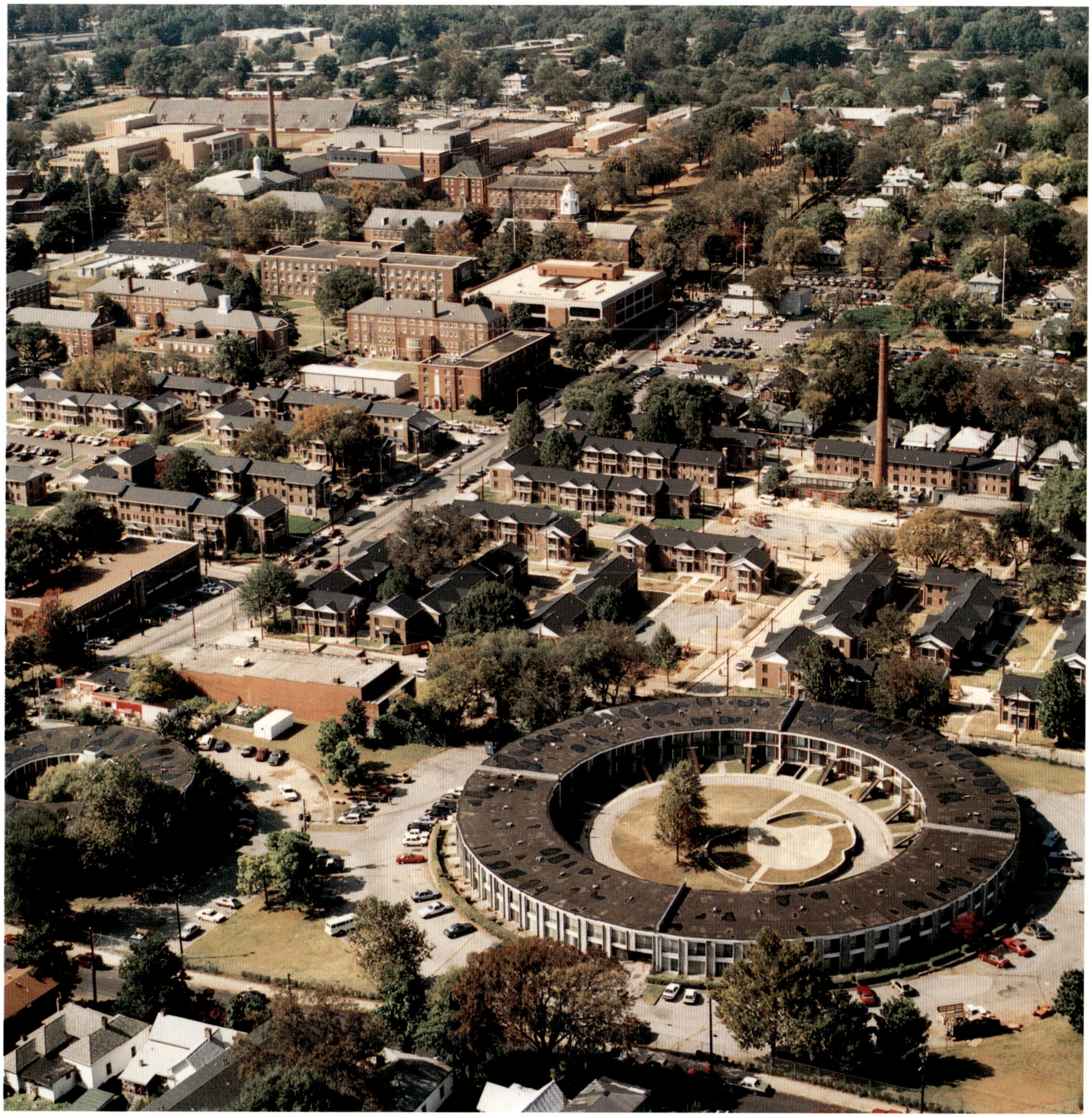

Atlanta University Center

Atlanta University can trace its genesis to classes offered in a railroad boxcar in 1865, having begun essentially as a grammar and high school for freed slaves. Today it is joined with Clark College (1869) and clustered in the Atlanta University Center with three other undergraduate colleges and two graduate schools on adjoining campuses just west of downtown. Morehouse College was founded in 1867, Morris Brown and Spelman Colleges in 1881. The Interdenominational Theological Center and a recent addition, the Morehouse College of Medicine, are graduate schools. The six original institutions became affiliated as Atlanta University Center in 1929. Each has its own administration, academic programs, dorms, and other facilities, but students may cross-register in all of the schools except the Morehouse College of Medicine. The six schools share a library, a career-planning and placement service, campus security, and other services. The campus boasts many historically significant buildings, including (left) the clock-towered Fountain Hall, dating to 1882, and the even older (1869) Gaines Hall, across the footbridge.

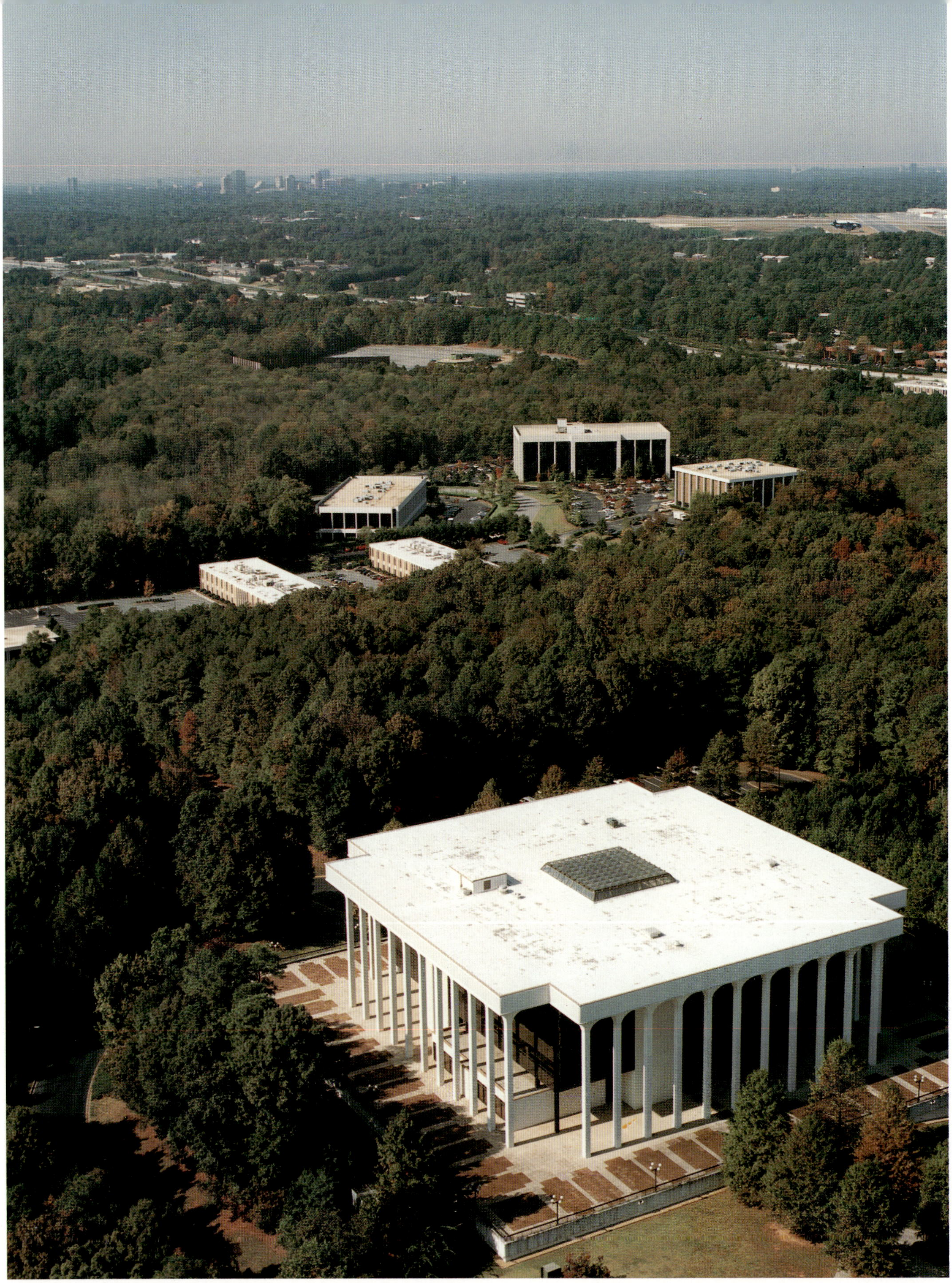

Mercer University in Atlanta

The original Mercer College was founded in 1833 in Macon. It merged with Atlanta Baptist College in 1972 and moved to this north Atlanta campus. Currently the school serves 1,800 students. The Baptist Center is a dramatic focal point, seeming to rise out of the trees on its gleaming white columns.

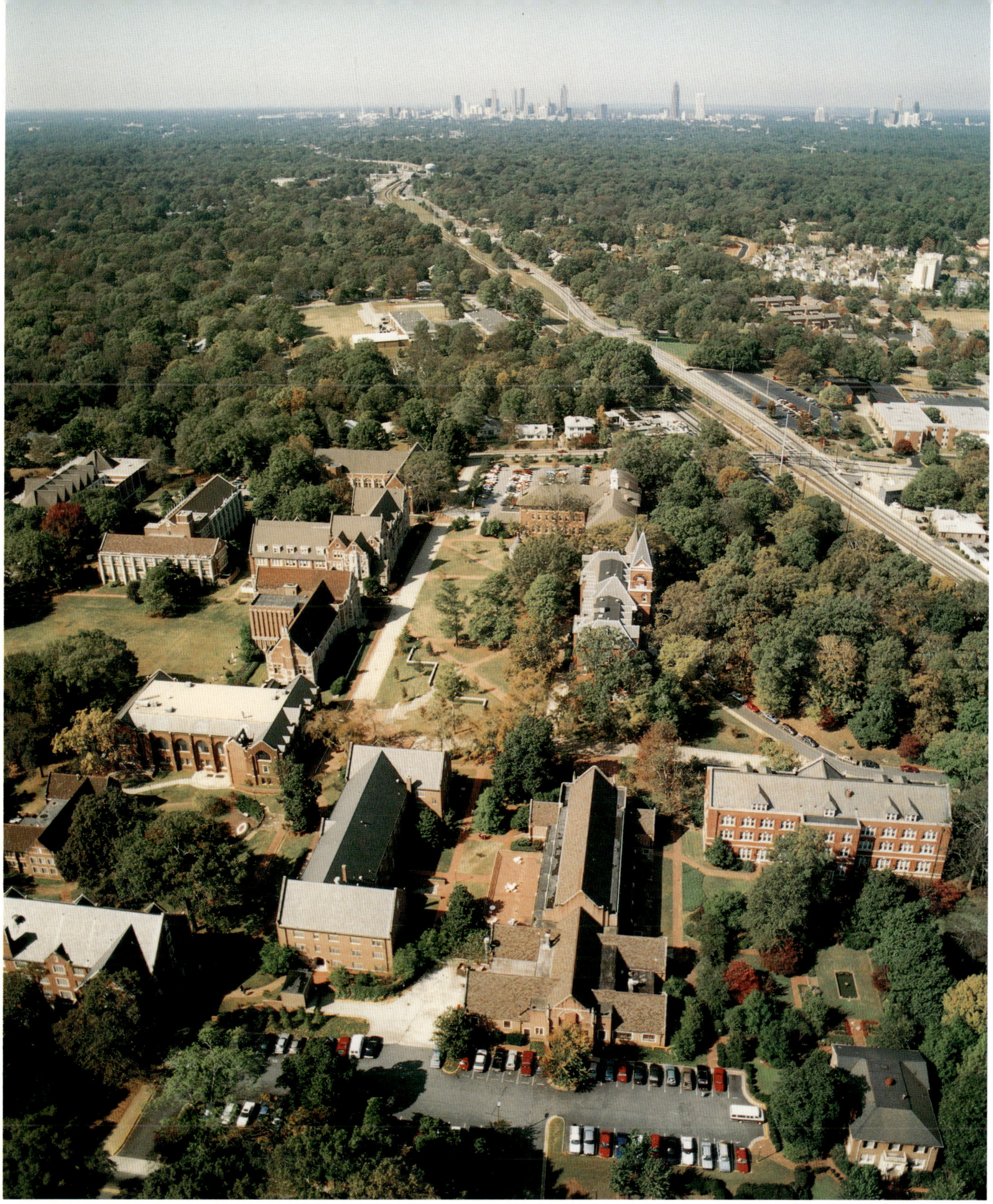

Agnes Scott College

Agnes Scott, originally the Decatur Female Seminary, opened in 1889 with sixty students. An early backer was George Washington Scott, a local industrialist from Pennsylvania who fought for the South in the Civil War, made and lost several fortunes, and named the school after his mother. Several original brick structures from the 1890s are still in use on the 105-acre campus six miles east of downtown Atlanta in the small-town ambience of Decatur. In its second century, the school continues to prepare young women for leadership roles.

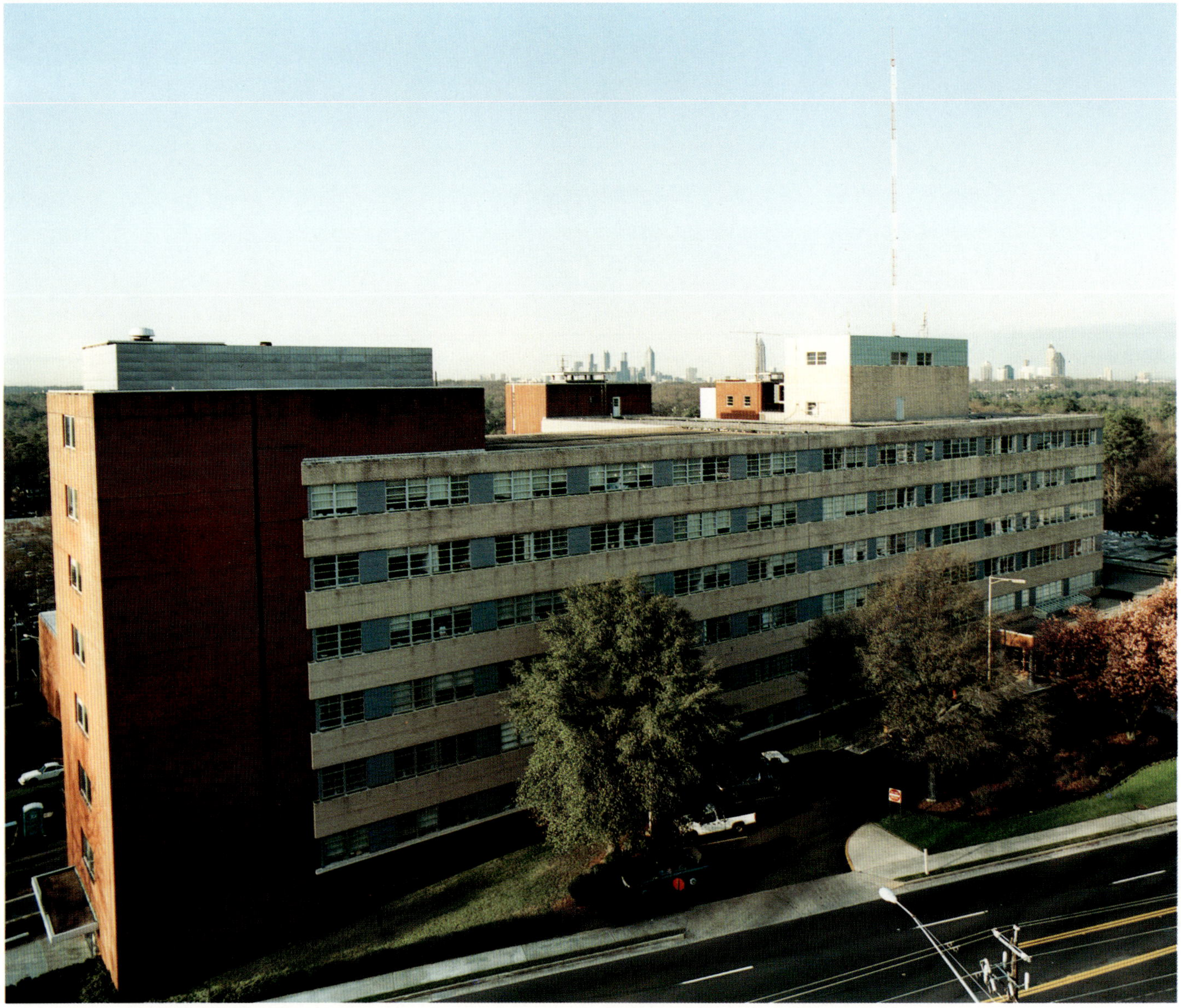

The Centers for Disease Control

Not strictly part of any university, but adjoining Emory and historically associated with the school, the internationally renowned Centers for Disease Control and Prevention provide vital health information and track down the sources of epidemics worldwide. Local lore traces the CDC's roots to the plight of a sick employee on Robert Woodruff's south Georgia plantation. The worker had come down with malaria, and Woodruff turned to Emory University Hospital for help. He carried back enough quinine to treat not only his own workers, but the rest of Baker County as well. Woodruff established the Malarial Research Foundation at Emory in the 1930s, financing doctors and nurses to eradicate the illness in south Georgia. He later helped convince President Franklin Roosevelt to set up a government agency to combat infectious diseases nationwide. The Malarial Research Foundation led to the establishment in 1946 of the Communicable Disease Center, the predecessor of today's CDC.

Part III

Midtown and Buckhead

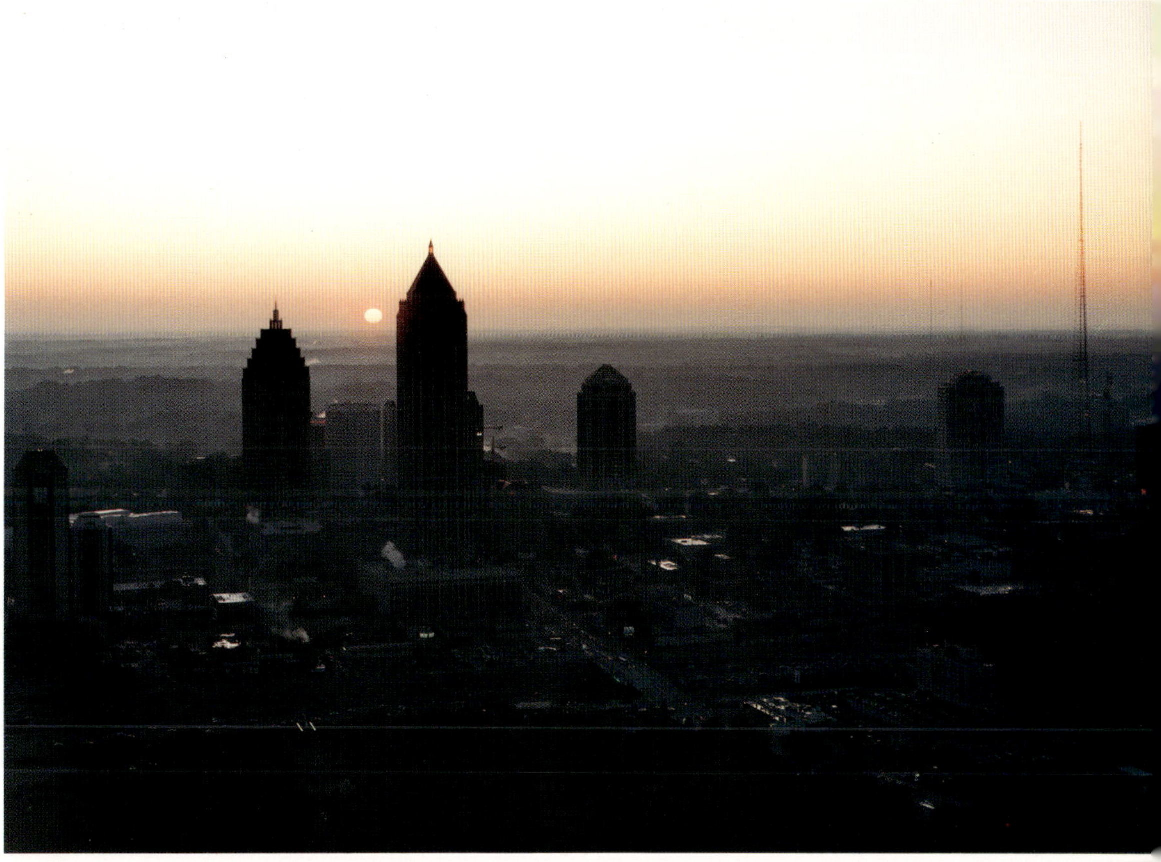

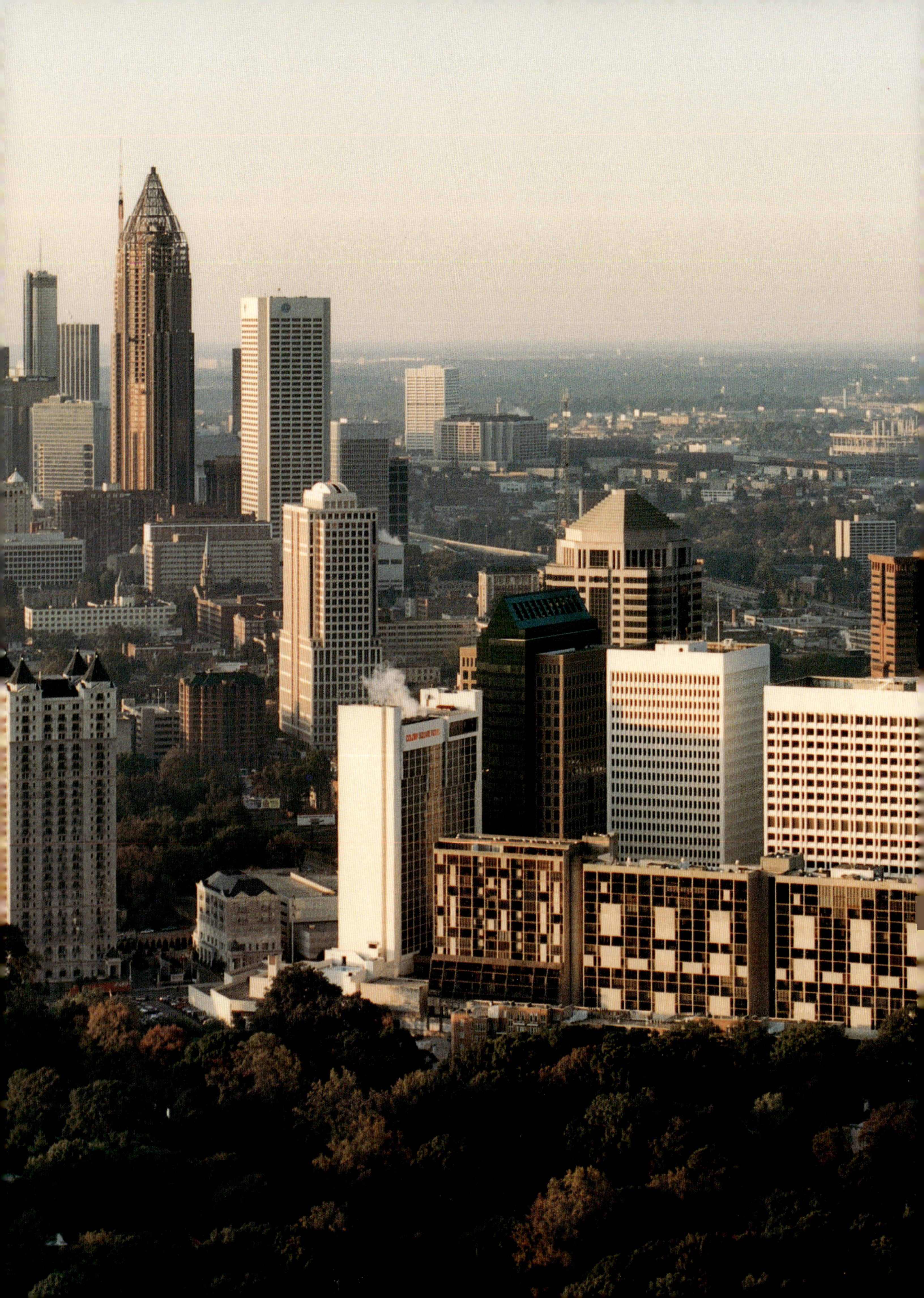

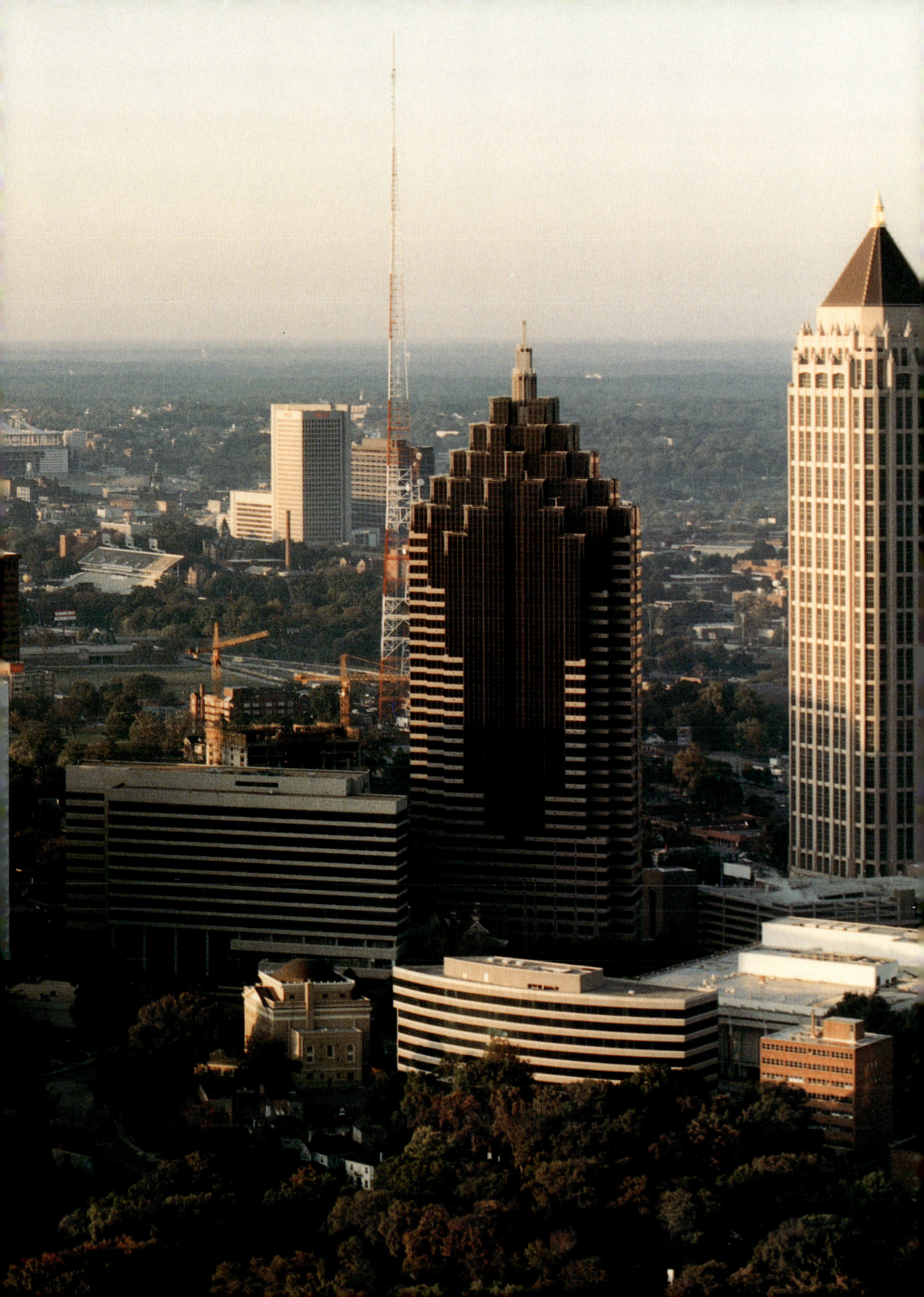

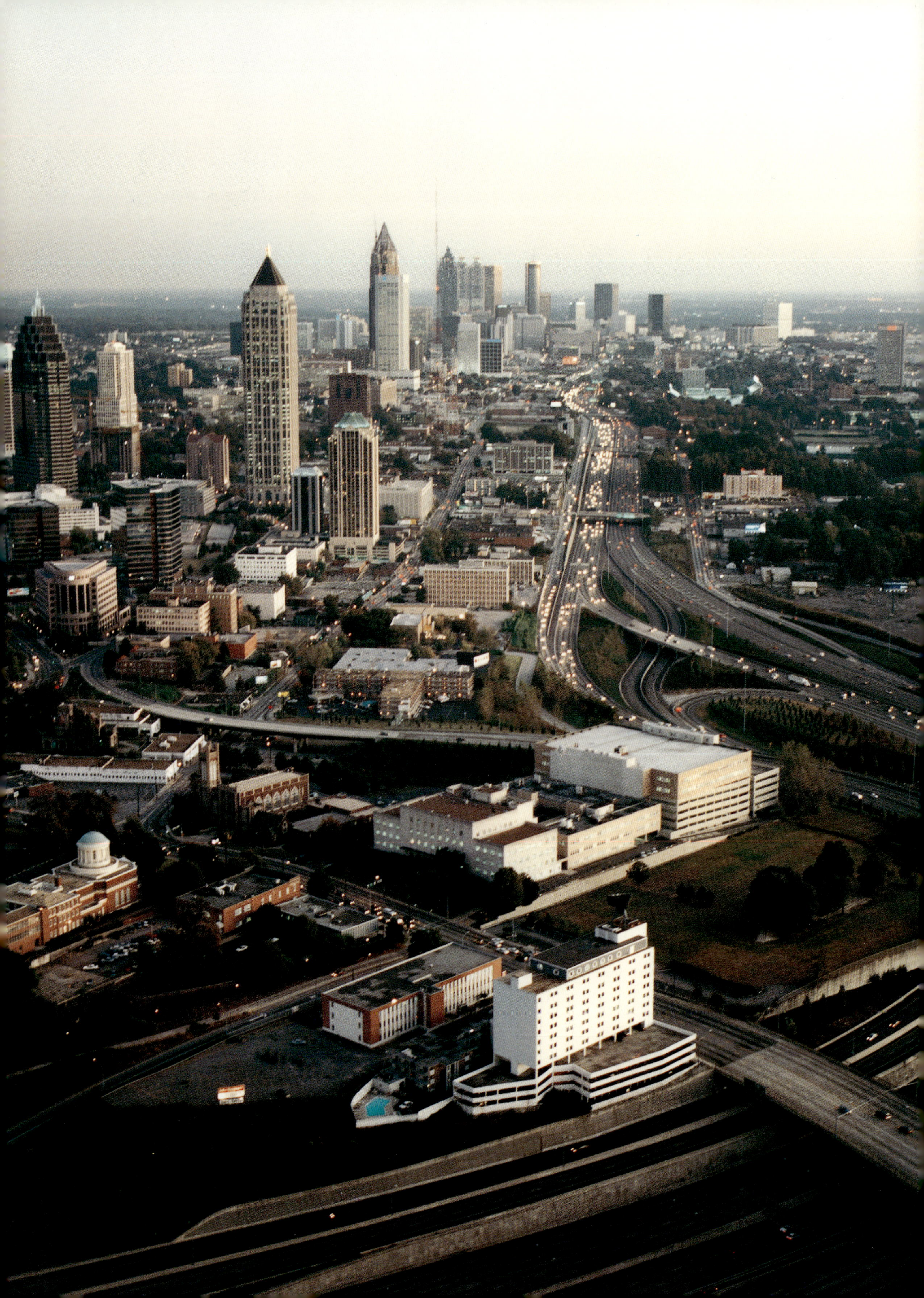

Midtown

In the early 1980s the Midtown area, north of the downtown business district, looked like a bombed-out war zone, with boarded-up buildings and graffiti-sprayed walls. Today it is a bustling business and residential district with its own distinctive skyline. Its hallmark building is the fifty-story One Atlantic Center (upper left center), completed in 1987 to house the Atlanta offices of International Business Machines and known as the IBM Tower until it was purchased by the Sumitomo Life Insurance Company. A much older landmark is the green-domed synagogue (lower left) of the Hebrew Benevolent Congregation. The Peachtree Street building, known simply as "The Temple," has been a center for Atlanta's Jewish community since its construction, to a Philip Shutze design, in 1920. A bombing in 1958 blasted a twenty-foot hole in the synagogue's walls—an incident depicted in the Oscar-winning film *Driving Miss Daisy.*

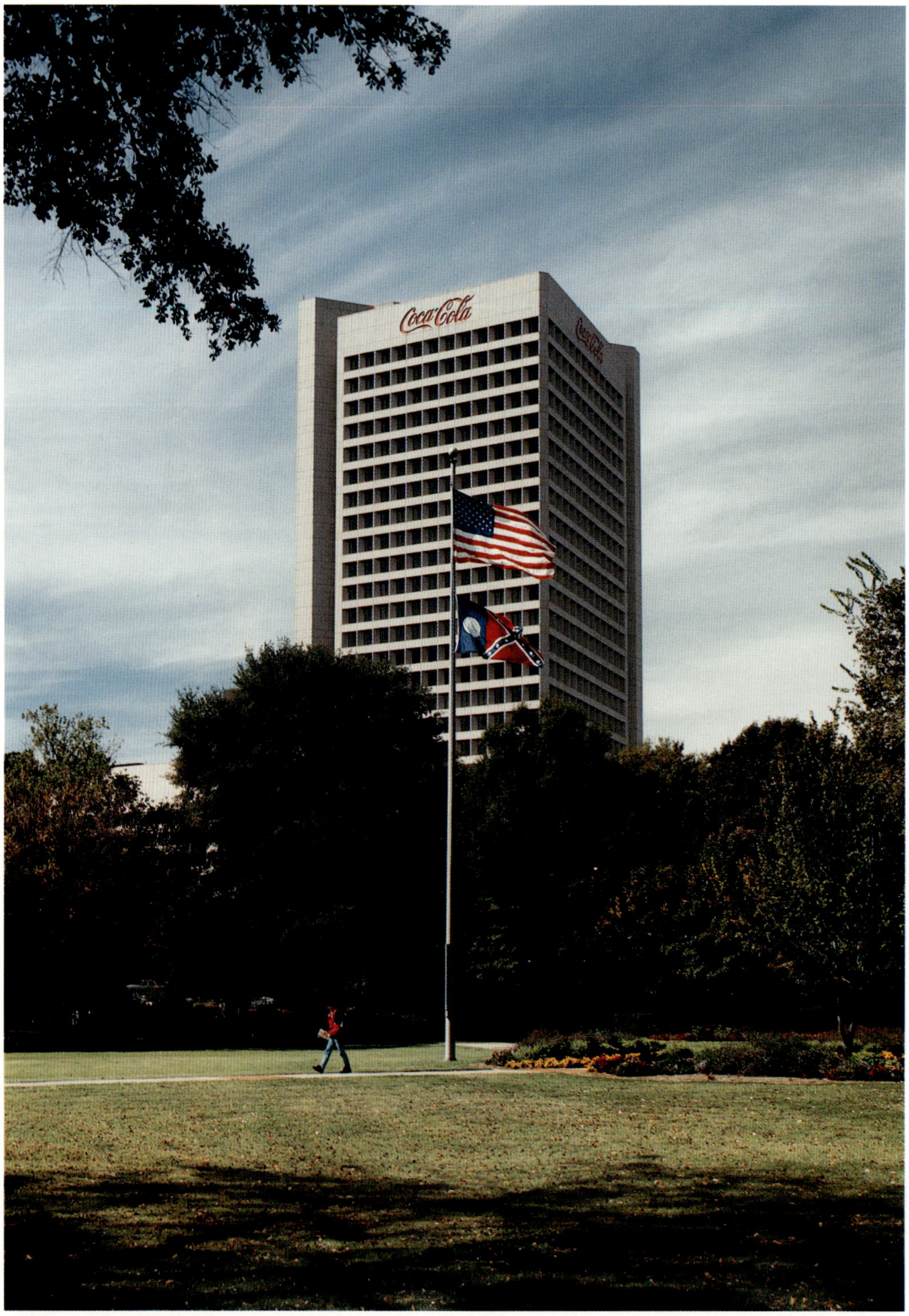

Coca-Cola Headquarters

The world's most famous soft drink was invented and first dispensed in 1886 at Jacobs' Pharmacy at Marietta and Peachtree Streets. Pharmacist John Pemberton came up with the name when he reformulated his French Wine Cola after Fulton County voted to go dry. The next year, Pemberton's fellow pharmacist Asa G. Candler bought the formula for $1,750. Candler resold it in 1919 to Ernest Woodruff, Samuel Dobbs, and other investors for $25 million. Robert Woodruff became president of Coca-Cola in 1923. Under him the company's aggressive marketing spread Coke throughout the world, particularly as the beverage followed the troops in World War II.

The Coca-Cola North Avenue Tower, shown here, is part of the company's world-headquarters complex just south of Georgia Tech.

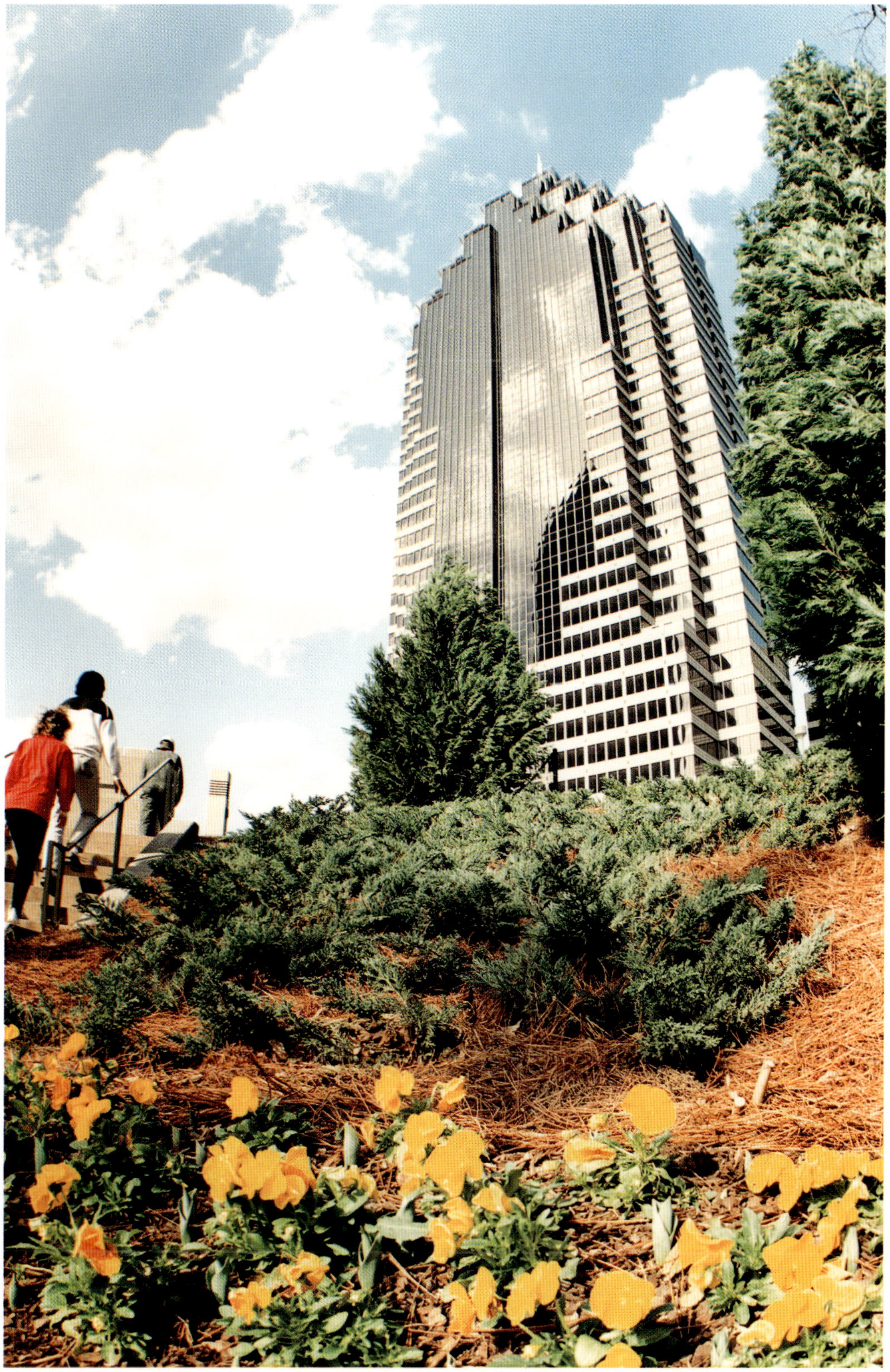

Promenade II

Adding a visionary skyscraper to the Midtown skyline, Promenade II was completed in 1990 as the regional headquarters for AT&T. Designed by the Atlanta firm of Thompson, Ventulett, Stainback and Associates, the thirty-eight-story structure was planned as part of a complex that will include two more towers and a retail and conference center. The building's exterior is granite sheathed in rose-tinted glass.

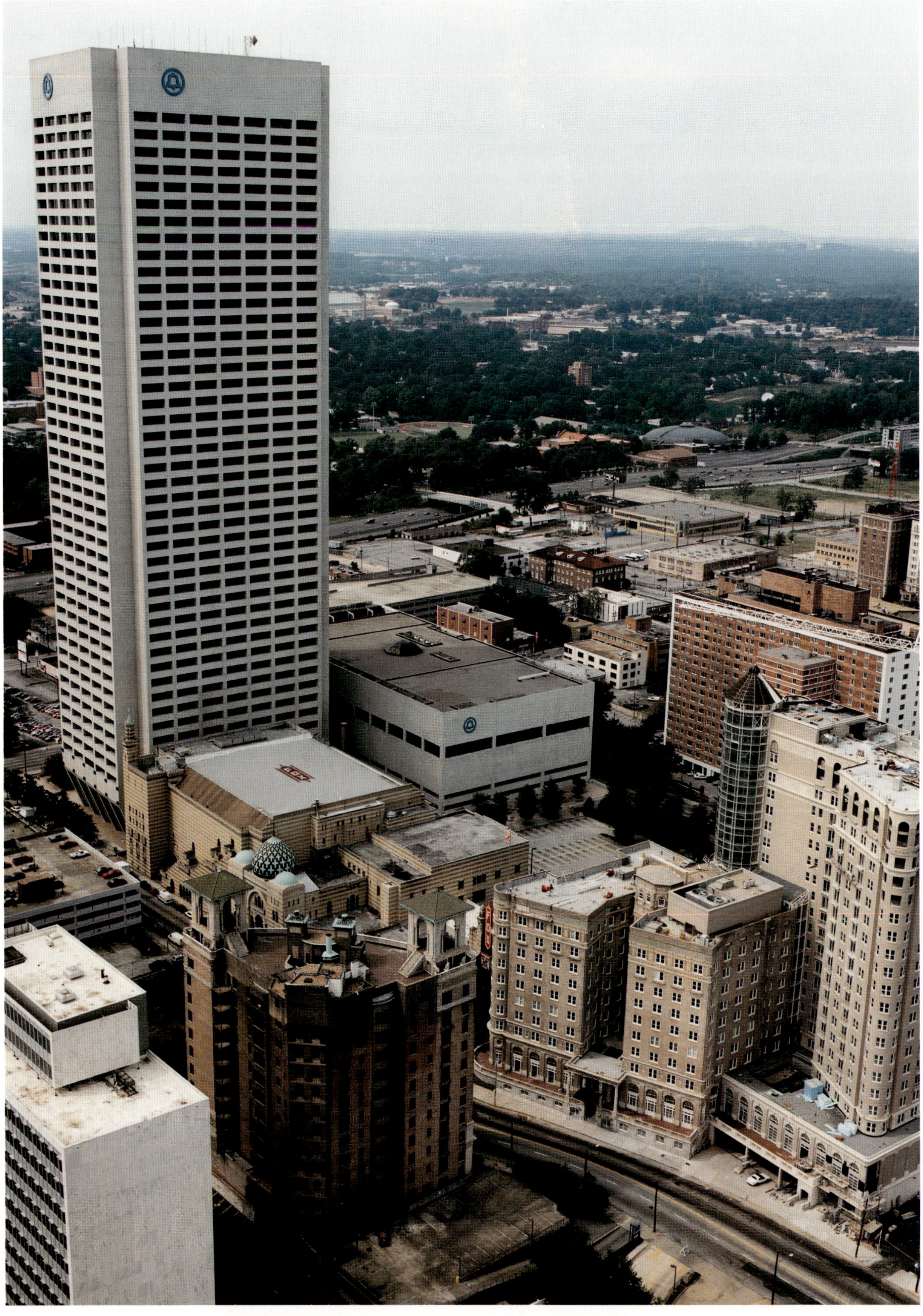

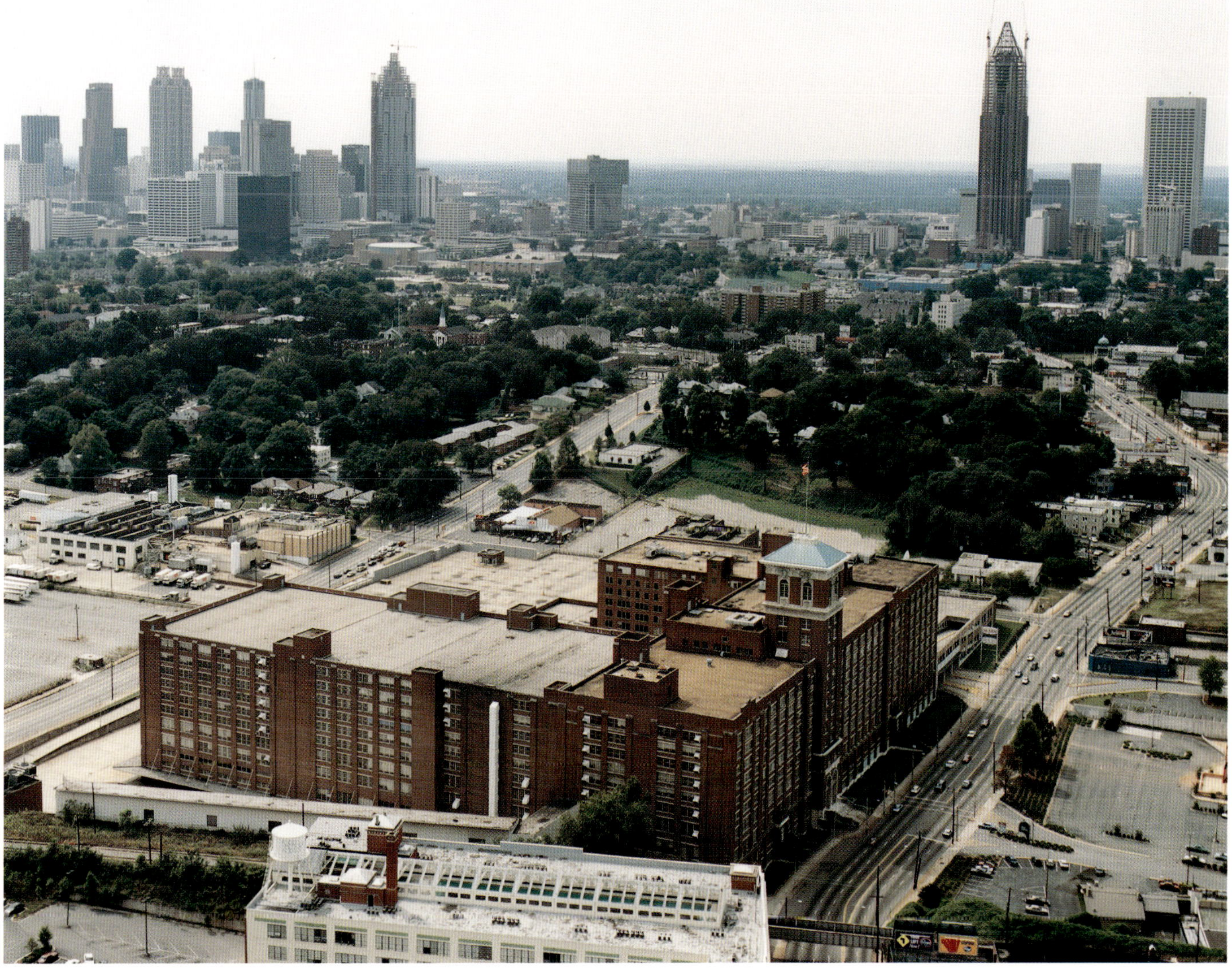

BellSouth Building (left)

This building's clean lines belie a complicated history. Completed in 1982 as the Southern Bell Center, the structure was built only after a total replanning necessitated by local preservationists' successful campaign to save the neighboring Fox Theatre, which Southern Bell had bought and targeted for demolition as part of the new project. To the lower right of the Fox (1929) is the old Georgian Terrace Hotel (1911) with its turreted 1991 addition, and across the street from that, the Ponce (1913), the city's oldest high-rise luxury apartment building.

Old Sears Building (above)

Sears, Roebuck was one of the first companies to use architecture as a form of advertising. Sears buildings nationwide were all designed by the same firm and given the same general architectural treatment, which followed that of the company's Chicago headquarters, built in 1904. In Atlanta, Sears opened this vast retail store and mail-order warehouse on Ponce de Leon Avenue in 1926. In the early 1990s, having vacated the building, Sears sold it to the city. It is now City Hall East.

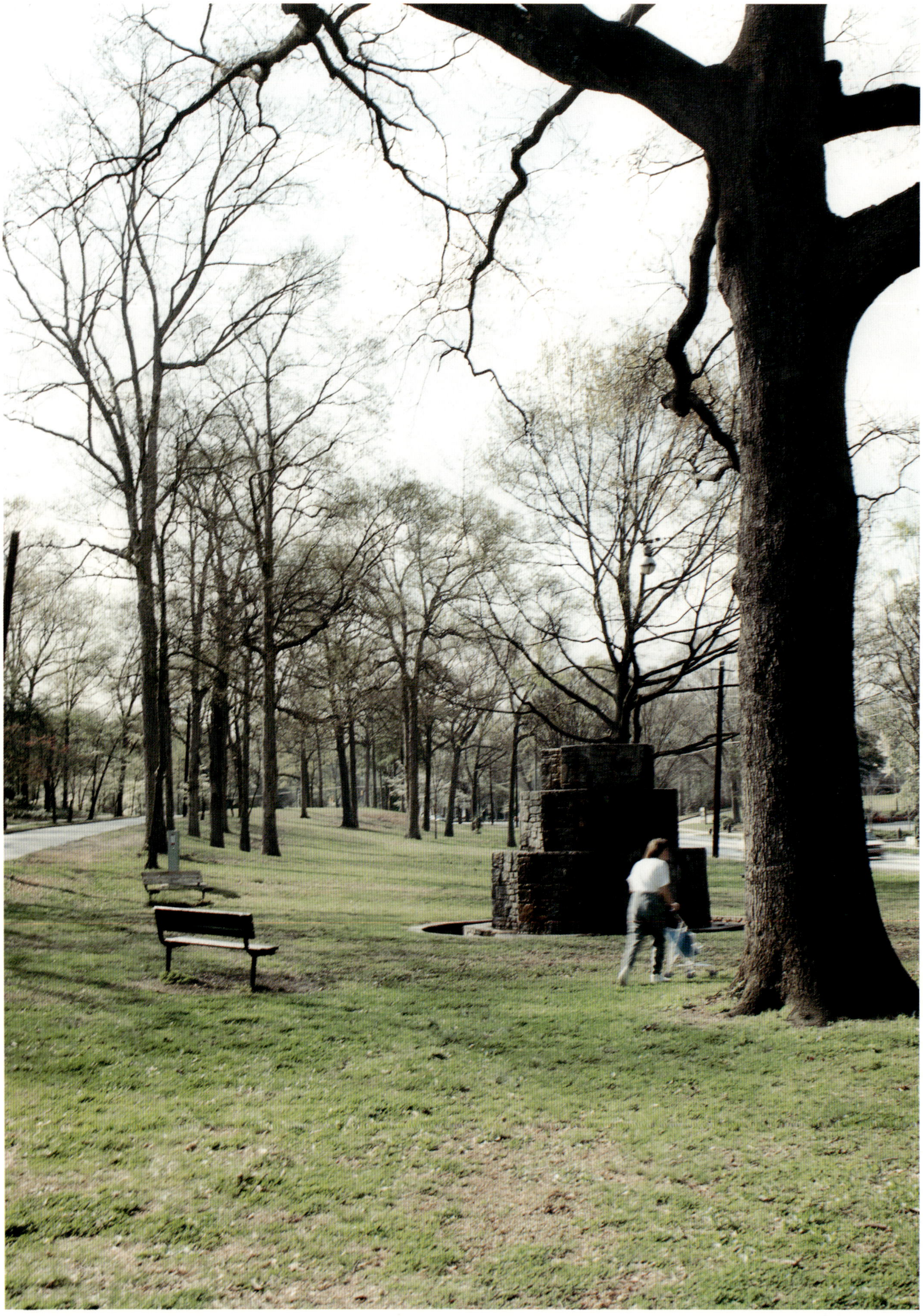

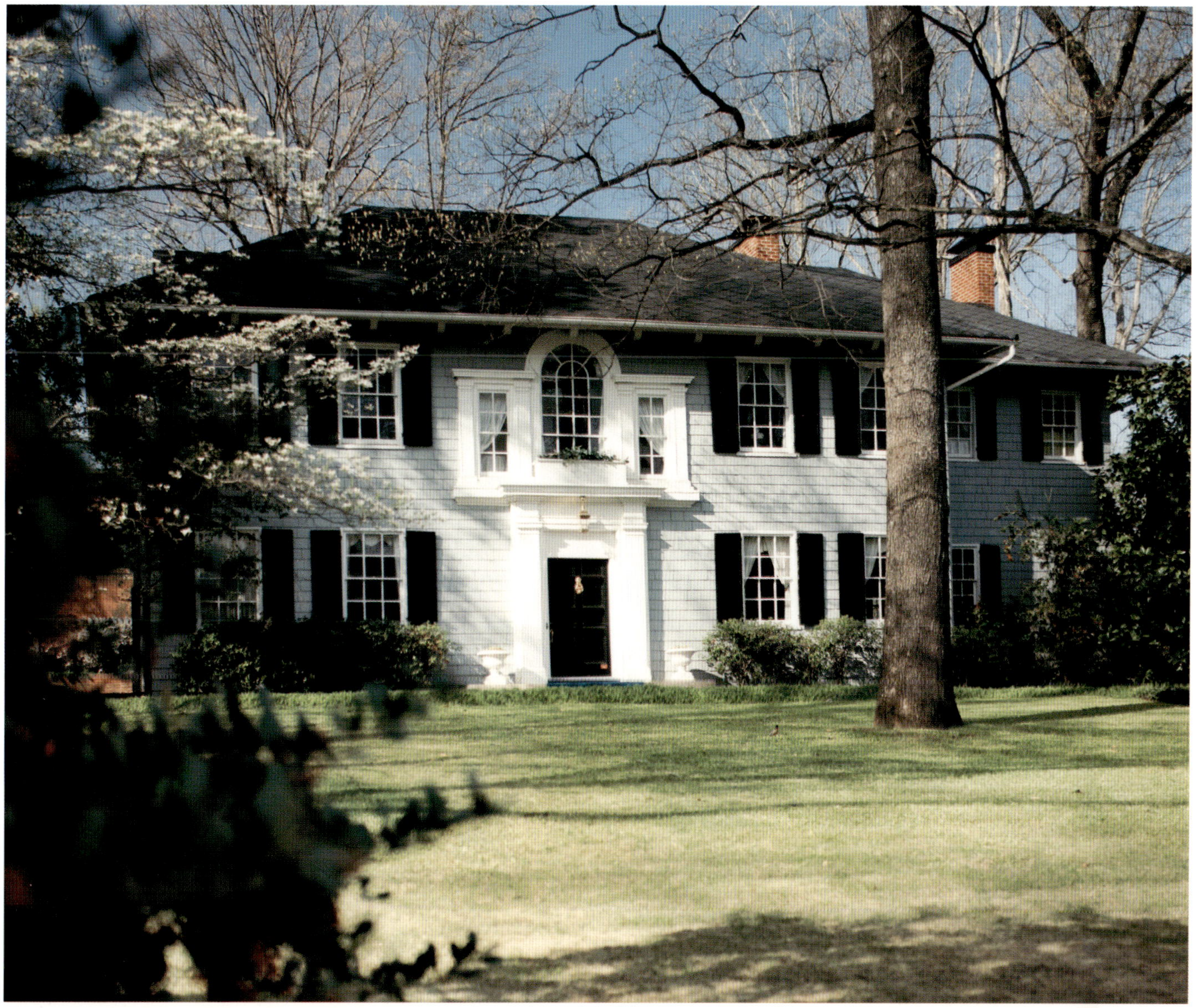

Ponce de Leon Parkway and Druid Hills

Flowing out of Midtown to the east, Ponce de Leon Avenue has become a busy commuter route, but residents can find solitude in the series of parks that line and define it. The parks were designed by Frederick Law Olmsted and his sons as the centerpiece of the Druid Hills development. The elder Olmsted, best known as the landscape architect of New York's Central Park, envisioned his creations as islands of pastoral refuge for urban dwellers.

Druid Hills itself was the brainchild of developer Joel Hurt, who recruited Olmsted to landscape the project in 1890 (Olmsted's sons took over after he retired in the mid-1890s). Hurt encountered financial difficulties and in 1908 sold Druid Hills to a group of investors headed by Asa Candler. Today the 1,500-acre development remains one of the city's most exclusive neighborhoods.

Among many architectural jewels, Druid Hills boasts several early residential designs by Neel Reid, later one of Atlanta's best-known architects. Reid designed the gray two-story house shown here for himself and his mother. The Palladian window over the door framed by Doric pilasters is an unusual touch.

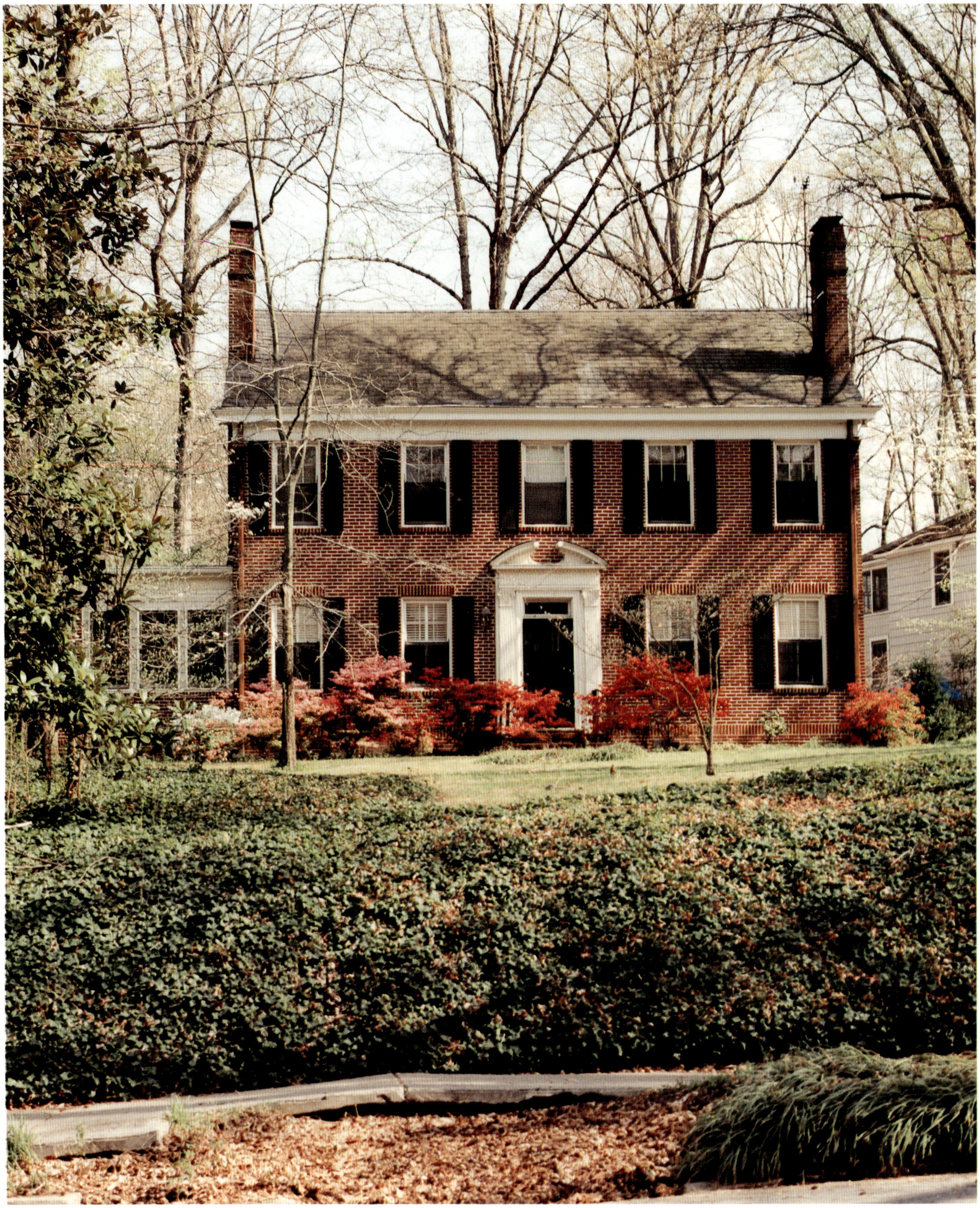

Spring in Druid Hills

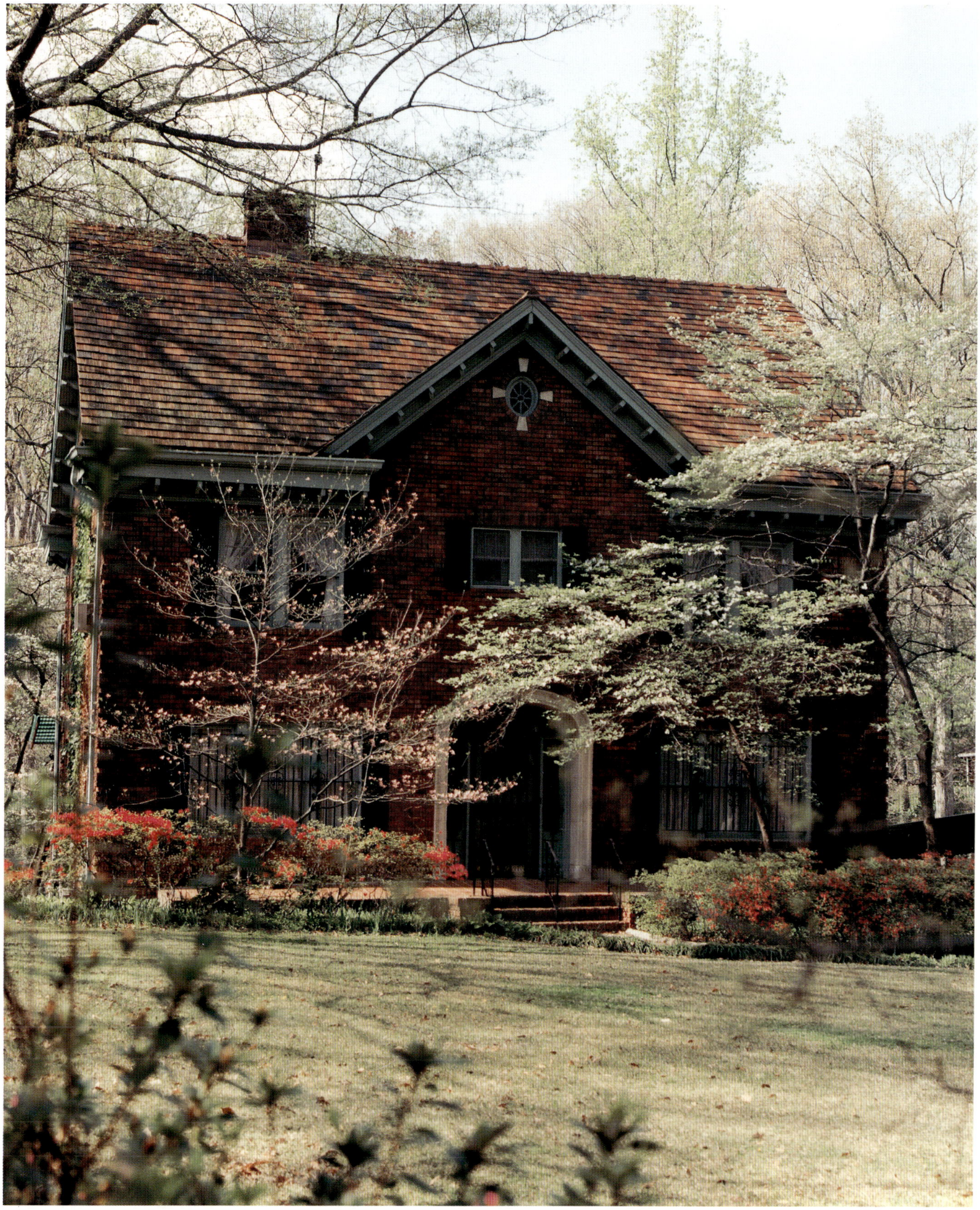

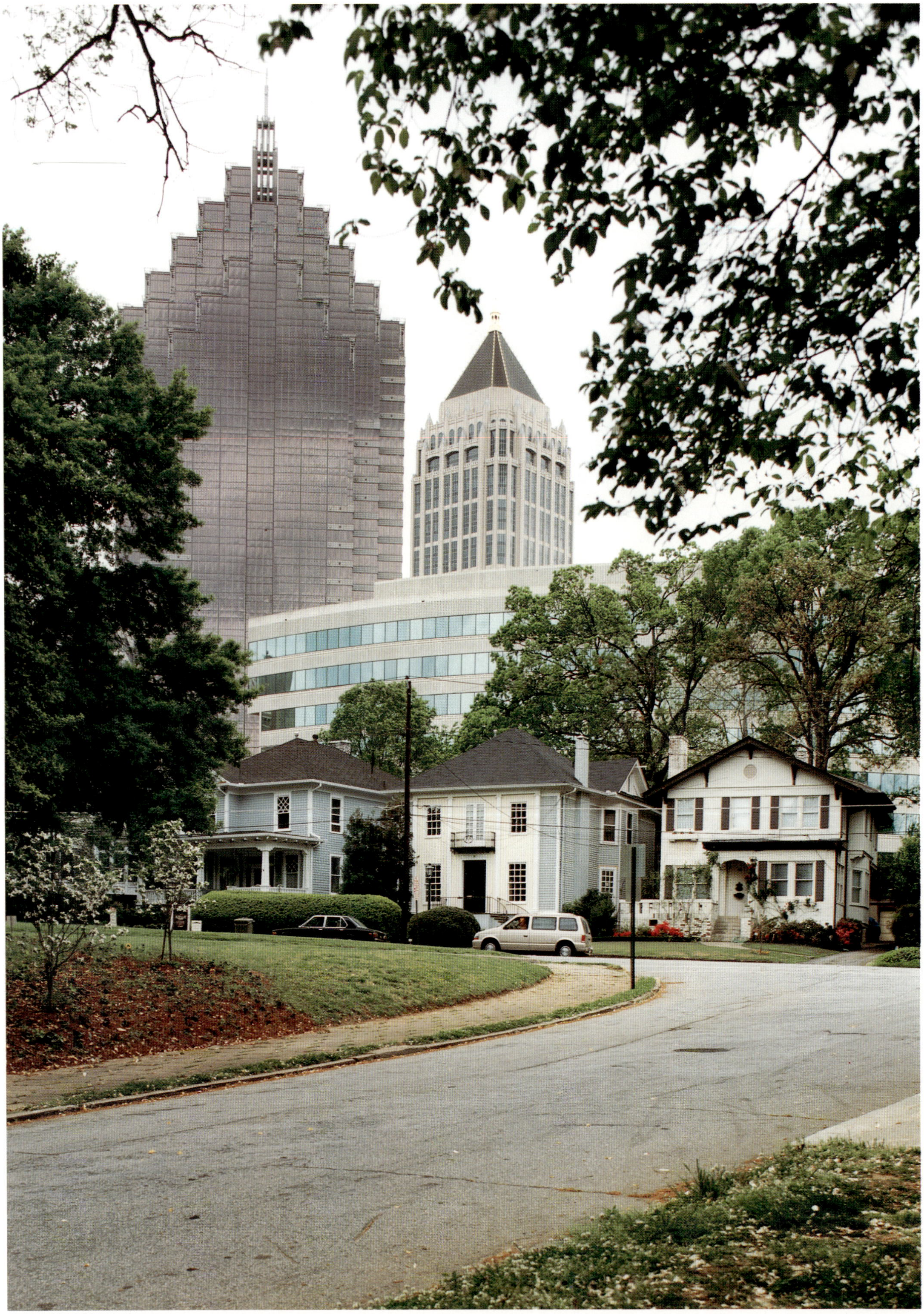

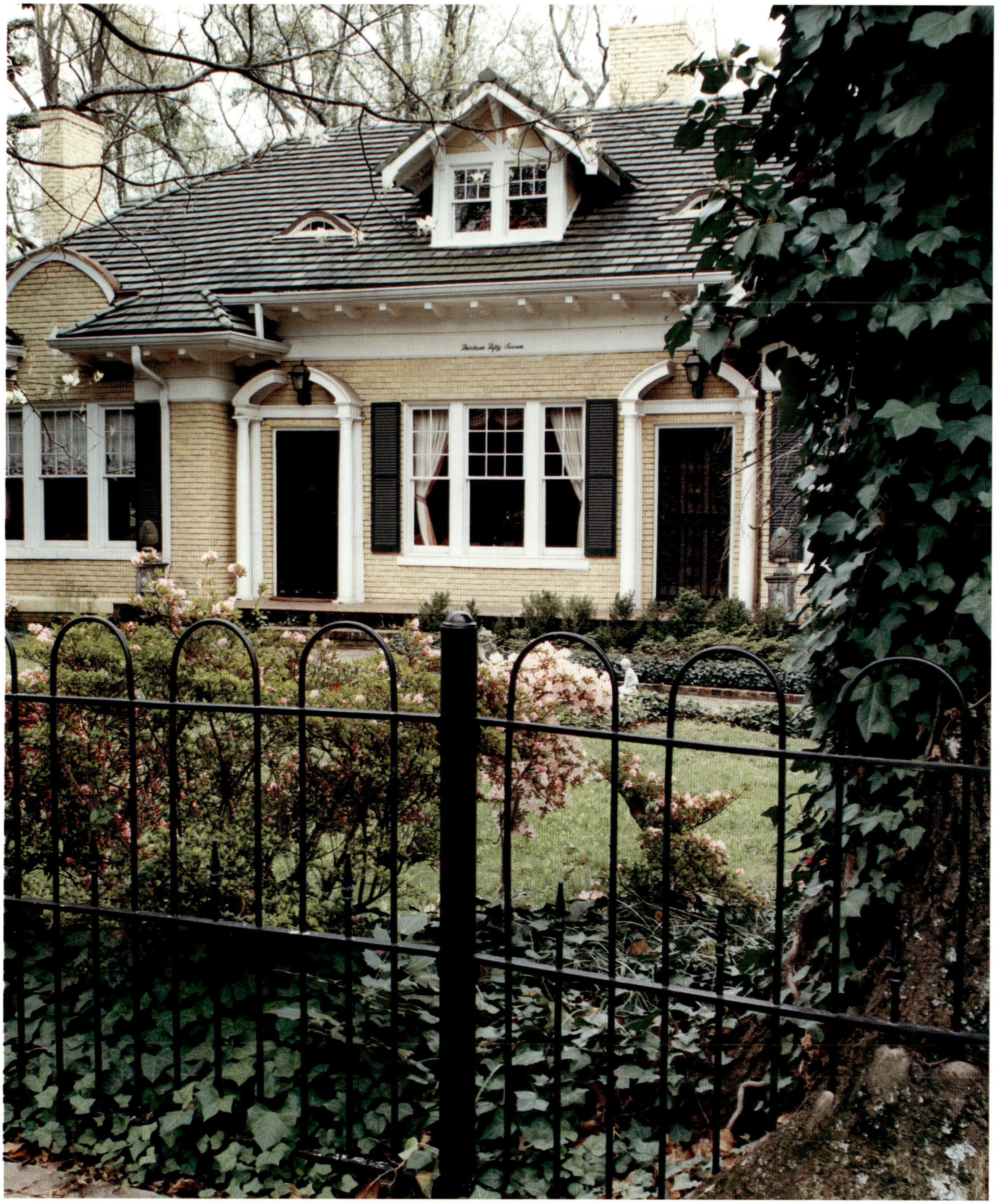

Ansley Park

Developed in several stages between 1904 and 1913, Ansley Park was the first Atlanta suburb to be laid out with the automobile, more than the trolley, in mind. Designed by Solon Z. Ruff, who had worked with Frederick Law Olmsted on Druid Hills, the neighborhood reflects the classic Olmsted influence, remaining a haven of greenery and quiet even in the shadows of Midtown's skyscrapers.

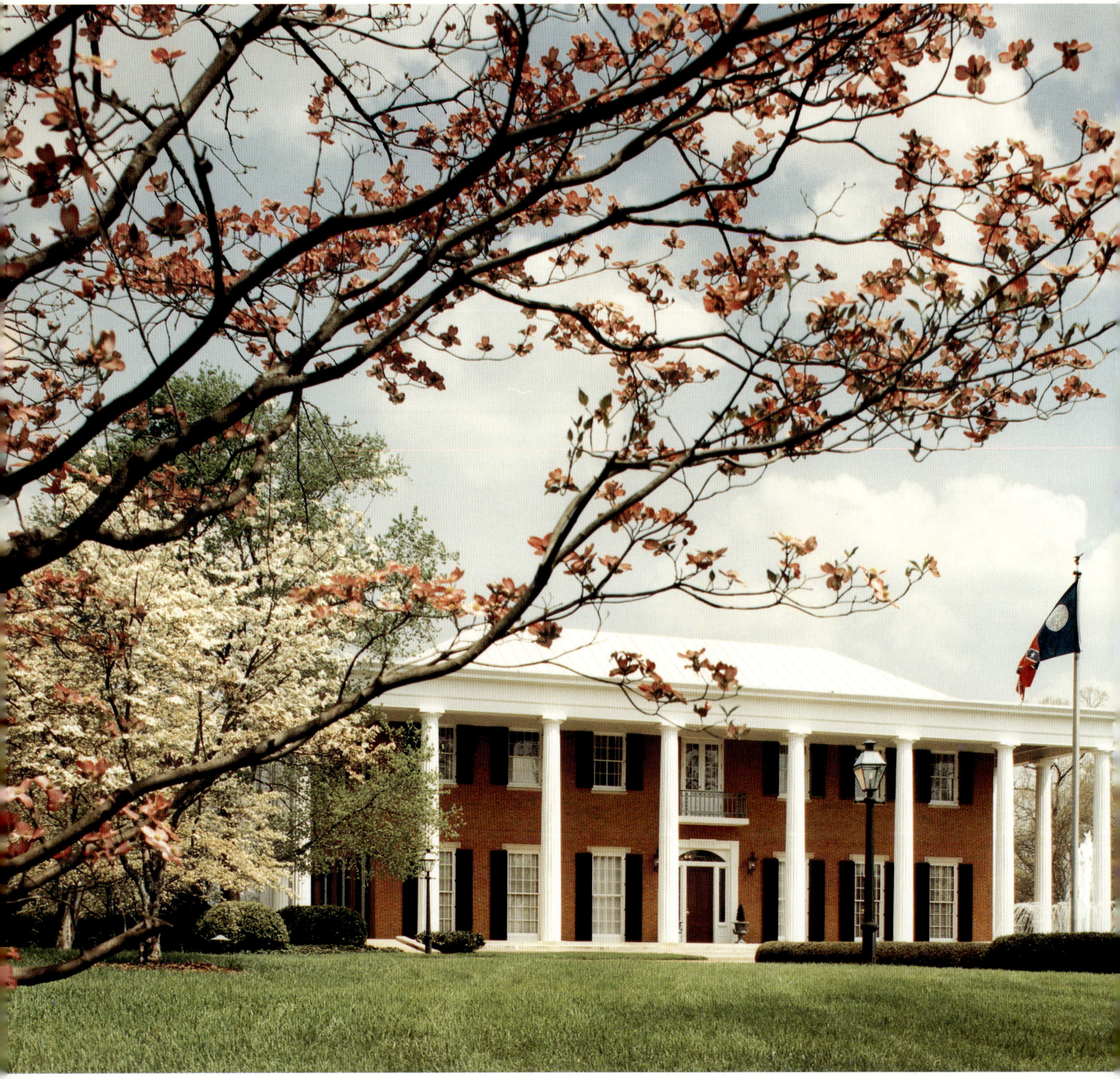

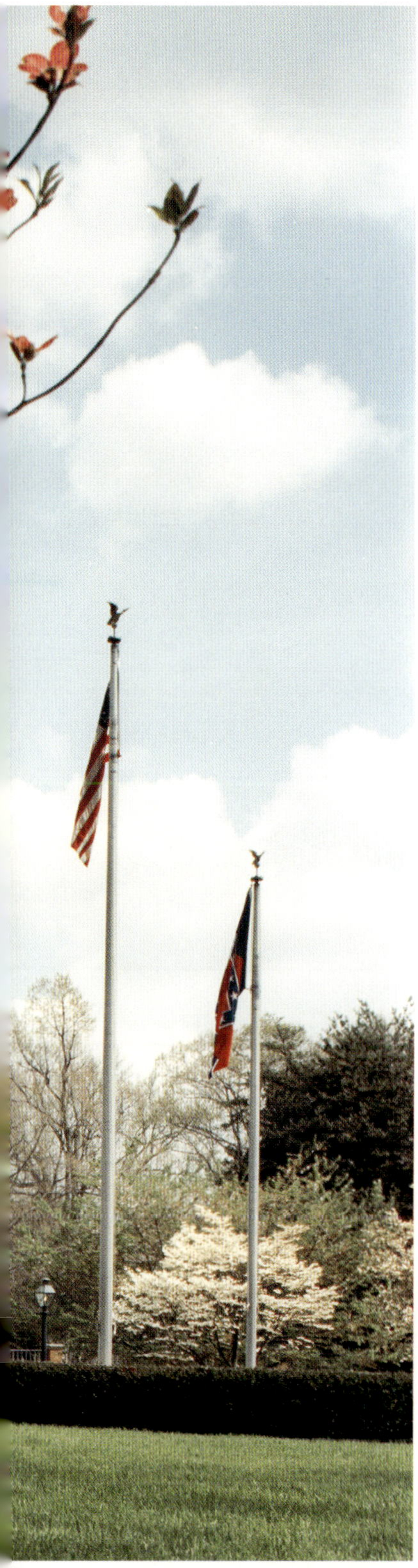

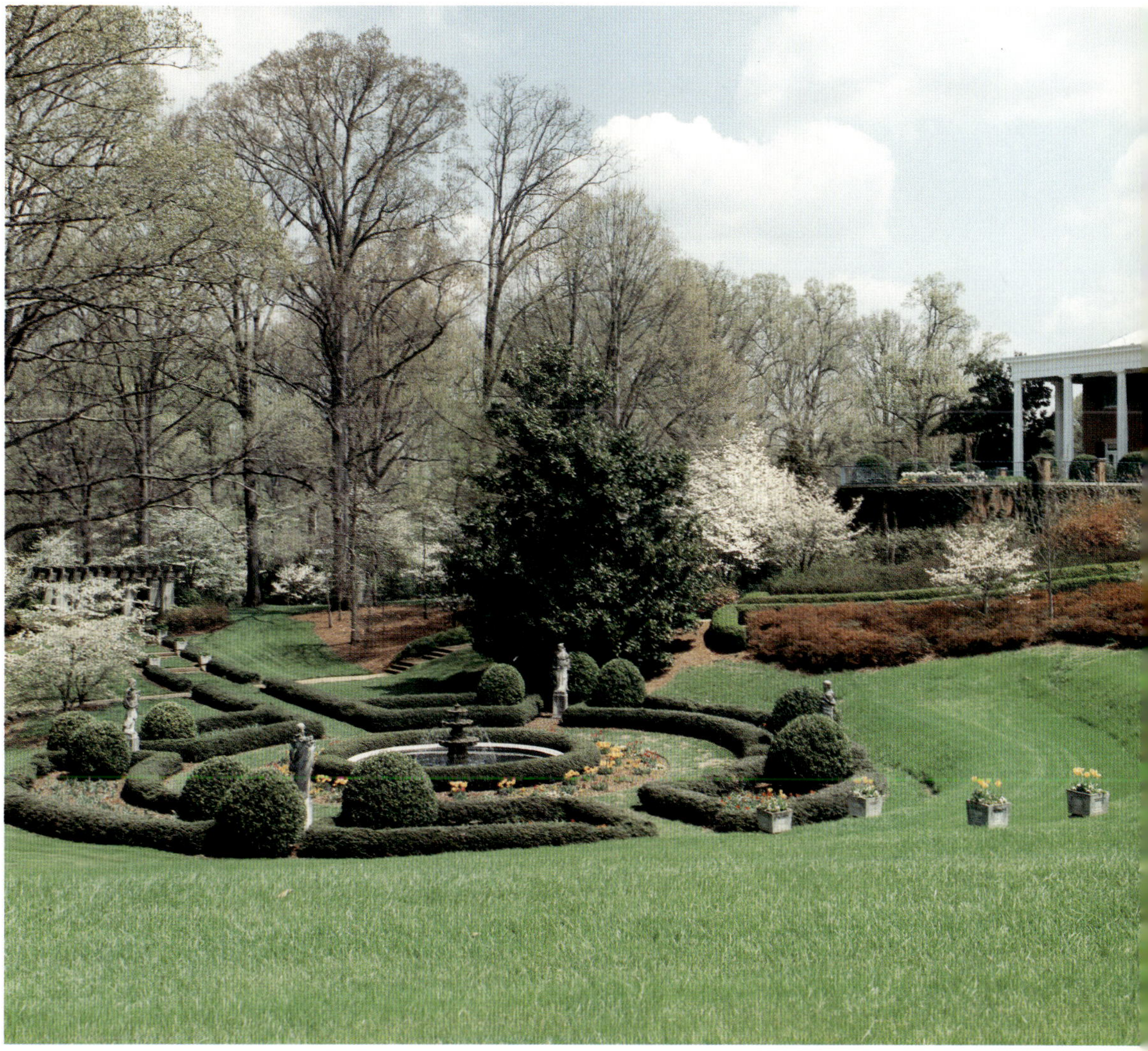

Governor's Mansion

Although it dates to only 1968, the official home of Georgia's governors, on West Paces Ferry Road in Buckhead, embodies the Greek Revival architectural style popular in the South before the Civil War. Dominated by dogwoods in early spring, the mansion's sculpted gardens are a place of joy and horticultural beauty in any season.

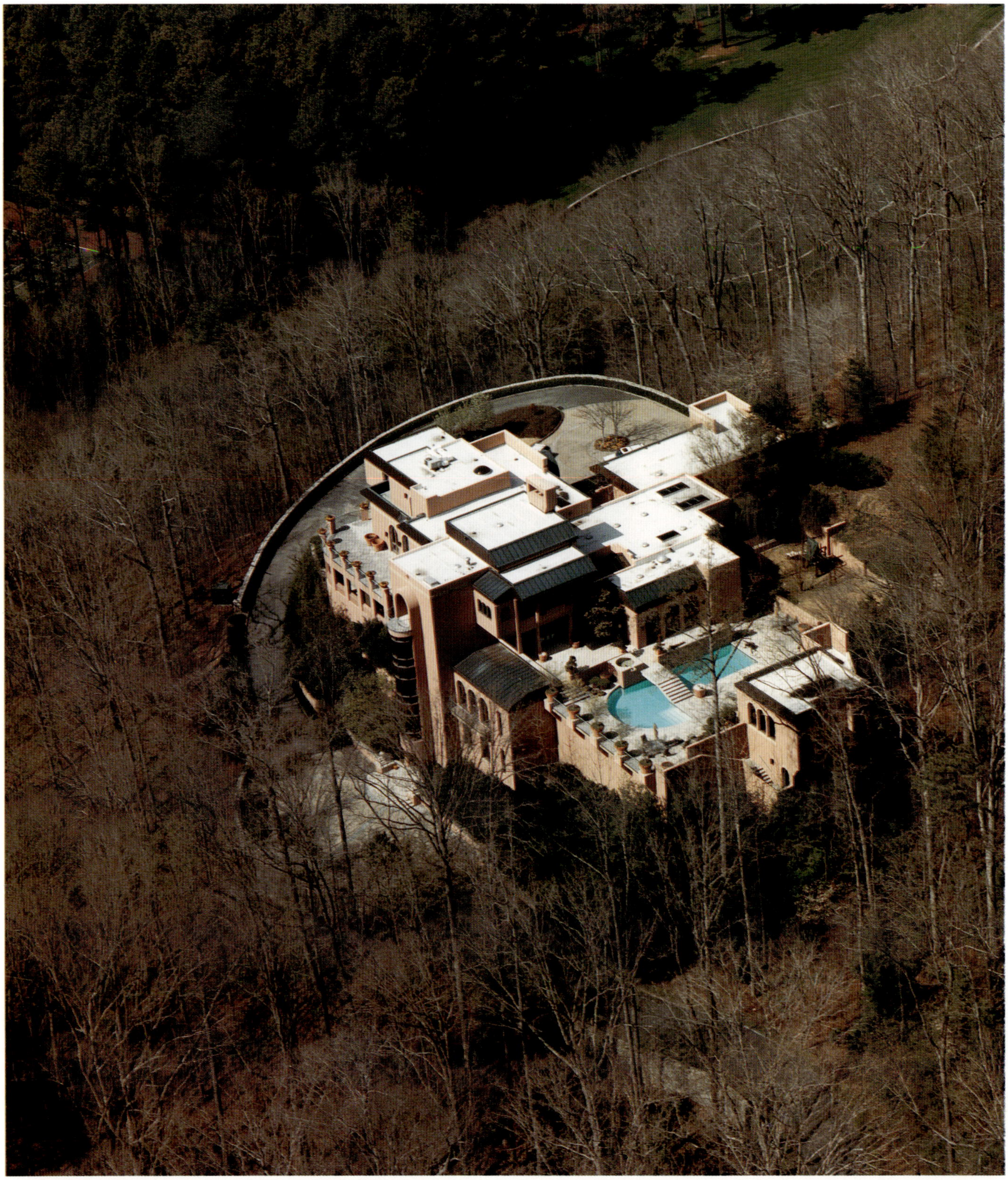

Buckhead Homes

When Atlantans think of Buckhead, they may conjure up images of the stylish restaurants and elegant shops at Phipps Plaza and Lenox Square, but they are even more likely to envision the area's impressive homes on large, beautifully landscaped lots. For all its luxury, Buckhead had a humble beginning as a little backwoods settlement centering on Henry Irby's tavern and grocery, at the junction of present-day Peachtree, Roswell, and West Paces Ferry Roads. The explanation most often heard for the community's name is that it derived from a deer's head that Irby mounted on a post at a nearby spring around 1840.

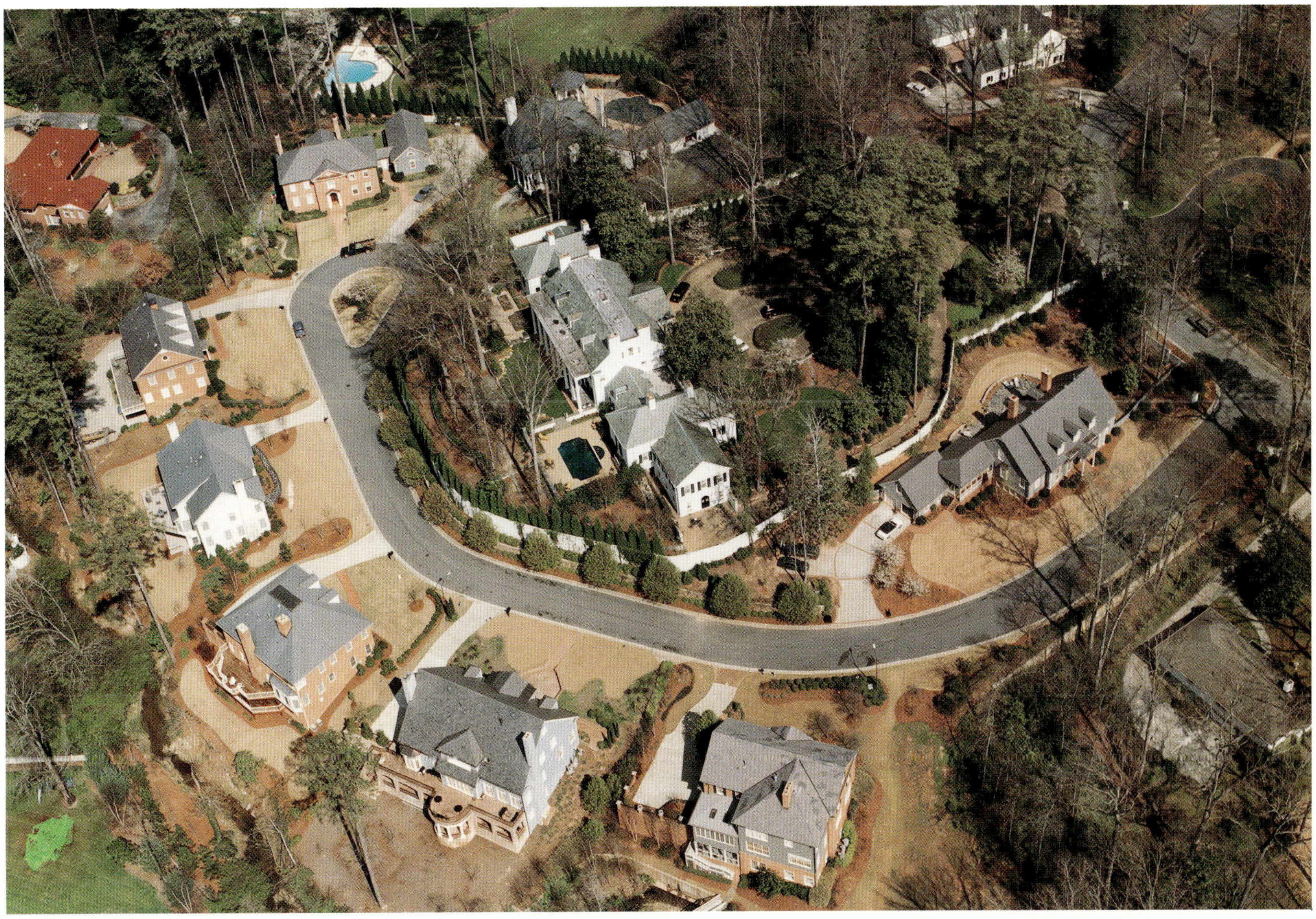

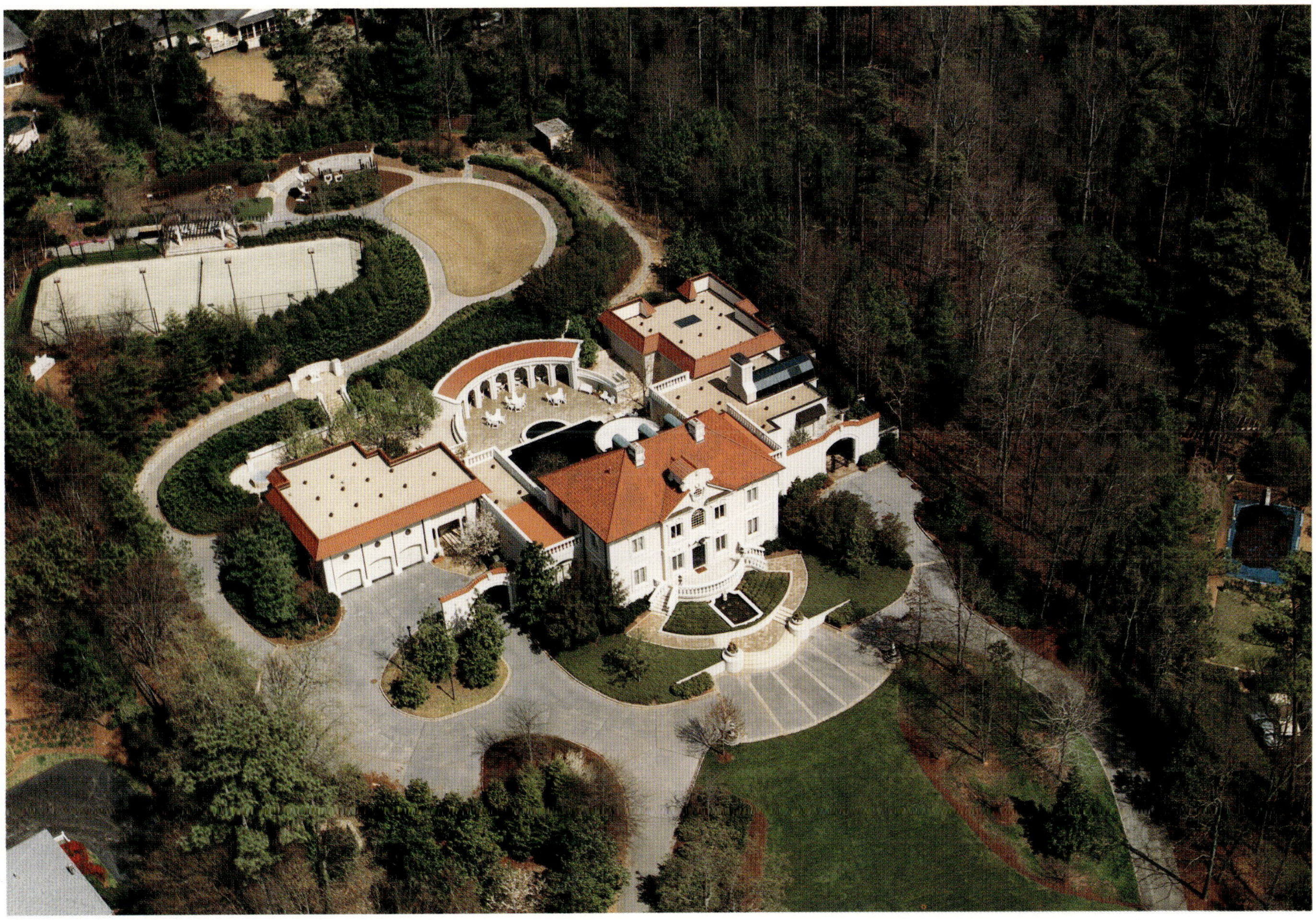

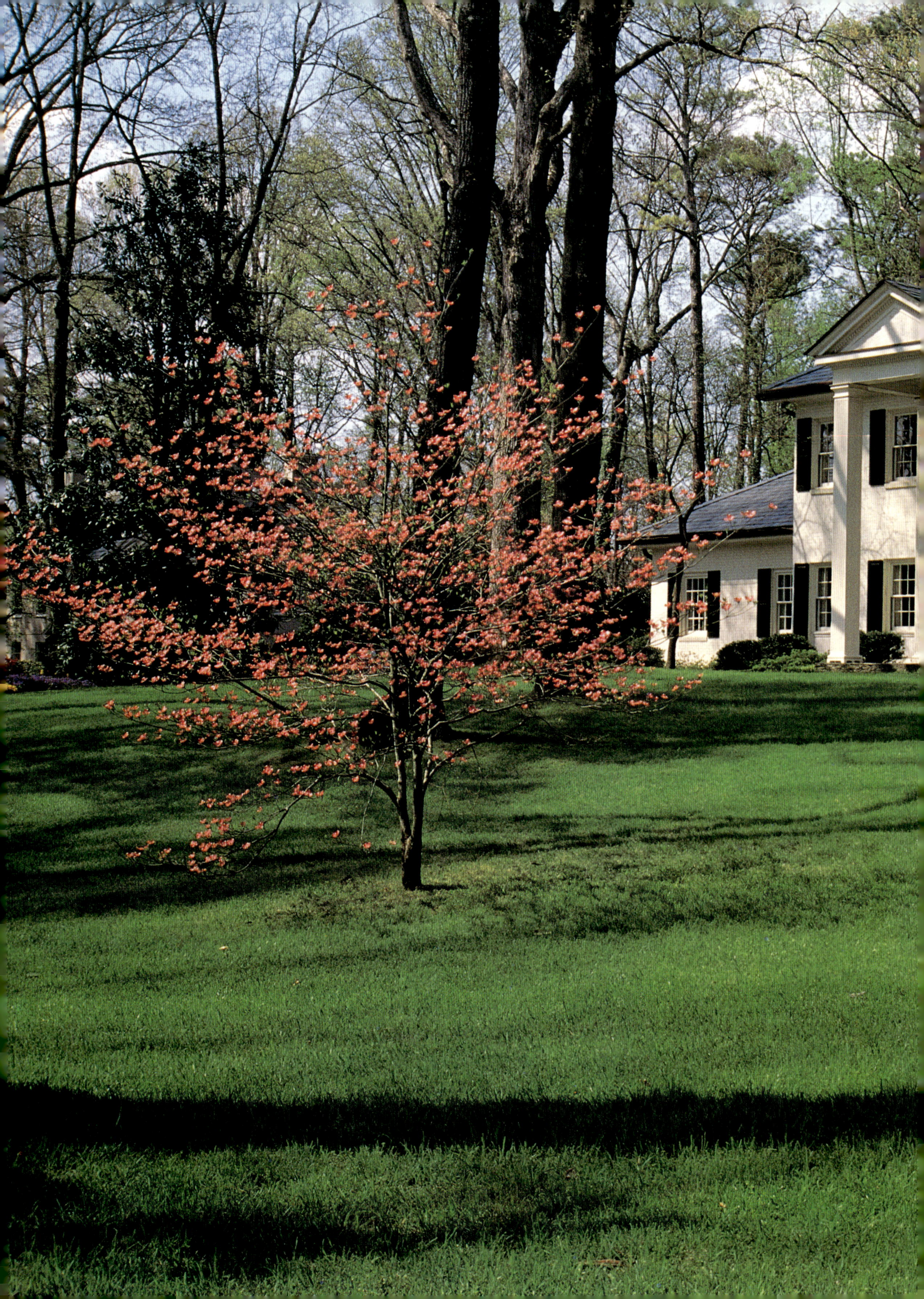

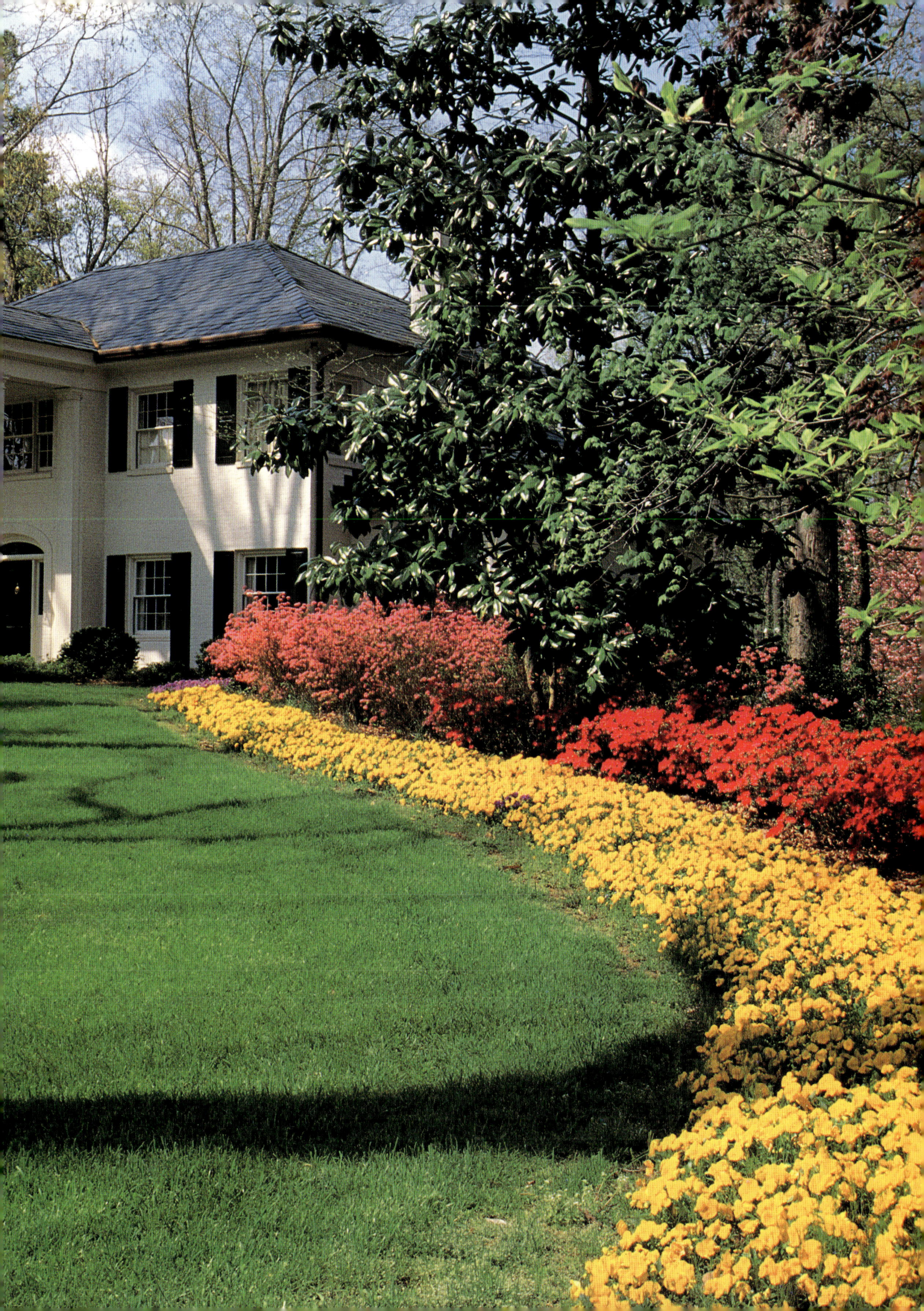

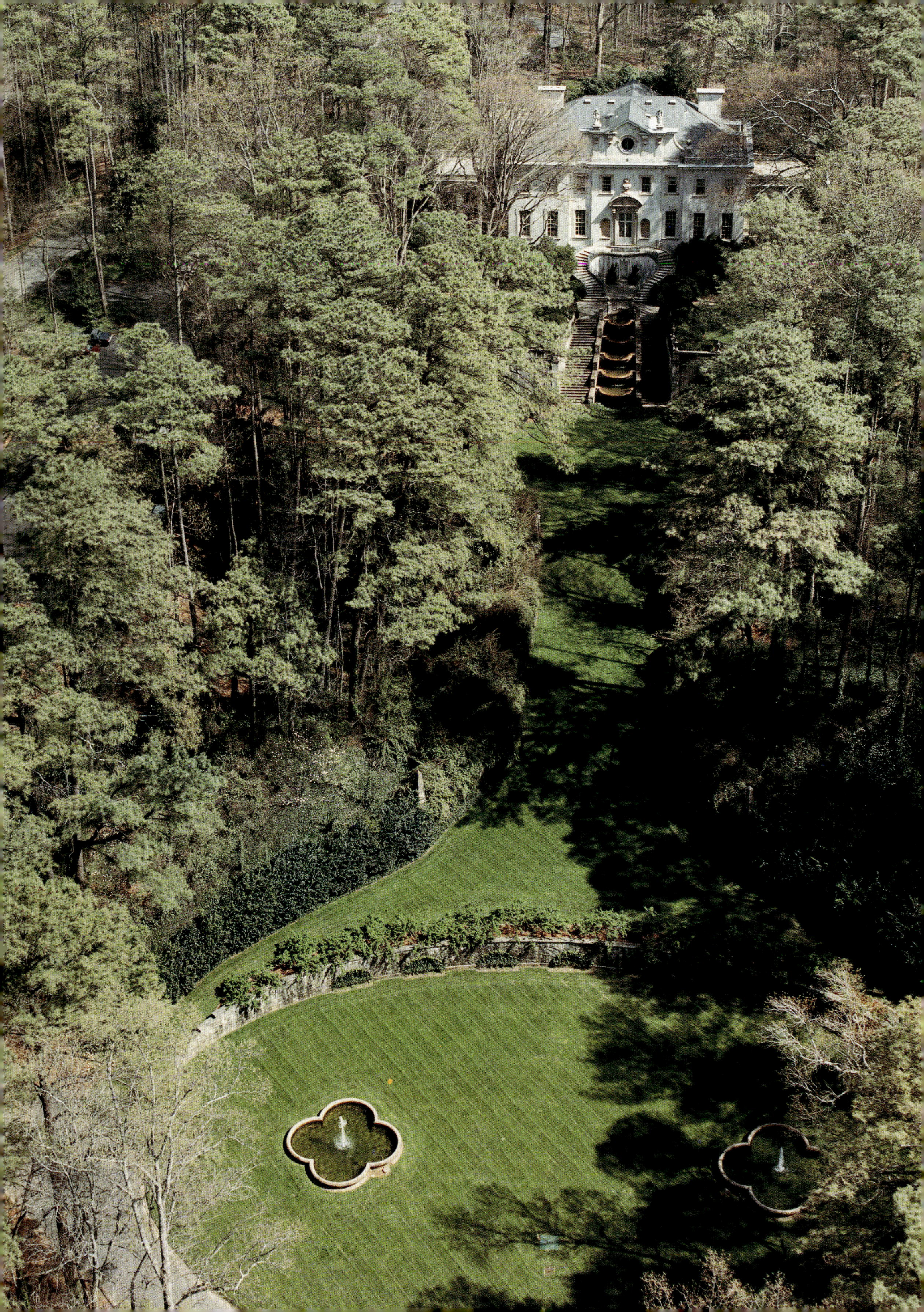

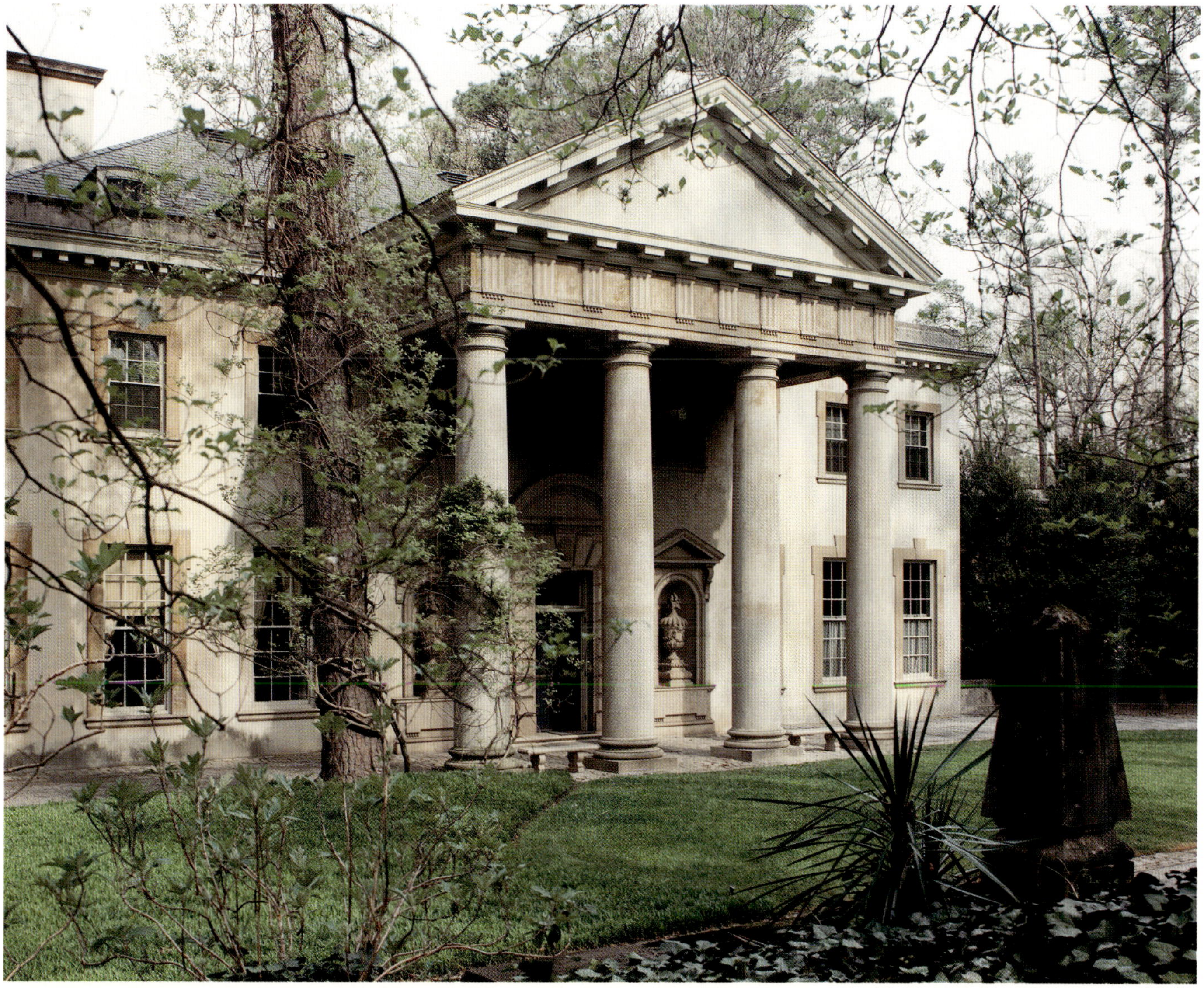

Swan House

Built between 1926 and 1929, this Buckhead mansion—considered by many to be architect Philip Shutze's masterpiece—combines Italian baroque and Anglo-Palladian features overlooking cascading terraces and a formal garden at the rear (left). The house, now part of the Atlanta History Center, gained its name from the swan theme that is repeated in many of its interior details and some of the exterior ones—for example, the swan's-neck curves of the terrace stairs.

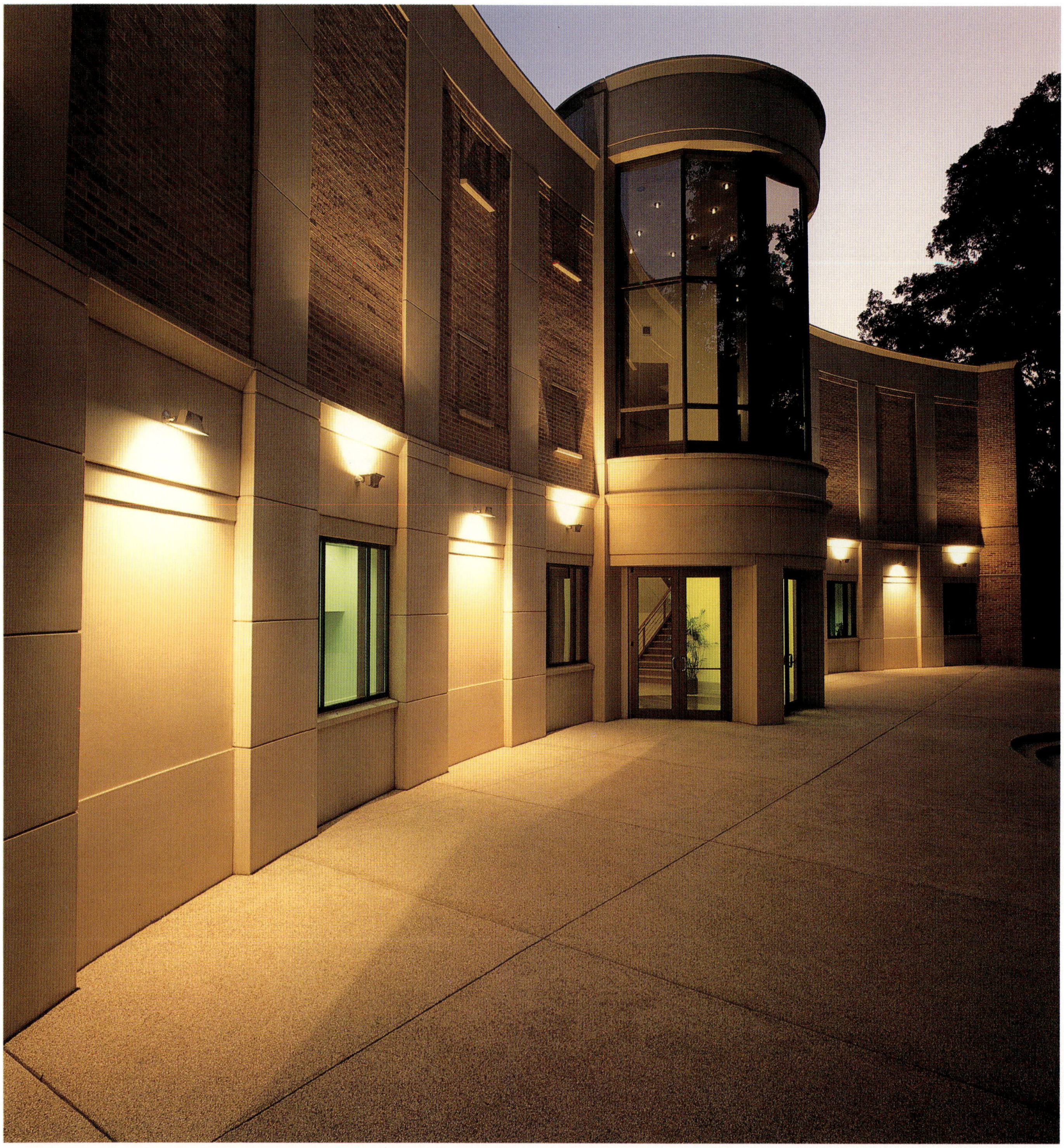

Atlanta History Museum

The $11-million Atlanta History Museum, which opened in 1993 as part of the Atlanta History Center in Buckhead, provides visitors with a panorama of the city's past and present. Temporary exhibits—prototypes for future permanent galleries—explore the Civil War, the growth of black enterprise, southern folk crafts, and ethnic and immigrant celebrations. A major permanent exhibit already in place, "Metropolitan Frontiers: Atlanta, 1835–2000," contains, among many other artifacts of the city's life, an authentic 1890s "shotgun" house, for decades a typical residence for poor families both white and black.

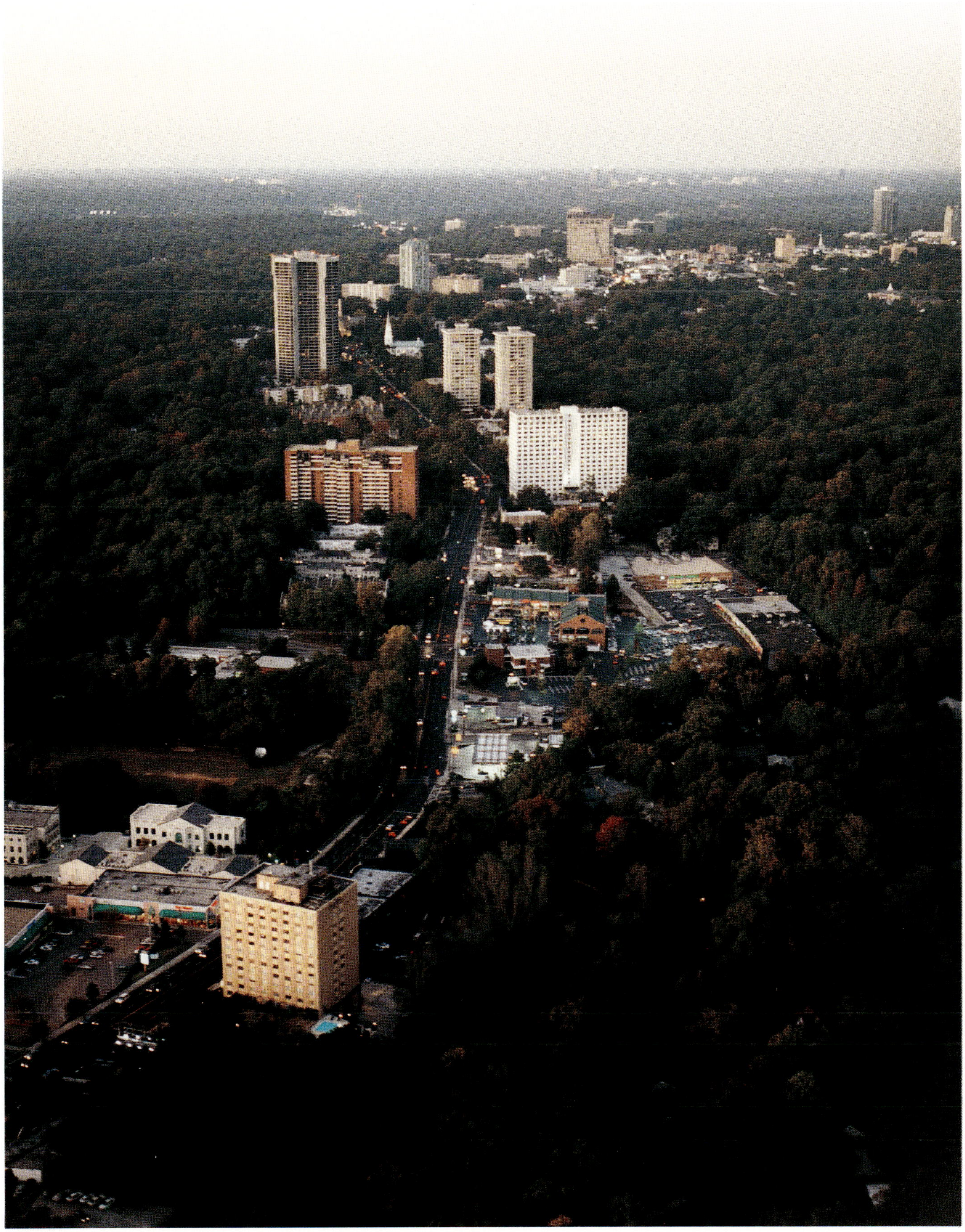

Peachtree Battle

Peachtree Battle, north of Midtown and just south of Buckhead, takes its name from the fierce combat that occurred along Peachtree Creek during the fight for Atlanta in July, 1864. Today it is a thriving neighborhood between Peachtree Road and Northside Drive.

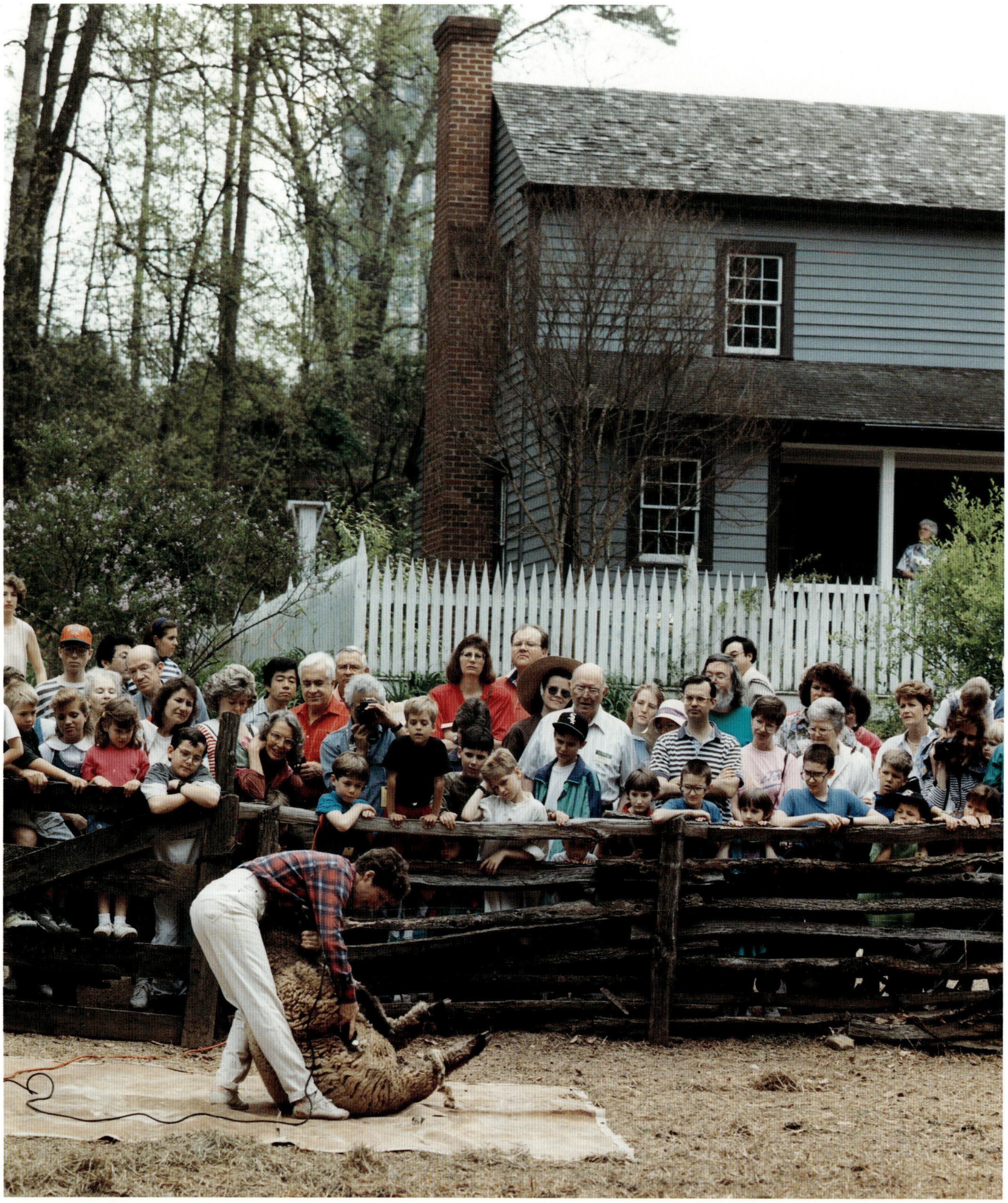

Tullie Smith House

When it was engulfed by shopping centers and an office park, the antebellum Tullie Smith House was moved in 1969 from DeKalb County to the grounds of the Atlanta History Society (now the Atlanta History Center) in Buckhead and restored. Built in the 1830s on a 1,000-acre farm, the "Piedmont plantation plain" home now sits amid its outbuildings with gardens and crops authentic to the antebellum period, and features demonstrations of plantation work such as wool shearing, spinning, and knitting during the annual "Sheep to Shawl" festival. The house is named for its last private owner, who died in 1967.

Part IV

Historic Atlanta

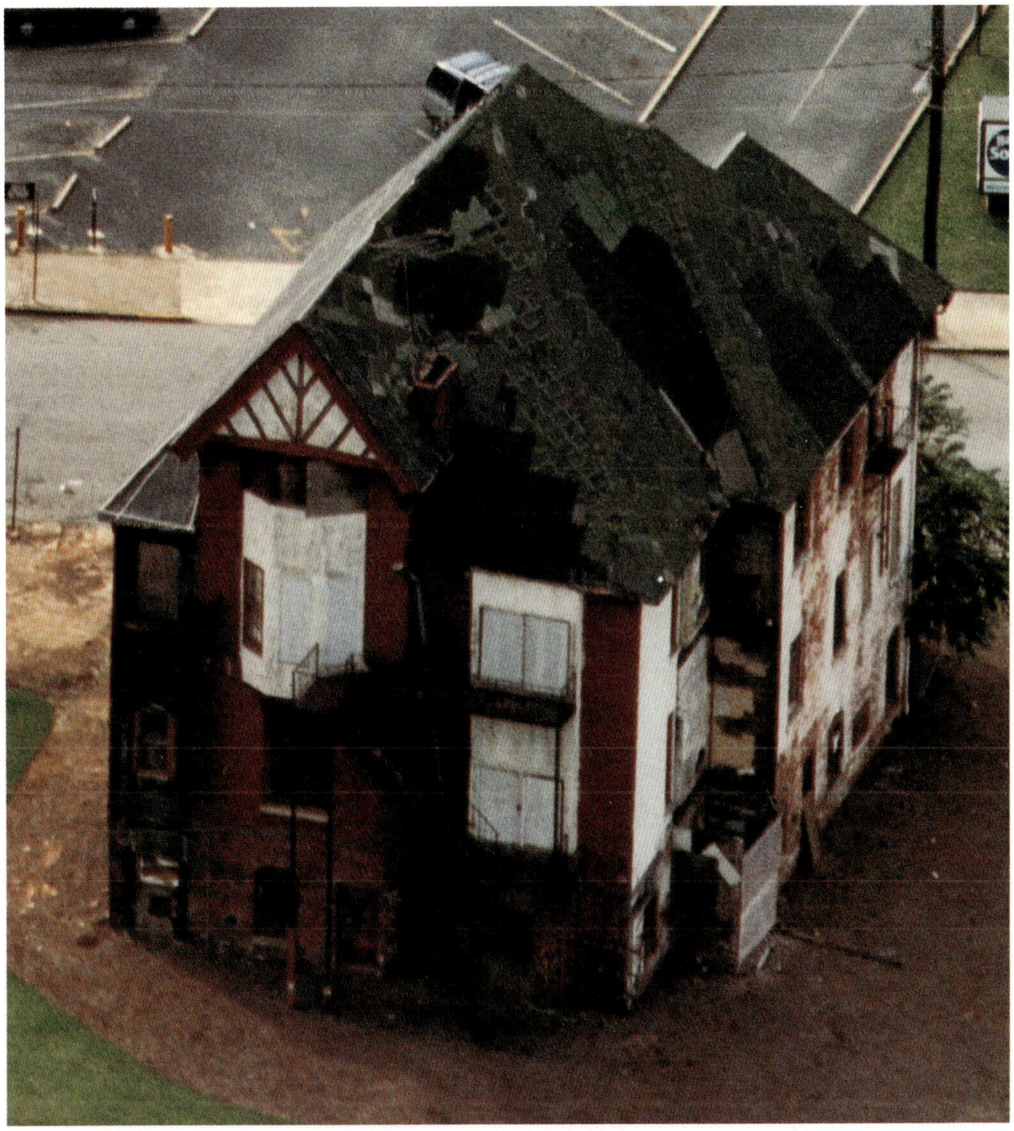

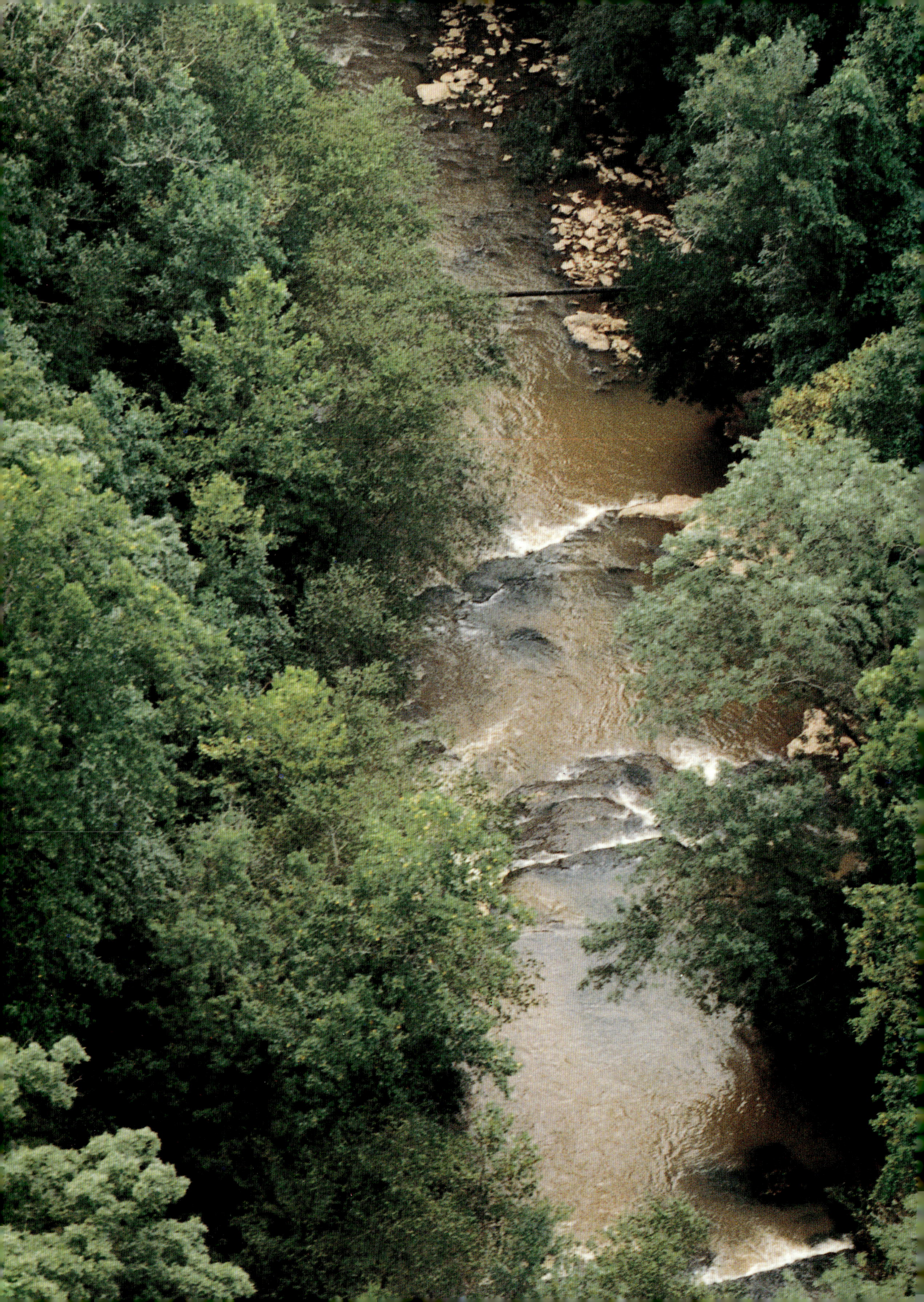

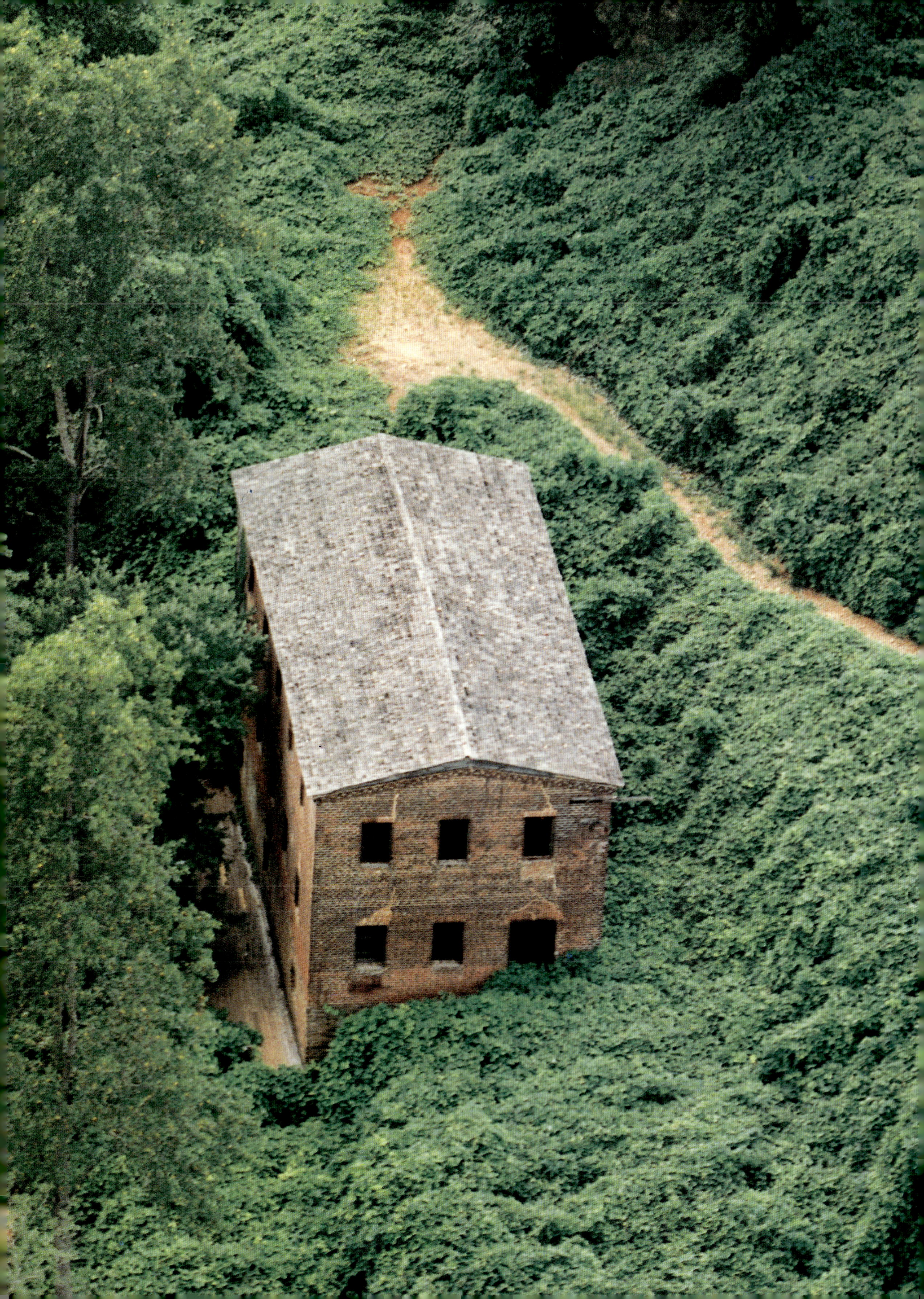

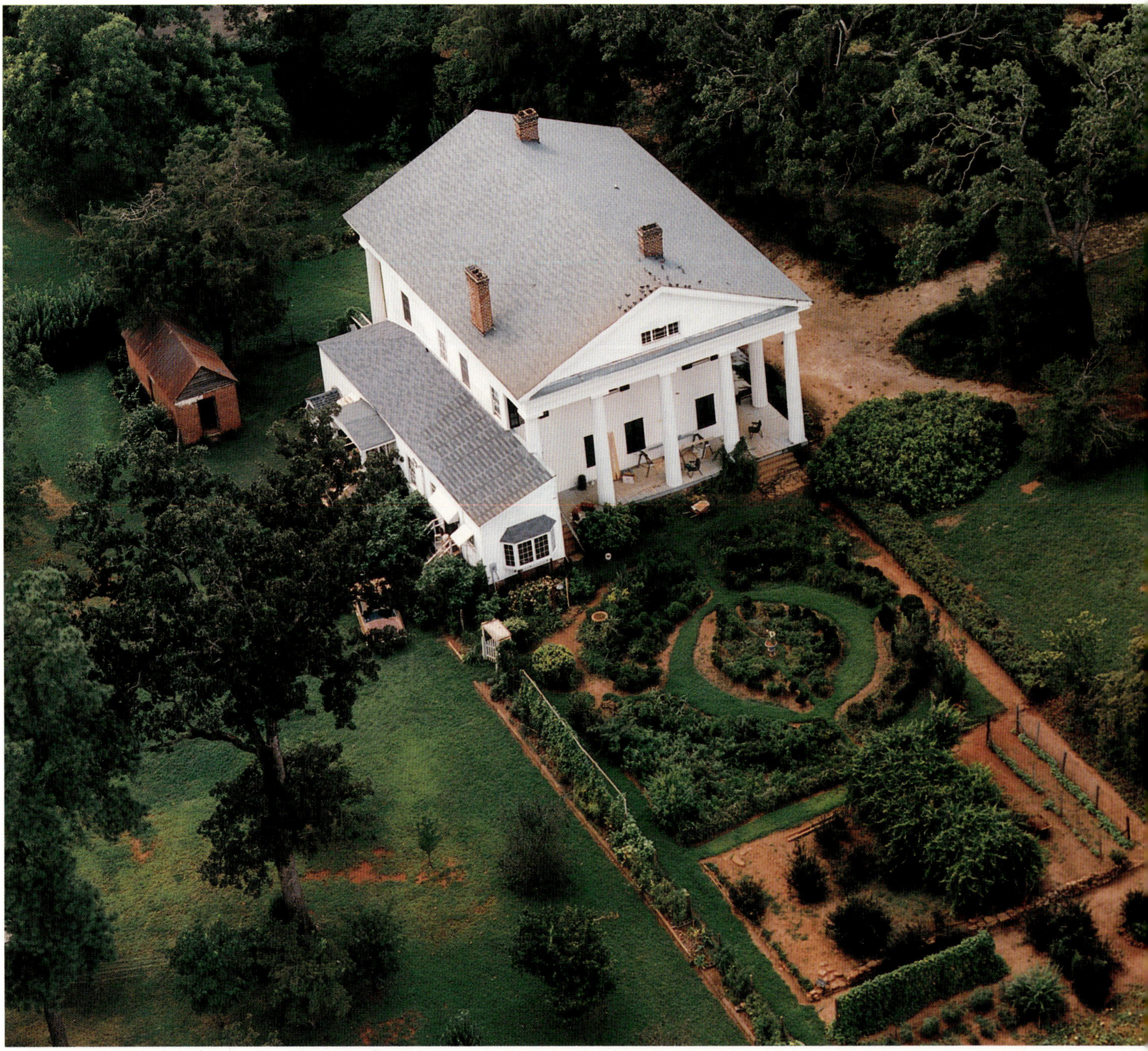

Bulloch Hall

A classic antebellum Greek Revival house in Roswell, north of Atlanta, Bulloch Hall was the childhood home of Mittie (Martha) Bulloch, Theodore Roosevelt's mother, having been built by her father, Major James S. Bulloch, in 1840. It is now in the National Register of Historic Places and is open for tours.

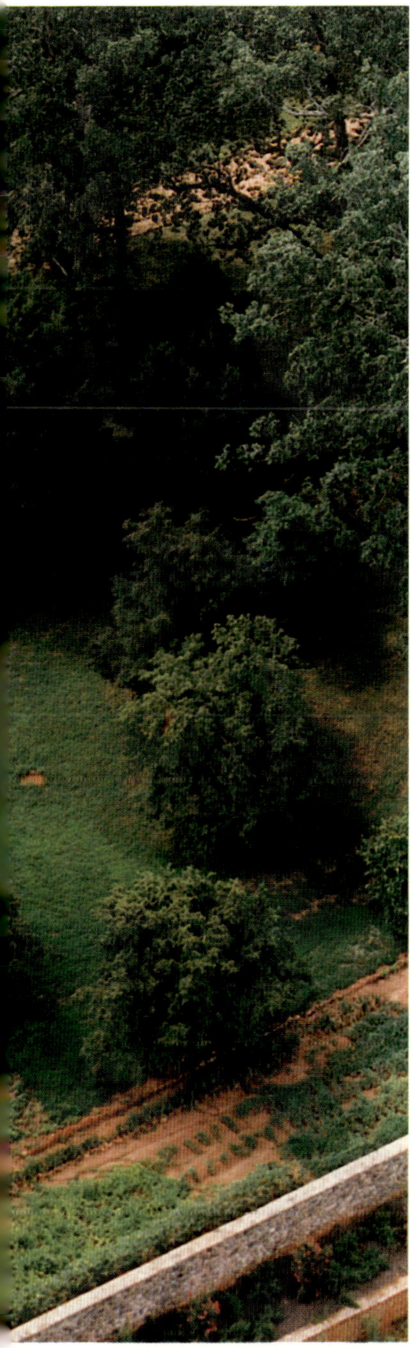

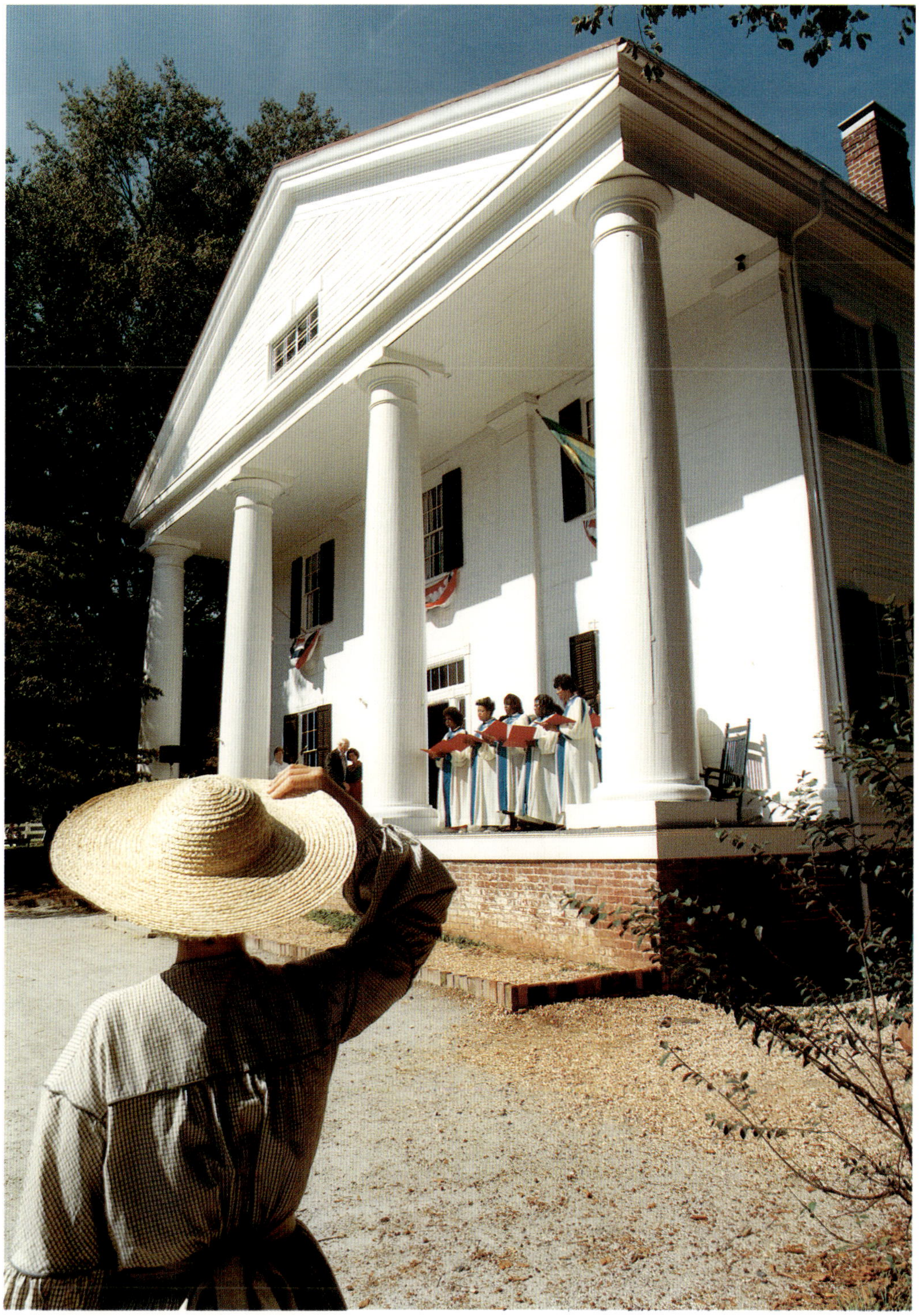

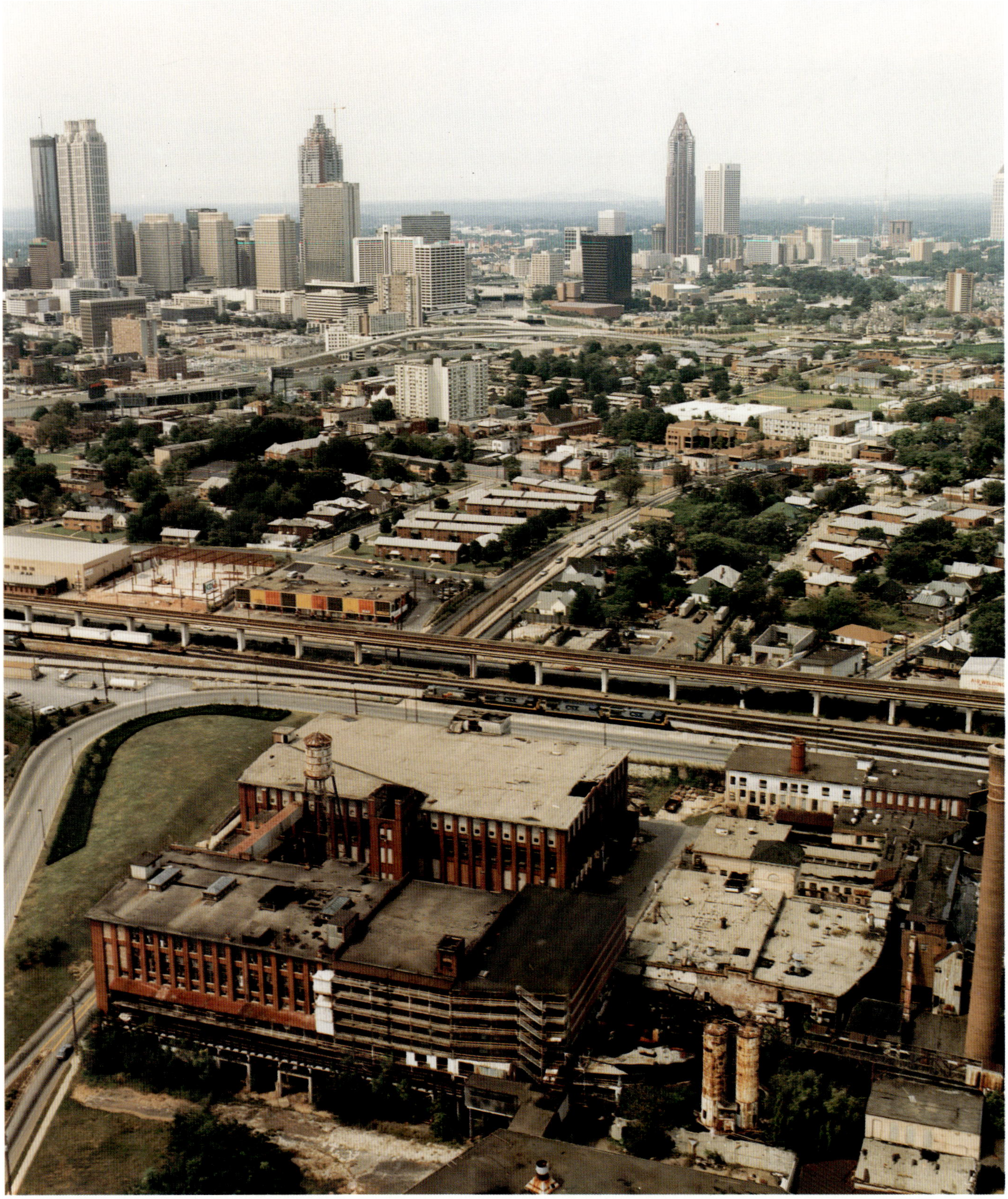

Fulton Bag and Cotton Mill and Cabbagetown

At its peak, in the 1940s, the Fulton Bag and Cotton Mill employed 2,600 workers, many of them from Appalachia, who crowded into small wood-frame houses in a six-block adjoining community called "Cabbagetown" (a corner of which is visible on the right in the photograph). The mill closed in 1976, but many of its former workers and their descendants still live in the neighborhood.

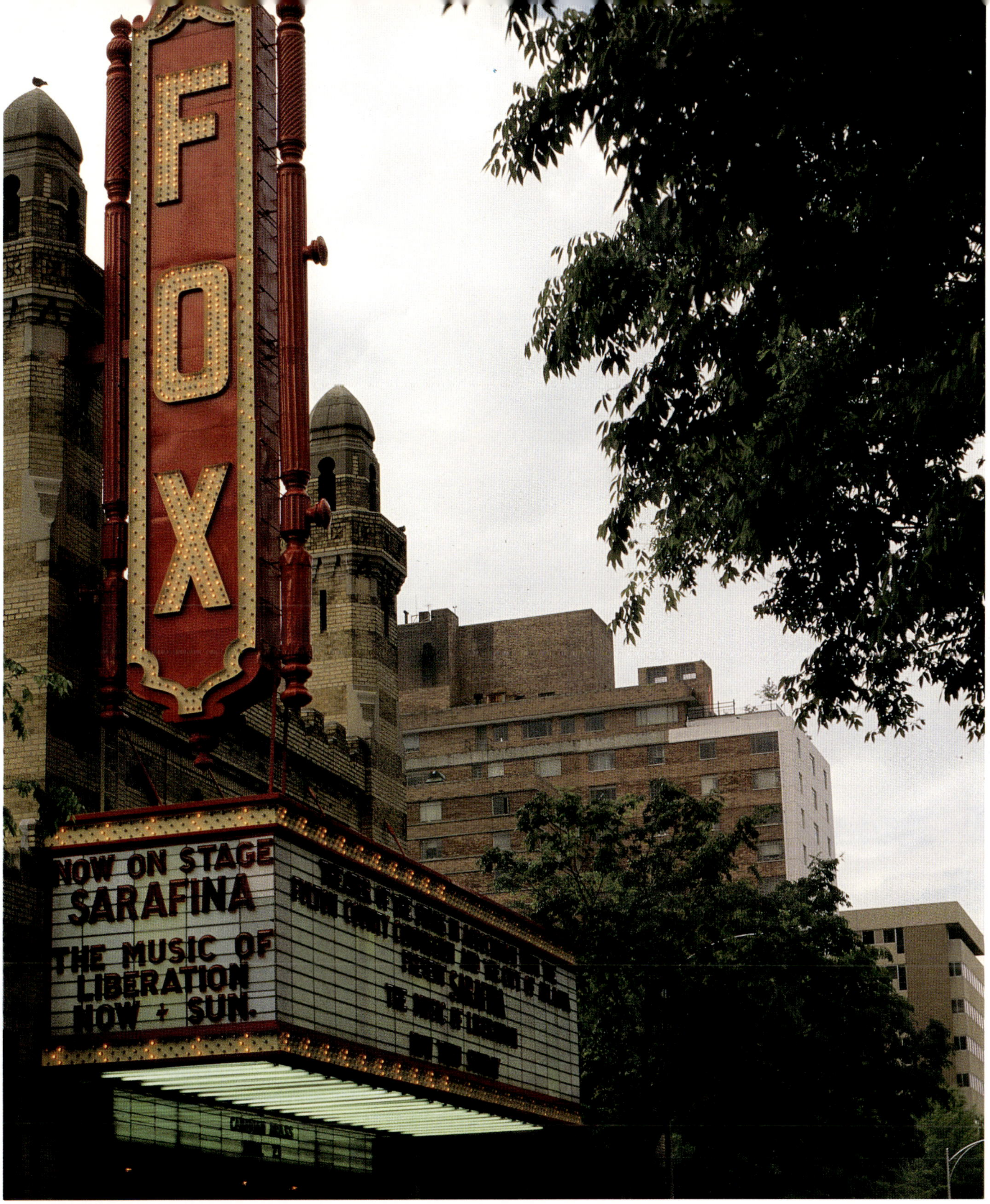

Fox Theatre

The last reminder in Atlanta of an age when movie theaters were works of art, the Moorish-Egyptian extravaganza of the Fox Theatre was actually designed as the local temple of the Order of the Nobles of the Mystic Shrine. The deal with the Shriners fell through, and movie magnate William Fox took over the project. The building's interior is, if possible, more elaborate than the exterior, giving theatergoers the illusion of being in the courtyard of a Middle Eastern palace, while lighting effects create sunrise, sunset, stars, and clouds on the ceiling. The theater is also famous for its 3,600-pipe organ, one of the world's largest.

Opening in 1929, at the dawn of the Great Depression, the opulent Fox ironically never made much money, and only a "Save the Fox" campaign preserved it from demolition in the late 1970s. Today the 4,000-seat theater is used for concerts, traveling plays, and family-film festivals.

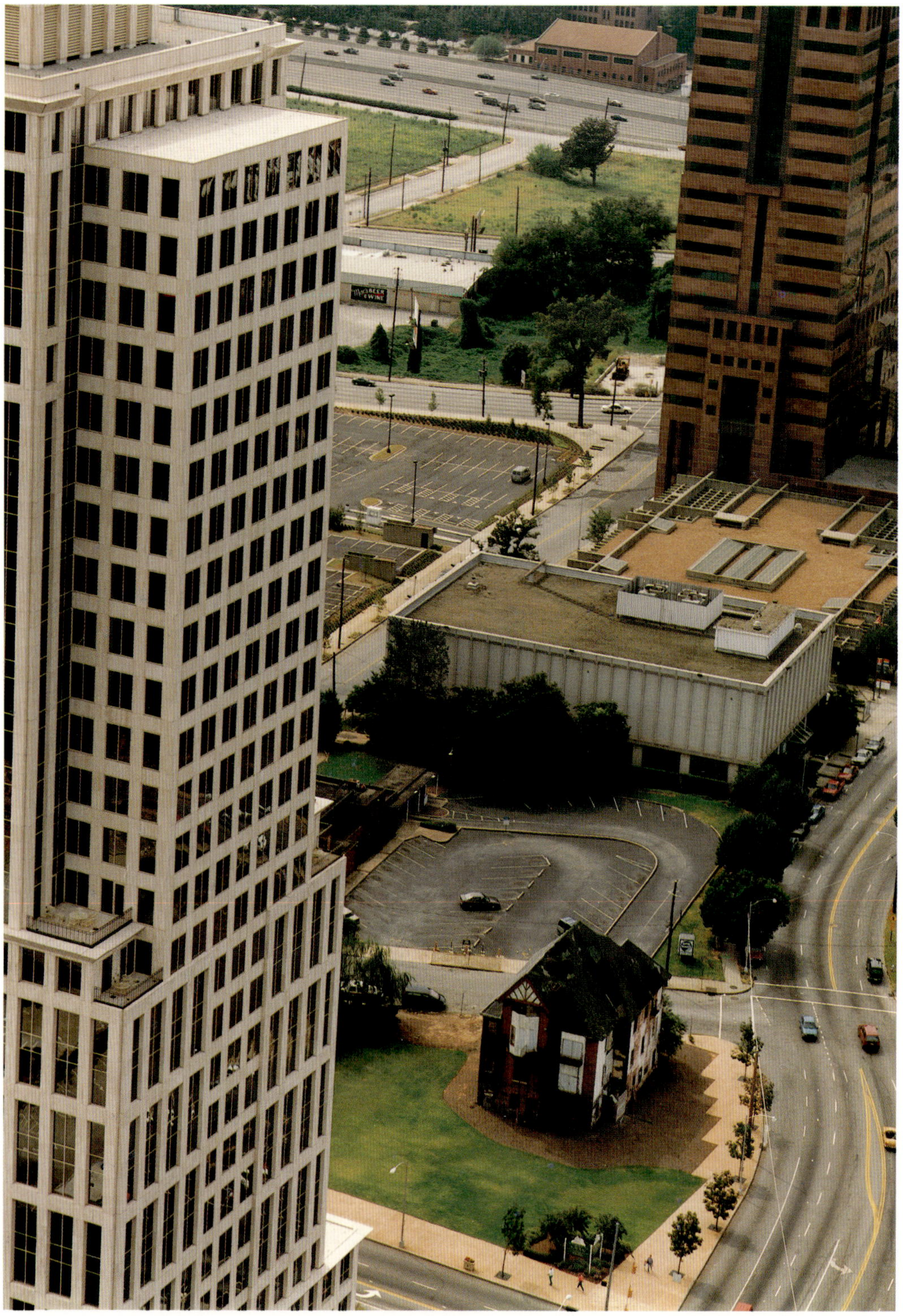

The Dump (Windsor House Apartments)

Termed "a dump" by its most famous resident, and a candidate for the wrecking ball a few years ago, the house where Margaret Mitchell wrote *Gone with the Wind* is being restored, thanks to a group of dedicated preservationists. Built in 1899 as a single-family residence, the house, on Crescent Avenue just off Peachtree Street, was converted to apartments in 1919. Mitchell moved into Apartment 1 in 1925 and lived there for seven years, during which she created her masterpiece.

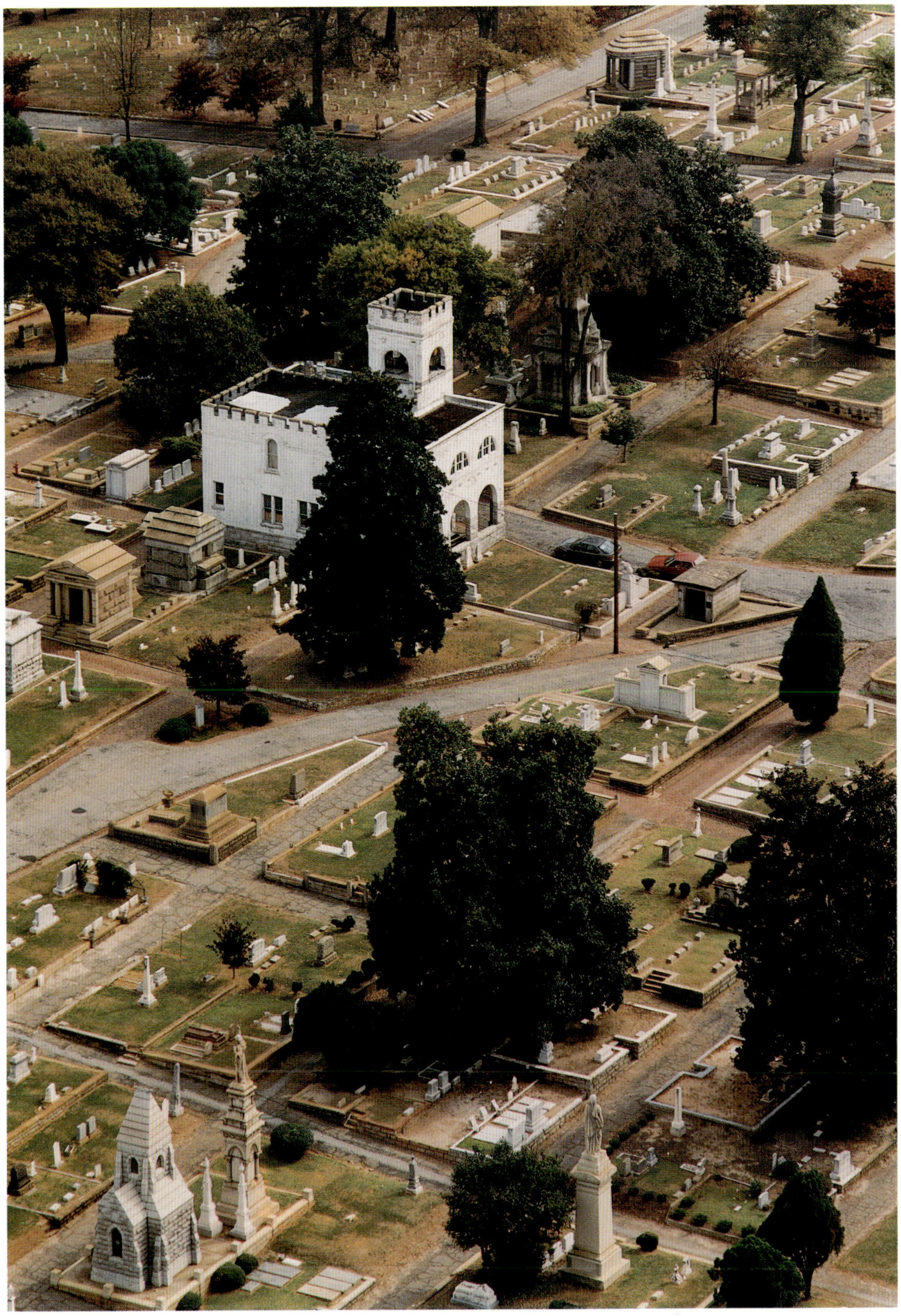

Oakland Cemetery

Nineteenth-century Atlantans often spent Sunday afternoons tending family plots and picnicking under the tall oaks of the city's oldest cemetery, established in 1850. The parklike setting, with its statuary and marble mausoleums adorned with stained glass, still offers visitors an opportunity to dip into local history and Victorian art while walking among the resting places of golf great Bobby Jones, author Margaret Mitchell, Civil War dead, and many governors and generals. The east line for the Metropolitan Atlanta Rapid Transit Authority skirts the cemetery.

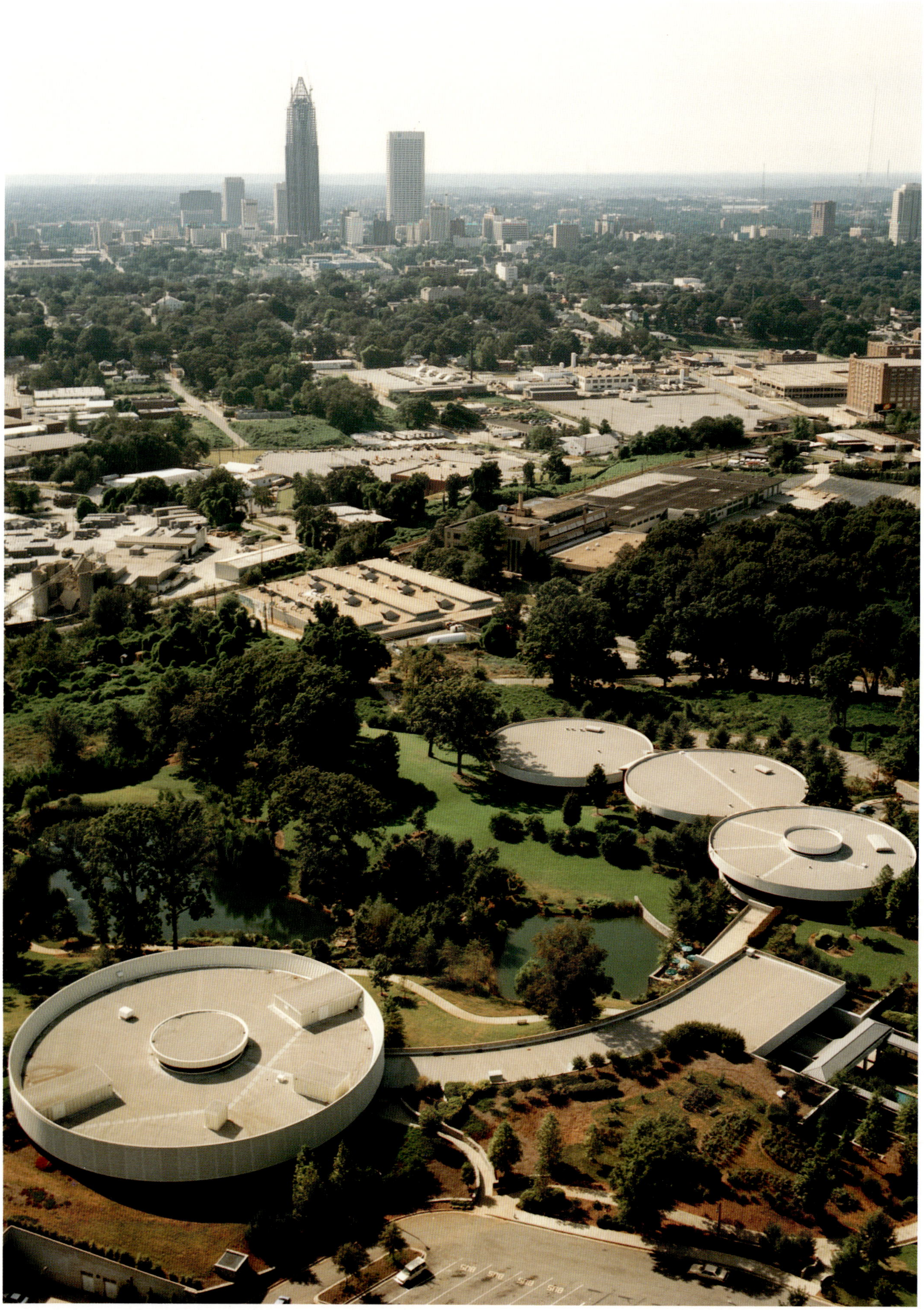

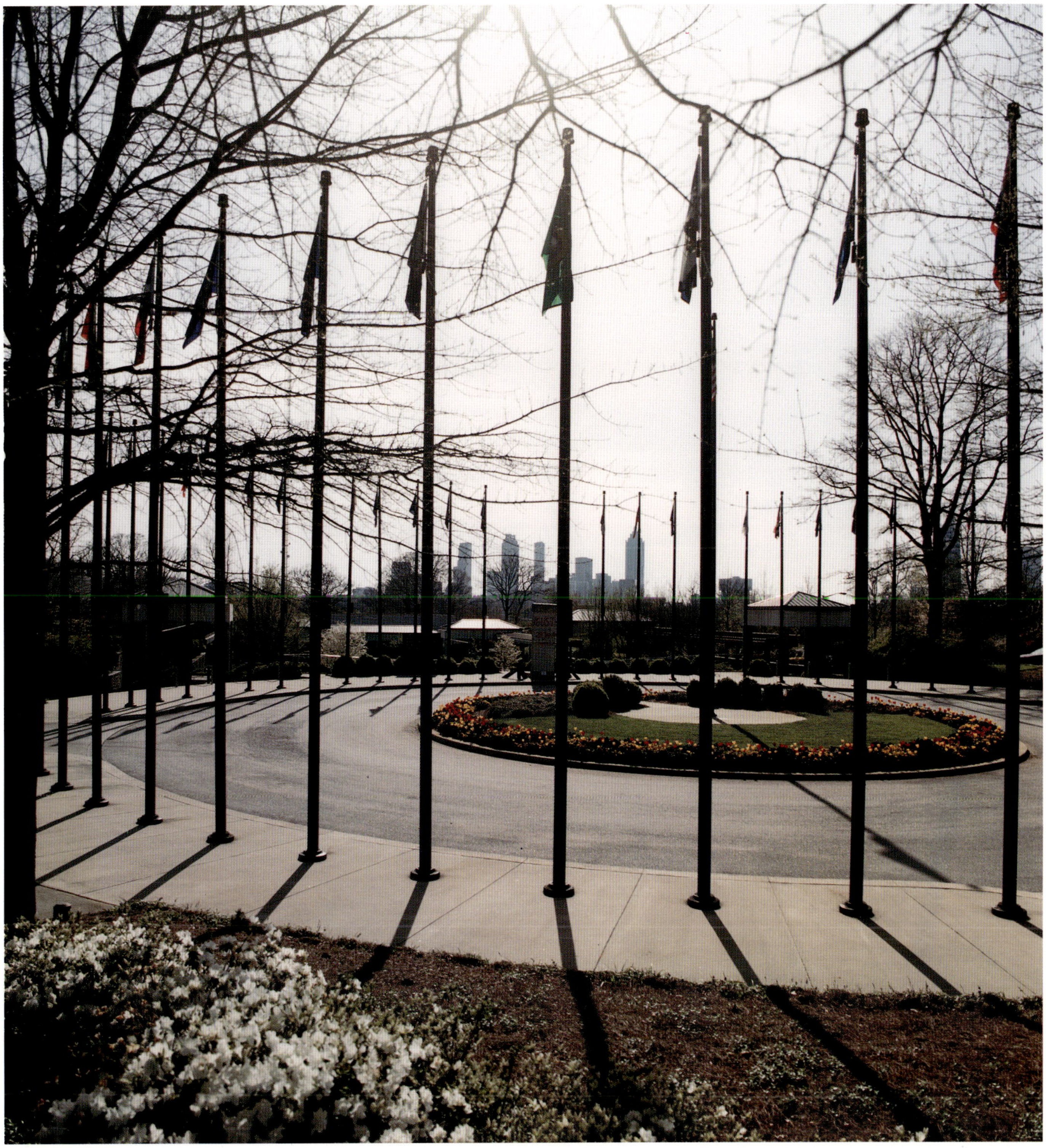

Carter Presidential Center

One of the newest additions to Atlanta's collection of historic places is the Carter Presidential Center. Some of the world's leading thinkers and statesmen have gathered here to discuss global problems at the invitation of former president Jimmy Carter. The eastside research facility and museum, off Cleburne Avenue just north of Inman Park, includes photos, mementoes, and millions of pages of documents from Carter's life and presidency. The complex, entered through the flag-circled Court of the States, also contains a restaurant and a Japanese garden with a stunning view of the Atlanta skyline.

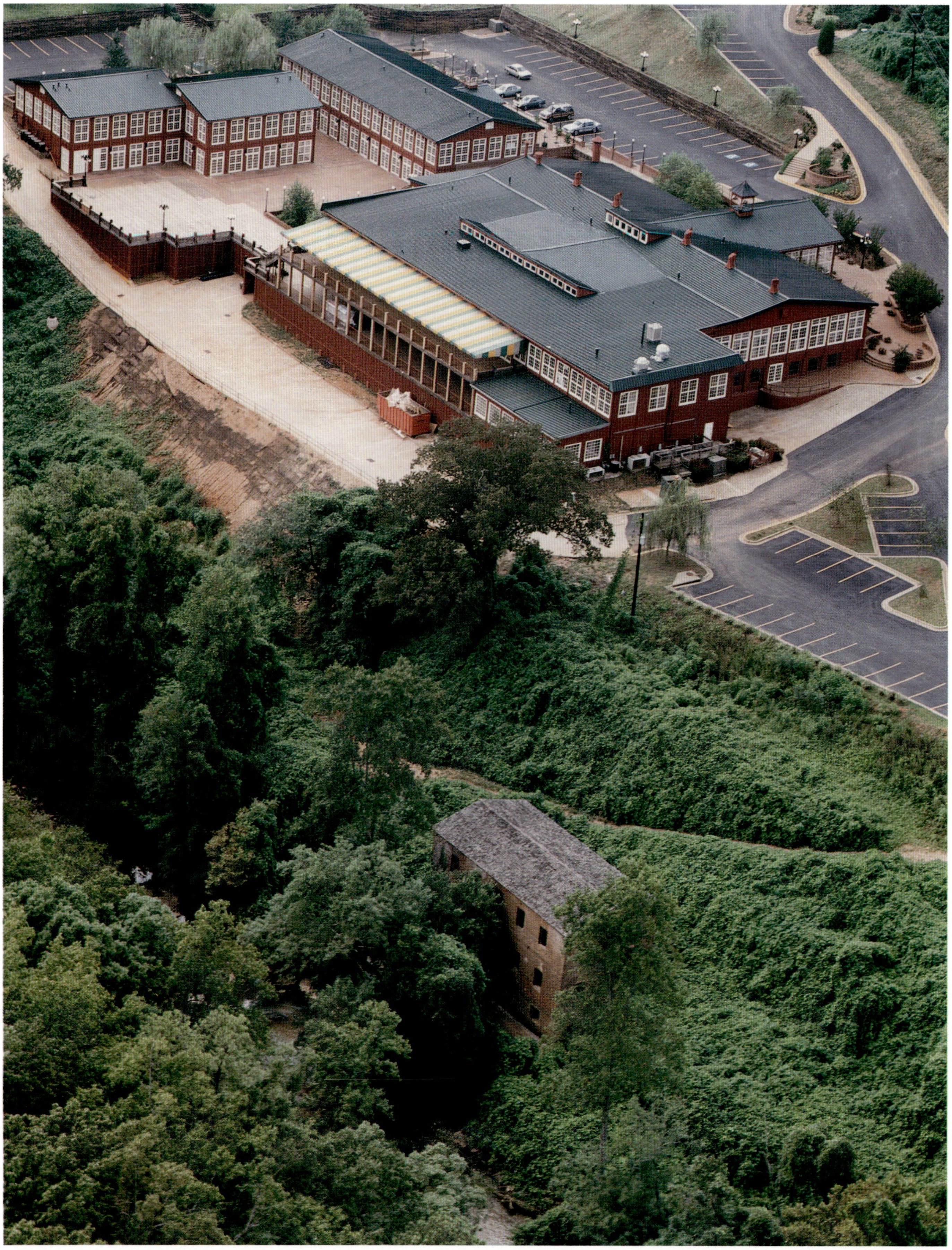

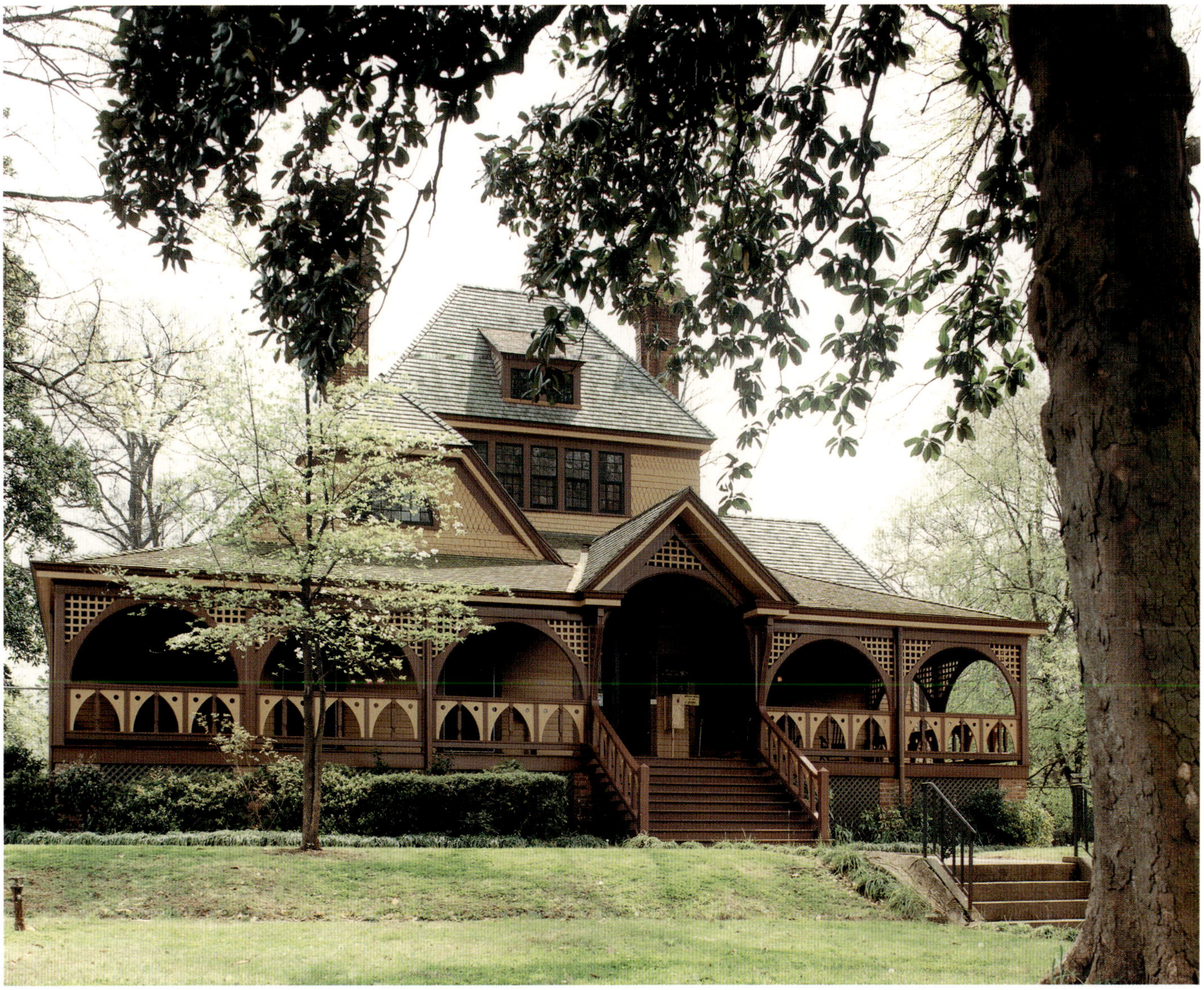

Roswell Mill (left)

Founded by Roswell King in Roswell, the original mill produced woolen and cotton cloth until it was destroyed by advancing Union troops in July, 1864. Arguing that the mill and others nearby had been turning out war supplies, General Sherman ordered four hundred of their female employees sent north to Indiana. Today the rebuilt Roswell Mill contains shops and restaurants.

Wren's Nest (above)

The southwest Atlanta home of author, newspaperman, and Uncle Remus creator Joel Chandler Harris is a reminder of the city's Victorian legacy. Harris, known for his stories of Br'er Rabbit and Br'er Fox, which were based on African-American folktales, was an associate editor at the Atlanta *Constitution* when Henry Grady was managing editor. Bought by the Harris family in 1880, the Wren's Nest is now a National Historic Landmark open to the public for tours and storytelling. Original furnishings, photographs, and a slide show provide a glimpse into the life and times of Harris, who supposedly gave the house its name after a wren built a nest in the mailbox.

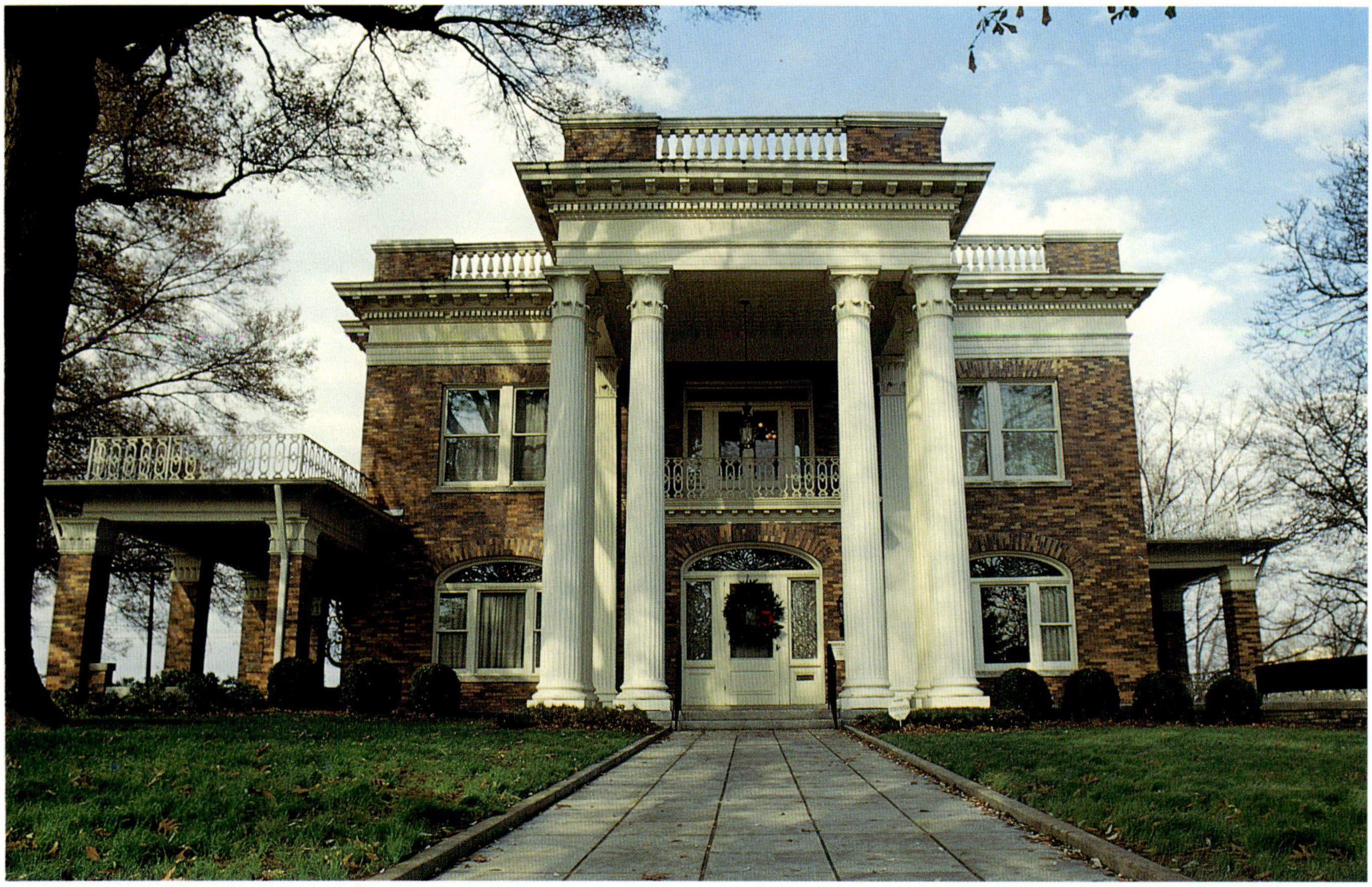

The Herndon Home

Alonzo F. Herndon, a former slave, after the Civil War became the first black millionaire in Atlanta by starting a series of successful businesses ranging from a luxurious barber shop to the Atlanta Life Insurance Company. Herndon and his wife and young son were part of Atlanta's black elite in a strictly segregated society at the turn of the century. In 1910, on land purchased from Atlanta University, he completed this *beaux arts* classical home, built by black craftsmen. In it he displayed the treasures he and his wife brought back from trips to Europe. The family collection of furniture, clothing, memorabilia, photographs, and documents is preserved here.

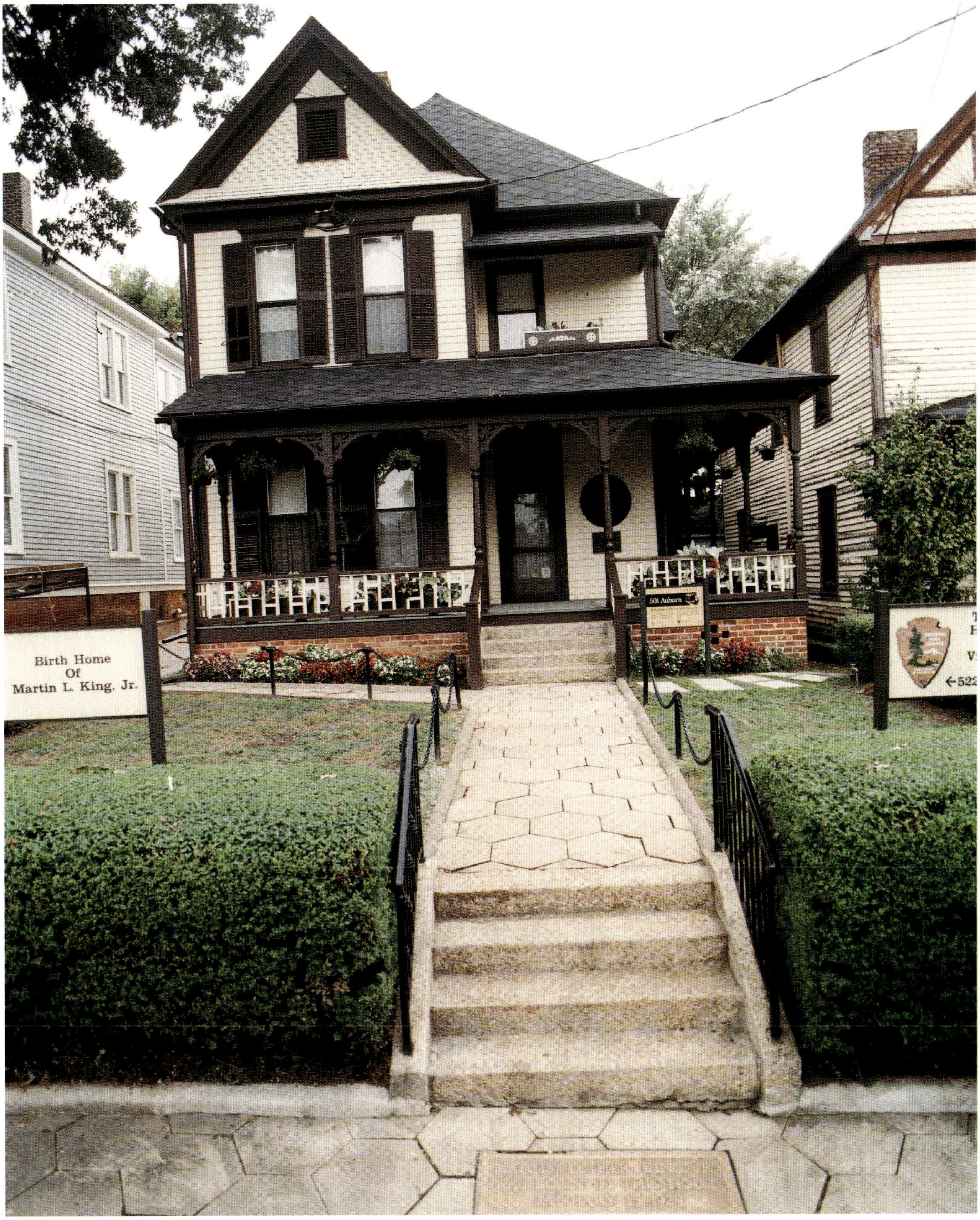

King Birthplace

Martin Luther King, Jr., was born in 1929 in this house on historic Auburn Avenue downtown. The house, where the Kings lived until 1941, was restored beginning in 1974 by the National Park Service, which has also revivified several other historic buildings in this neighborhood of homes, businesses, and churches.

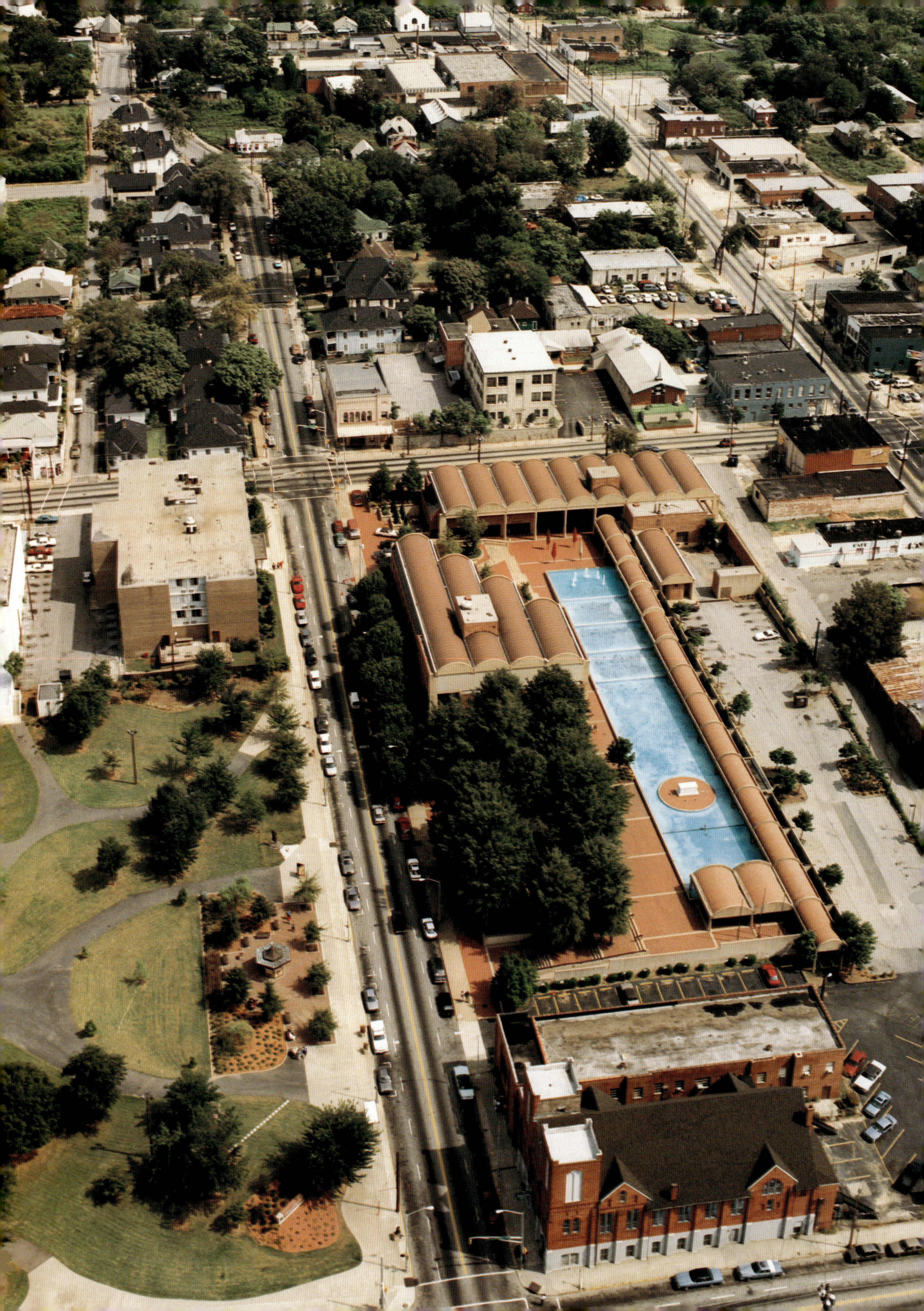

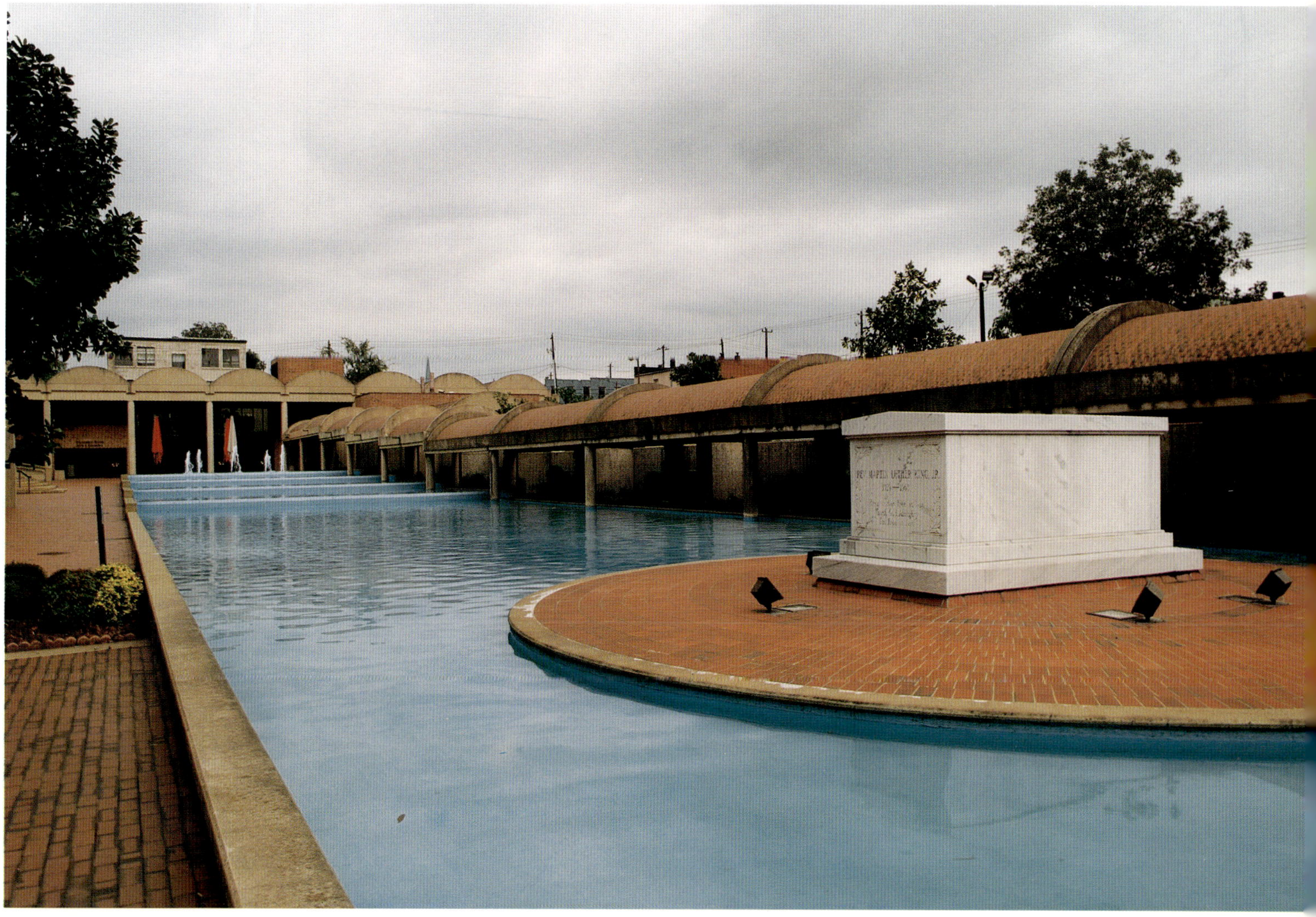

Martin Luther King Center

Just down the street from Martin Luther King's birthplace, the Martin Luther King, Jr. Center for Nonviolent Social Change hosts more than a million visitors a year. The center offers programs telling the story of the civil rights movement and workshops teaching the nonviolent methods of Atlanta's Nobel Peace Prize winner. On the grounds, King's simple marble tomb rests in the middle of a quiet reflecting pool. The epitaph it bears is based on the conclusion of King's famous "I Have a Dream" speech: "Free at last. Free at last. Thank God Almighty, I'm free at last."

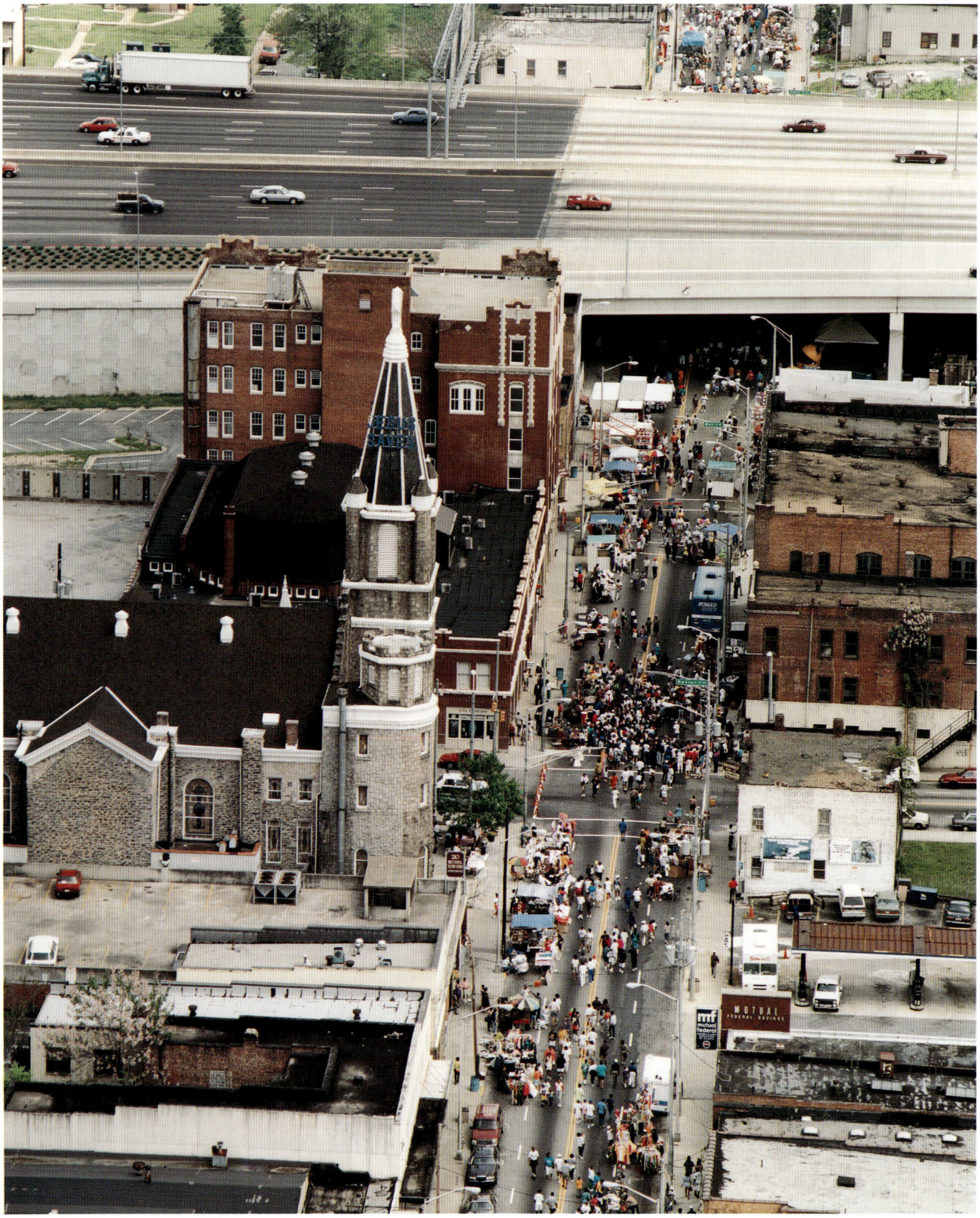

Sweet Auburn Festival

Every year, the Sweet Auburn Festival celebrates the social, political, musical, and culinary history of black Atlantans. Auburn Avenue was a nucleus for black business development and cultural activities in the city from the 1890s through the 1940s.

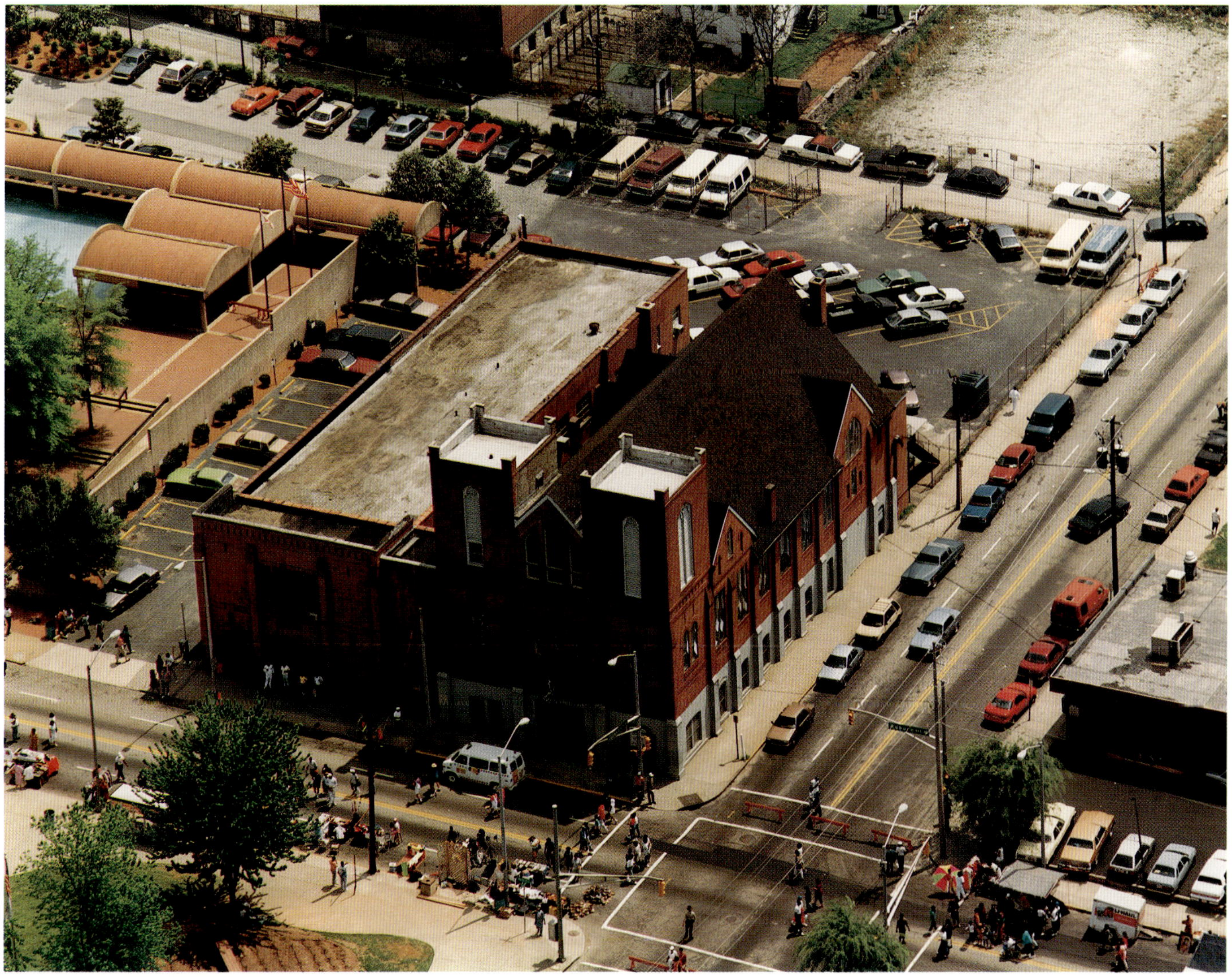

Ebenezer Baptist Church

The current building on Auburn Avenue was completed in 1922, but as a congregation Ebenezer Baptist dates to 1886. The Reverend Martin L. King, Sr., served as the church's pastor for many years, having succeeded his father-in-law, the Reverend A. D. Williams. Martin Luther King, Jr., was also pastor of the church and preached some of his most eloquent sermons from its pulpit.

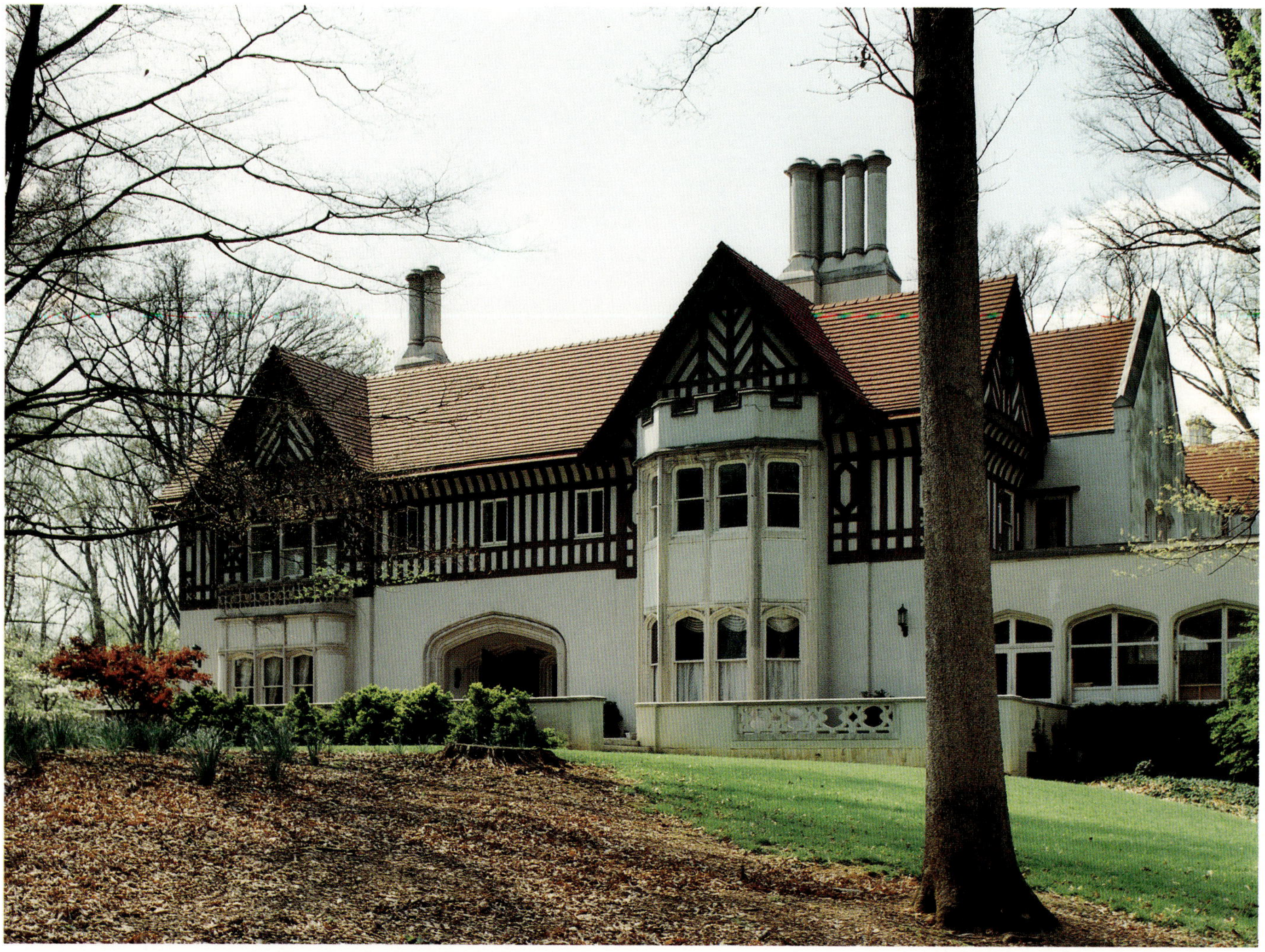

Callanwolde (above)

The Druid Hills home of Charles Howard Candler, Asa Candler's eldest son and long-time chairman of the board of Coca-Cola, Callanwolde is now a DeKalb County fine-arts center hosting art classes, musical performances, and rehearsals by many local groups. The mansion's styling, reminiscent of many a stone-and-timber Tudor home in England, is deceptive: the architect, Henry Hornbostel, believed in modern materials and methods, and the construction is steel and poured-in-place concrete. Callanwolde was completed in 1921.

The Roosevelt (Franklin D. Roosevelt High School)

Built in 1924 as Girls' High School and later renamed for the president, this striking example of Byzantine Revival architecture on Rosalia Street, southeast of downtown, closed in 1985 but was soon converted into a ninety-unit apartment building.

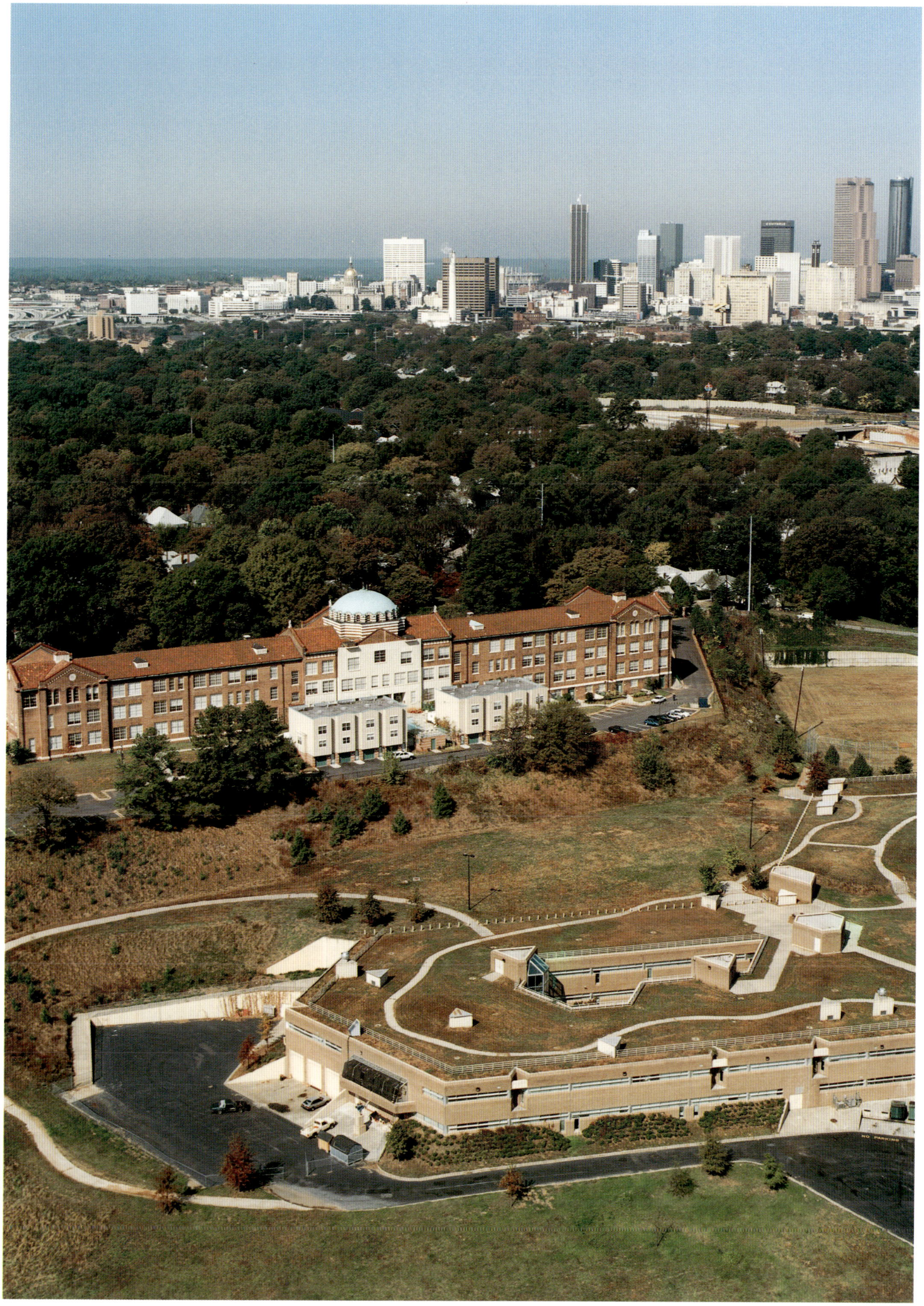

Callan Castle

Built in 1903, Asa Candler's Callan Castle (*callan* being Irish for "candler"), combining Victorian, Greek Revival, and Colonial Revival influences, towers over Inman Park from a prominent corner location. Candler lived there until 1916.

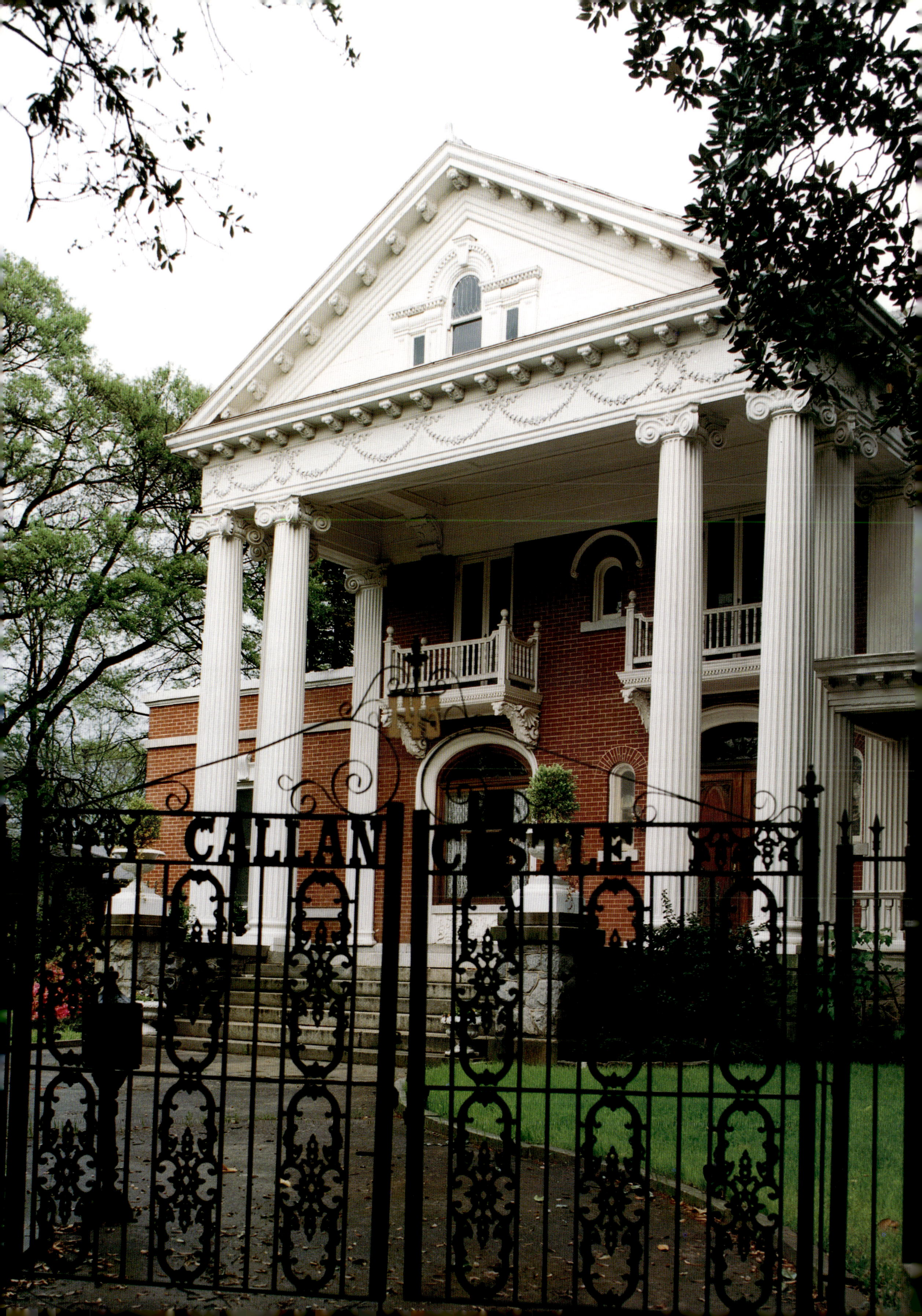
CALLAN

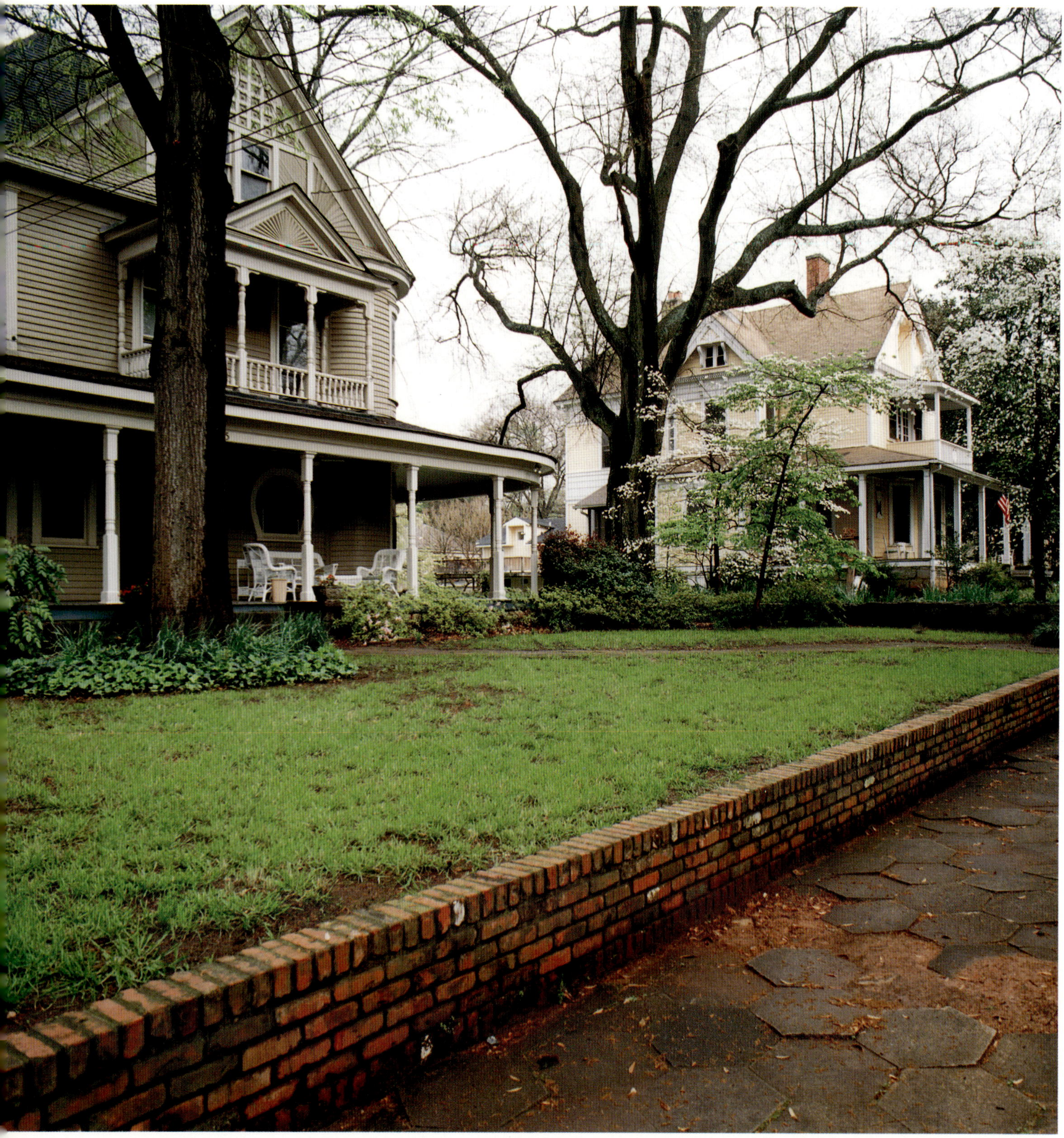

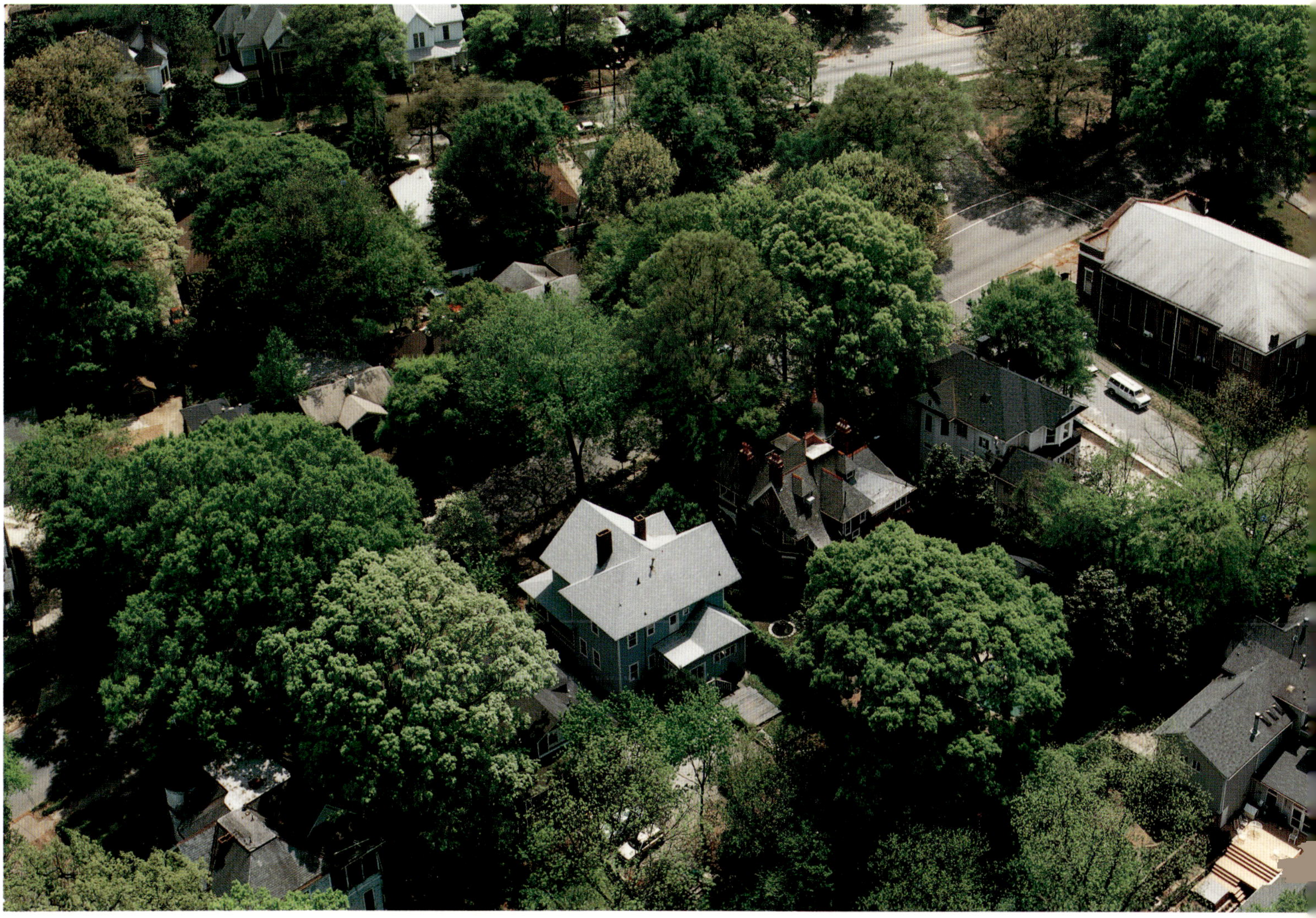

Inman Park

Begun in 1889 by developer Joel Hurt, Atlanta's oldest planned suburb contains many classic examples of Victorian architecture. The city's first electric trolley line ran from Inman Park to the downtown business district; the original 1889 trolley barn has been restored. The neighborhood began to decline in fashionableness by 1920 and suffered from urban flight in the 1960s, but a renewal began with the renovation of the remarkable Beath-Dickey house (red with three chimneys, above) in 1969. Today Inman Park is a showcase of restoration efforts and annually hosts a popular spring festival.

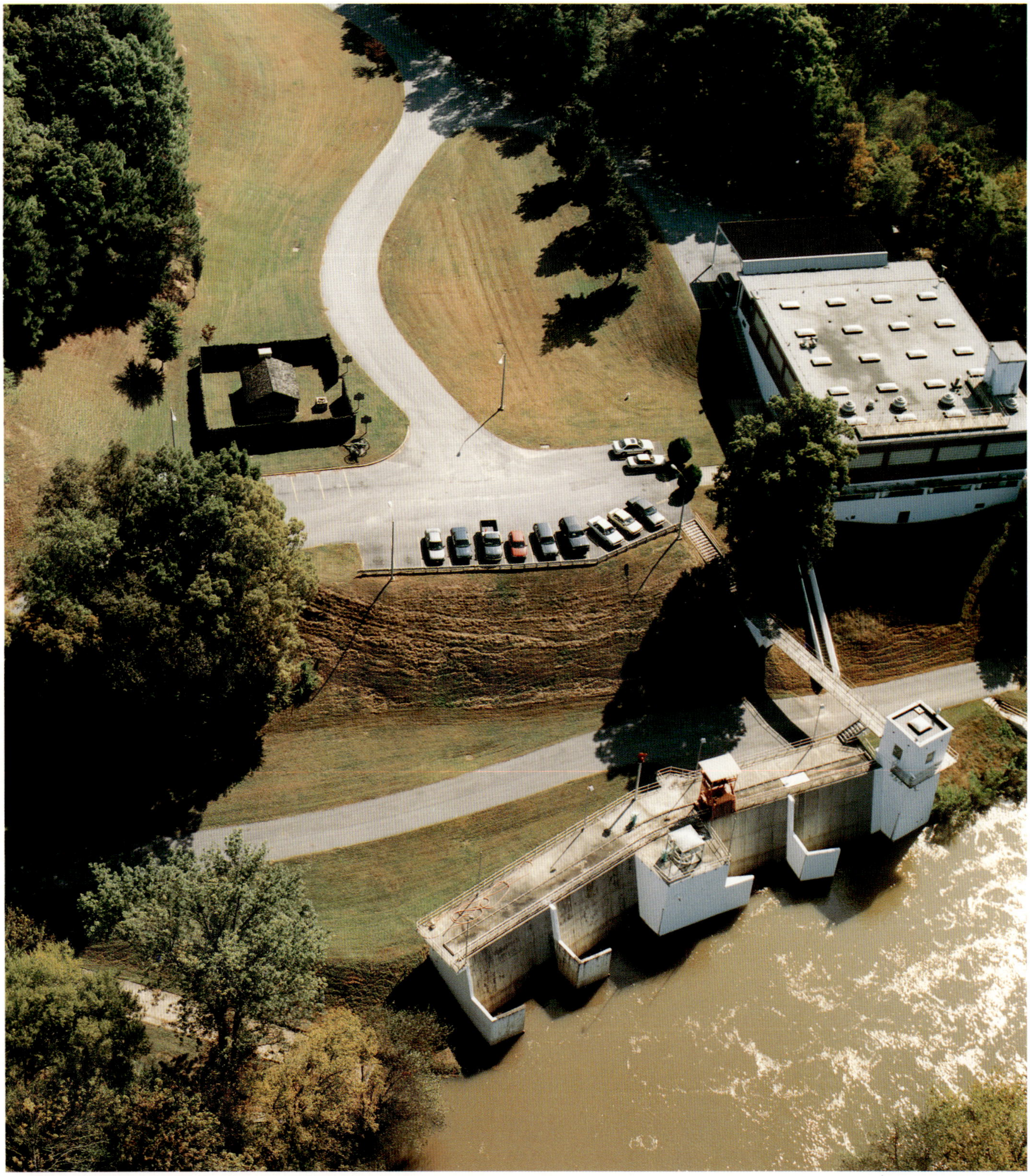

Fort Peachtree

Standing incongruous guard over a modern waterworks facility, tiny Fort Peachtree recalls a time when Atlanta did not yet exist. The fort is a fanciful re-creation of a stockade erected nearby in 1814 at the Indian trading post of Standing Peachtree. The site adjoined a shallow ford used by travelers crossing the Chattahoochee River on their way to or from even remoter outposts. The name "Peachtree," ubiquitous in Atlanta today, may have been derived simply from a peach tree, but it just as likely came from a *pitch* tree, a resin-rich pine. A trail between the trading post and Terminus eventually developed into Peachtree Road and Peachtree Street.

Part V

Leisure and Entertainment

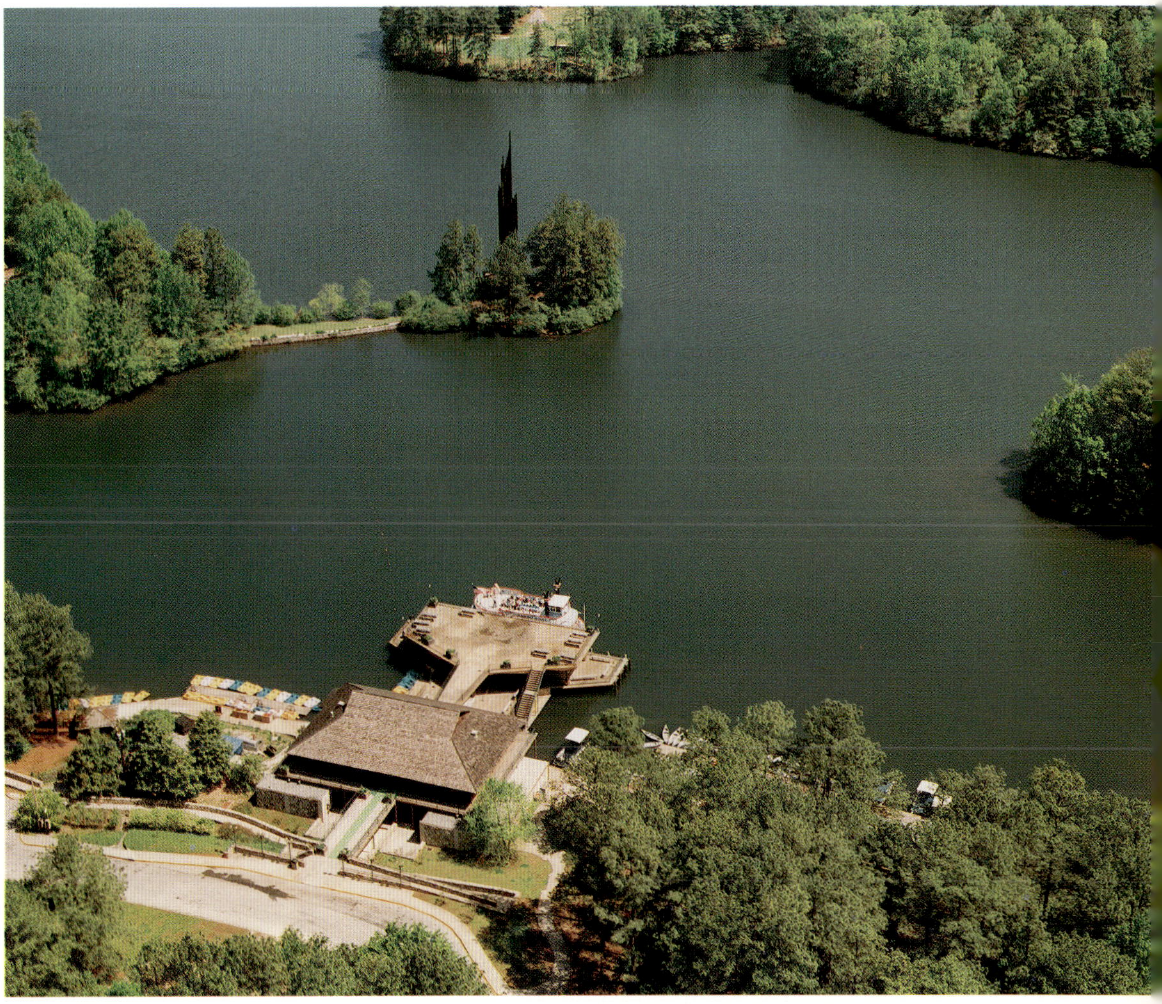

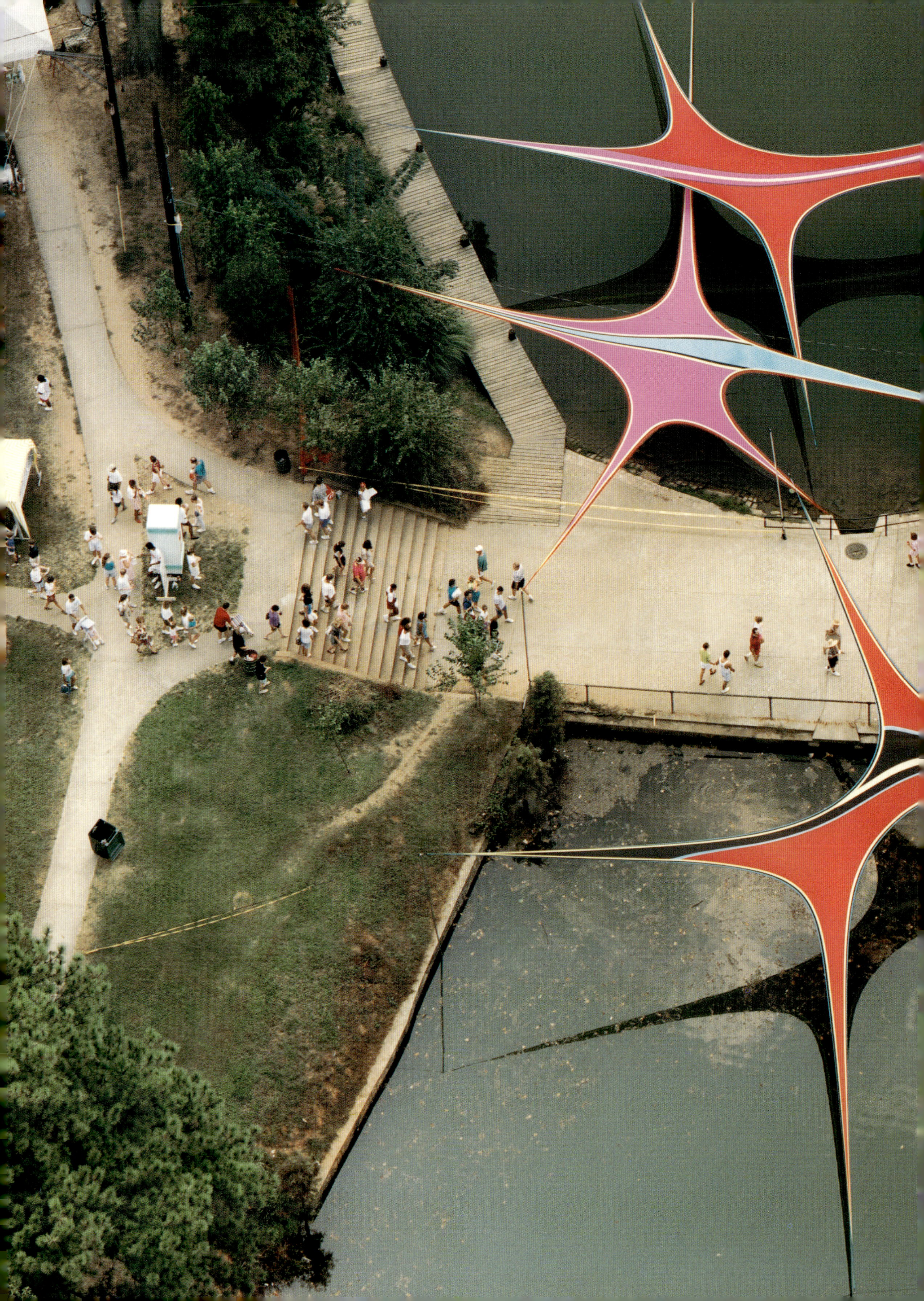

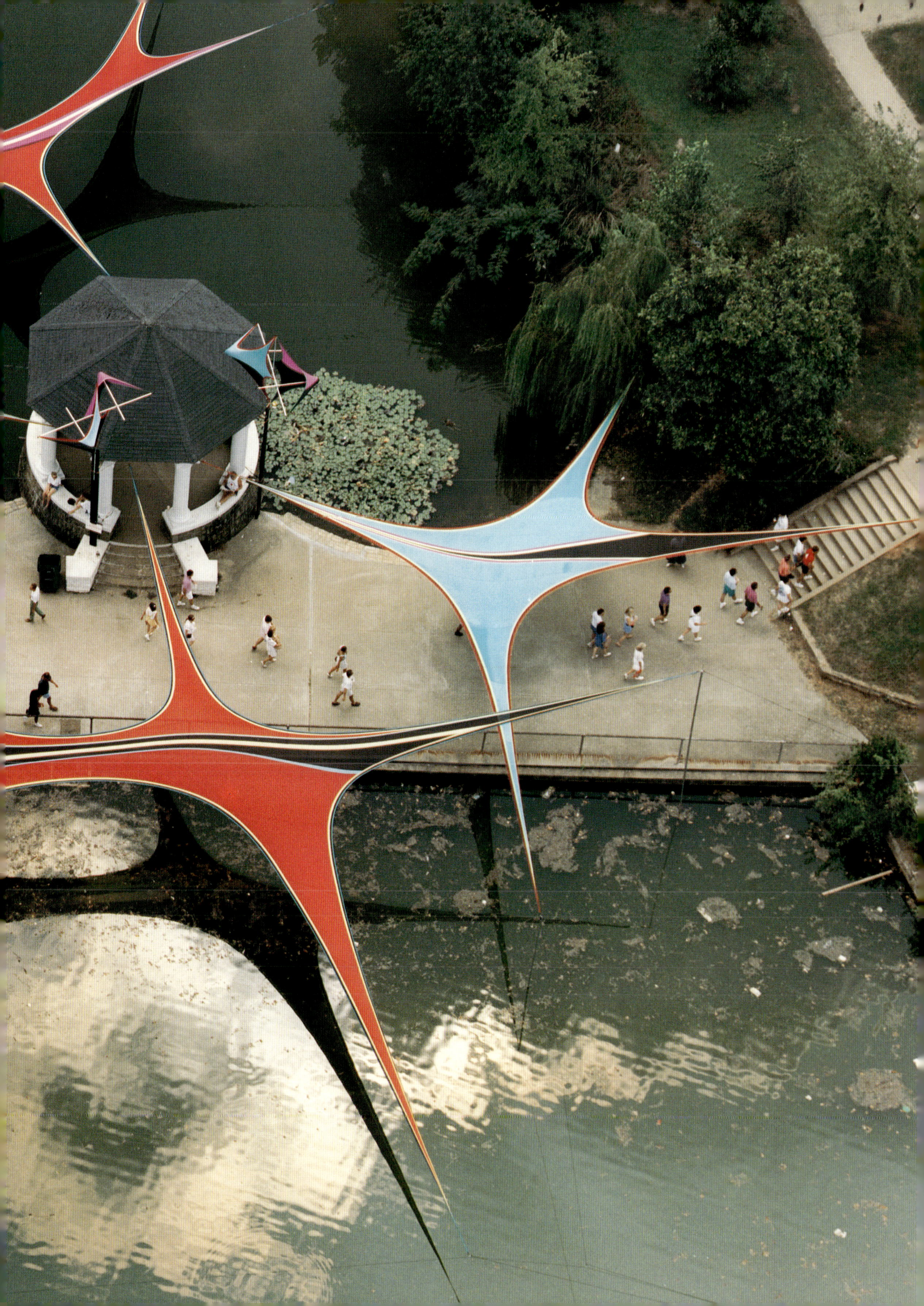

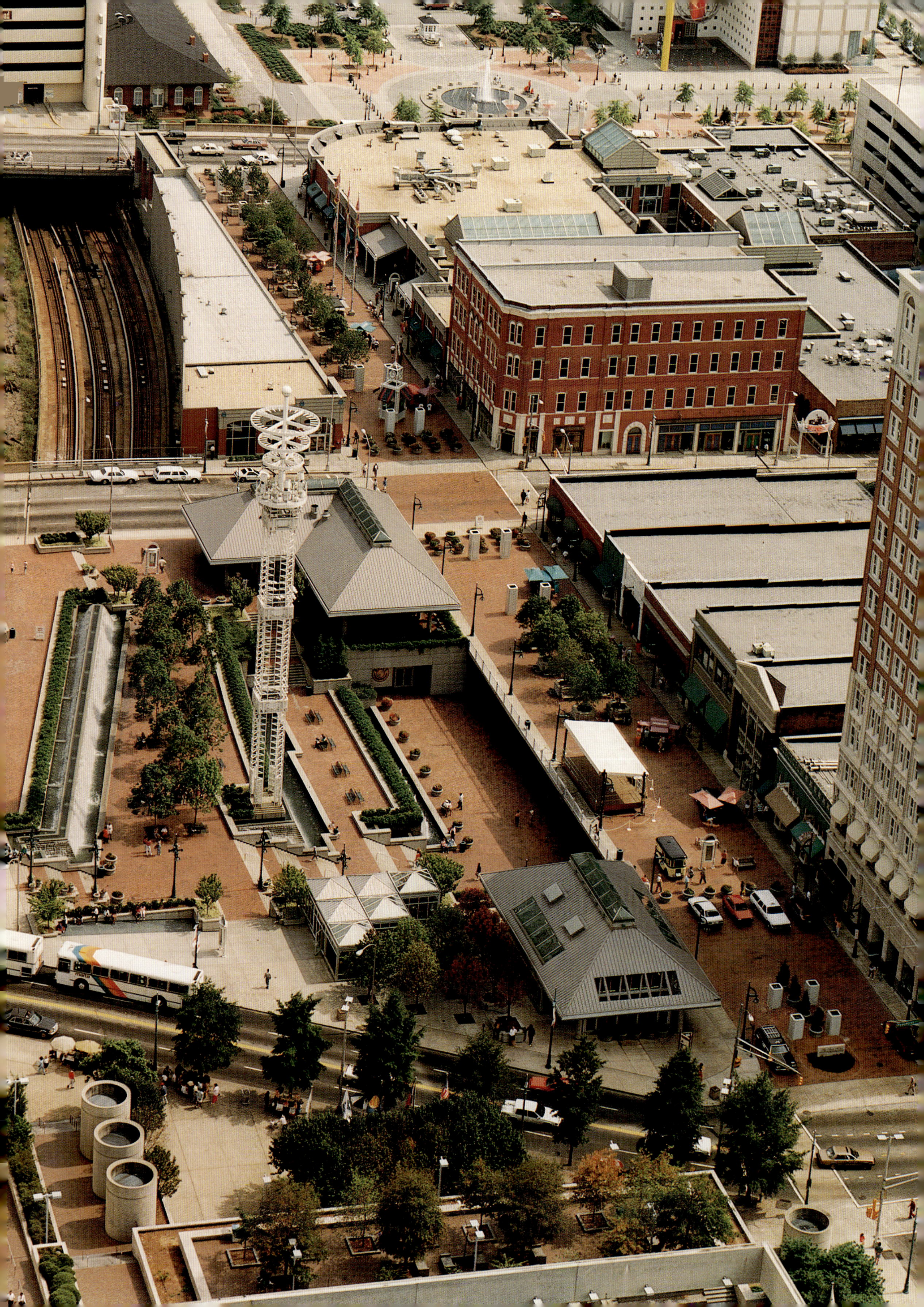

Underground Atlanta

Sheltered beneath Atlanta's bustling downtown streets stands a stone marker bearing the inscriptions *W*RR 138* and *W&A RR 00.* The letters refer to the Western & Atlantic Railroad; the numbers mark the final eastward mile and westward starting point of the line. Few cities can point to a single spot and say, "This is where it all began." Atlanta can: the Zero Milepost is the place.

Today the milepost is just across the tracks from the scene of a new beginning—the second reincarnation of Underground Atlanta (a smaller version thrived briefly in the 1960s and early 1970s before fading out). New structures and historic buildings blend in a festive six-block panoply of shops, restaurants, and nightclubs above and below street level. The terraced entrance at Peachtree Fountain Plaza, providing a unique view of downtown, covers Railroad Gulch, the tracks that once divided the northern and southern sections of the city. The futuristic light tower is a focal point for New Year's Eve revelers, who cheer and count down the seconds while a giant peach descends from the top as midnight approaches. One of the most popular attractions year-round is Kenny's Alley, a street of nightclubs with musical entertainment ranging from jazz and rock to reggae and country.

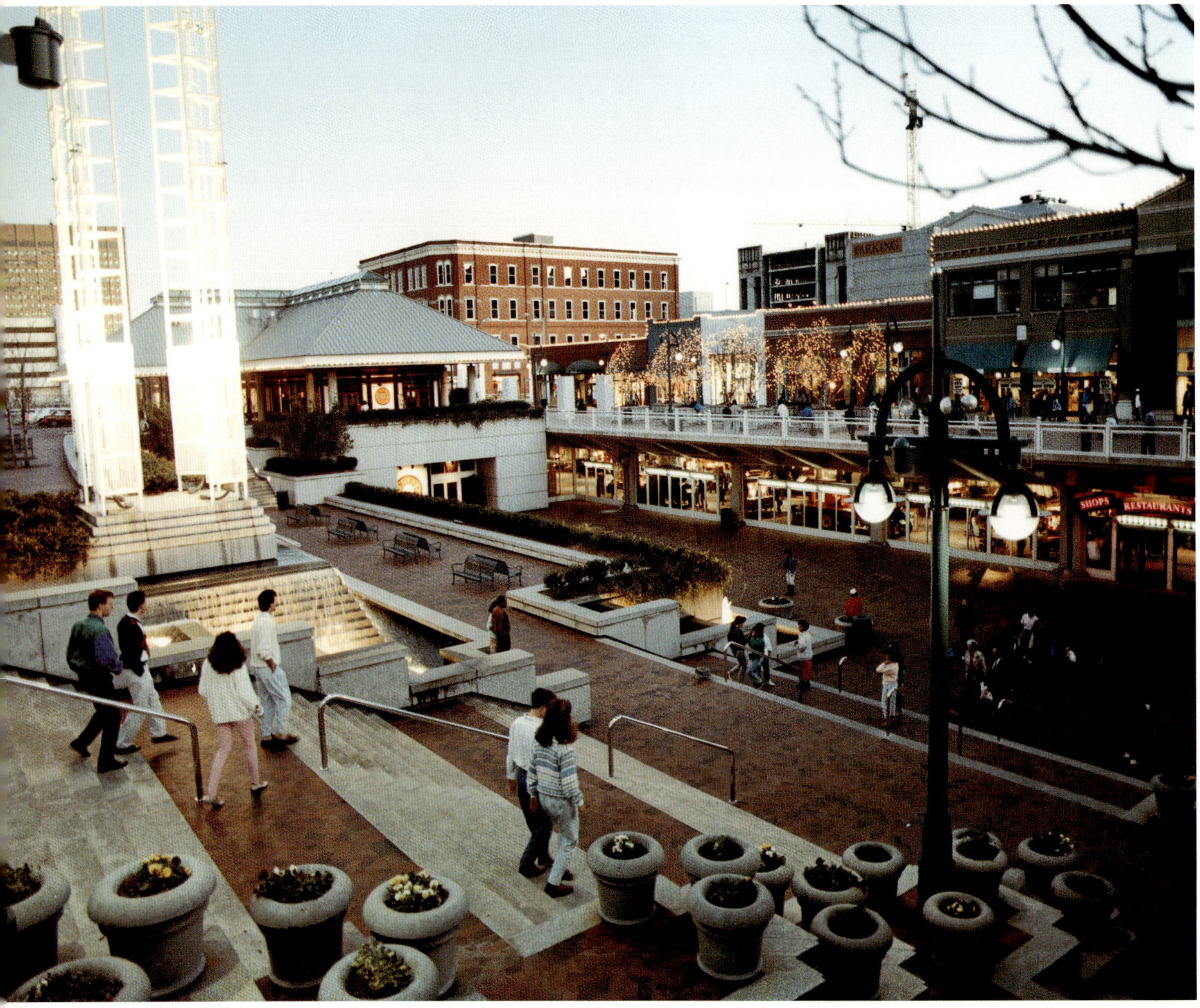

Fountain Plaza, Underground Atlanta

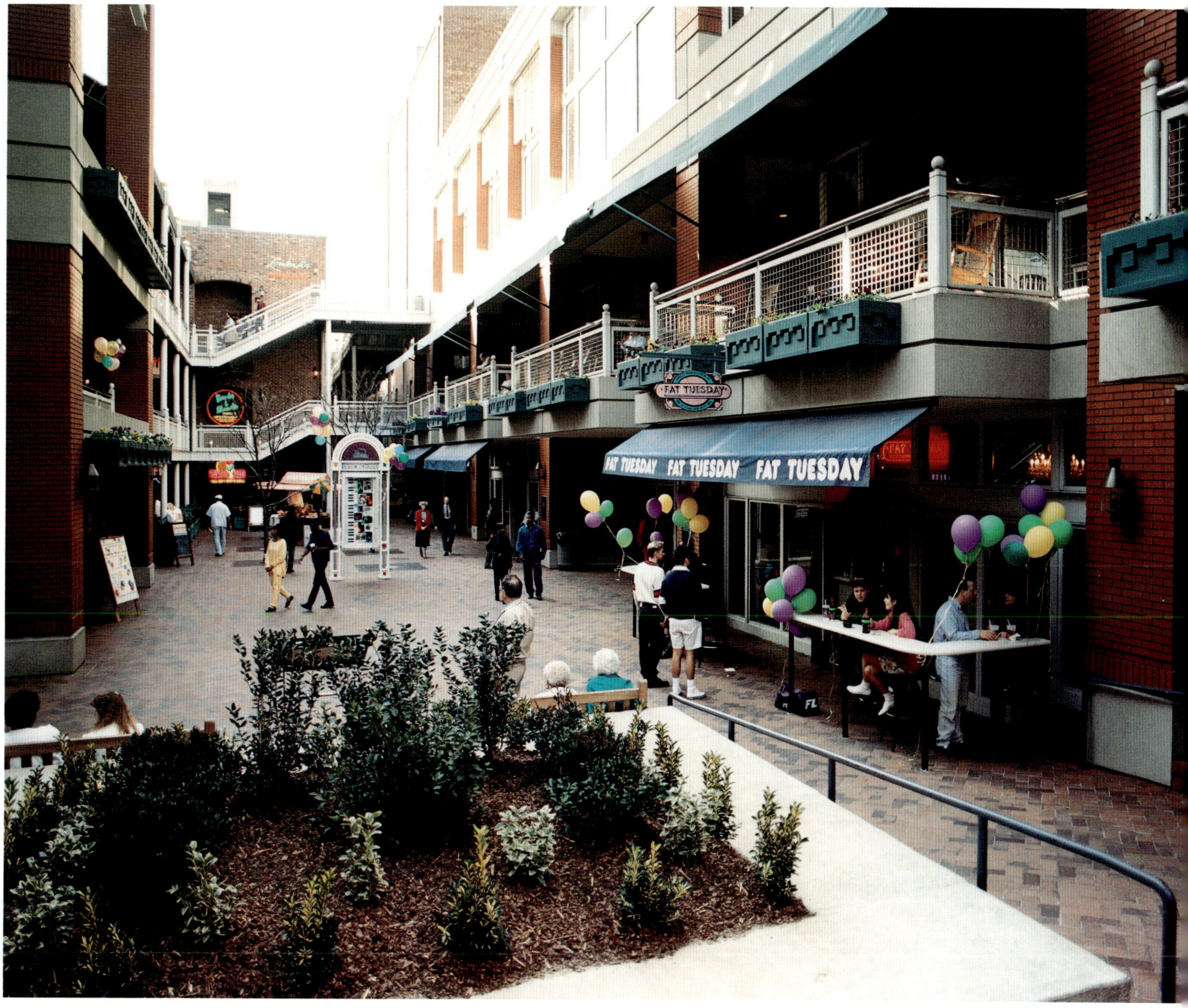

Kenny's Alley

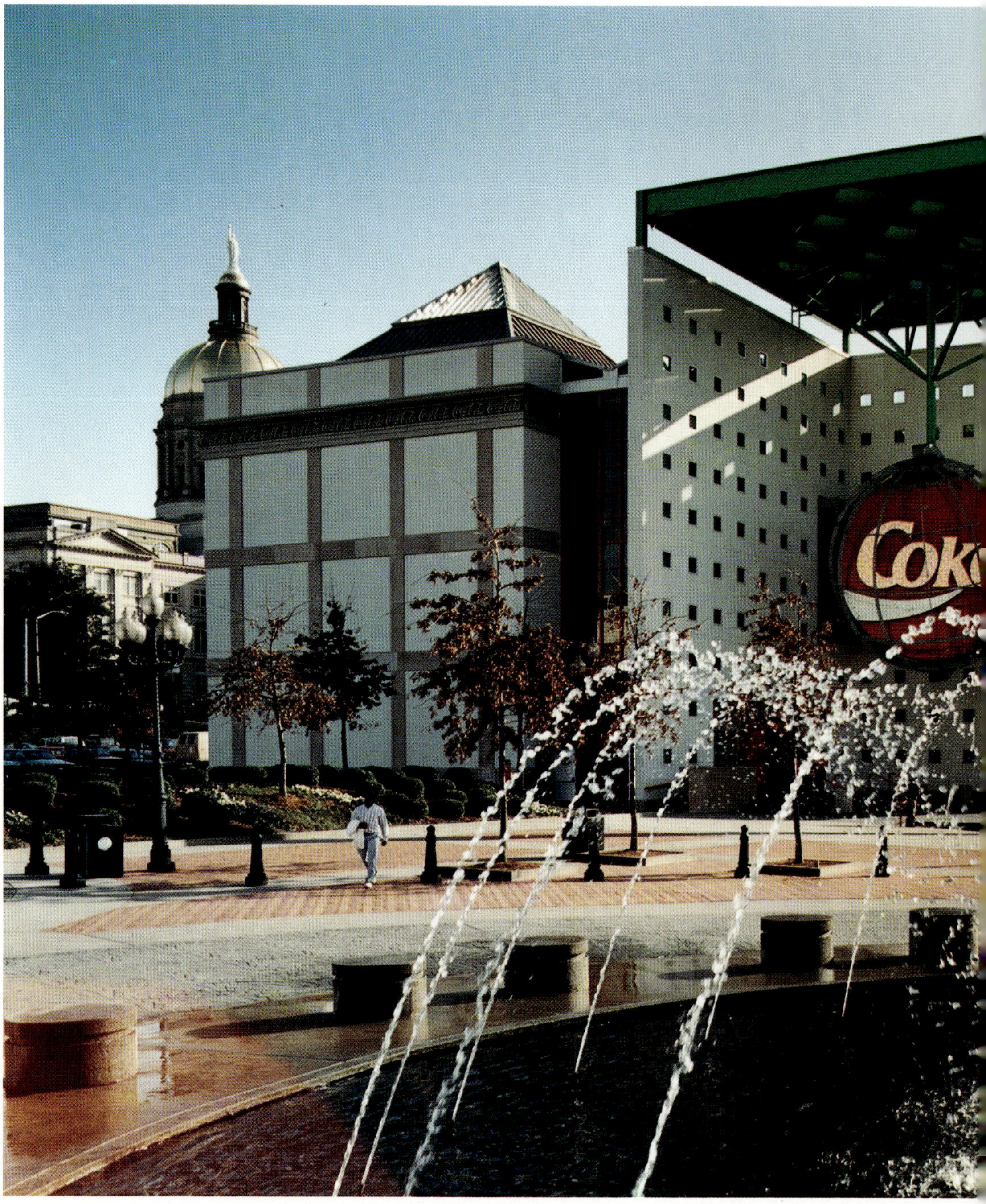
Coke

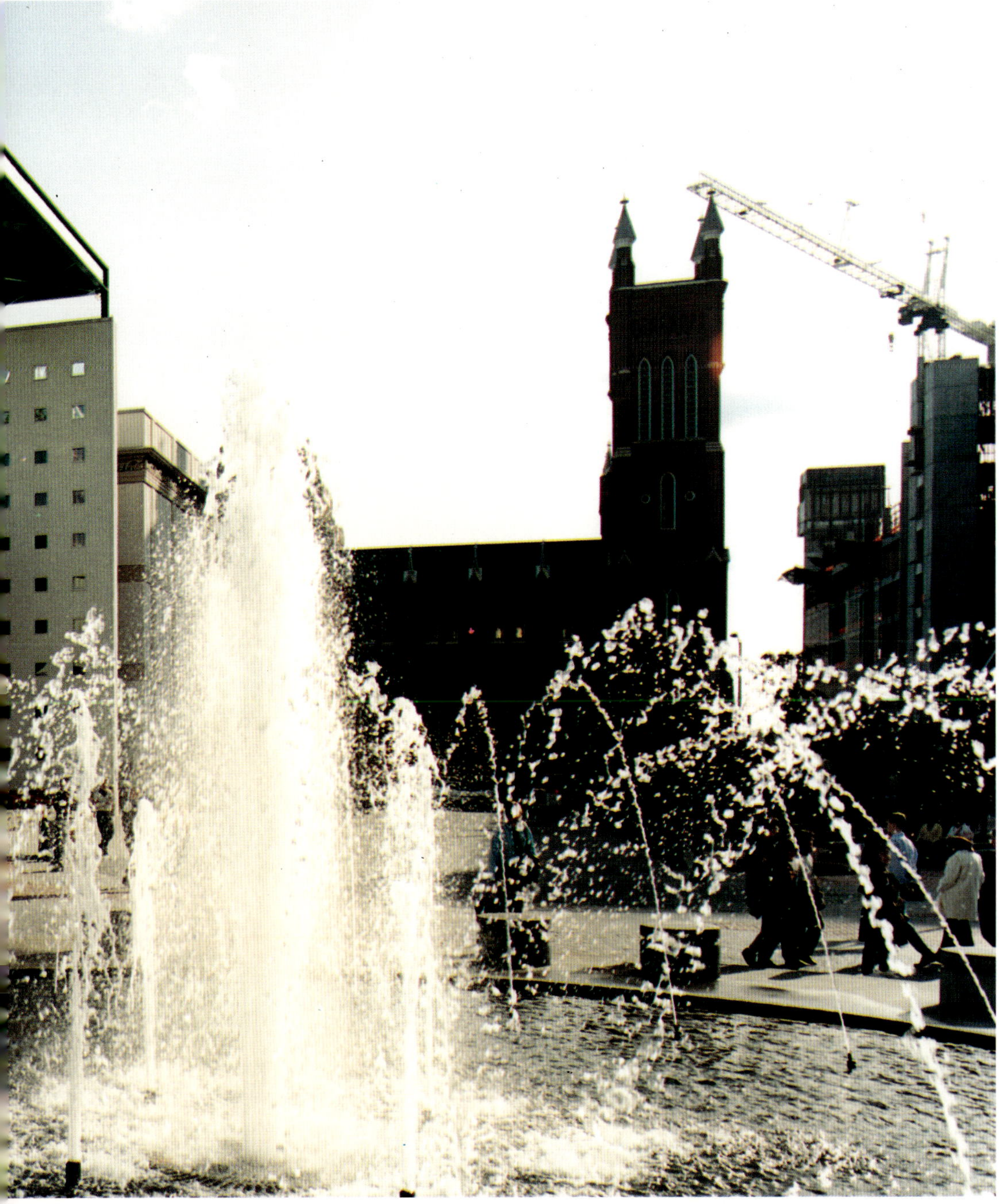

World of Coca-Cola Pavilion

Cheek-to-cheek with Underground Atlanta, the World of Coca-Cola stands just three blocks from the old pharmacy where the first Coke was served. Exhibits inside the pavilion trace the soft drink's history with an incomparable collection of Coca-Cola memorabilia and samples from around the world. The curious can learn, for instance, that the famous Coke-bottle shape was taken from an *Encyclopaedia Britannica* drawing of a cola nut, or that Asa Candler, who made millions after buying the Coke formula cheap, was not always so shrewd: in 1899, convinced that the beverage's future was in soda fountains, he sold the bottling rights for one dollar.

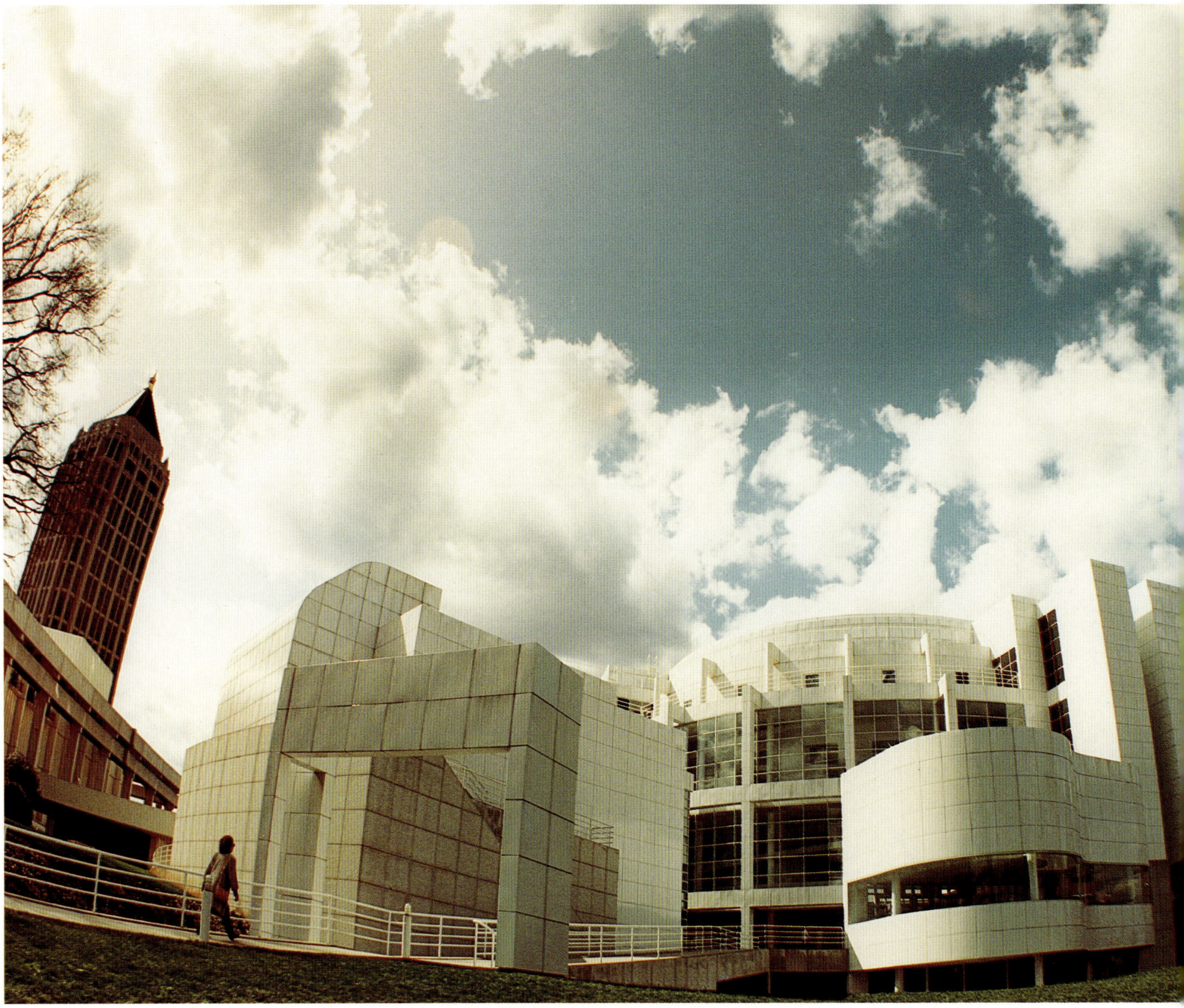

High Museum of Art, Woodruff Arts Center

The original arts-center building was the residence of Mrs. J. M. High, a widow who ran her husband's dry goods store for fifteen years after his death. She donated her house in 1926 to be called the High Museum of Art. The spectacular new version of the High Museum, designed by Richard Meier and opened in 1983, is a work of art in itself. Sharing the museum's location at Sixteenth and Peachtree Streets is the Robert W. Woodruff Arts Center, also known as the Atlanta Memorial Arts Building (left of the High Museum in the photo). Constructed in memory of 106 Atlanta arts patrons who died in a 1962 plane crash in Paris while returning from a High Museum–sponsored tour of Europe, the Woodruff Center houses the Atlanta Symphony Orchestra, the Alliance Theater, and the Atlanta College of Art.

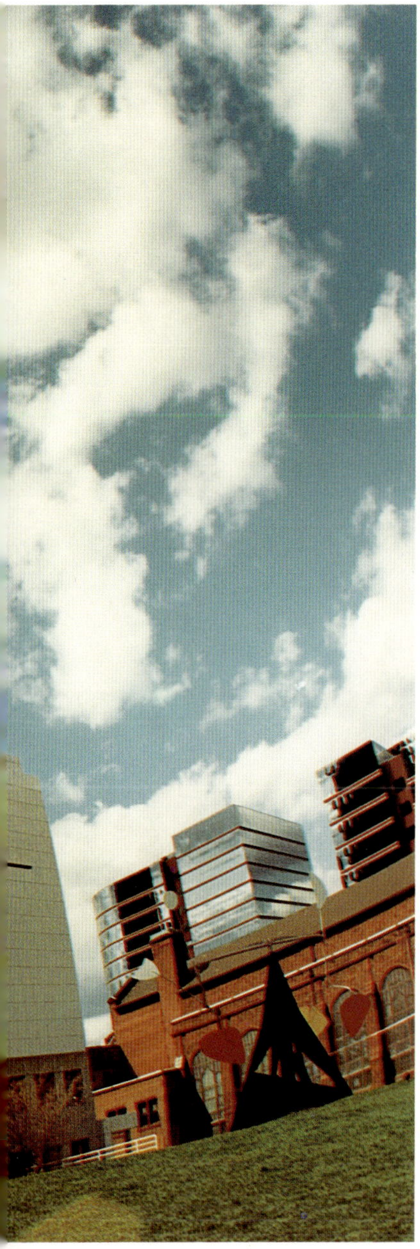
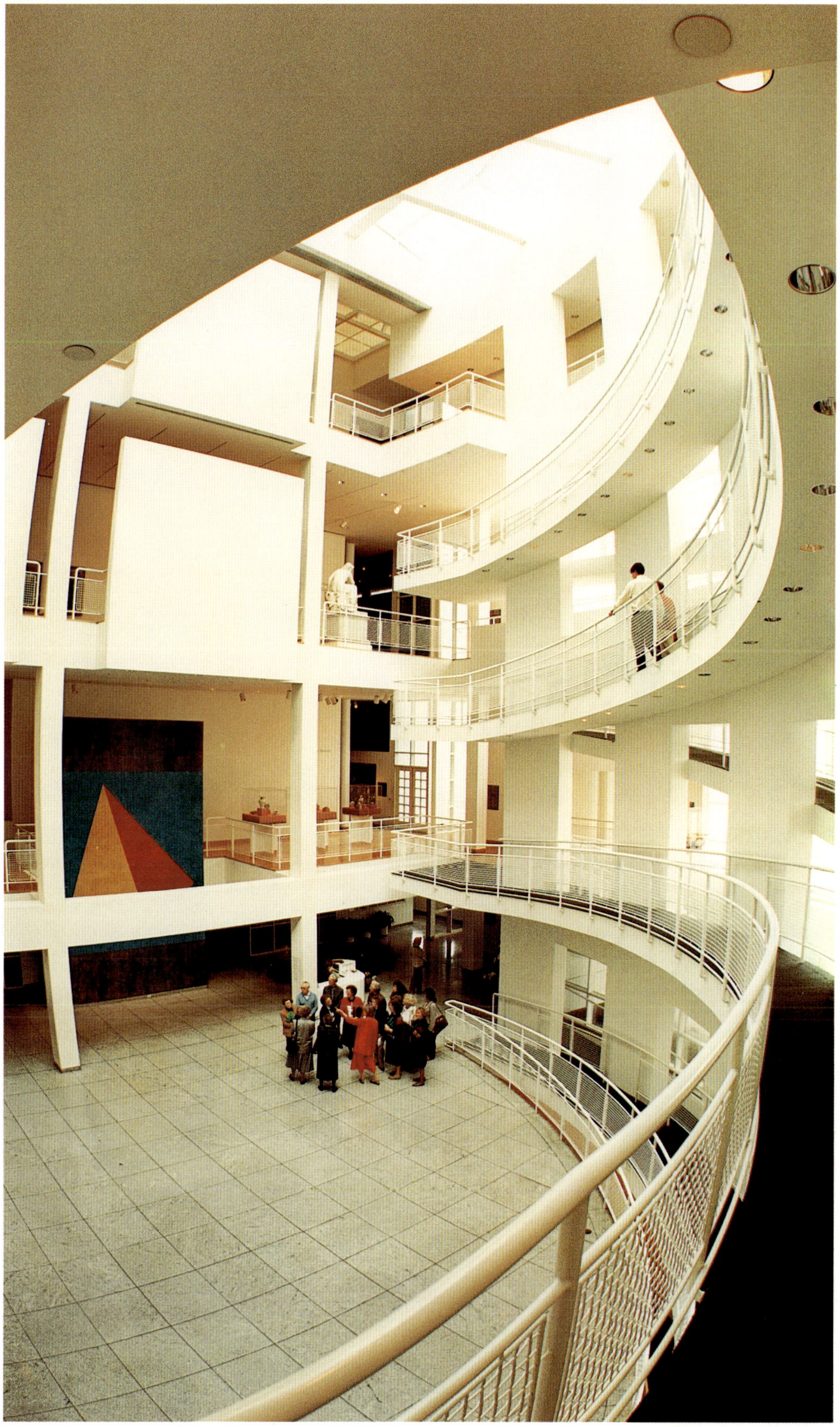

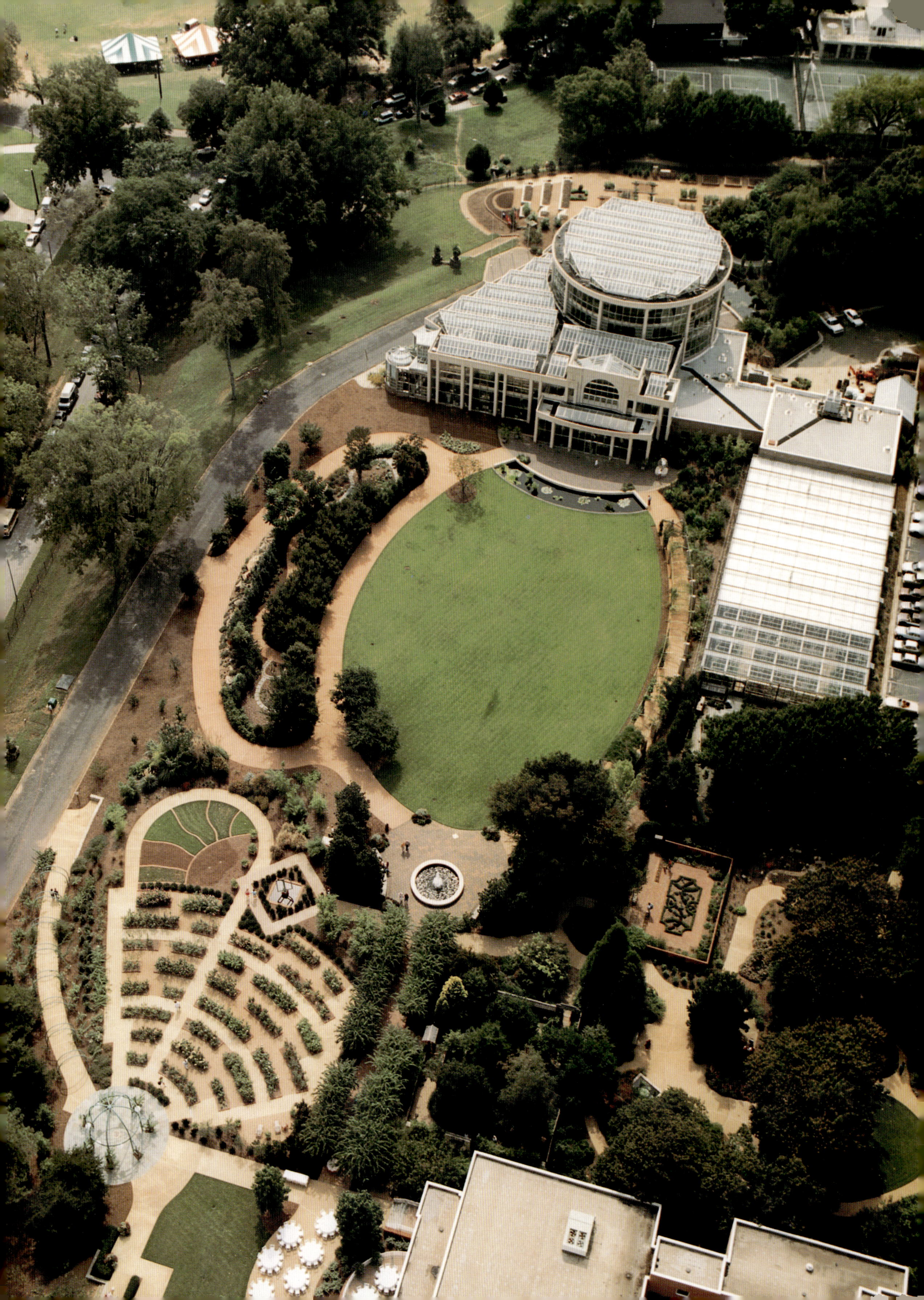

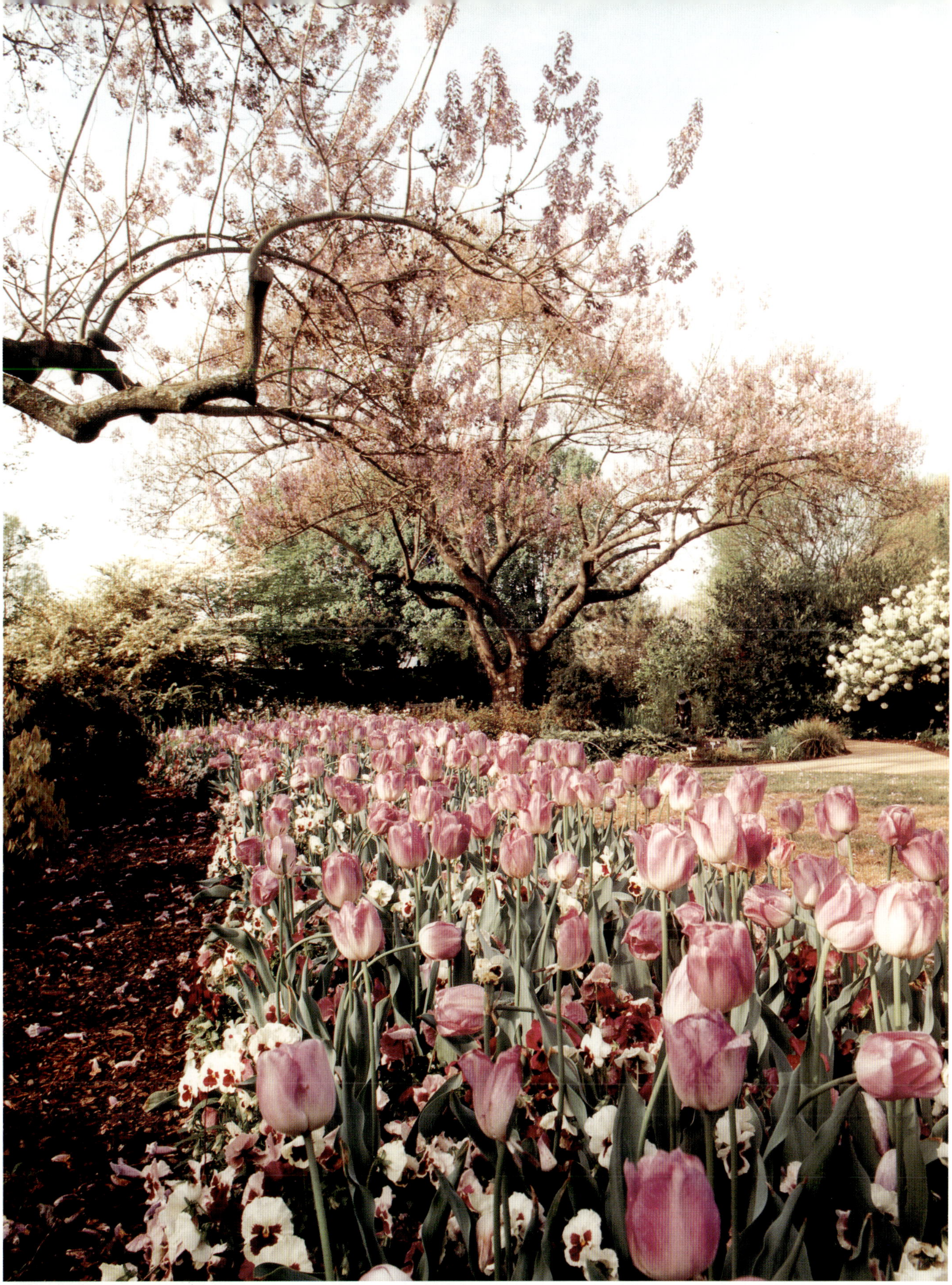

Atlanta Botanical Garden

Atlanta is proud of its trees and greenery, and no place is greener than the Atlanta Botanical Garden in Piedmont Park. Outdoors, the plant lover will find seasonal flowerings of many varieties, herbal and Japanese gardens, and a nature trail through fifteen acres of woodland. Indoors, thousands of tropical, desert, and endangered species flourish year-round in the vast greenhouse of the Dorothy Chapman Fuqua Conservatory.

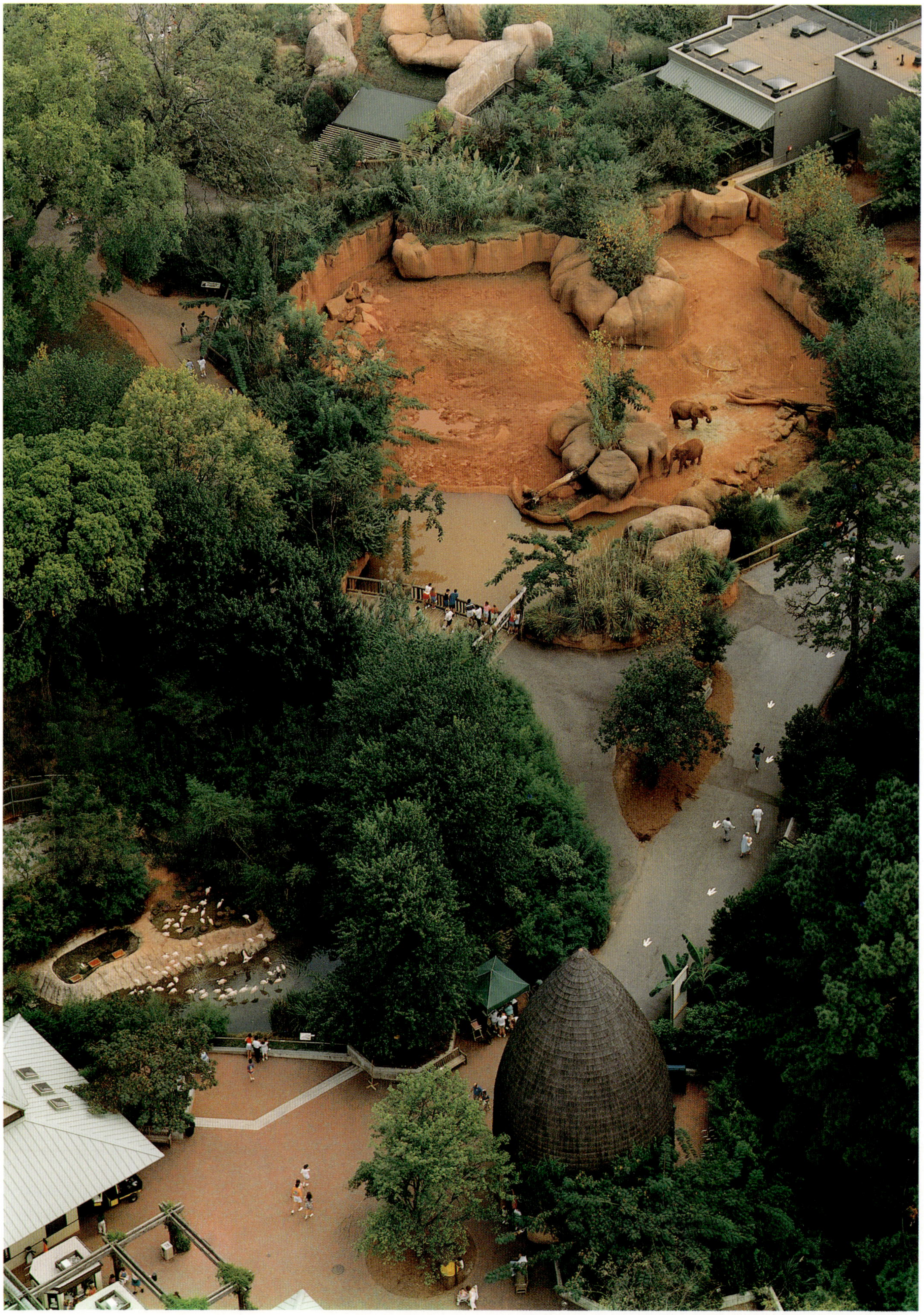

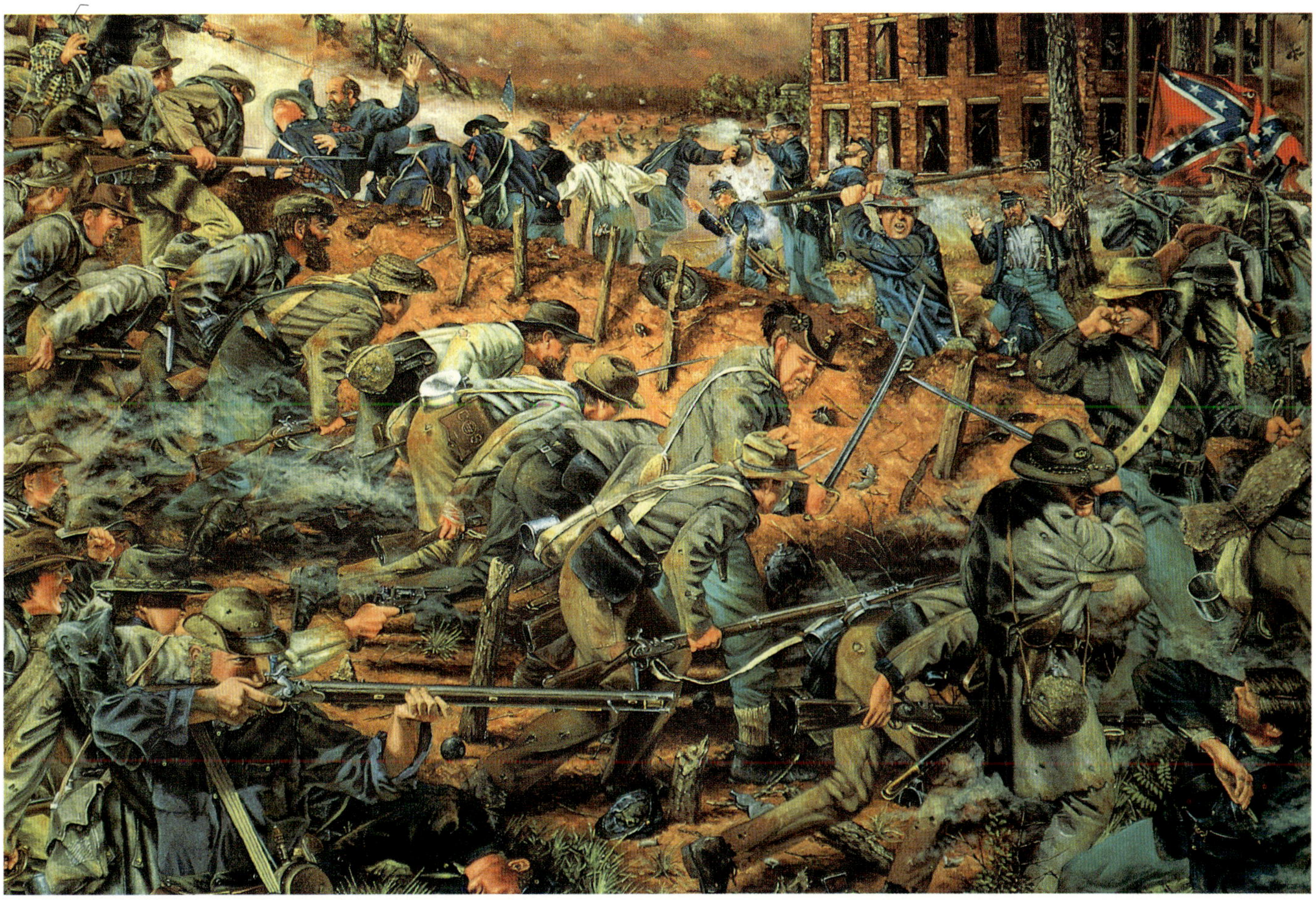

Zoo Atlanta and Grant Park (left)

Zoo Atlanta has been transformed from a sad collection of caged animals several years ago to an acclaimed natural-habitat facility with areas such as the African Rain Forest, Asian Rain Forest, and West African Aviary. The zoo is located southeast of downtown in Grant Park, one of the oldest and largest city parks, named for Lemuel P. Grant, who donated the land in the 1880s. Grant, a civil engineer who helped construct several railroads in the area, also designed and built the fortifications that surrounded Atlanta during the Civil War.

Cyclorama (above)

The Cyclorama at Grant Park houses a circular painting, 42 feet tall and 358 long, of the Battle of Atlanta. Painted in 1884 and sent on a tour of northern cities, the monumental work was eventually acquired by the city. In 1921 it was installed in the present building, which after years of neglect required a massive renovation-rescue in 1981. The figures, mannequins, and models in front of the painting, giving it a three-dimensional effect, were added in the 1930s. The Cyclorama is one of the most consistently popular attractions in Atlanta, for locals as well as out-of-towners.

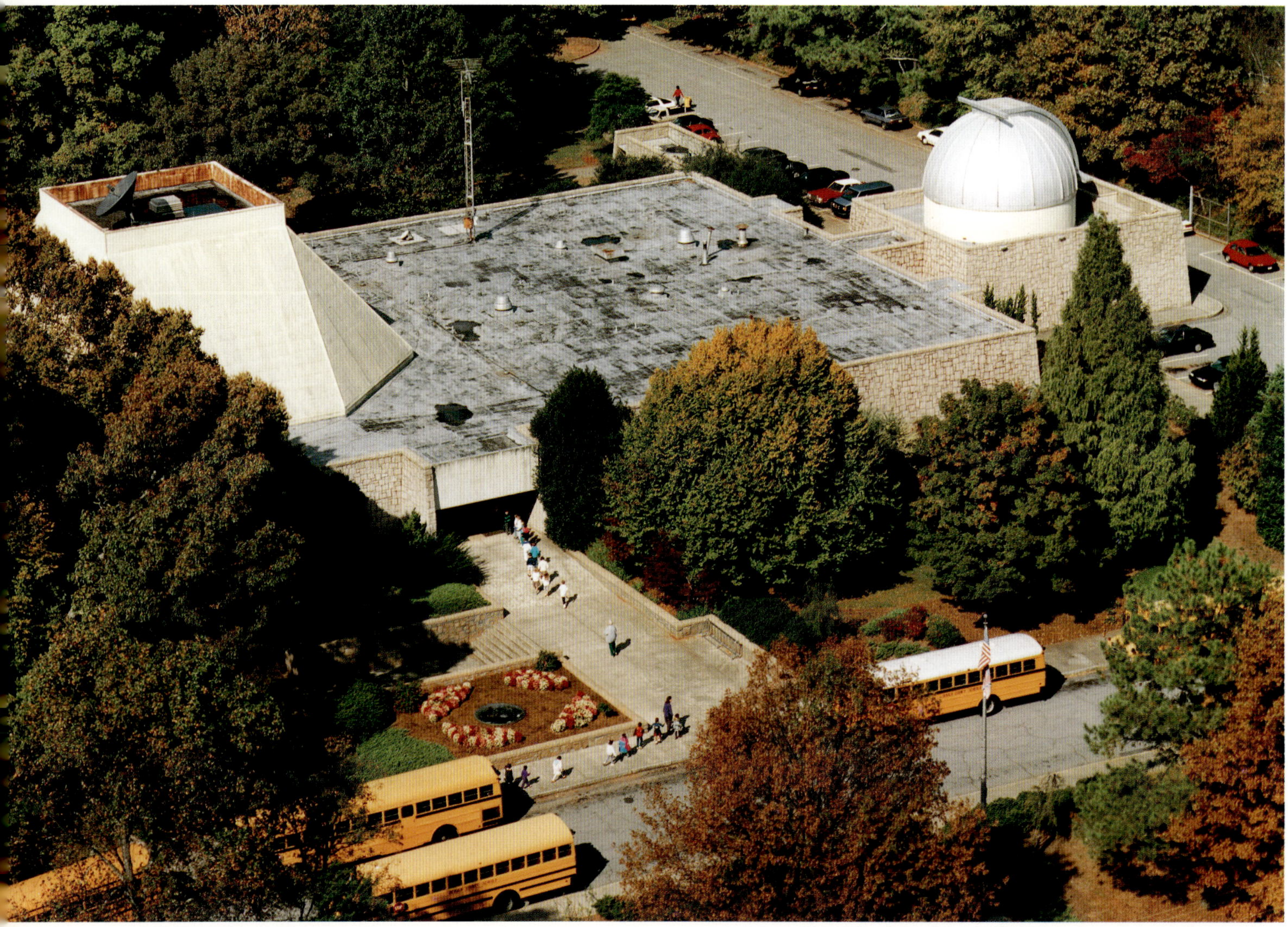

Fernbank Science Center

Located near Emory University, the Fernbank Science Center, an educational complex of the DeKalb County school system, provides a steady stream of students access to a planetarium, an observatory, and the sixty-five-acre Fernbank Forest.

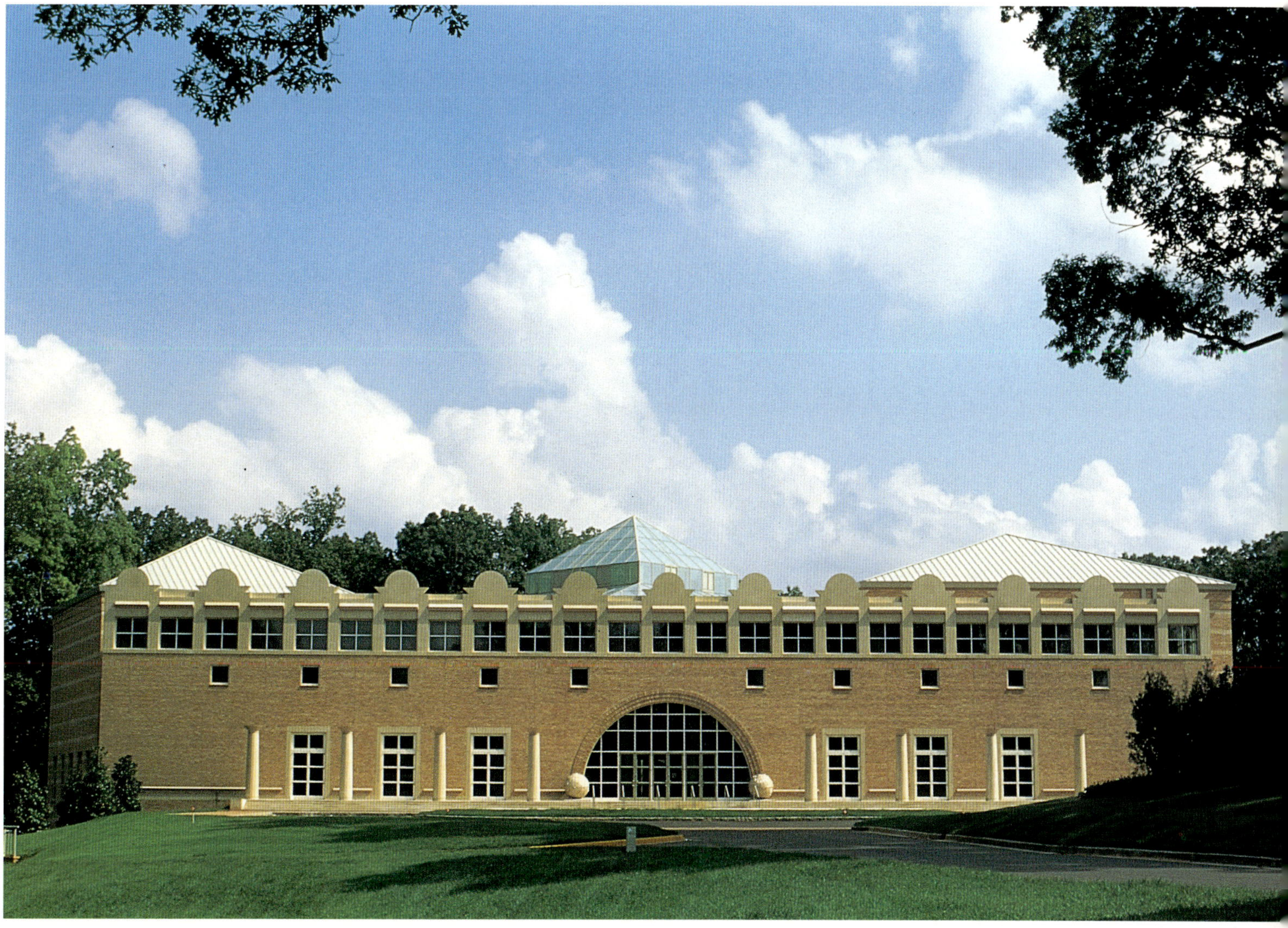

Fernbank Museum of Natural History

Completed in 1993, this magnificent facility on the edge of the Fernbank Forest features a permanent exhibit tracing the natural history of Georgia. Visitors can participate in an interactive light-and-sound exhibit and view spectacular nature films on the five-story screen of the museum's IMAX theater.

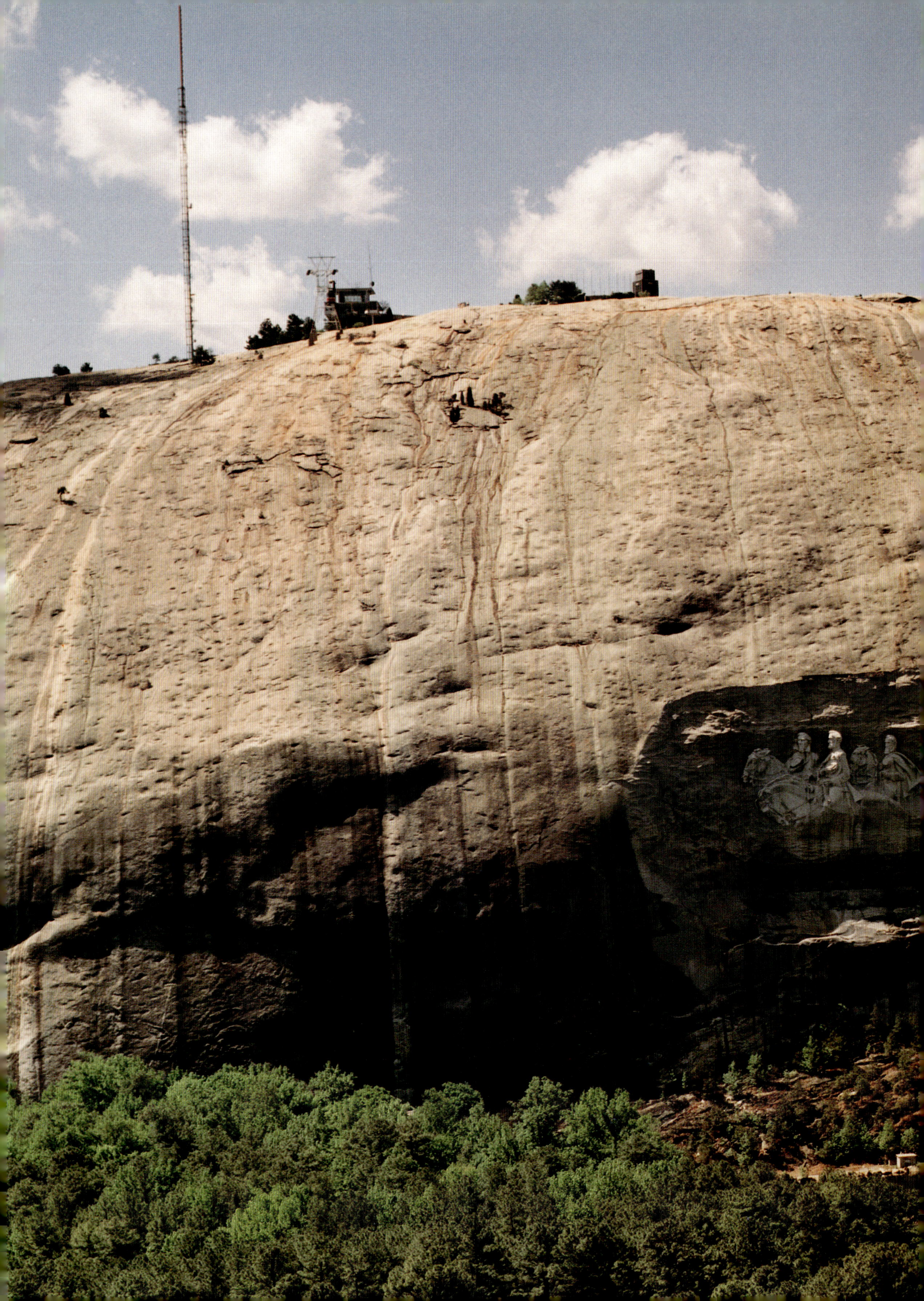

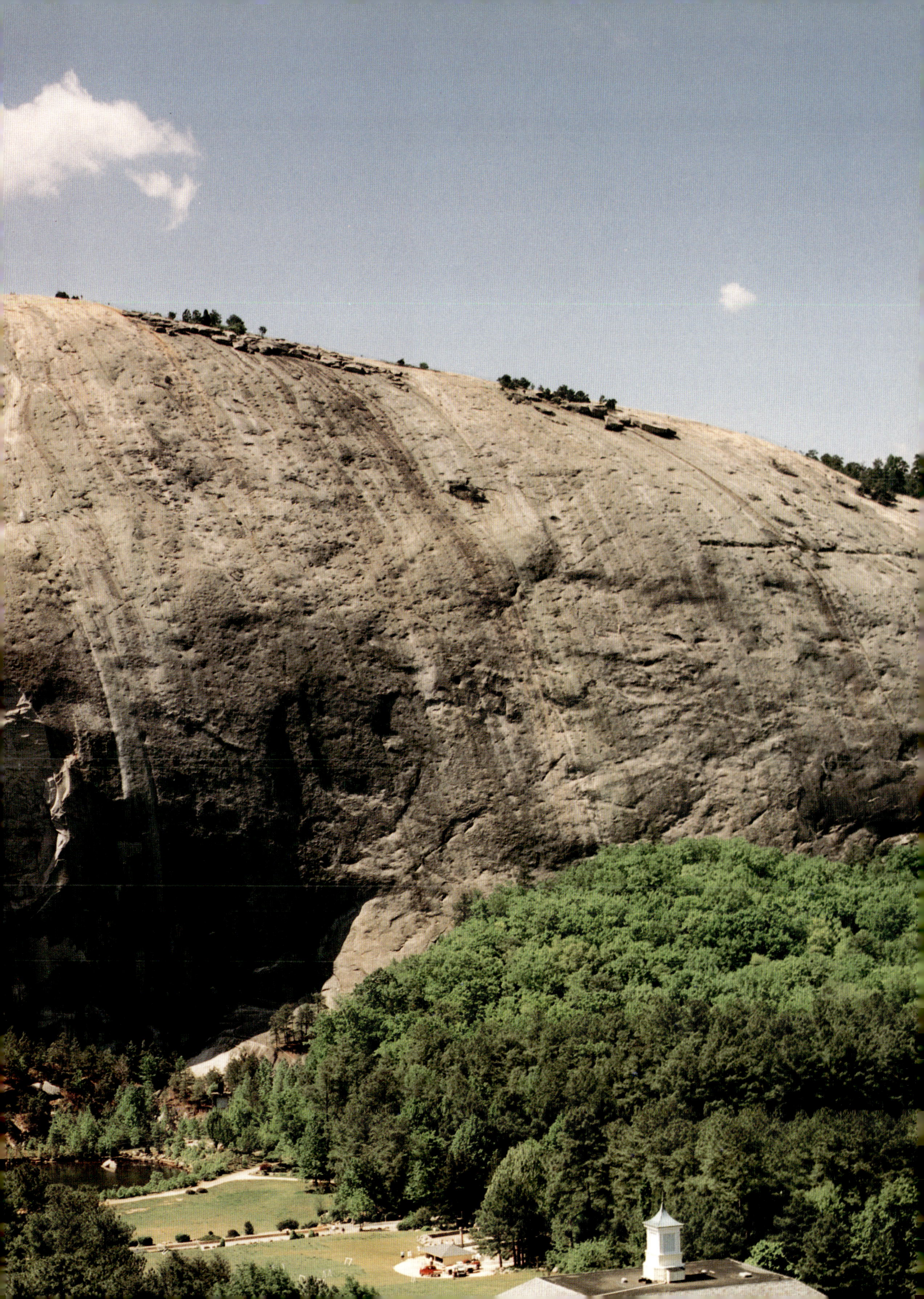

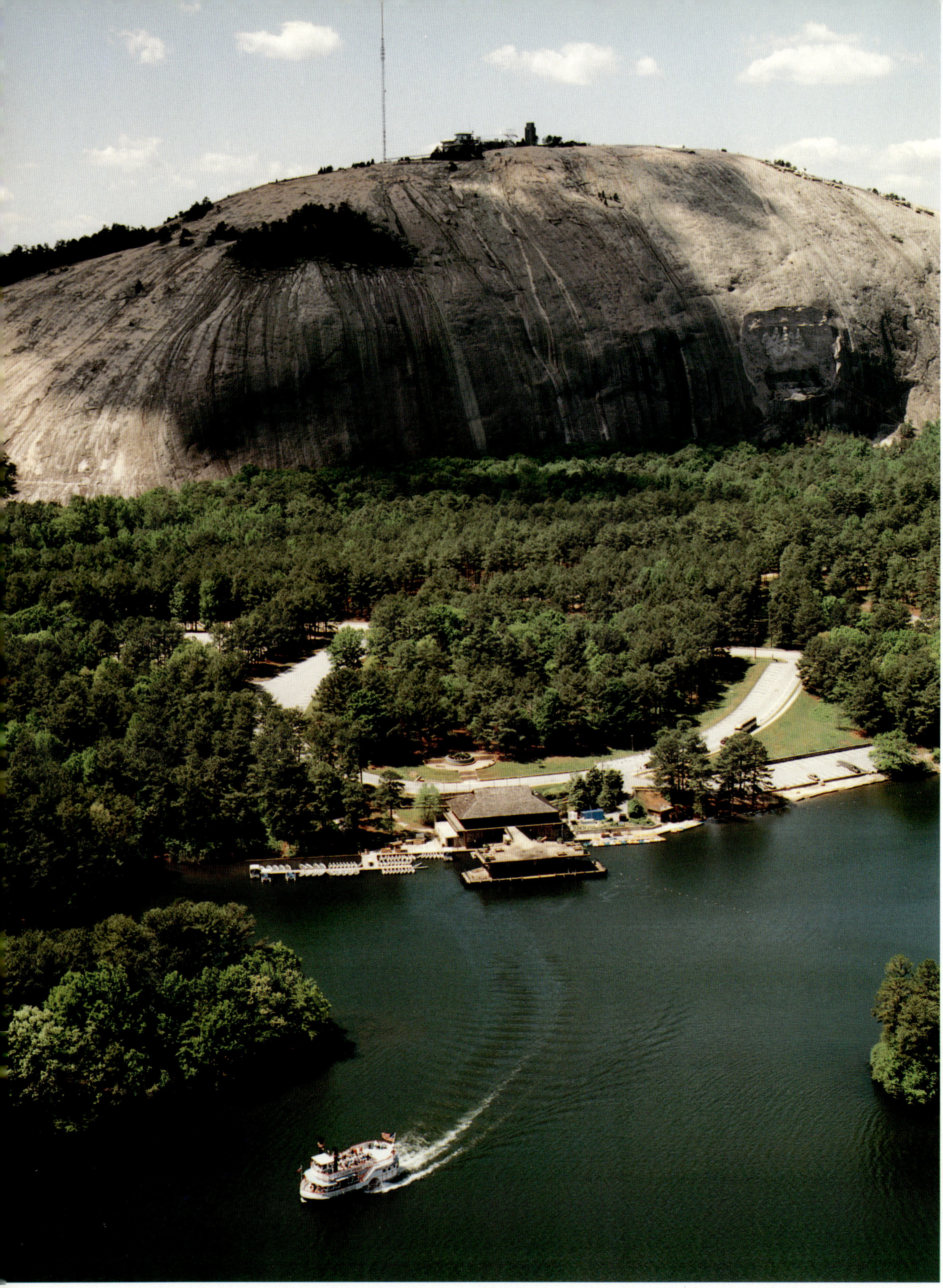

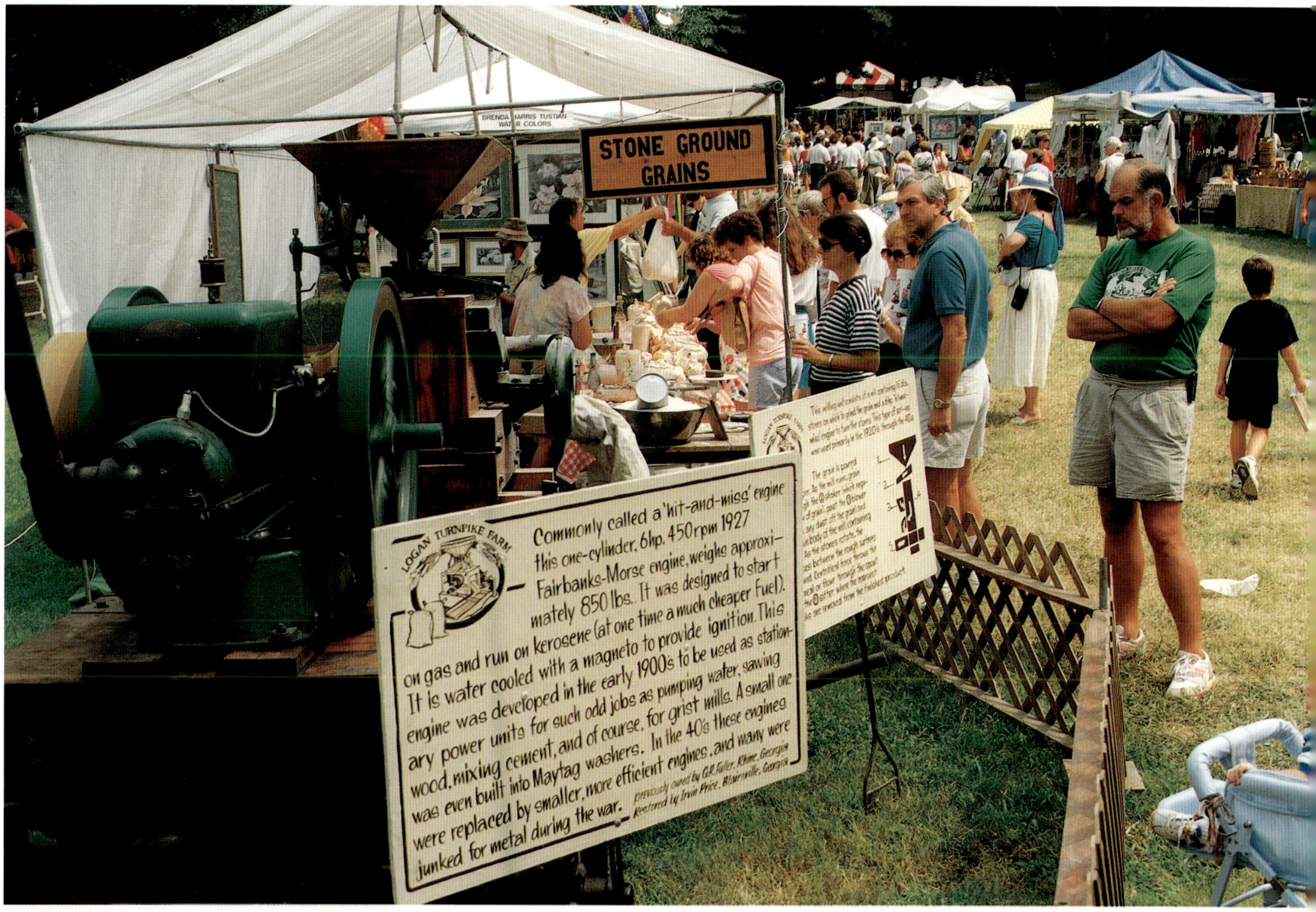

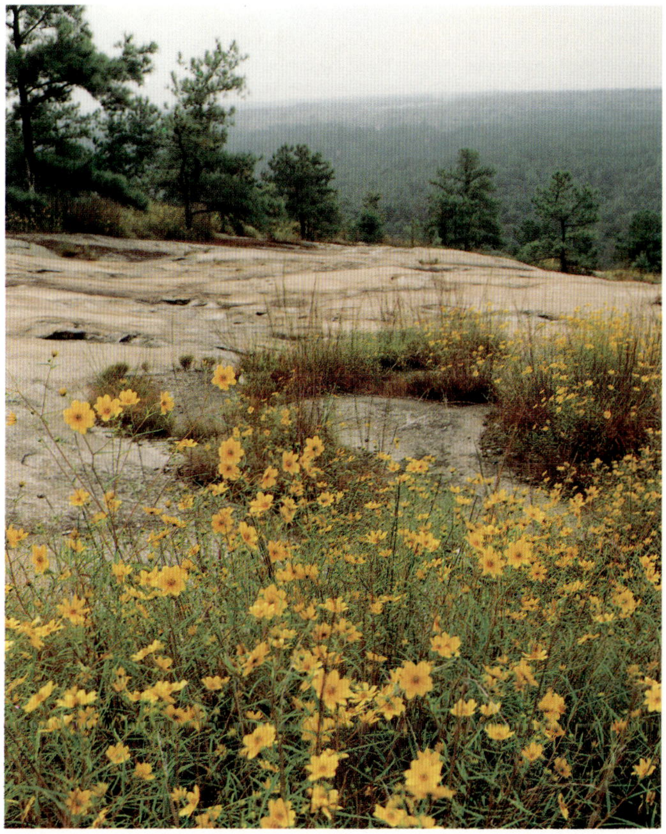

Stone Mountain Park

The mountain itself is impressive—the world's largest outcropping of granite, five miles in circumference, 825 feet from top to bottom, and 300 million years old—but even more eye-catching are the horseback figures of Confederate heroes Jefferson Davis, Robert E. Lee, and the aptly nicknamed "Stonewall" Jackson carved into the sheer rock. Sculpted by three different artists from 1923 to 1928 and 1964 to 1970, the carvings overlook a 3,200-acre park with swimming, picnicking, golf, a skylift to the mountain's summit, a paddlewheeler, a scenic railroad with three old-time steam locomotives, a resort hotel, and an antebellum plantation. In the fall, the Yellow Daisy Festival brings together craftspeople from all over the South. The festival celebrates a daisy that grows only in the vicinity of Stone Mountain.

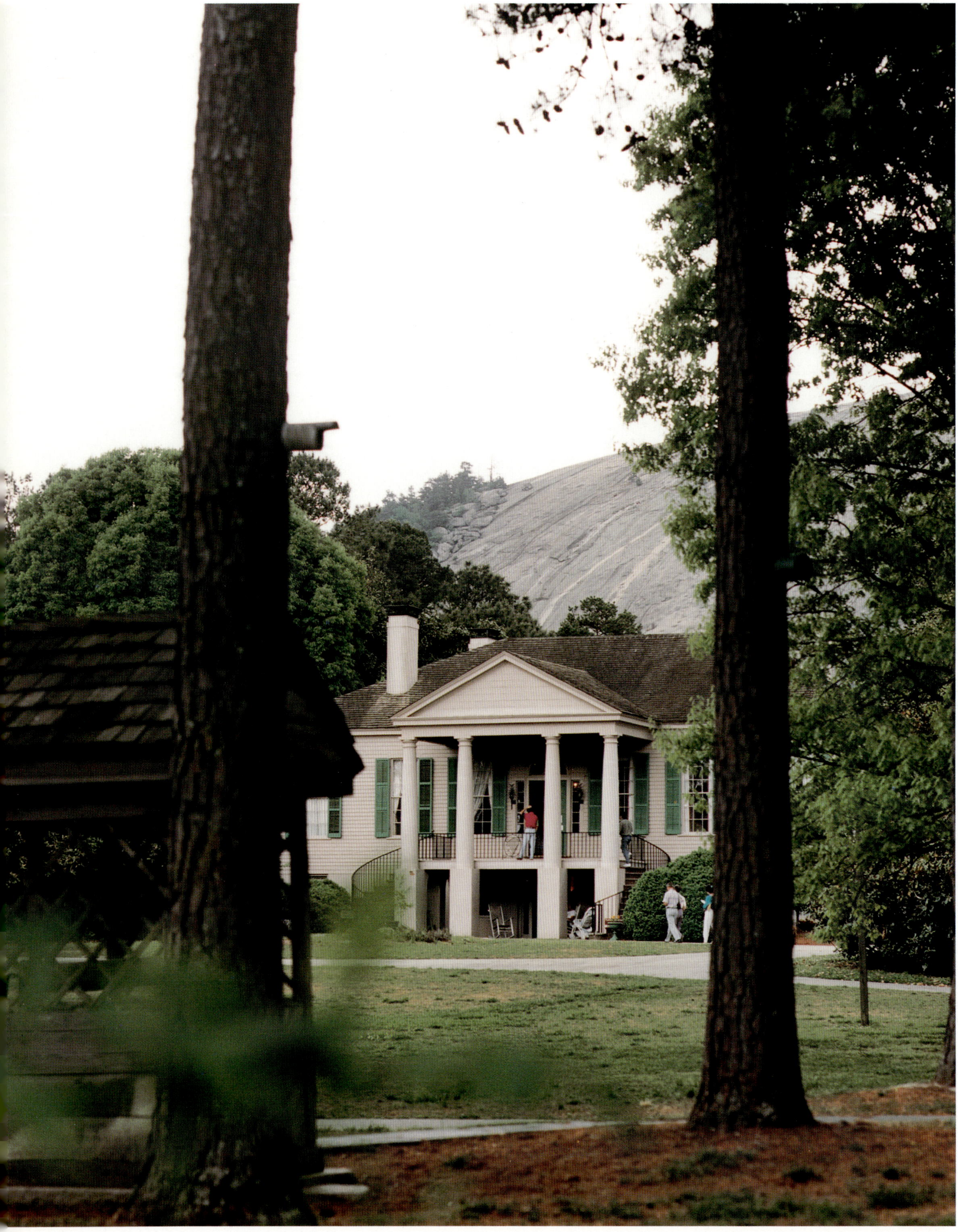

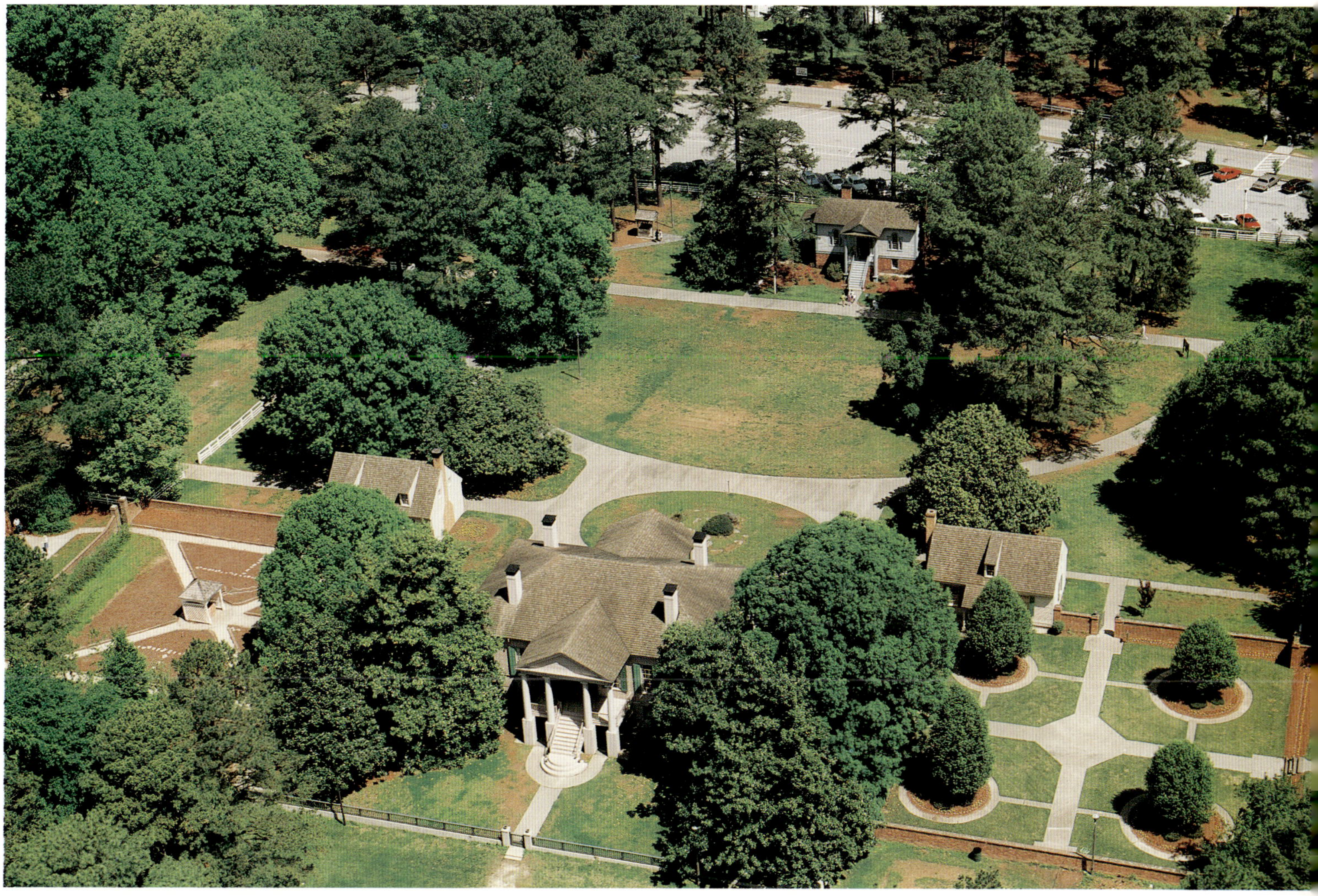

Stone Mountain Plantation

Nineteen authentic antebellum buildings, including a main house, overseer's house, slave cabins, country store, and other structures, were moved from their original sites all over Georgia and furnished in period to create a representative southern plantation at the foot of Stone Mountain. Demonstrations of early-eighteenth-century cooking and other plantation work are conducted throughout the year. The Stone Mountain Park complex is less than half an hour east of downtown Atlanta.

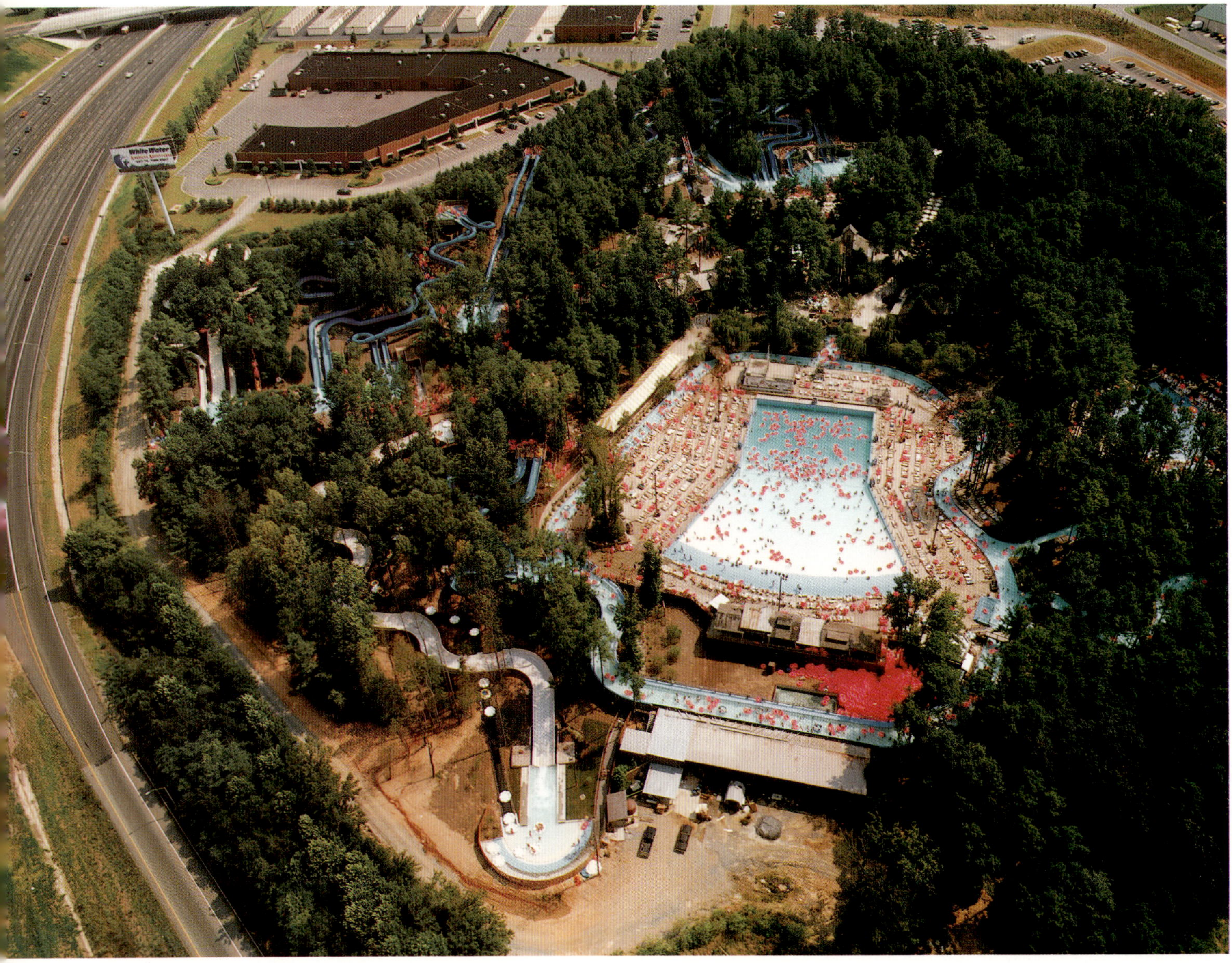

White Water Park and American Adventures

These side-by-side amusement parks north of Marietta provide family fun with wet-and-wild rides, miniature golf, a penny arcade, and dozens of other activities.

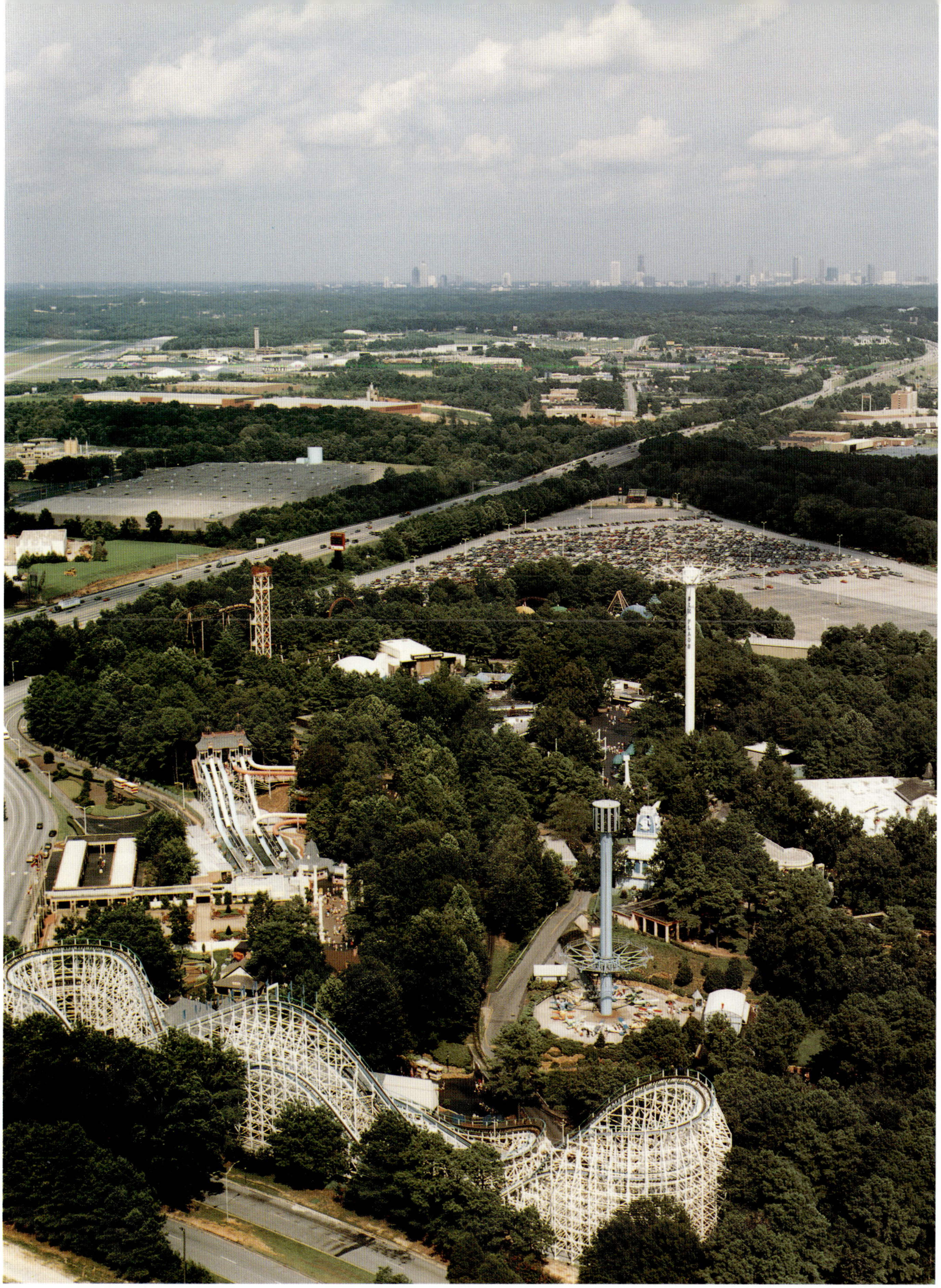

Six Flags over Georgia

Home of the Scream Machine, the Georgia Cyclone, Ragin' Rivers, and 100 other heart-stopping rides, this 330-acre amusement park twelve miles west of Atlanta also offers musical performances, Looney Tunes Land, a dolphin and sea lion show, and other attractions for all ages.

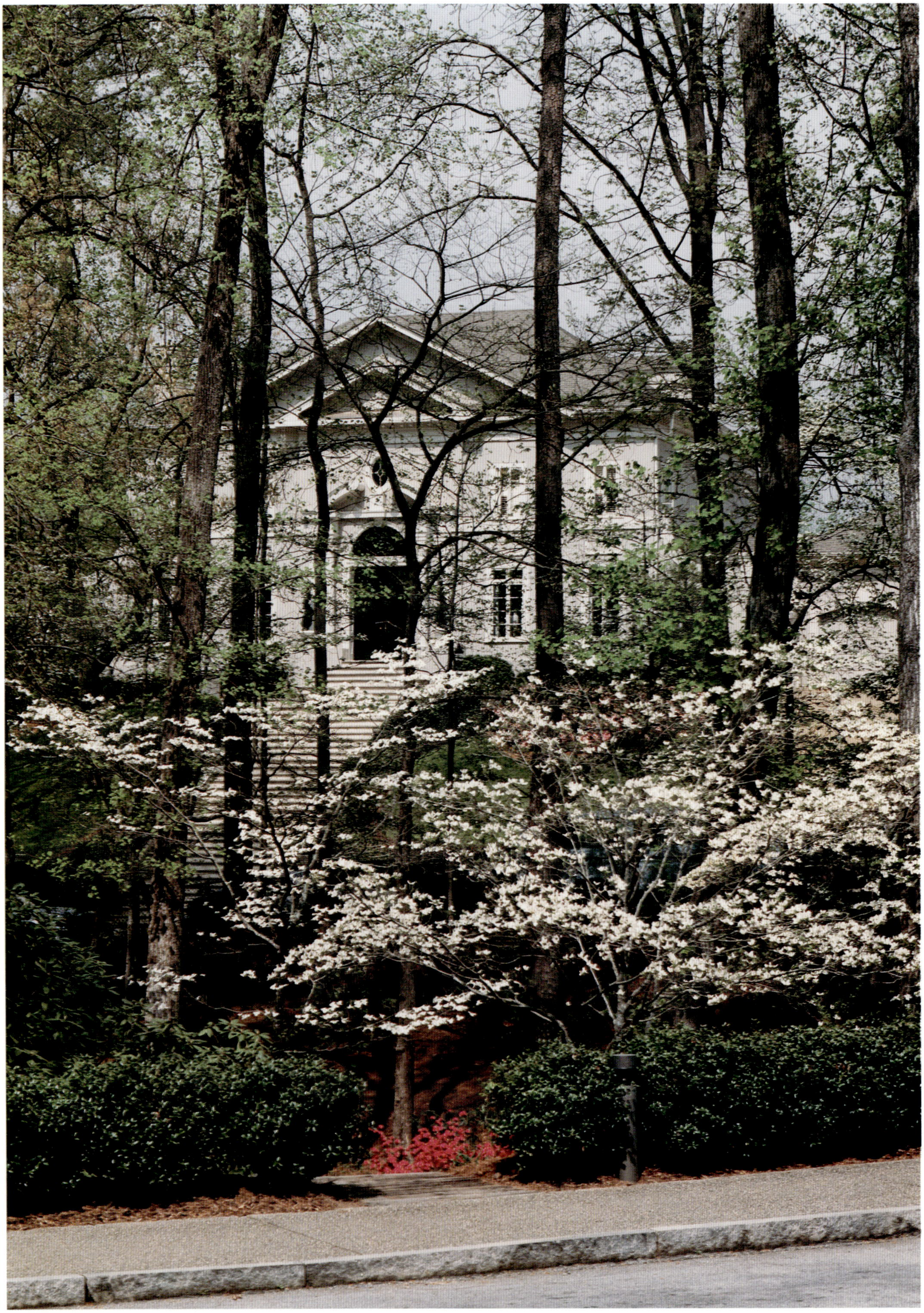

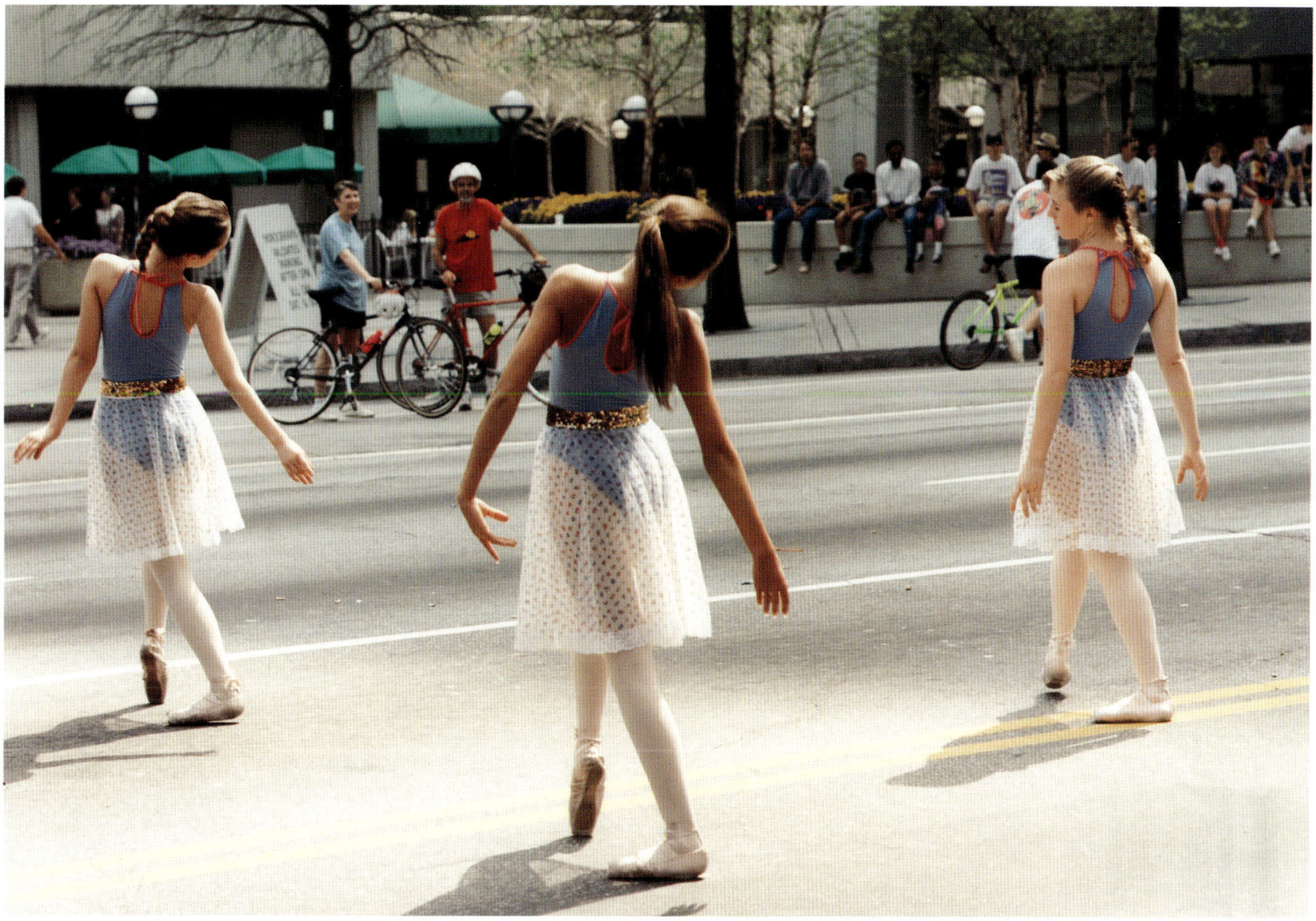

Dogwood Festival

When the dogwoods bloom in April, there's no prettier place to be than Atlanta. Celebrating the annual burst of white and pink blossoms, the citywide Dogwood Festival presents an equally delightful array of dancing, parades, concerts, exhibits, and competitions ranging from canine Frisbee championships to hot-air-balloon races.

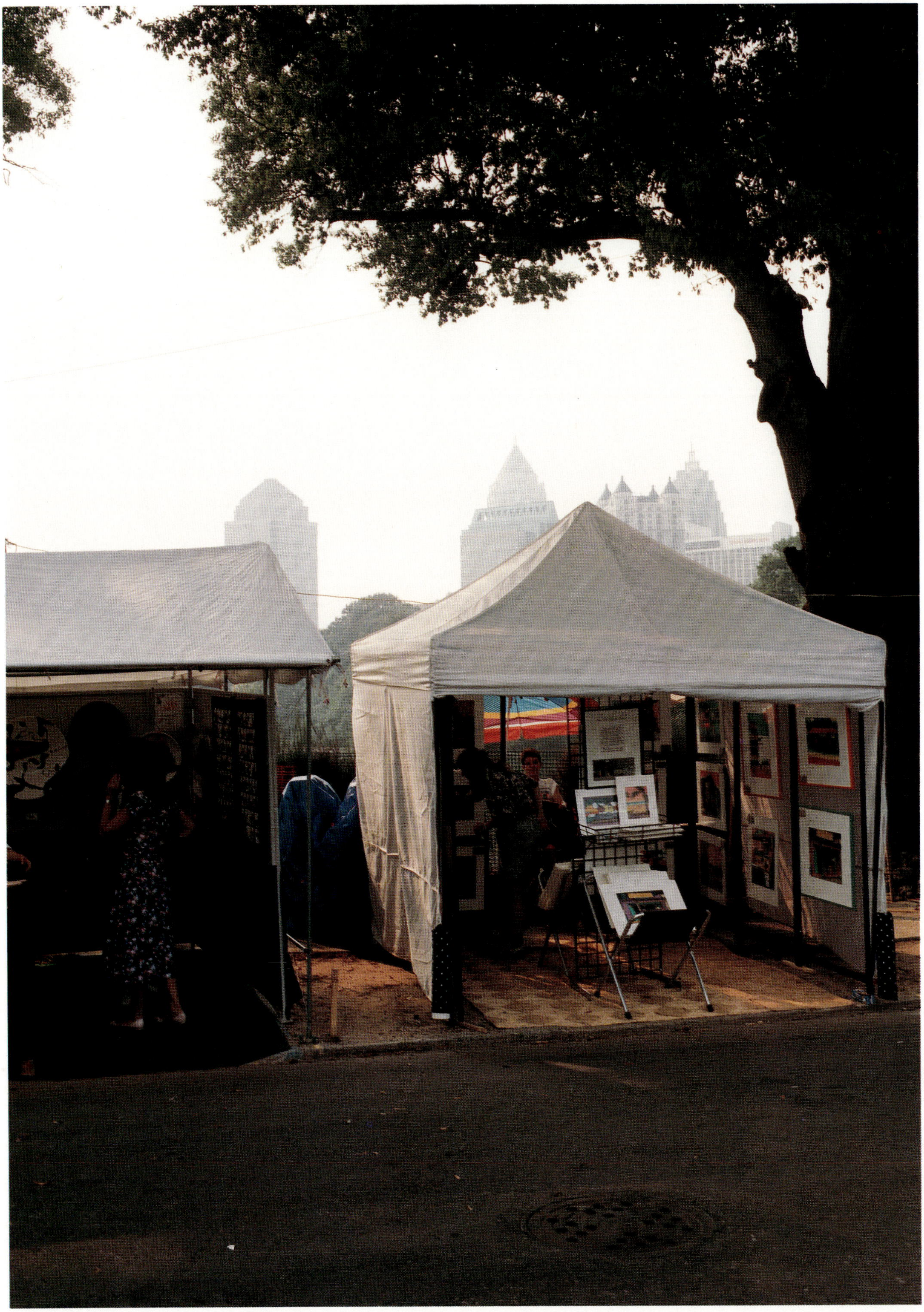

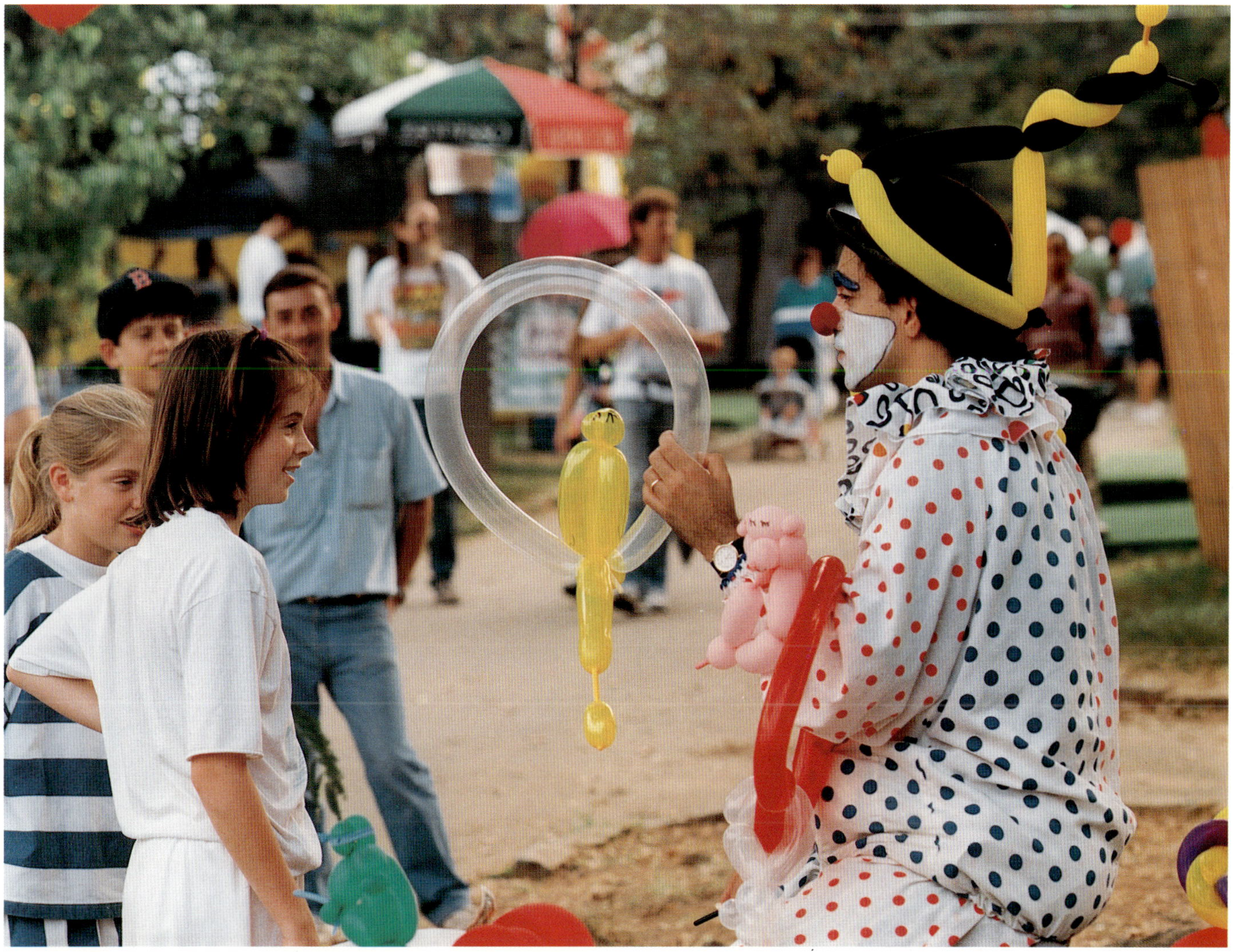

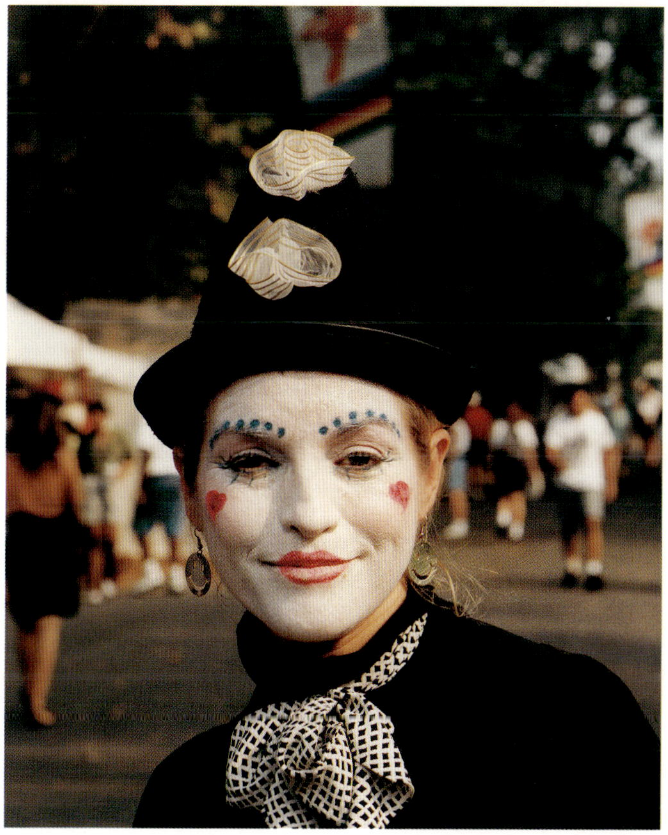

Arts Festival, Piedmont Park

The largest of the city's parks is worth a visit anytime, but especially during the Arts Festival of Atlanta every September. The week-long festival, a local favorite for more than forty years, brings visual arts, performing arts, and family activities to a beautiful outdoor setting landscaped by the Olmsted Brothers in the early 1900s. The 185-acre park stretches east of Piedmont Road in Midtown.

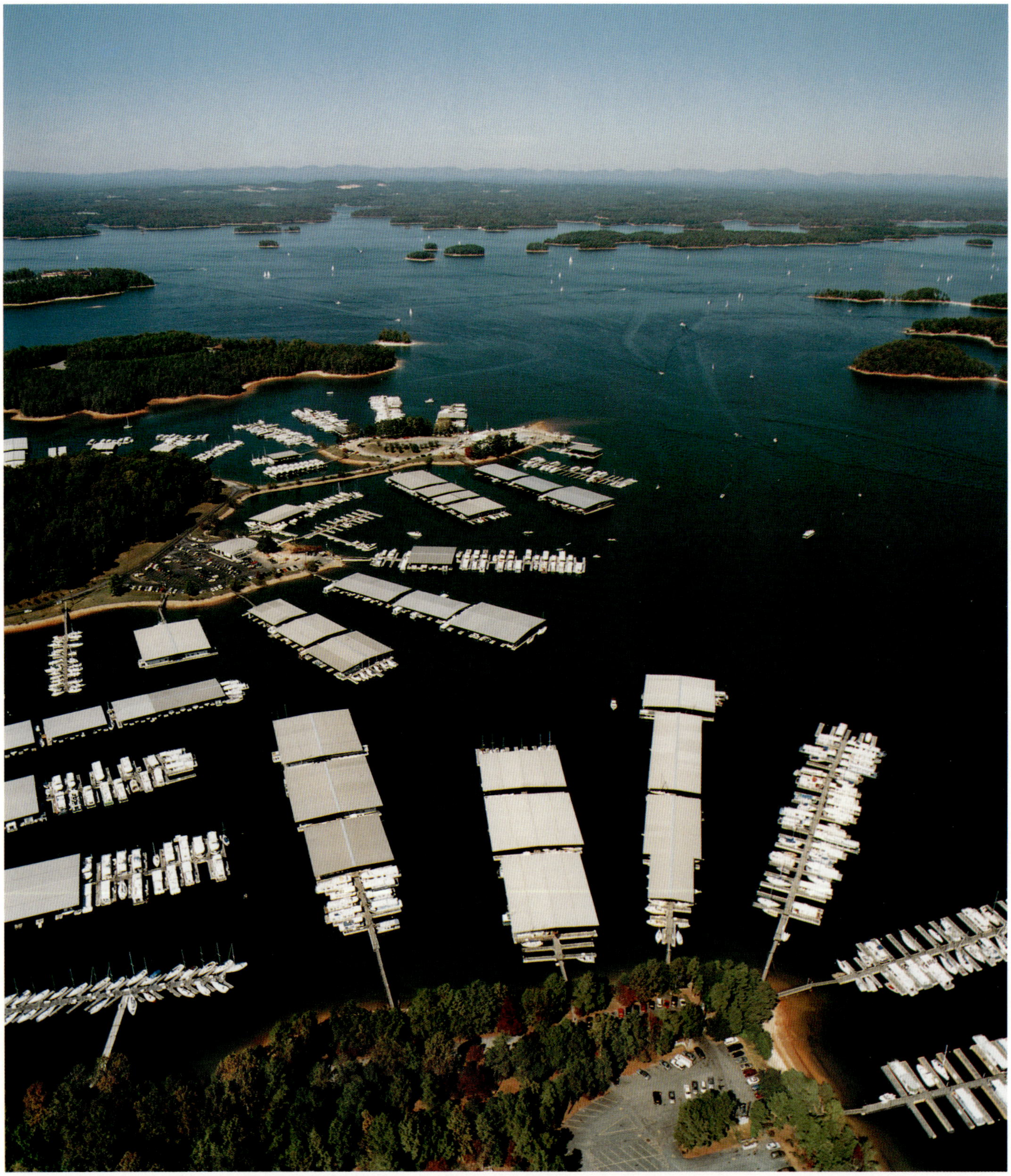

Lake Lanier and Lake Lanier Islands

One of the most popular lakes in the region, Lake Sidney Lanier was created when the United States Army Corps of Engineers dammed the Chattahoochee River to provide flood control, hydroelectric power, and a water-supply reservoir. In recent years, utilitarian lakes like Lanier have also become important recreation areas. Lake Lanier is the most visited Corps lake in the nation. The 38,000-acre reservoir, with its 550 miles of shoreline and scores of islands that once were hilltops, is about an hour's drive north of Atlanta, near Buford. Four of the largest islands form the resort area known as Lake Lanier Islands. The lake offers boating, camping, fishing, and swimming, with a hotel, restaurants, and golf course at Lake Lanier Islands.

Part VI

The Sporting Scene

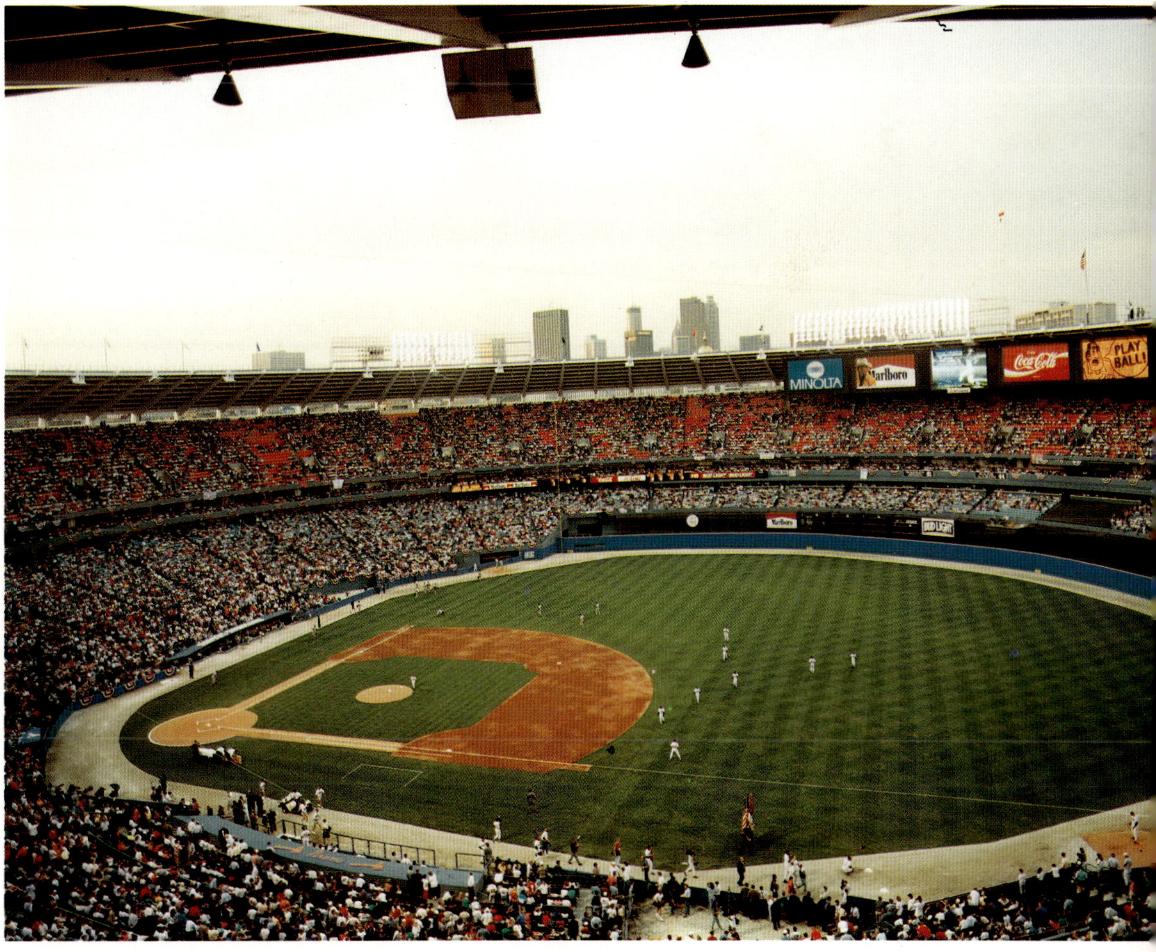

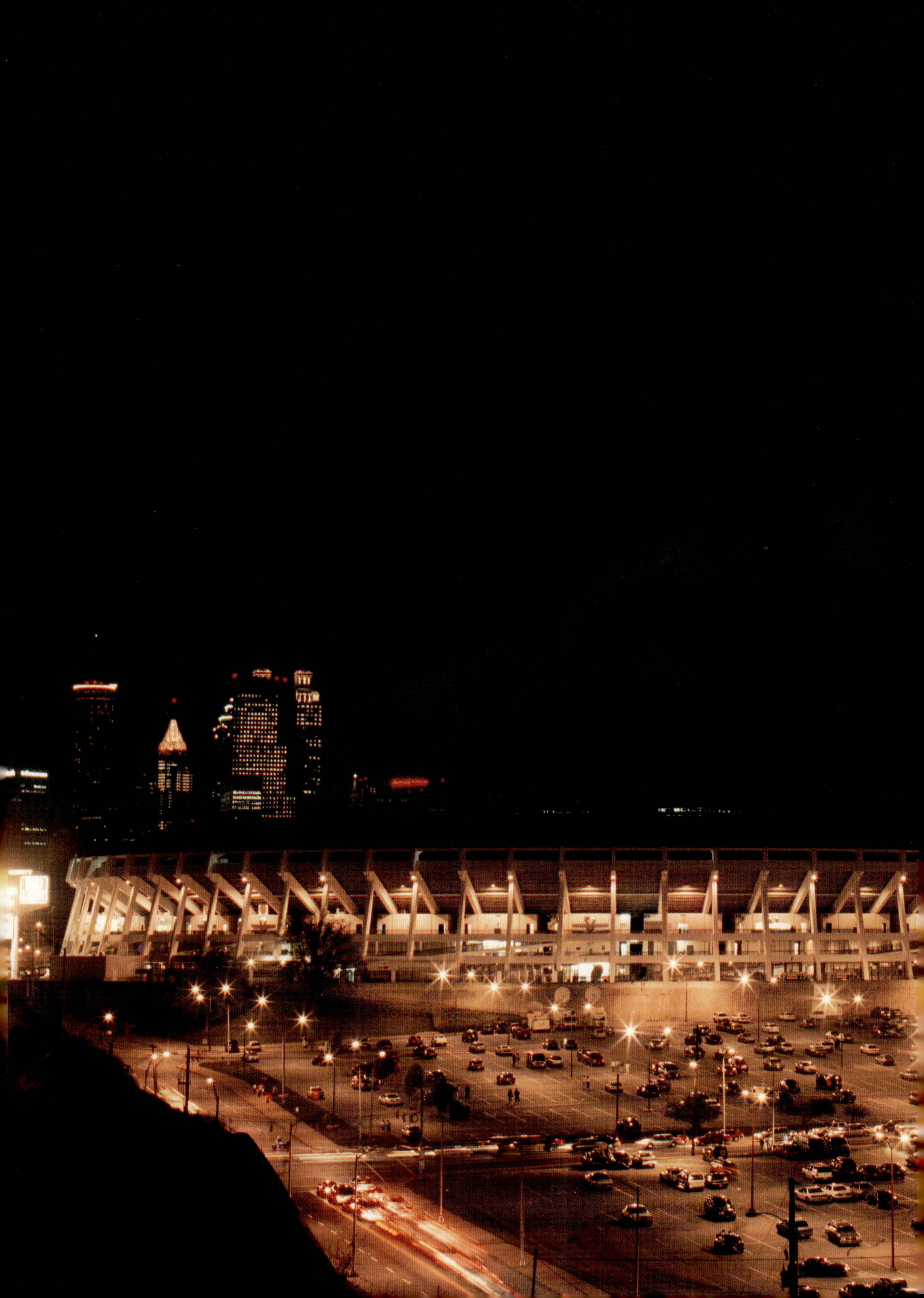

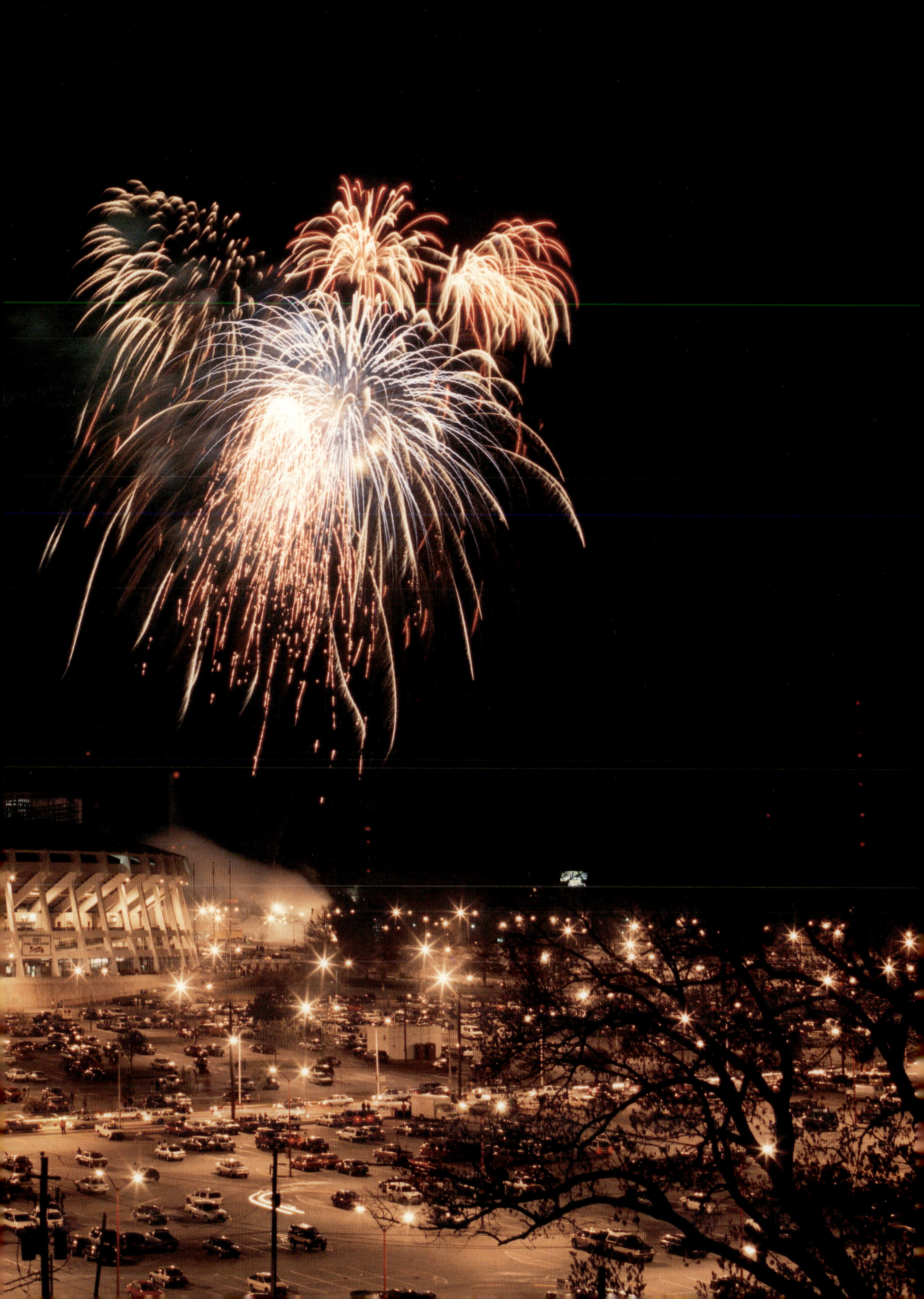

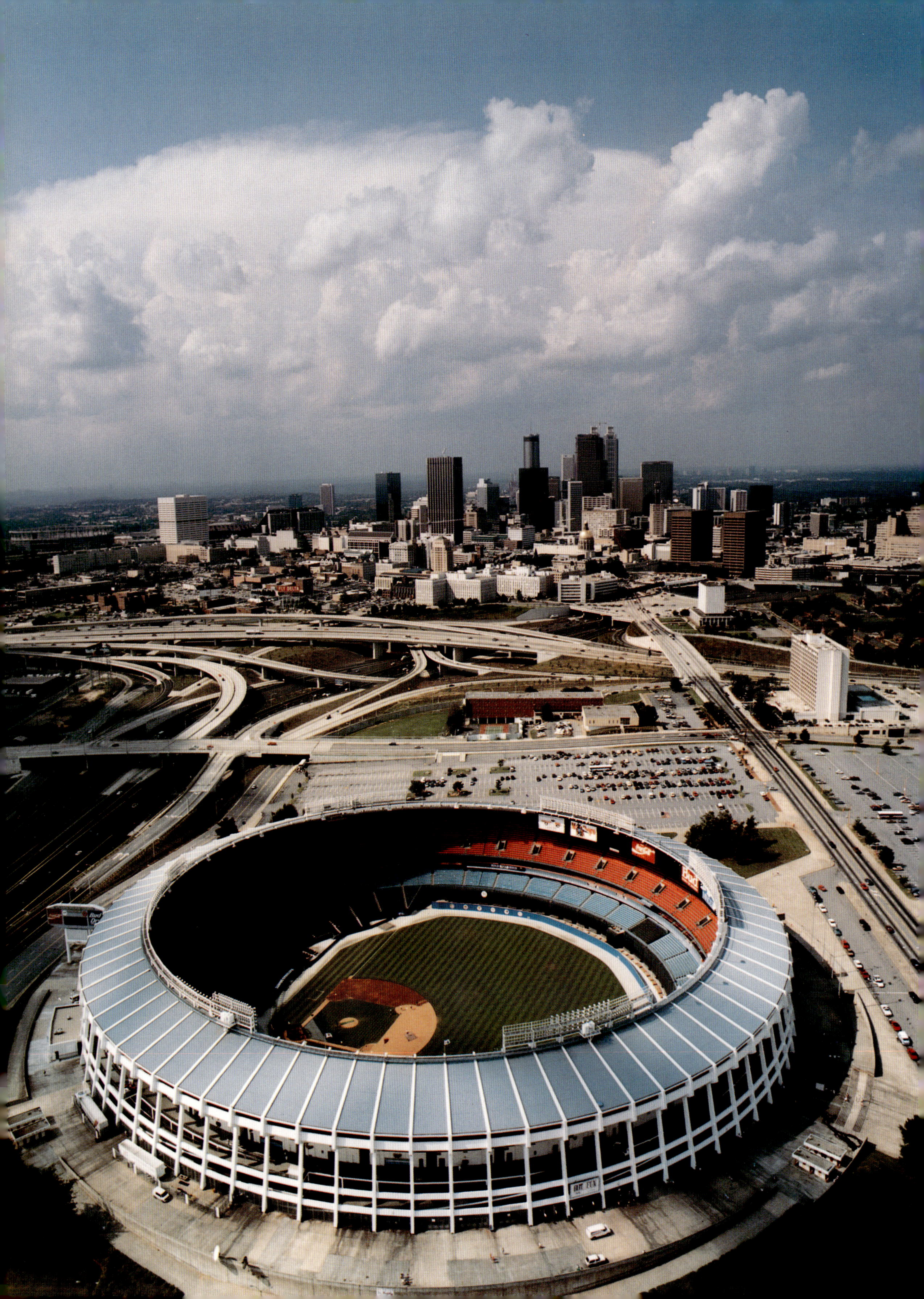

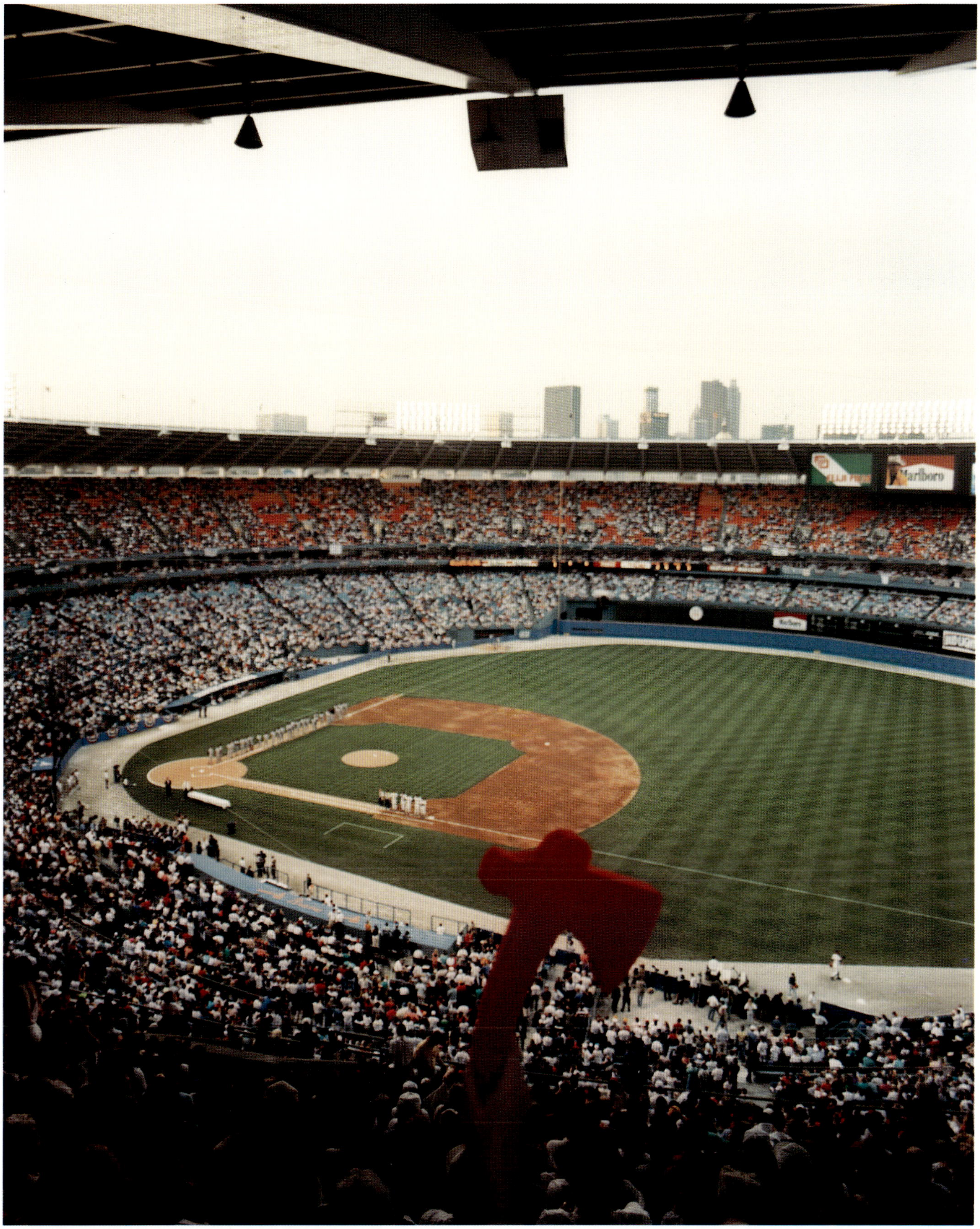

Atlanta–Fulton County Stadium

More than three million fans pack the Chop Shop each baseball season to wave tomahawks, eat hot dogs, and cheer on the Atlanta Braves. The first World Series in Atlanta history was played here in 1991, the second in 1992. Braves fans hope there are more in the near future, but after the 1996 Olympics their team will be playing in Olympic Stadium. The old facility will be torn down and the site made into a park.

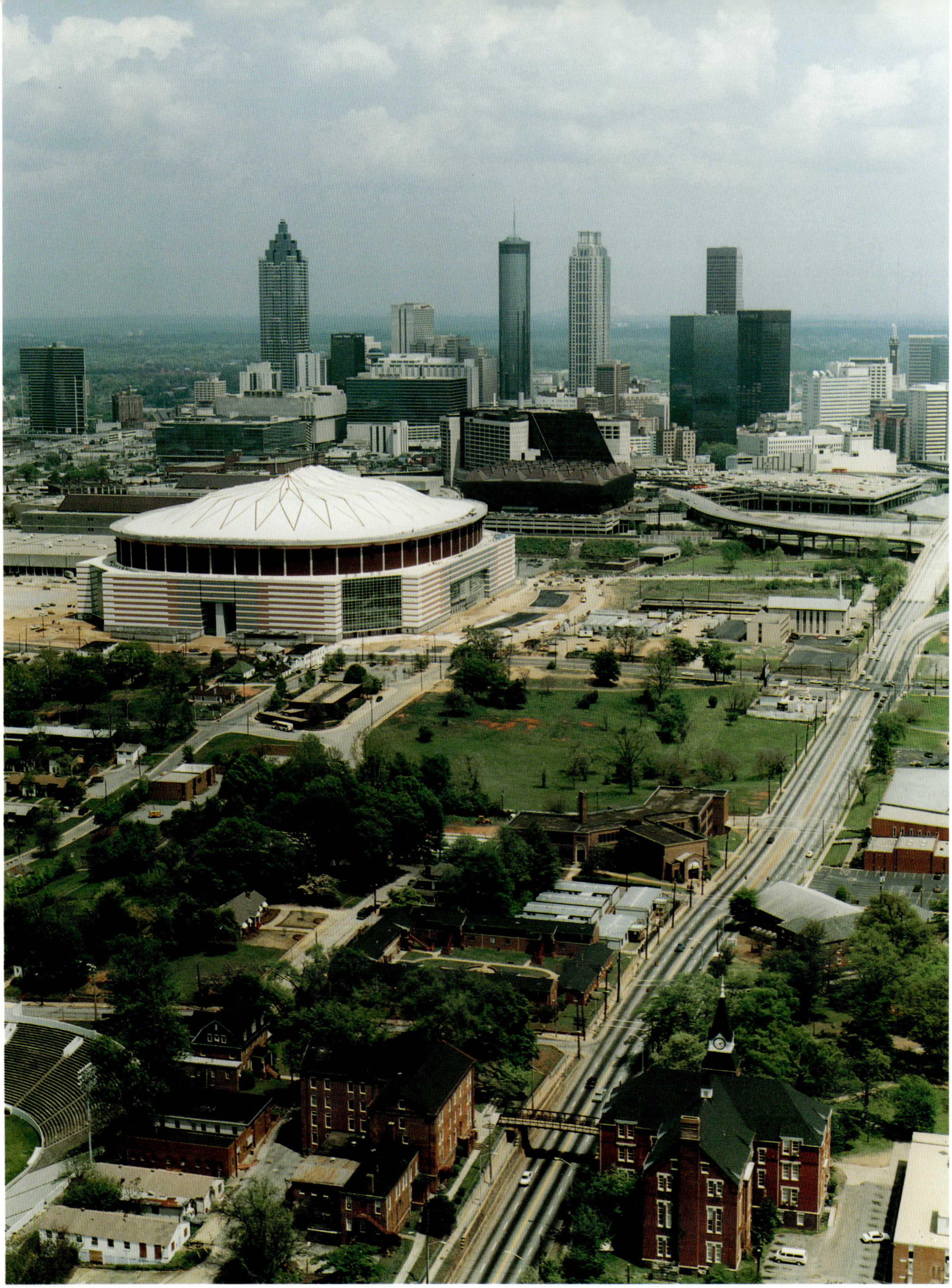

The Georgia Dome

Home of the Atlanta Falcons professional football team and site of the 1994 Super Bowl, the Georgia Dome opened in 1992. The largest cable-supported oval dome in the world covers the 70,500-seat stadium just west of the downtown area.

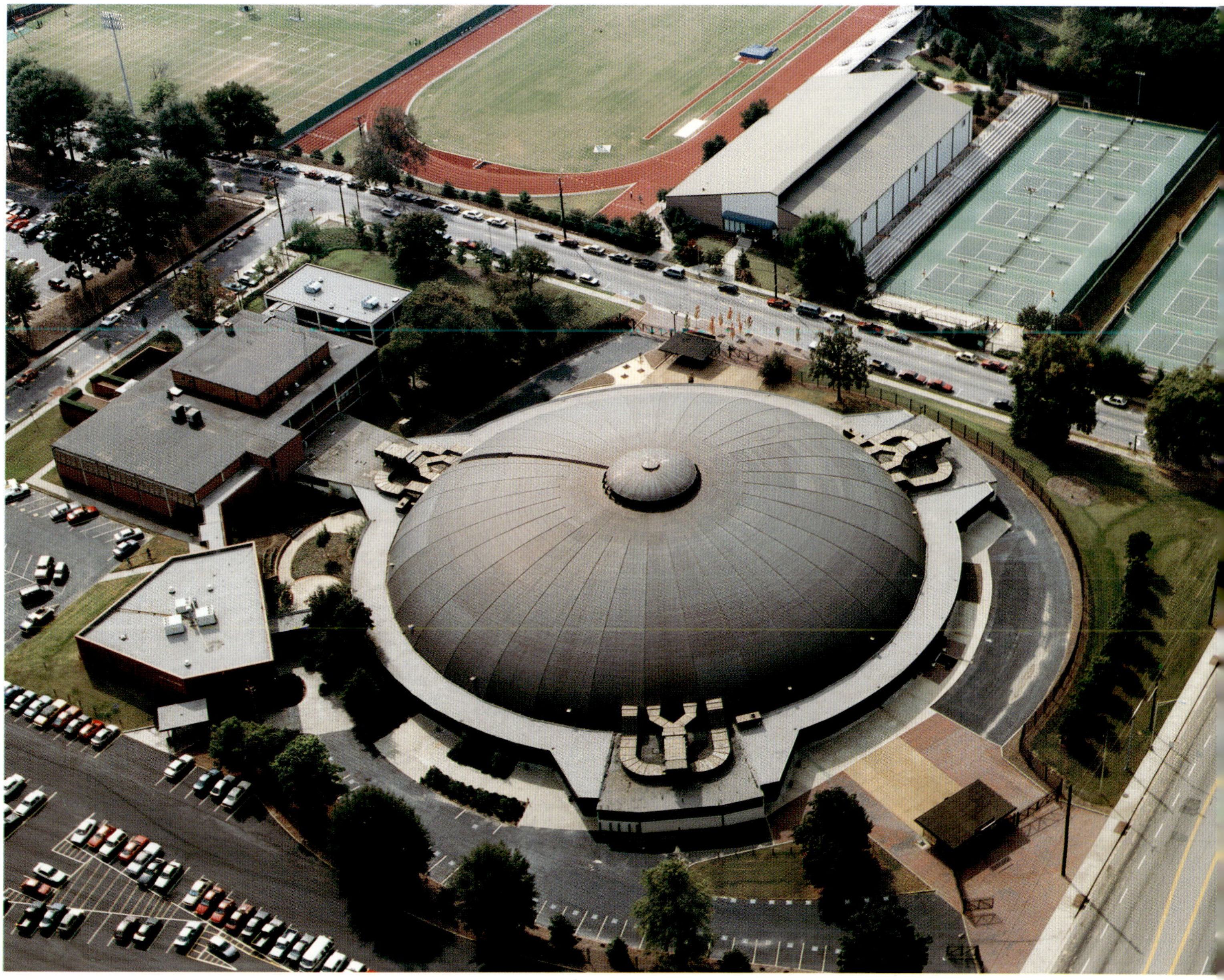

Alexander Memorial Coliseum

The shieldlike dome on the edge of the Georgia Tech campus shelters the battlefield for basketball wars between the Yellow Jackets and Atlantic Coast Conference foes Duke, North Carolina, North Carolina State, Maryland, Wake Forest, Virginia, Clemson, and Florida State.

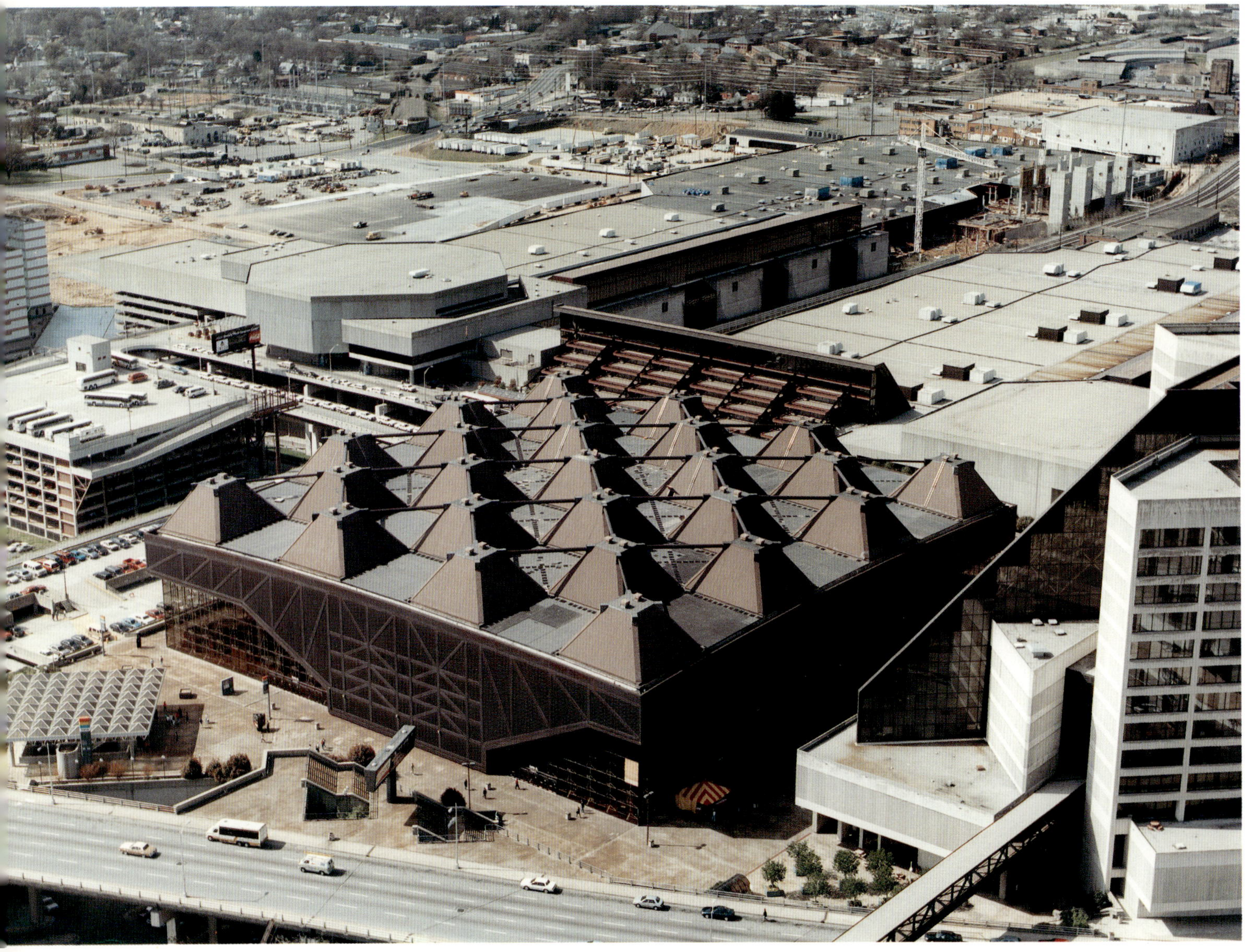

The Omni

The 16,500-seat Omni, near the Georgia Dome, is the home of the Atlanta Hawks basketball team and the Atlanta Knights hockey team, as well as the venue for dozens of special events such as ice skating, rock concerts, circuses, and (in conjunction with the nearby Georgia World Congress Center) the 1988 Democratic National Convention.

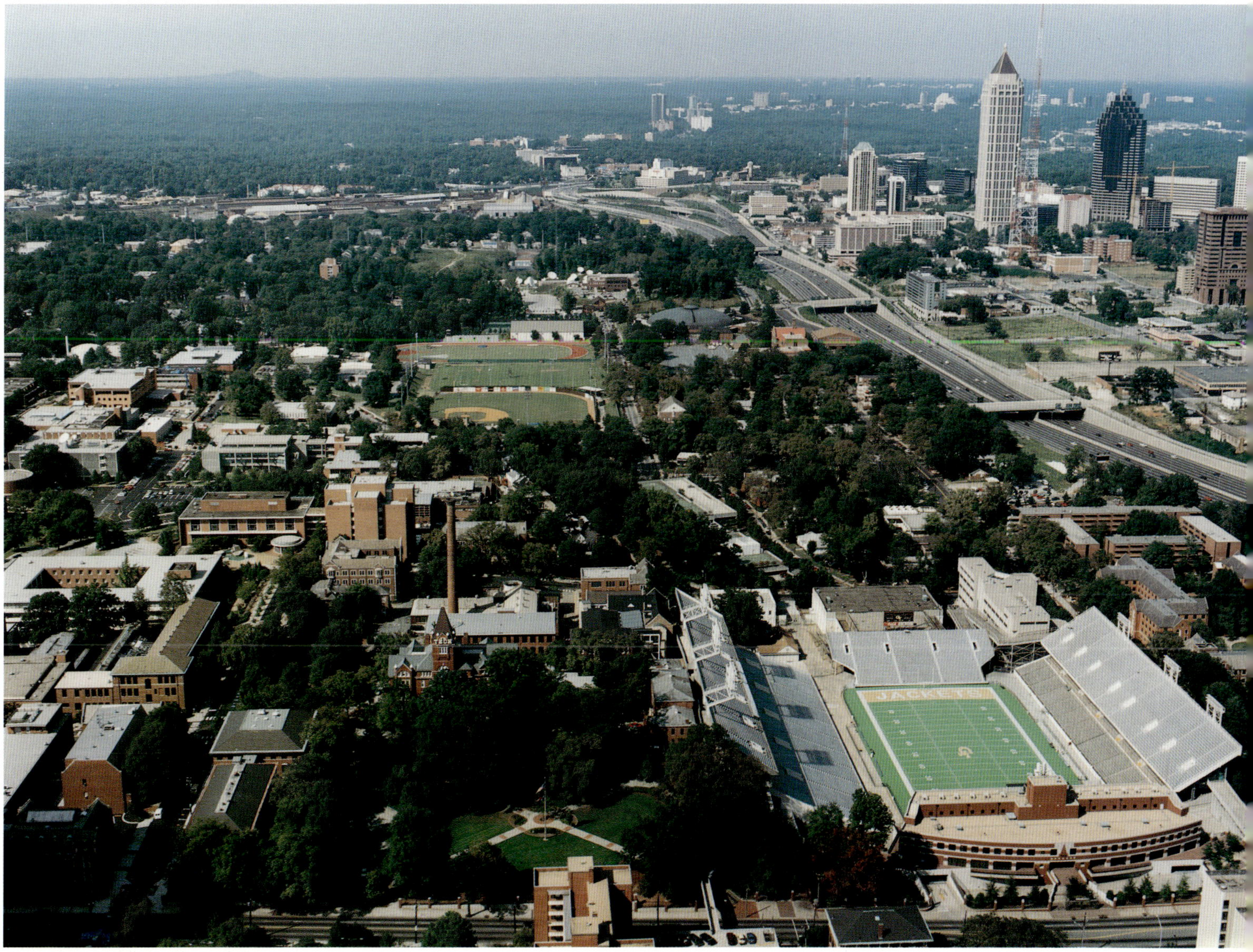

Bobby Dodd Stadium

When the Georgia Tech football team is playing at home, the cheers of its fans float on the night air from Midtown to downtown. The Yellow Jackets rewarded their faithful with a national championship in 1990.

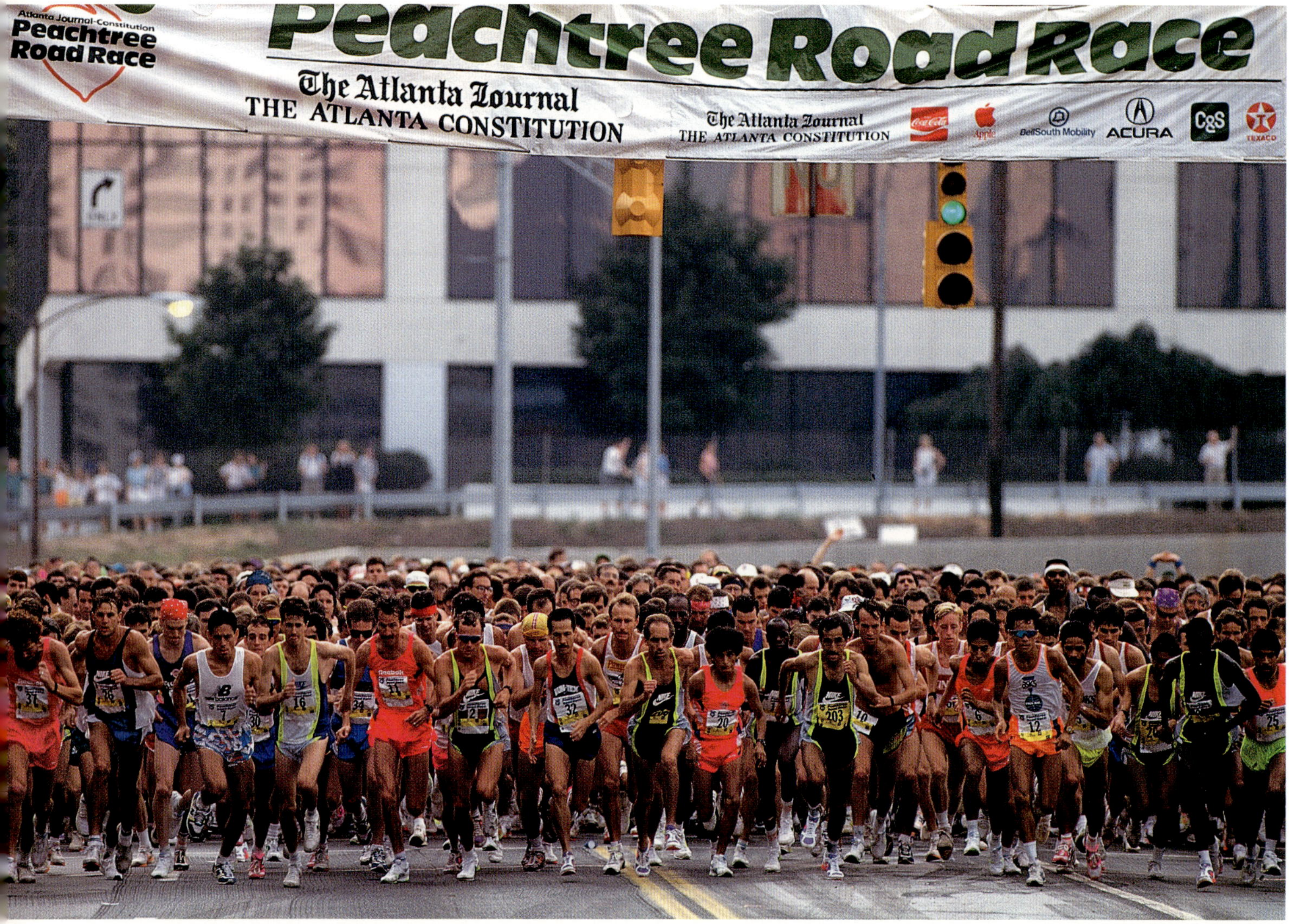

Peachtree Road Race

Held every Fourth of July, the Peachtree Road Race has evolved from a loosely organized street run to one of the largest 10K races in the world. Braving the heat and humidity of a midsummer morning in Georgia, upwards of 45,000 contestants run, jog, walk, and stumble from Buckhead to Piedmont Park in hopes of earning a T-shirt. The event includes separate wheelchair competitions and races for kids.

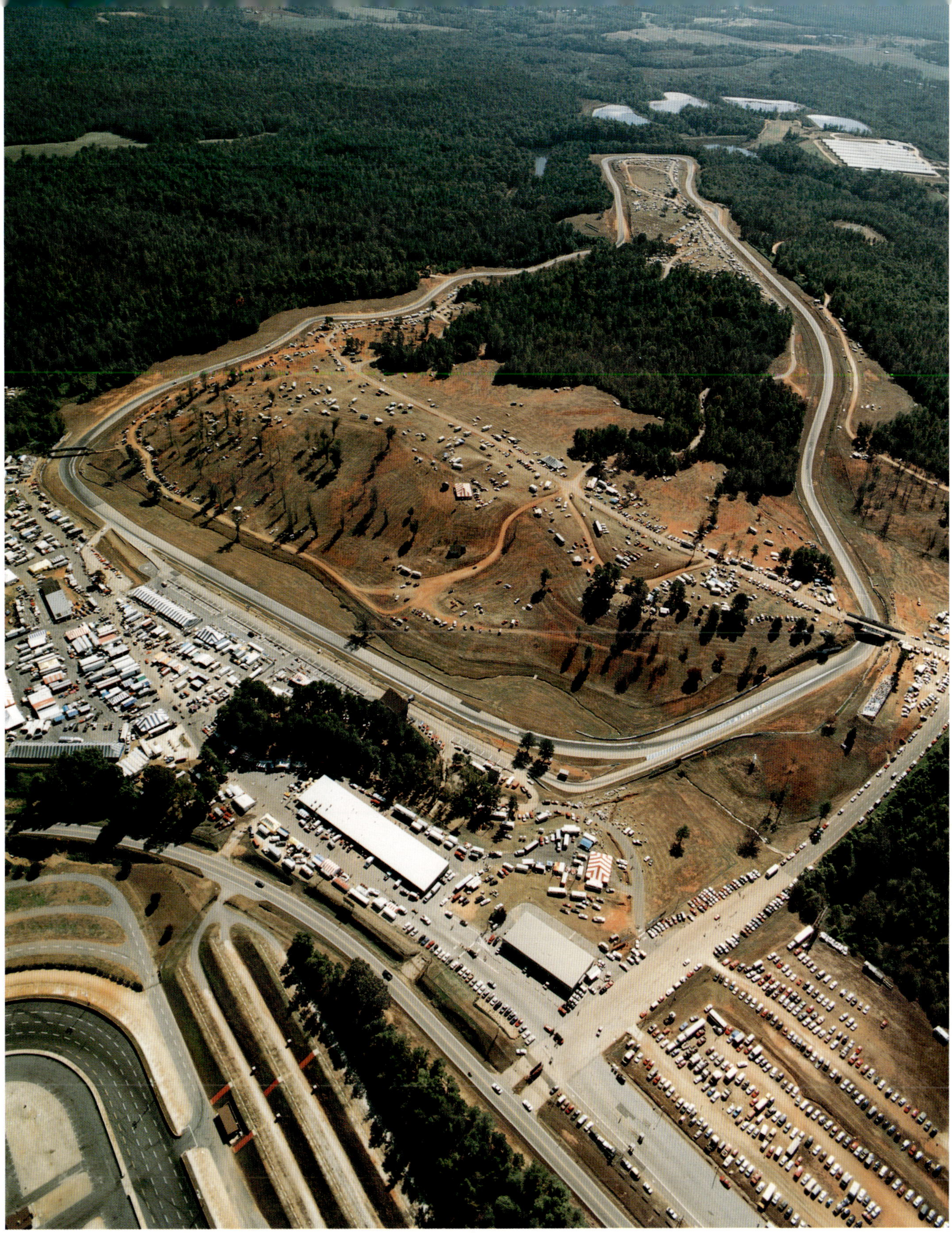

Road Atlanta

The largest Grand Prix racing facility in the Southeast, Road Atlanta conducts sports car, Formula One, motorcycle, and motocross competitions on and around its 2.52-mile track. Famous amateur drivers Tom Cruise and Paul Newman sometimes show up among the professionals. The track is 39 miles northeast of Atlanta, near Braselton.

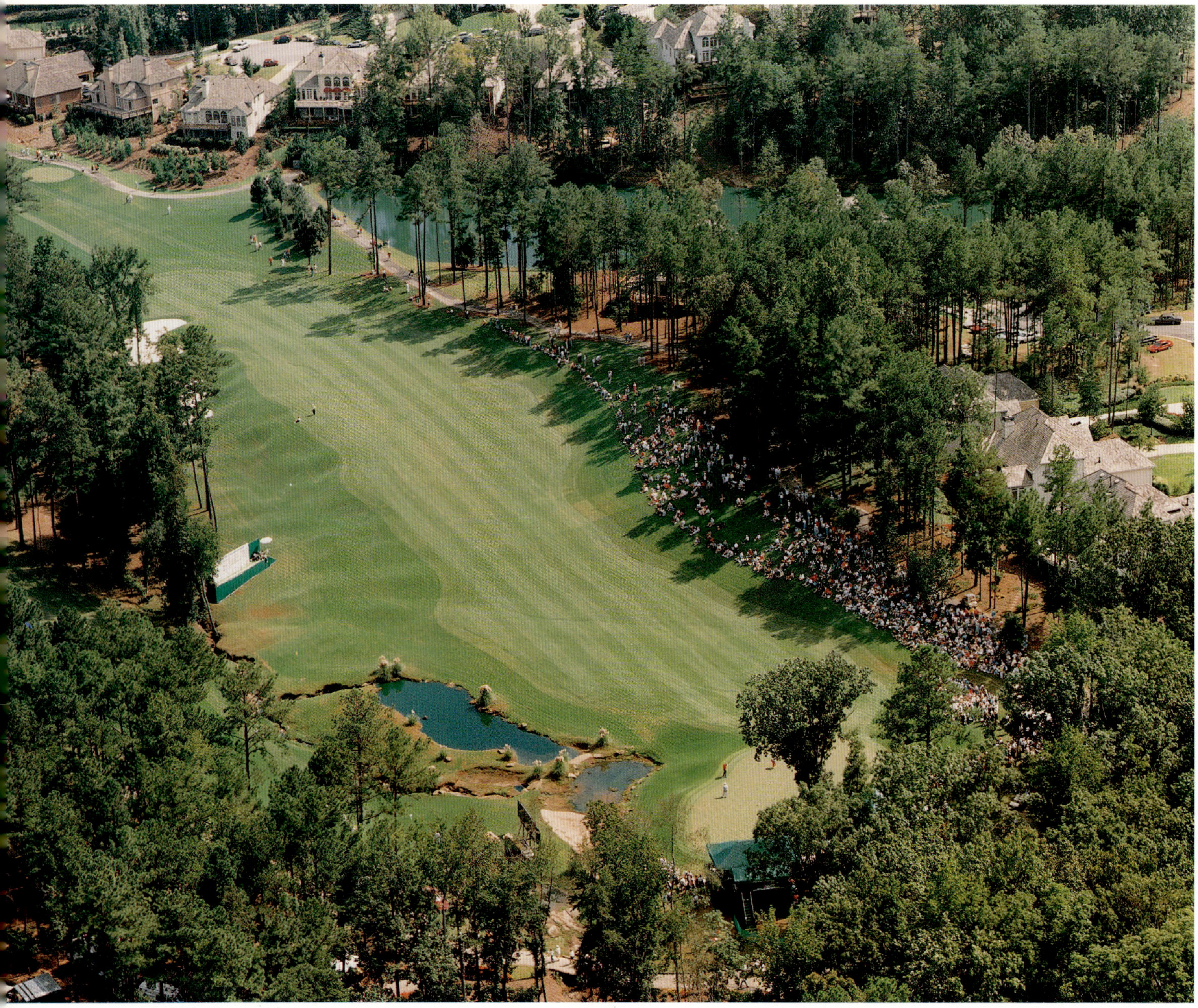

Country Club of the South

Spectators line a fairway during a professional golf tournament at the Country Club of the South in Alpharetta, north of Atlanta. The course, designed by Jack Nicklaus, is rated among the finest in the region.

PART VII

The Environs

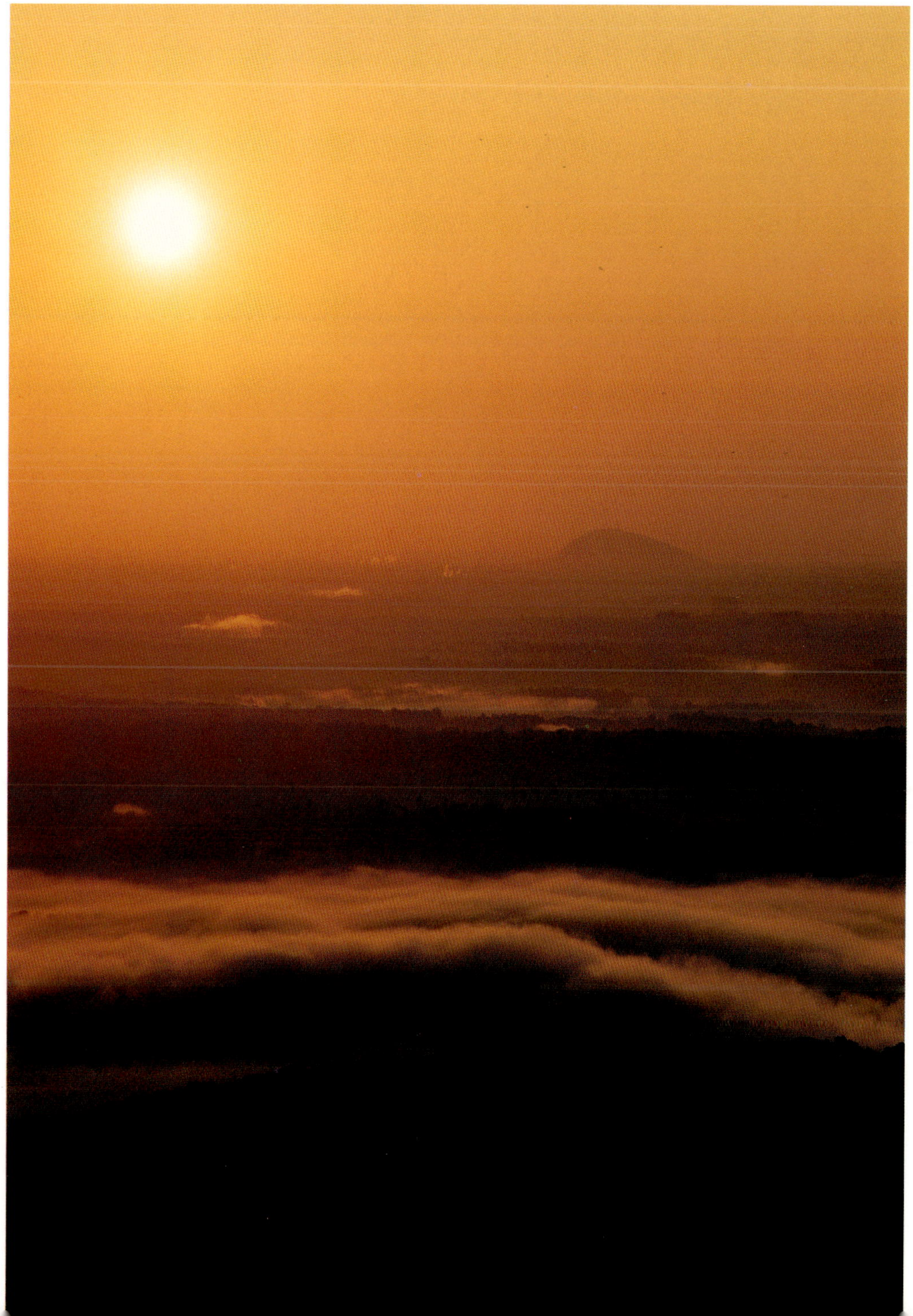

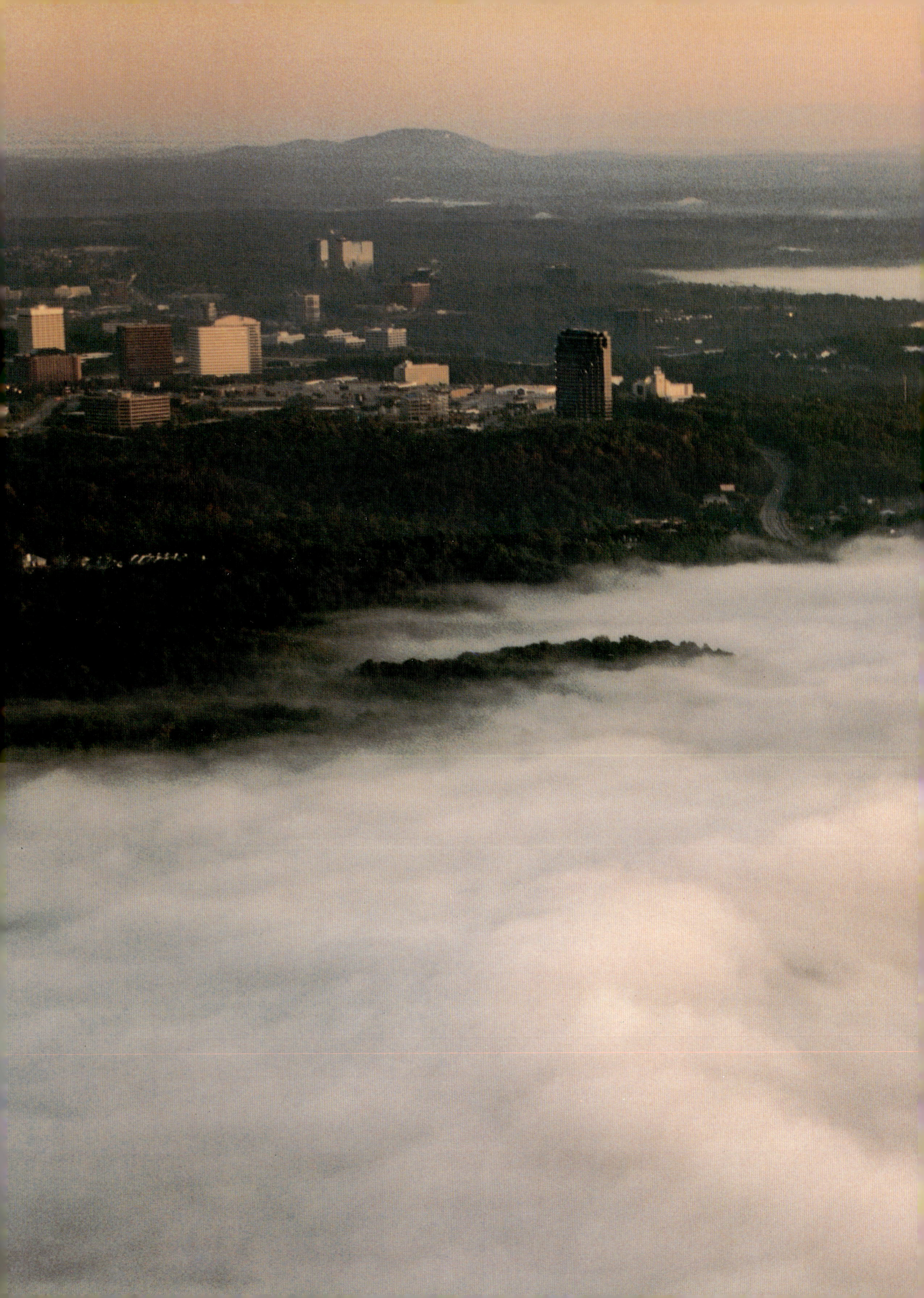

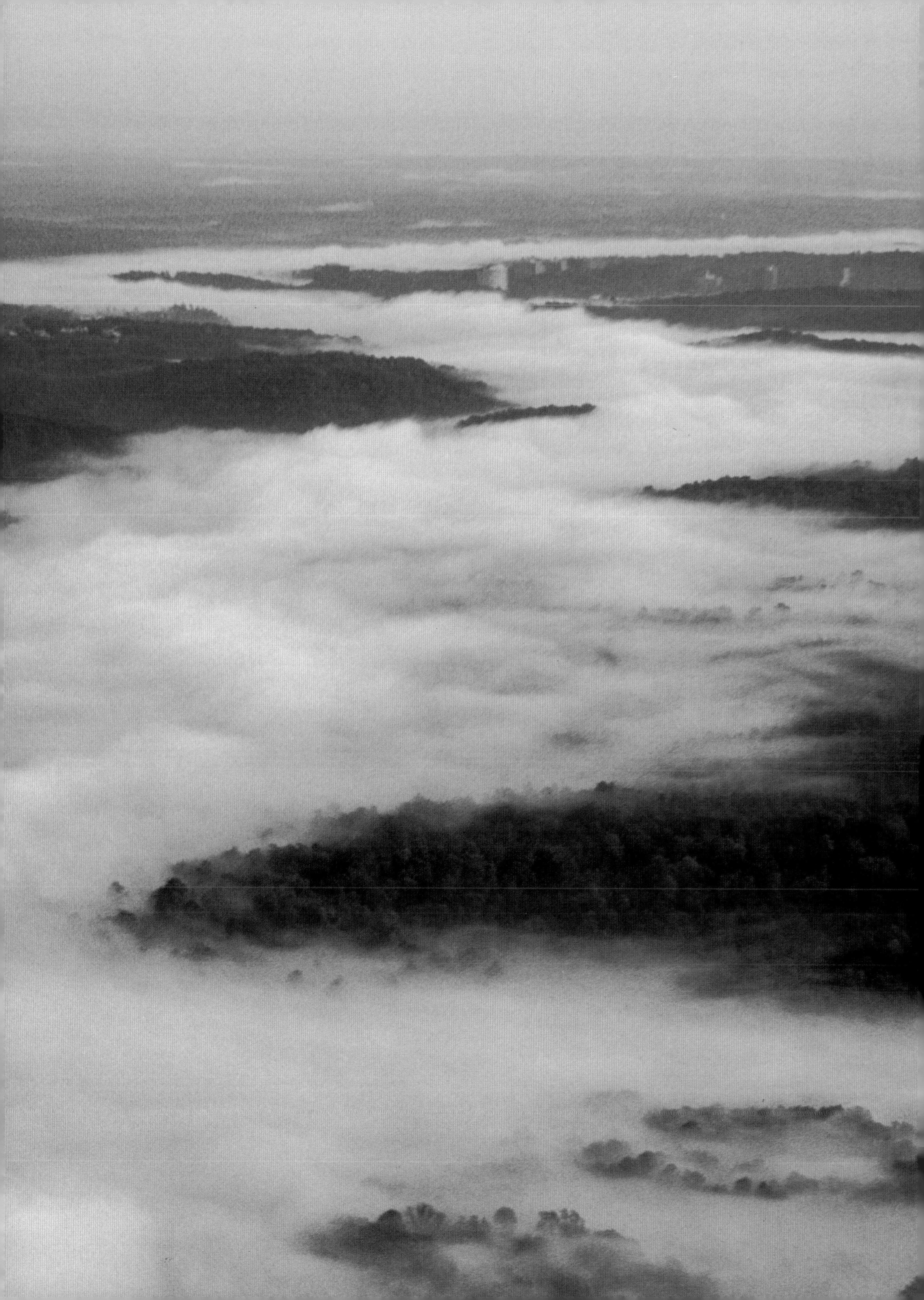

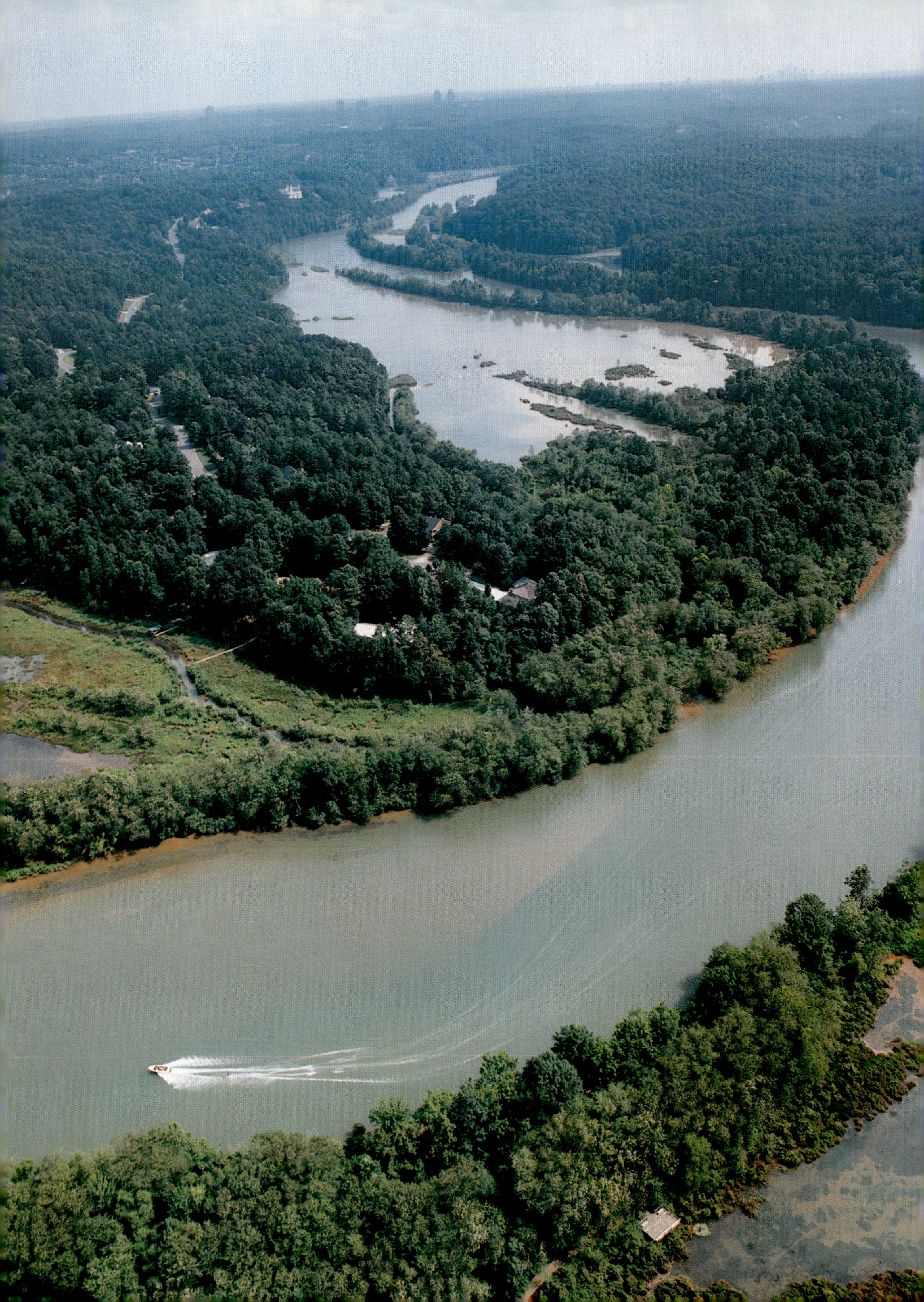

Chattahoochee River

When the state of Georgia commissioned civil engineer Stephen H. Long to mark a terminus for the Western & Atlantic Railroad, he chose a spot six miles from the nearest reach of the Chattahoochee, but Atlanta has long since expanded to embrace the river, and Atlantans have adopted it as their own, whether their affection is expressed in a moment's glimpse from the bridge during a hurried commute along Interstate 75, in an afternoon of boating along the river's winding course, or for the lucky few, in daily contemplation of its many moods from a clifftop mansion.

In the early days, there was interest in developing the Chattahoochee as a canal, but the stream's shallows forced the engineers to declare it unnavigable. Atlanta thrived on railroads instead, and to the delight of its citizens today, the river remained a piece of nature, rather than an avenue of commerce.

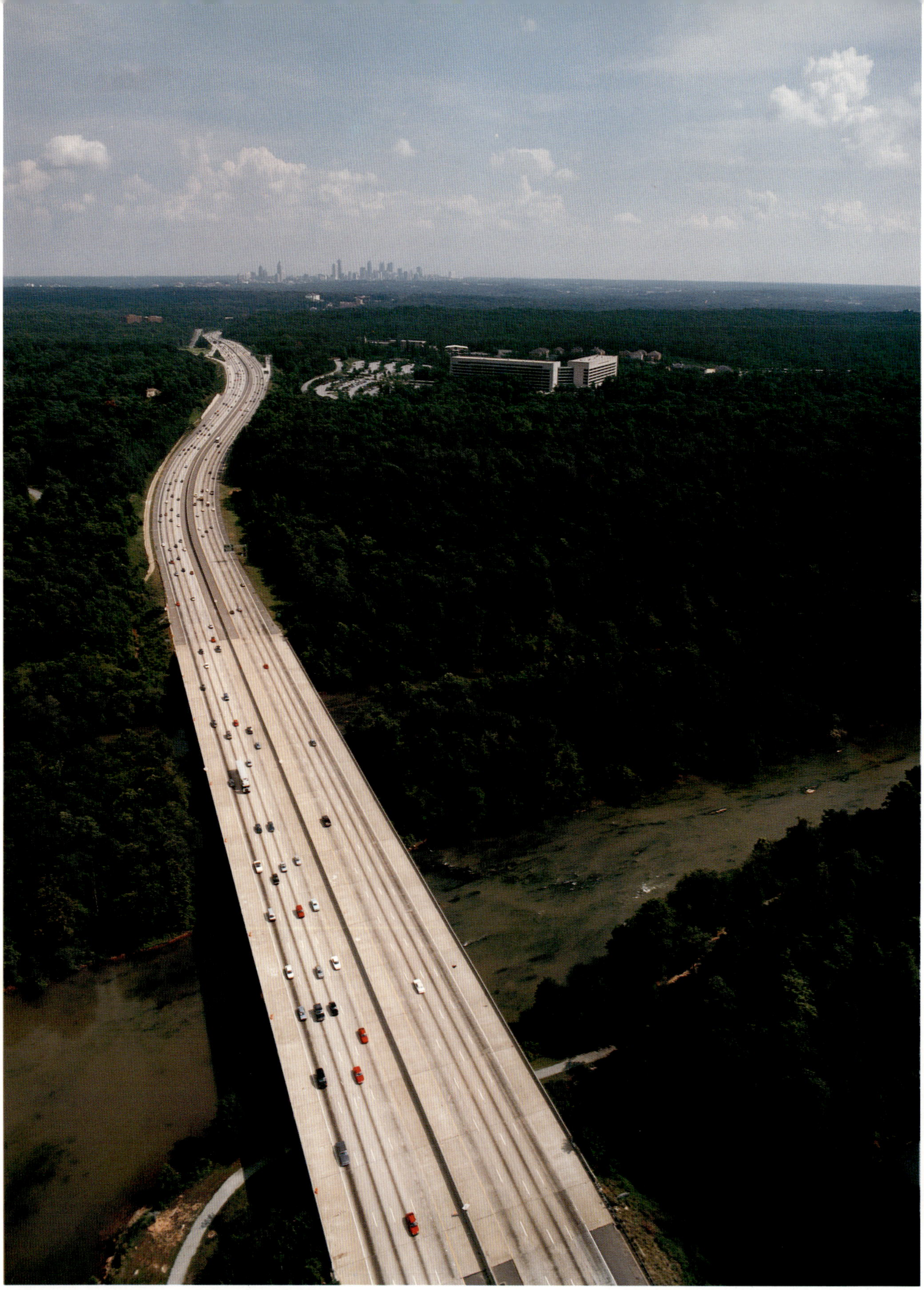

I-75 crossing the Chattahoochee

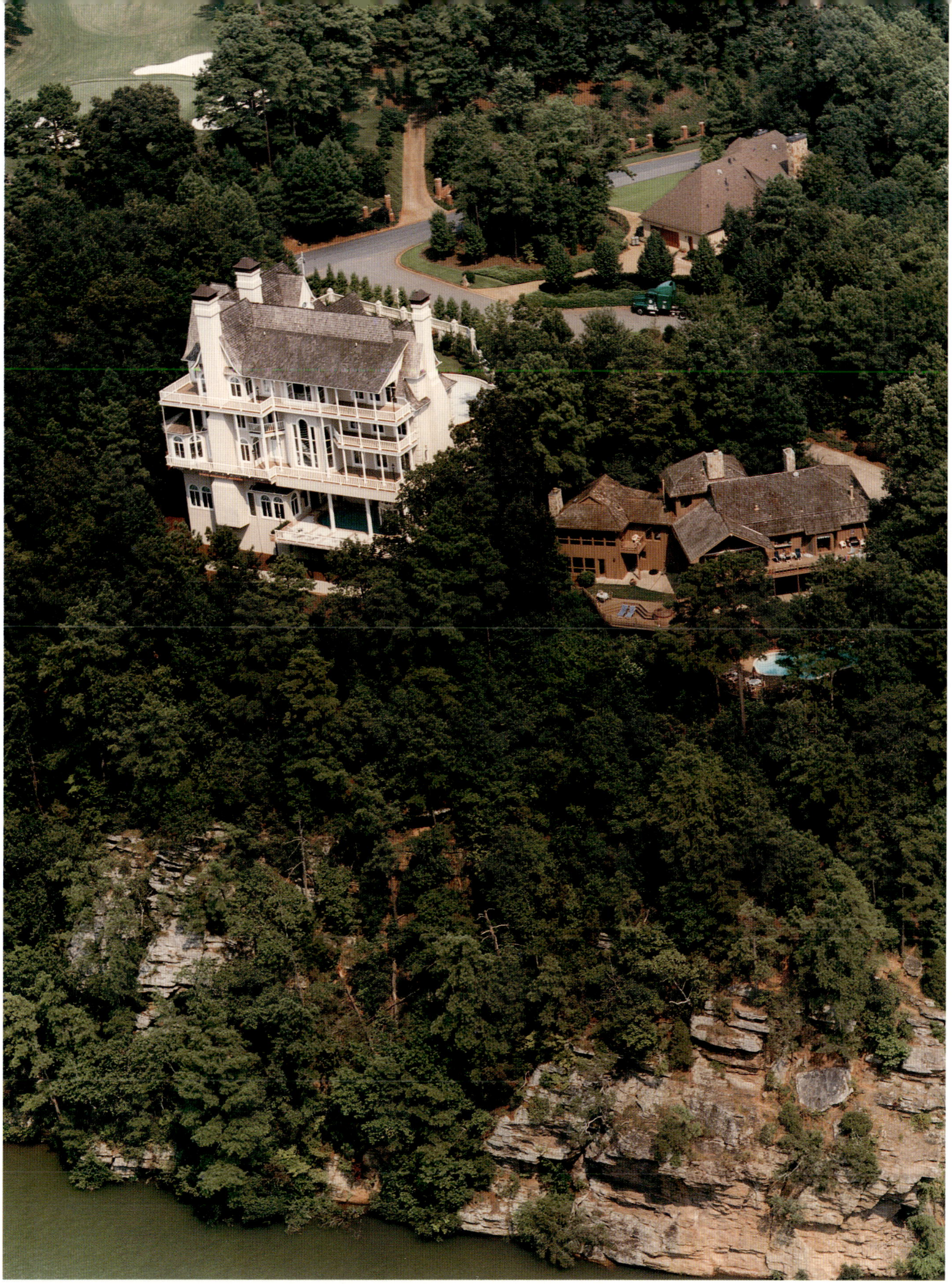

Cliff houses, Chattahoochee River

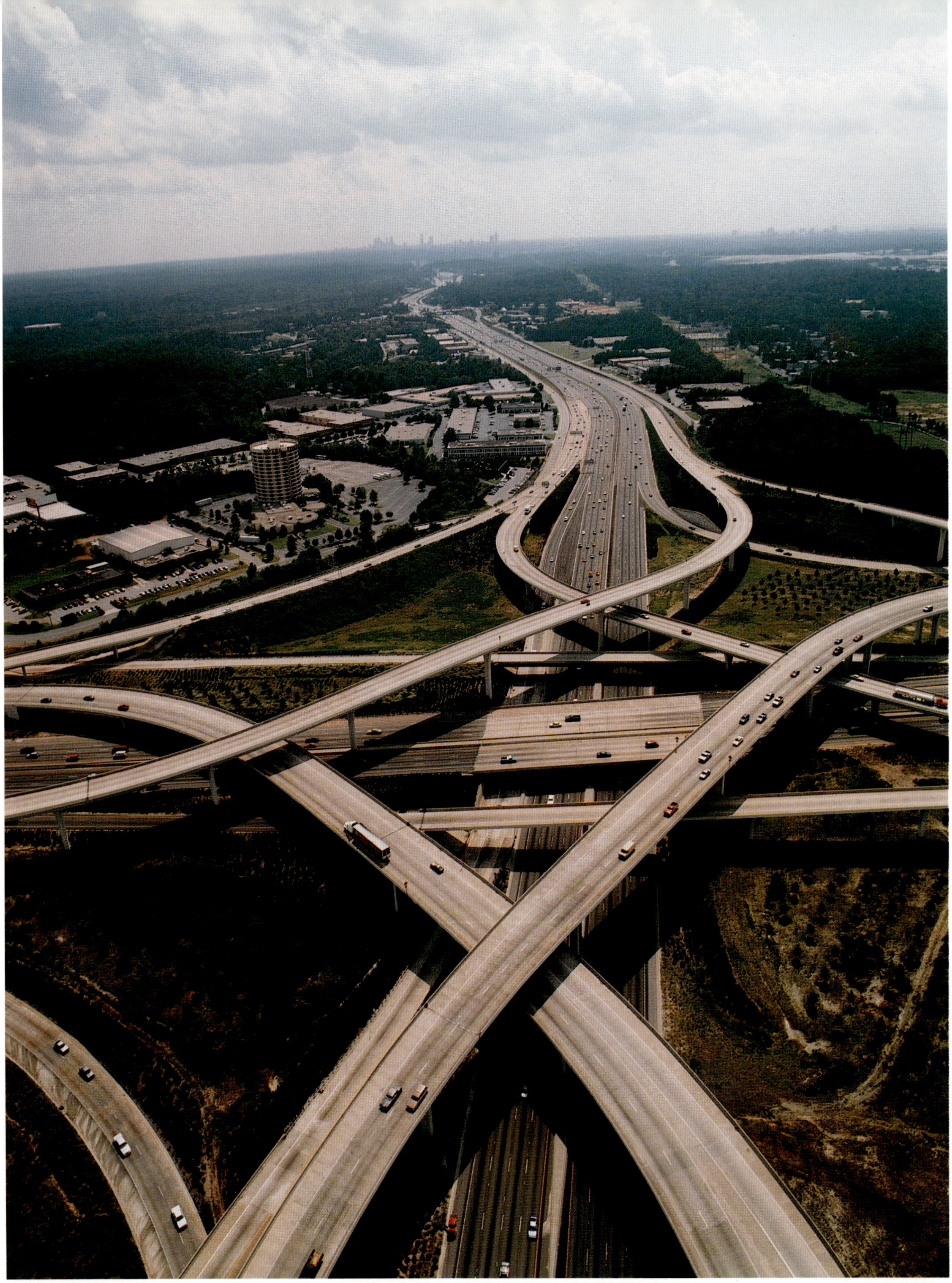

Spaghetti Junction

The Tom Moreland Interchange—"Spaghetti Junction," as it is known locally—connects Interstates 85 and 285 by way of twelve ramps and fourteen overpasses. Even the most jaded commuter can appreciate its soaring architecture on a clear summer's day, but feelings about it change rapidly when an ice storm comes to town.

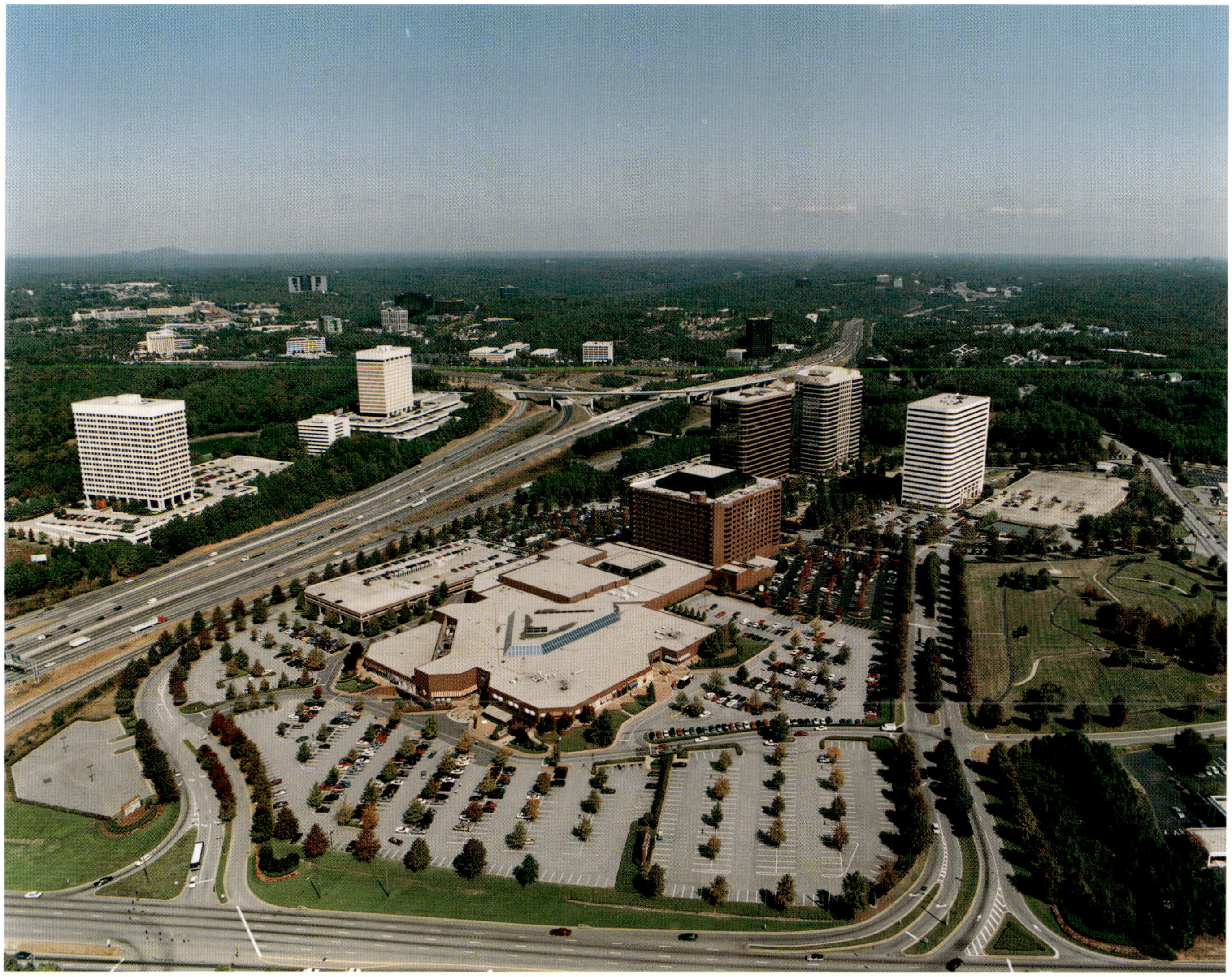

Galleria Mall

The Galleria, a mixed-use complex midway between Atlanta and Marietta, featuring the Waverly Hotel and the attached Galleria Shopping Mall, attracts shoppers and conventioneers more comfortable in a suburban than an urban environment. Future expansion plans include a new Galleria Civic Center for Cobb County.

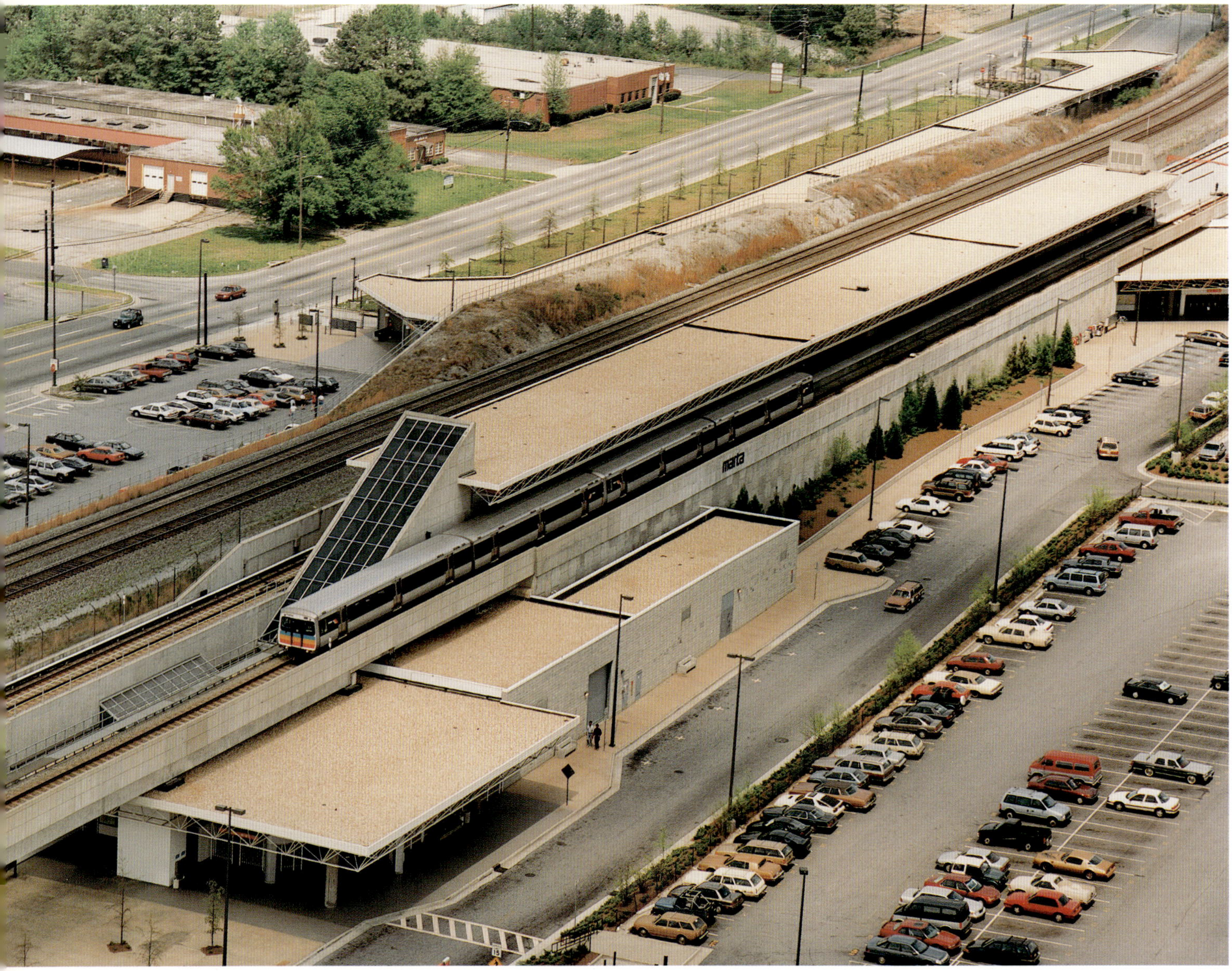

MARTA Station at Chamblee

The Metropolitan Atlanta Rapid Transit Authority operates more than 680 buses and 240 rapid rail cars, serving more than 70 million riders a year in DeKalb and Fulton Counties. The Chamblee station is one of the northernmost stops on the rail line.

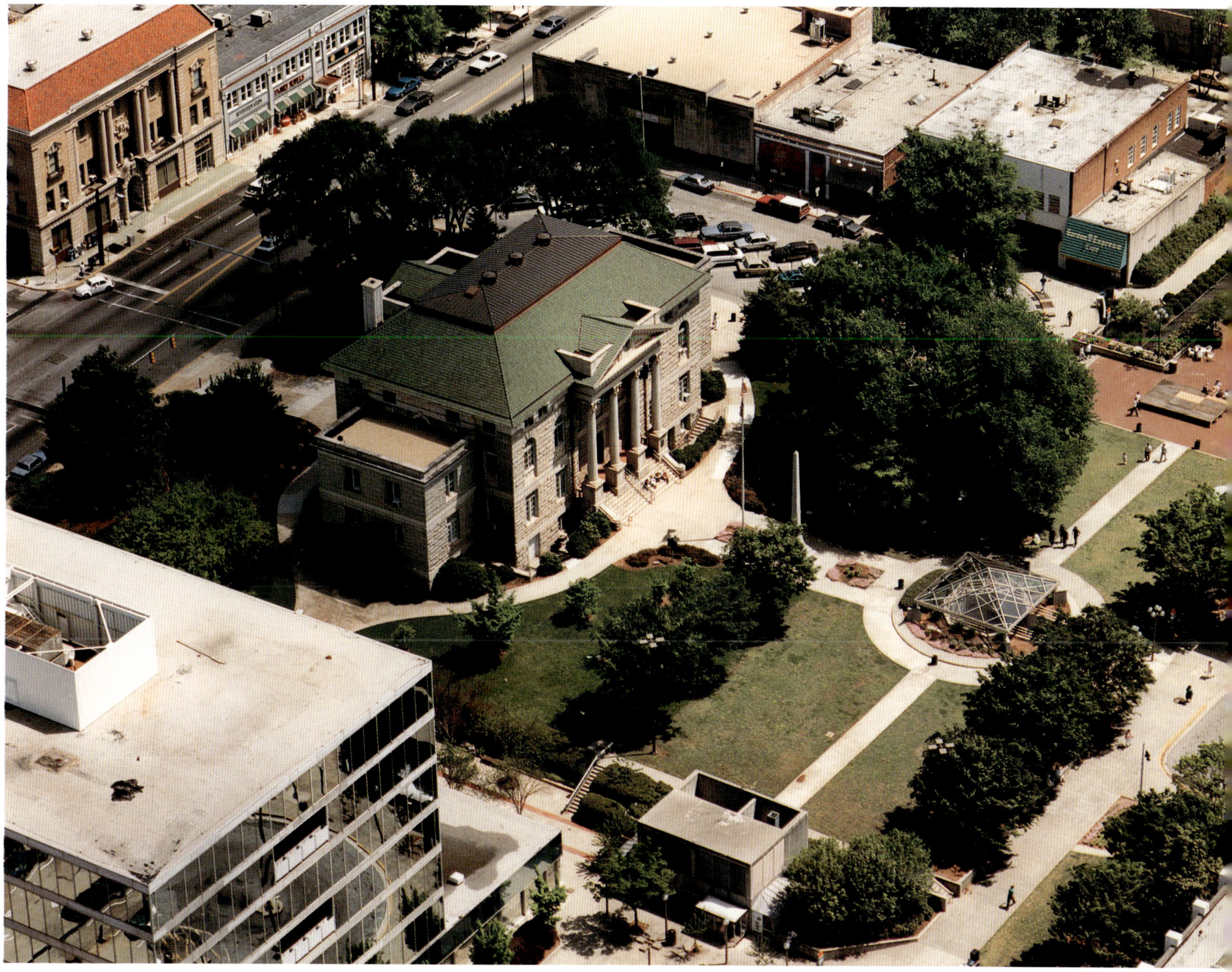

Decatur Courthouse Square

Years before Atlanta was founded, Decatur was already a prosperous small town—so prosperous that its citizens could afford to tell the Western & Atlantic Railroad to locate its noisy, smoky train line elsewhere. Today Decatur, some six miles east of downtown Atlanta and surrounded by its younger neighbor's sprawl, still retains a small-town atmosphere, exemplified by the DeKalb County Courthouse Square at its center.

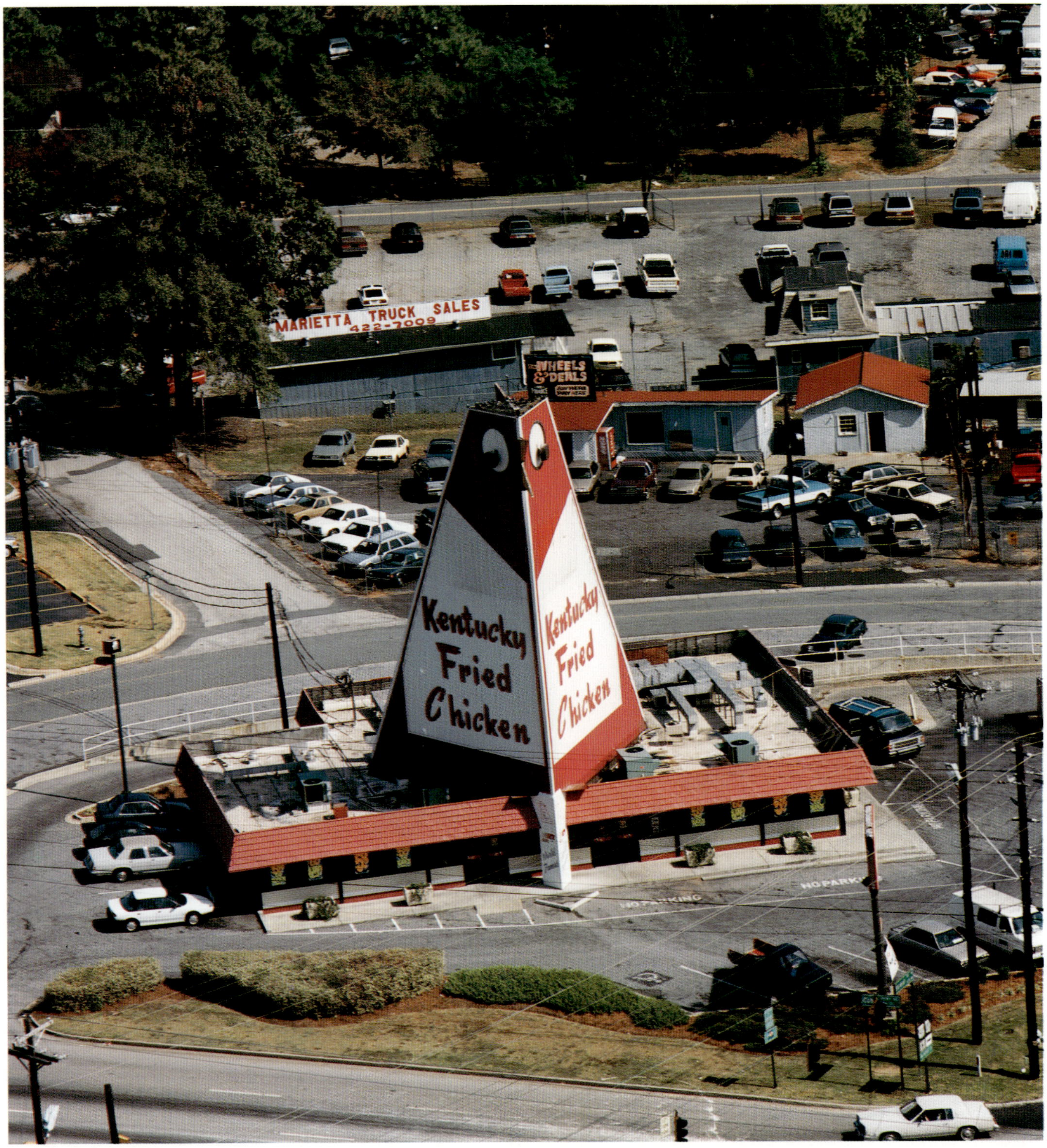

The Big Chicken

For years, a fifty-six-foot-tall highly stylized metal chicken has been perhaps the most unusual landmark in the Atlanta area. Perched in the middle of Marietta, the Big Chicken has come to symbolize not only a fried-chicken franchise, but also the community. It is so well known nationally that it was used in a clue on the TV quiz show *Jeopardy*. The fowl shown here is the original; damaged by high winds in 1992, it was replaced with an updated version in 1994.

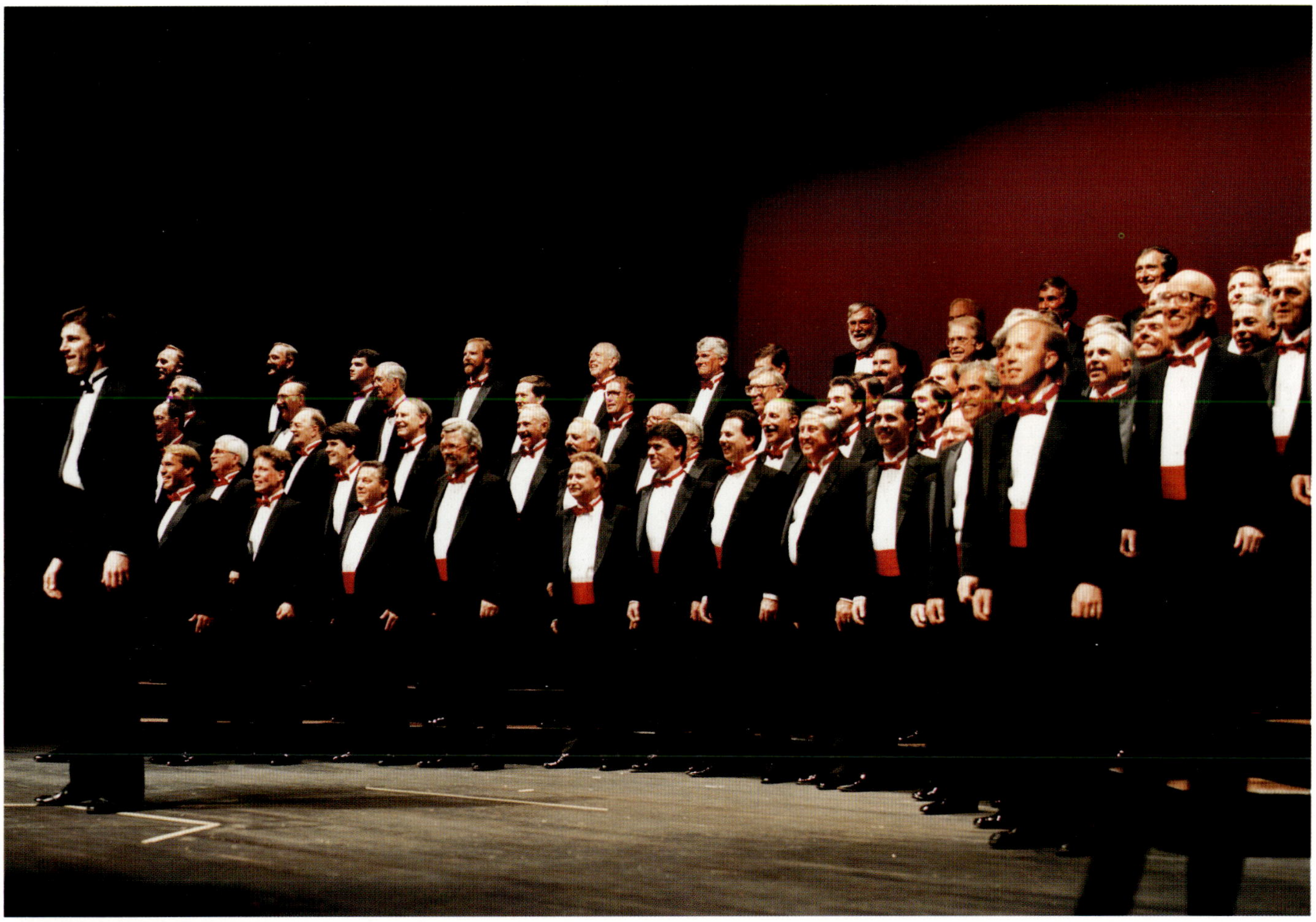

Big Chicken Chorus

Taking their name from the local landmark, a group of Mariettans in 1986 formed the Big Chicken Chorus, which has gone on to become a perennial winner of barbershop-style singing competitions.

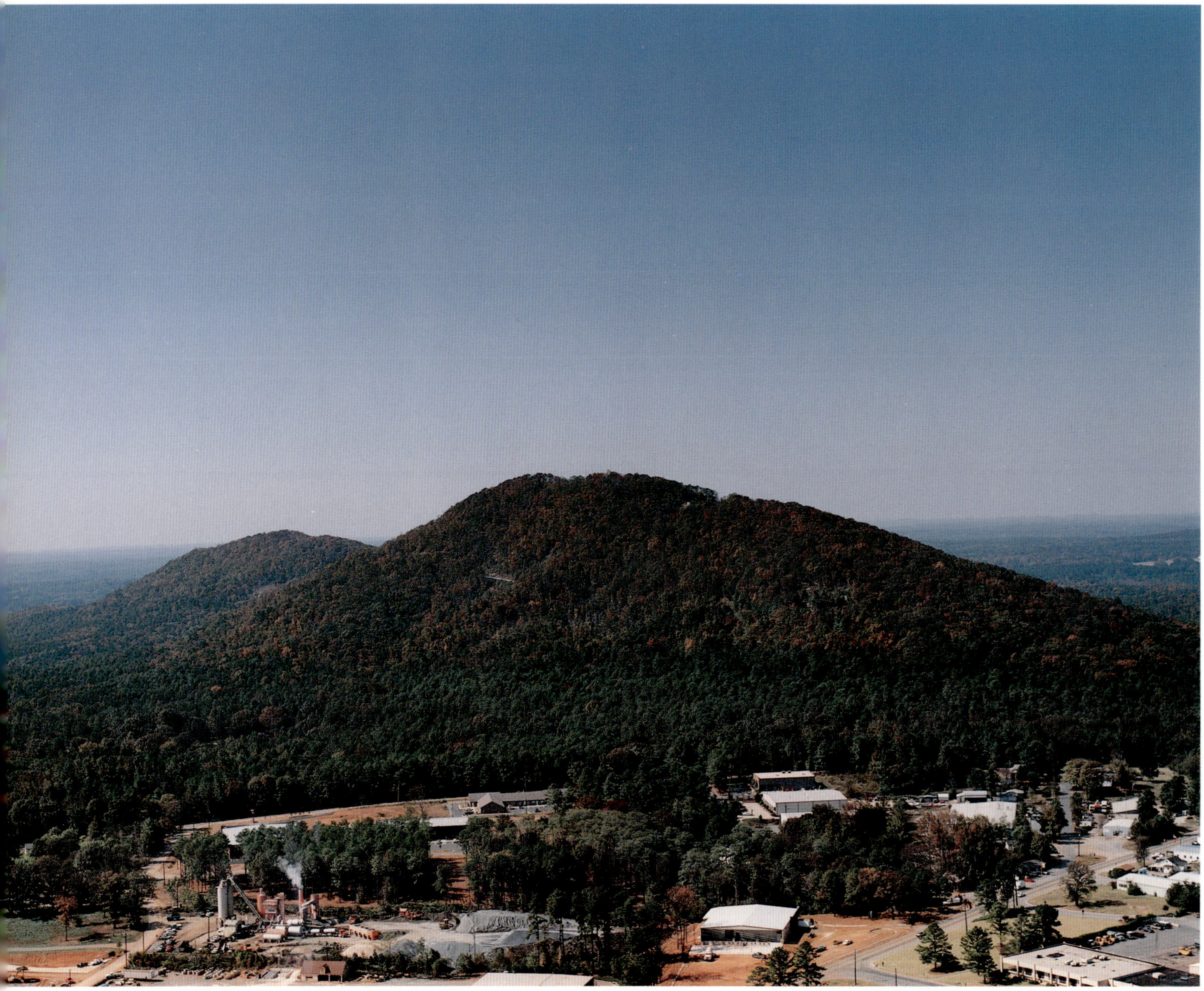

Kennesaw Mountain National Battlefield

This unassuming slope just north of Marietta became a little corner of hell on June 27, 1864, when Sherman's invaders tried to push General Joseph E. Johnston's Confederates from a strong defensive position. The northerners were driven back with severe losses, but a flanking movement by Sherman soon forced Johnston to withdraw anyway.

The mountain, a national park, is one of the few major Civil War sites to have escaped commercial or residential development. Visitors can peruse the historical markers, note the lines of fire, and study the terrain for a better understanding of this important battleground in the Atlanta campaign.

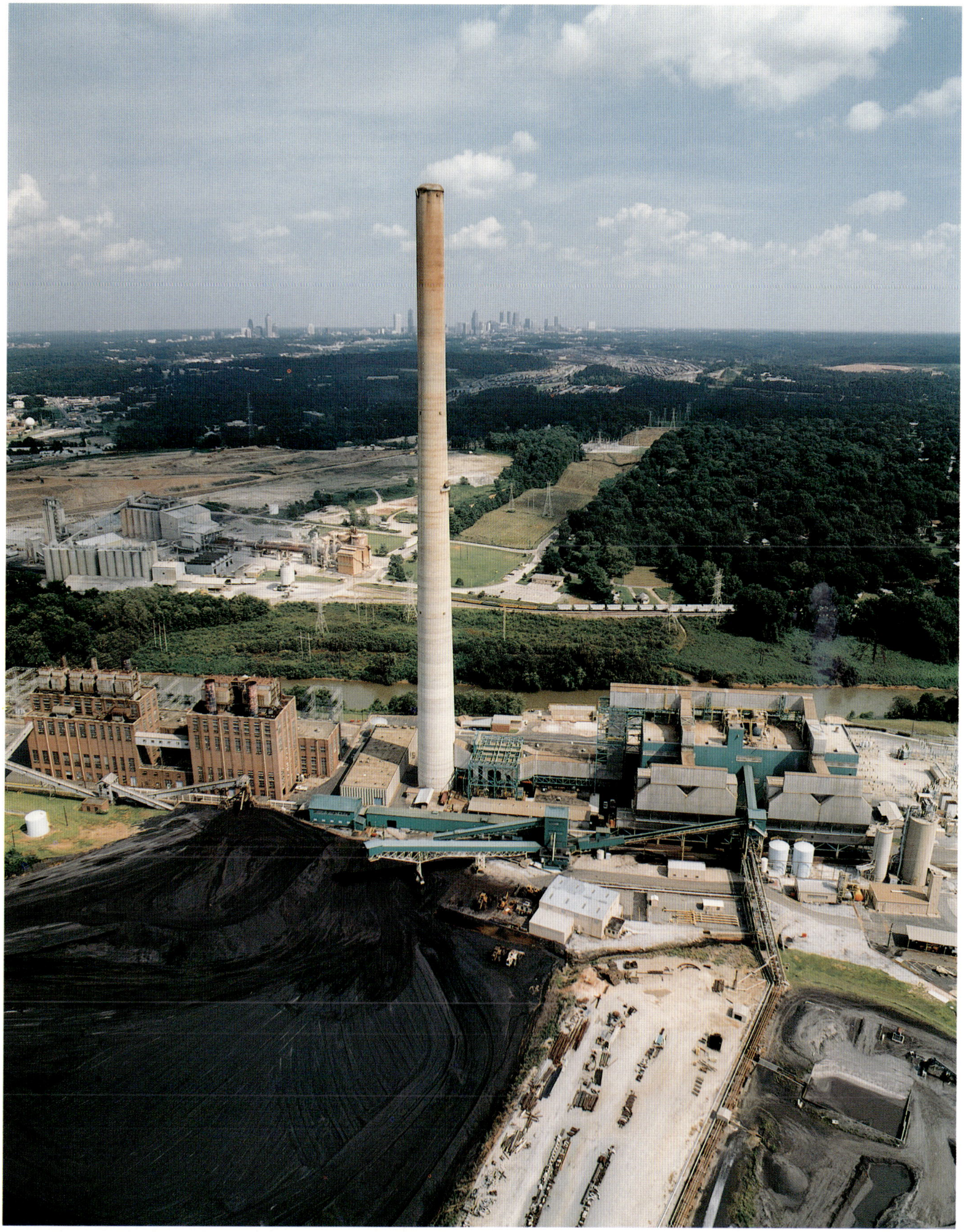

Georgia Power Plant

High-tension wires leading south from the Georgia Power Company's Plant Atkinson, in Cobb County, carry electricity to the metropolis on the horizon.

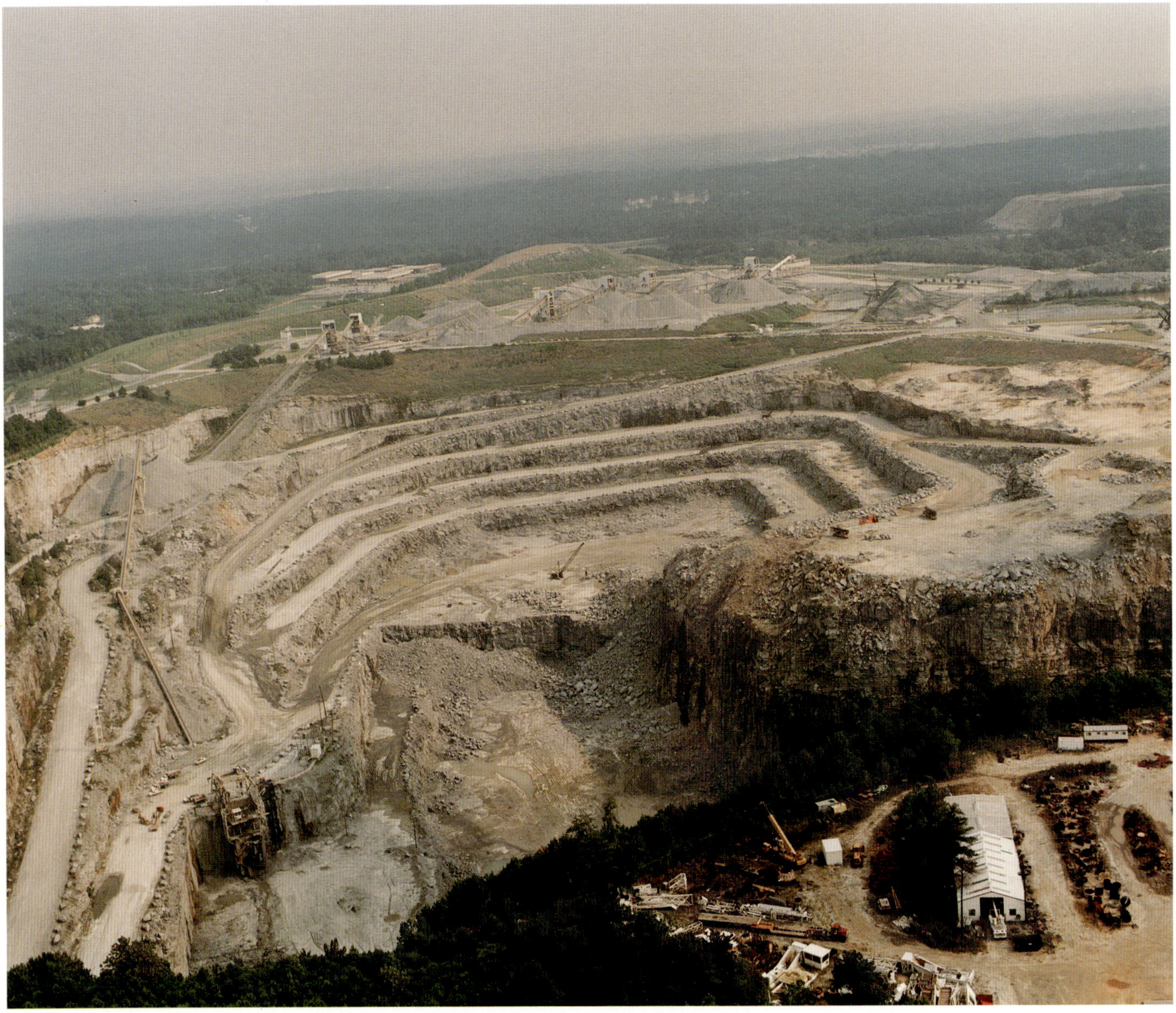

Vulcan Quarry

From above, the Vulcan Materials Company granite quarry in suburban Gwinnett County looks like a child's sandbox strewn with toy trucks and cranes. Awash in volcanic magma eons ago, north Georgia is today one of the nation's chief suppliers of granite.

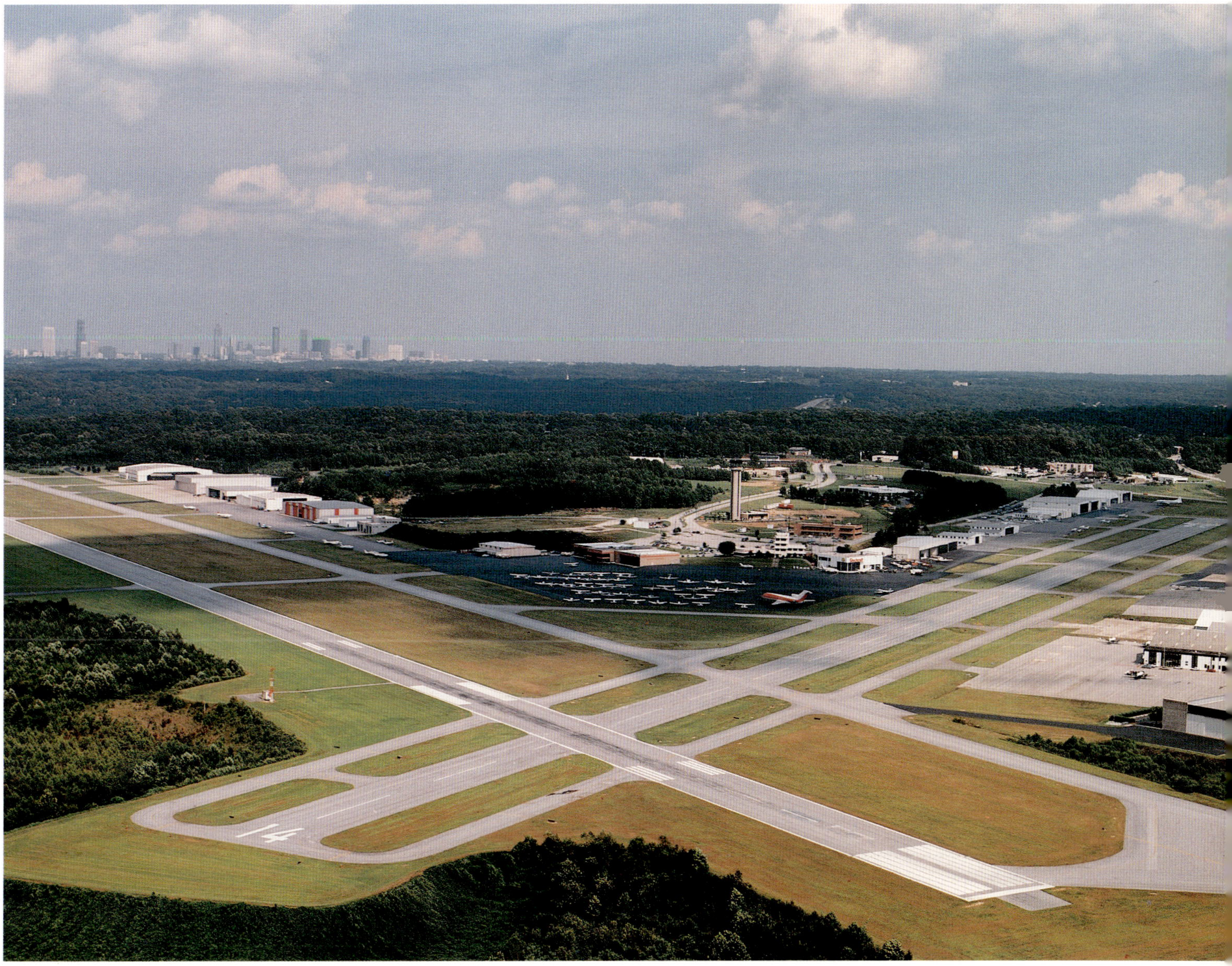

Charlie Brown Airport

This small airport in Fulton County flourishes only a few miles from giant Hartsfield International Airport.

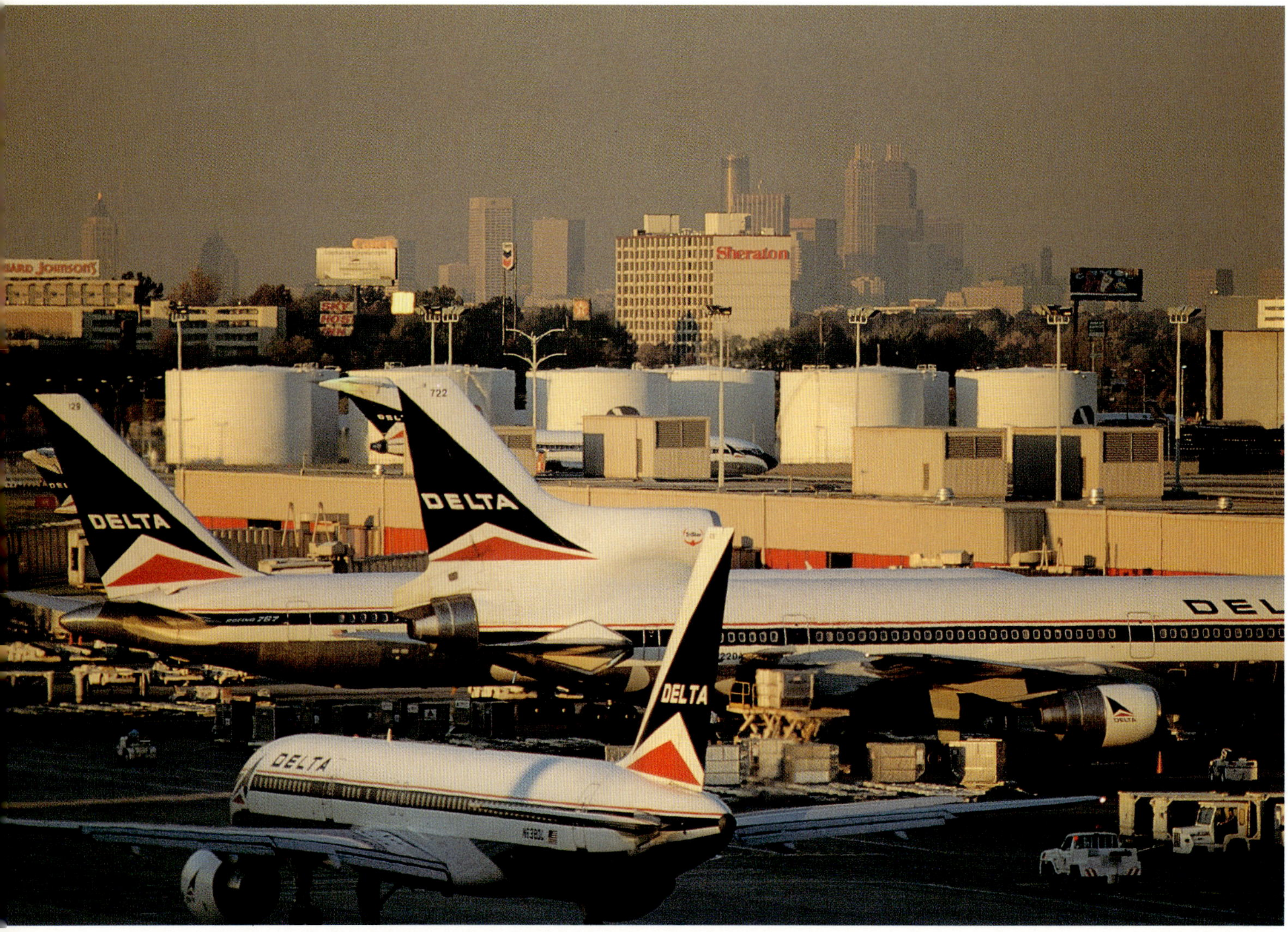

Hartsfield International Airport

Nine miles south of the downtown business district and named for former mayor William B. Hartsfield, Atlanta's principal airport is among the busiest in the world. Delta Airlines, which is headquartered here, and twenty-two other carriers provide service to more than 150 locations in the United States, as well as to thirty foreign cities in seventeen countries. The airport's importance as a hub is enshrined in an old regional joke proclaiming that when southerners die, they have to change planes in Atlanta on the way to their next destination.